PROSE IN PRACTICE
a rhetorical reader

IN PRACTICE a rhetorical reader
second edition

James William Johnson

The University of Rochester

Harcourt Brace Jovanovich, Inc.

New York   Chicago   San Francisco   Atlanta

Waldenbooks, Orland Square 2-25-85 .99

ISBN: 0–15–572272–7

Library of Congress Catalog Card Number: 75–39397

Printed in the United States of America

For
Claire and Bill Reed

Foreword

The purpose of this collection of essays is suggested by its title: *Prose in Practice*. Good writers are made, not born; they become good through the steady practice of combining words and ideas into effective, vital prose. By examining the ways in which accomplished writers practice their craft, students gain a valuable sense of words and style even as they encounter new ideas. And by formulating their own ideas into oral or written criticism of what they have read, apprentice writers practice the art of prose writing in the most profitable way.

The selections in *Prose in Practice* are arranged in two parts. Part One, Methods of Development, has nine sections with four or five selections in each: Defining, Classifying, Comparing and Contrasting, Analyzing, Describing, Characterizing, Illustrating and Exemplifying, Demonstrating Causality, and Reasoning. Part Two, Modes of Discourse, has four sections that show how the methods are used: Exposition (Arranging Information); Narration (Recounting Events in Time); Explanation (Showing Relationships); and Argumentation and Persuasion (Proving Opinion). With the exception of the dictionary definition from the Oxford English Dictionary and a short selection by Sir James Jeans, "Why the Sky Looks Blue," selections are full-length essays and short stories.

Each section begins with a discussion of the method of development or mode of discourse and ends with four or five pages of questions grouped under Diction and Structure, Style and Rhetoric, and Theme and Viewpoint.

In this new edition, many of the selections have been changed to combine topics of special concern, interest, and occasionally humor in the 1970s with perennially outstanding examples of expository writing. The essays include fictional and factual materials: their subjects range from stress to Mickey Mouse, from the women's movement to television, from death to fighting and love. Almost all the selections, written during the past thirty years, deal with timeless problems and utilize timeless rhetorical techniques. They demonstrate that the best writing incorporates the best thinking, that ideas remain inchoate unless they are clearly expressed, and that "style" without thought is meaningless. The practitioners of prose included here are a heterogeneous lot, in techniques as well as in interests, yet the reader will find that they supplement each other's views and represent a variety of rhetorical methods.

James William Johnson

Contents—
by form

part one—Methods of development

Defining   3

Illustrating and exemplifying   171

Demonstrating causality   216

Reasoning   245

part two—Modes of discourse

Exposition: arranging information   287

Narration: recounting events in time   329

Explanation: showing relationships   369

Argumentation and persuasion: proving opinion   414

Contents—
by subject matter

The secrets of our emotions

Sexual roles and sexual attitudes

Varieties of Americans

Minority groups and political action

Race and racial attitudes

Ways of getting educated

The "popular" culture

Science and scientists

Contents—
by technique
and style

The nature of language

Words: their qualities and uses

Definition

Levels of diction

Technical

Formal

Informal

Argot

Sentences

Conversational

Grammatical

Declarative

Interrogative

**Imperative and
  exclamatory**

Rhetorical

The rhetorical question

Paragraphs

Developing the paragraph

See "Contents by Form"   ix

Introductory paragraphs

Transitional paragraphs

Concluding paragraphs

Special paragraphs

Dialogue

The total essay

Style and tone

part one

Methods
of development

Defining

"I hate definitions!" declared a character in a now-forgotten, nineteenth-century novel without giving her reasons why. Perhaps most of us feel a similar, if milder antipathy toward defining words, even as we admit the need to define unless our ideas are to become a meaningless muddle. The first English lexicographer, Dr. Samuel Johnson, however, saw very clearly one of the difficulties in defining: he wrote, "It is one of the maxims of the civil law, that definitions are hazardous." Certainly, the hazards of making legal definitions overly specific and thus overly exclusive is obvious today with controversy over what constitutes "equal rights" or "discrimination" or "pornography." Politicians meet equal hazards when they try to define "national security" or "national interest"; as do Black Nationalists when they talk of "power" and college students when they seek "relevance." Even meanings of such common words as "inflation," "crime," "delinquency," "justice," and "love" are hard to pin down. If any of these generalized, somewhat vague terms are narrowly defined, they lose some of their effectiveness, if not their very reason for existence.

On the other hand, Mark Twain realized that, difficult as

it may be to give words clearcut meanings, the dangers of leaving them indefinite are also great.

> Much energy has been spent in an effort to determine where the West begins. The definitions of poetry and luncheon clubs are unsatisfactory: vagueness should not be invoked when a precise answer is possible. The West begins where the average annual rainfall drops below twenty inches. When you reach the line which marks that drop—for convenience, the one hundredth meridian—you have reached the West.

This ingeniously humorous marking of boundaries illustrates quite well the essential qualities of definition. ("Definition" means "the setting of bounds.") Defining a word is setting up limits of signification which that word has or may have; it is done for the sake of understanding; and it is often arbitrary, depending upon the choice of some essential principle that seems to suggest natural limits. As map-makers draw lines indicating geographical boundaries, so dictionary-makers—like Dr. Johnson and Noah Webster—draw verbal boundaries past which a word's claim on meanings should not go. Even the nonexpert may stipulate the limits of word meanings as he or she uses them for particular purposes.

Nevertheless, not all words can be clearly delimited; and even those that can, shift and change with the passing of time, just as physical boundaries reflected on a map alter with erosion or upheavals. Thus the boundaries must be revised regularly, for maps *and* words. Why do meanings alter? Simply because words are used by people to indicate things, places, relationships, feelings, intentions, and other elements in life, both tangible and intangible. Even when a word is widely understood to indicate one person, place, or thing—for example, "Truman," "Rome," "glasses"—the multiple objects signified by that word may lead to misunderstanding: "Truman" might refer to a literary figure in eighteenth-century drama; "Rome" to Rome, New York; and "glasses" to "spectacles" as well as drinking tumblers. All words have more than one reference, as a glance at any dictionary shows; and many words are so abstract, general, or widely unknown that a universal agreement among their users as to one meaning is all but impossible. Kemp Malone, one of the leading word specialists, or etymologists, of this century, once tried to collect all the meanings of the word "mahogany" as people used it; after gathering 1,500 written passages including the word, he concluded that it had eight different meanings but that even his extensive sampling was not truly an accurate indicator of the widest and most popular usage. Yet, for a professional, the way of defining was clear if ultimately hopeless:

> The English language, like every other living language, is democratic in its form of government. The meaning of a word in general use . . . is determined, not by pundits, still less by official action of any kind, but by the people. It is the duty of the professional linguist to find out, by investigation, what the usage of the people is. . . . The investigator must go straight to the primary sources of information.

Since most of us are not professional linguists, Malone's statement might seem to provide us with complete freedom to make a word mean whatever we want it to, like Humpty-Dumpty in *Alice in Wonderland*. Of course we cannot. Language is a social instrument, useful only when it establishes communication between people; therefore, if definitions are arbitrary, they nonetheless have more or less discernible boundaries of meaning. By consulting any dictionary of current usage, one can find the possible range of meanings for a given word that other people will understand. Old words may shift meanings or drop usage; new words may be coined to fill a need. Nevertheless, to establish the meaning—or signification—of any given word at any specific moment, one or more of several basic methods of defining will be used.

Definition by root meaning traces the etymological origins of the word and states its original or first meanings. Thus *anthropomorphic* comes from the Greek words meaning *man shape; lunatic* is derived from the Latin *moonstruck;* and *idiot* comes from the Greek term for *an ignorant person.* Fascinating as root definitions may be—and some dictionaries specialize in historical roots and meanings—defining solely in root terms is seldom possible because words change their meanings through usage. The English word *idiom* comes from the same root as *idiot,* but the two now mean different things. Furthermore, it may be interesting to know that *impediment* means *baggage* in Latin, but in English a speech impediment means something more abstract. Similarly, words like *silly, very, psychology, livid,* and *aesthetic* now mean something quite removed from their roots.

Definition by synonym is the most simple and direct way of defining: *flimflam = nonsense, soil = earth, nutriment = food.* Many foreign terms that have been incorporated into English may be translated into their English synonyms and thus defined: *nolo contendere* = *I do not dispute it*, *welt-schmertz* = *world weary*, *gaffe* = *blunder*, *hydrocephalic* = *water on the brain*. Yet, for a definition by synonym to be useful, the definition must be more obvious or simple than the term to be defined; and some English words of necessity are the most simple term for the thing they stand for. Such simple words as *go*, *fall*, and *try* may have multiple meanings but they cannot be defined with synonyms simpler than the words themselves.

Another method, definition by illustration, is particularly apt where intangible or abstract qualities are concerned. It is possible, to be sure, to define *purple* simply as *a color*, *hot* as *a characteristic*, and *sweet* as *a quality*; but such definitions are too inclusive (there. are colors other than purple!) and therefore vague. They will be of very little use to anyone who wants a precise idea of what the words mean. Therefore, *purple* is best defined by illustration; that is, by citing objects in which the color appears: the kind of mollusk from which a dye comes, an emperor's robes, a crocus.

Definition by negation involves isolating a term by telling what it does not include. *War* can be thus defined as *the absence of or violation of a peaceful state*. Words like *dark*, *nothing*, *nonsense*, and *empty* also lend themselves to being circumscribed by what they are not.

By far the most common format for a definition, however, is that observed by dictionaries and lexicons: the term to be defined is placed into a group or "family" (*genus*) that shares some common, outstanding quality and then its differences (*differentia*) from the rest of the family are indicated. Thus, *Communism* may be put into the *genus*, "an economic system," and then distinguished from Capitalism, Socialism, and other economic systems by its *differentia*, "in which all property is owned by the community as a whole." Definition by *genus* and *differentia* is so useful a format that other methods of defining may be cast into it; for instance, *purple* is *that color to be found in shellfish of the porphyra variety*, where *color* is the *genus* and the remainder of the definition the *differentia*.

To use language intelligently and purposefully we must have some established sense of the meaning of the words we use. Even a simple idea or sentence will convey little, perhaps nothing at all, unless each of its words is used according to some commonly acknowledged or stipulated definition. The most subtly planned and elaborately written essay will collapse into nonsense unless the writer makes plain the meanings of the key words used. Many an essay, therefore, begins with some version of definition or later interjects definitions when new terms are introduced. Defining is a basic way of developing one's ideas; unless it is used, directly or indirectly, the writer risks alienating and losing readers rather than attracting their attention and engaging their minds.

Some of the uses of definition—and some of its pitfalls—are set forth in the selections following. The definitions of *prose* from the *Oxford English Dictionary* observe the concise format of standard lexicography; they also show how meanings have changed through the centuries and how experts have used the same term to mean different things. Herbert J. Muller's essay reminds us that no matter how authoritative the format of a definition, it is still a highly tentative statement of meaning. Helen Nowlis illustrates some of the problems involved in setting up an acceptable definition for a very common word. And the extended definitions given by Dr. Hans Selye and F. L. Lucas demonstrate how an entire essay can be devoted to defining a term that represents an idea which is subtle, abstract, or complicated.

Prose

Prose (prō^uz), *sb.* ME. [a. F. *prose,* ad. L. *prosa* (*oratio*), lit. straight-forward discourse, sb. use of fem. of *prosus,* for earlier *prorsus.*] 1. The ordinary form of written or spoken language, without metrical structure; esp. as a division of literature. Opp. to *poetry, verse, rime,* or *metre.* b. with *a* and *pl.* A piece of prose; a prose exercise. Now only in school or college use. 1589. 2. *Eccl.* A piece of rhythmical prose or rimed accentual verse, sung or said between the epistle and gospel at certain masses; also called a *sequence* 1449. 3. *fig.* Plain, simple, matter-of-fact, (and hence) dull or commonplace expression, quality, spirit, etc. 1561. 4. a. A prosy discourse or piece of writing 1688. b. *Old colloq.* Familiar talk, chat; a talk 1805. 5. *attrib.* (often hyphened). a. Consisting of, composed or written in prose 1711. b. Composing or writing in prose 1668. c. *fig.* = PROSAIC 2. 1818.

1. Things unattempted yet in P. or Rhime MILT. The definition of good p. is—proper words in their proper places COLERIDGE. b. When my tutor fond supposes I am writing Latin proses 1901. 3. A broad embodiment of the p. and commonplace of her class 1900. 4. b. Long p. with the Duke of Portland till one in the morning 1807. 5. a. Bunyan . . is the Ulysses of his own prose-epic 1875. b. Poets and prose-authors in every kind SHAFTESB.

Comb.: p.-poem, a. p. work having the style or character of a poem; so -poet, -poetry; -writer, an author who writes in p.

Prose (prō^uz), *v.* late ME. [f. prec.] 1. *trans.* To express in prose; to translate or turn into prose. b. *intr.* To compose or write prose 1805. 2. To talk or write prosily; *old colloq.* and *dial.* to chat, gossip 1797.

1. Al schal passyn þat men p. or ryme CHAUCER. b. I've rhymed I've prosed. . In short done everything 1834. 2. Eternally prosing about the weather 1879.

PROSE From *The Shorter Oxford English Dictionary on Historical Principles,* Third Edition, edited by C. T. Onions. Reprinted by permission of the Clarendon Press, Oxford.

Herbert J. Muller

A Note on Definitions

"The one great Bible which cannot lie," wrote Froude, "is the history of the human race." Unhappily, there remains the problem of exegesis. The text is cited to support all sides of all questions: history teaches everything, history teaches nothing—these are head and tail of the same idea. The first impulse may be to cry tails. The record of the best that has been thought and said is also a record of endless contradiction and confusion. Yet one may get a simple lesson from it, for most of the confusion may be tracked to a single source. This is the arbitrary assumption that is taken for self-evident truth. It is an assumption involving other unconscious assumptions which, when explicitly stated, prove to be highly questionable or even demonstrably false. It is the universal habit that makes the whole process of proof seem incidental; for the argument implicitly assumes the idea to be proved, the conclusion is given at the outset. The chief cause of mischief throughout the history of thought has not been aces up the sleeve but jokers in the hole.

All human thought and behavior are necessarily based in certain assumptions, and the most fundamental of them—such as the existence of an external world—are not in themselves strictly logical or illogical, capable of absolute proof or disproof. Common sense is itself a metaphysic, learned before kindergarten, and a partly outmoded one at that; its "plain truths" are premises taken from Aristotle, Euclid, Augustine, Newton, Descartes, Kant, and other sources that might distress as well as surprise the "practical" man. Science, too, begins with a leap into metaphysics. But the recent revolution in science has resulted from the exposure and criticism of its basic assumptions—the notions of absolute time and space, for example, that Kant regarded as necessary modes of thought—and from the recognition that they are strictly *assumptions*. In all thought, more important

A NOTE ON DEFINITIONS From *Science and Criticism* by Herbert J. Muller. Reprinted by permission of the Yale University Press. Copyright © 1943 by Yale University Press.

than the premises themselves is this clear awareness of them and behavioristic attitude toward them. What goes without saying is what especially needs to be said. And so a thinker's first effort should be to discover and drag out into the open all his silent premises. He should lay his cards on the table face up, so that he as well as his readers may look at them.

Hence we approach the problem of definition, the terms in which the assumptions are buried. We can seldom be sure that we know just what a man means by his key terms, or that he himself knows; obviously we need to know if we are really to get together. But it is not enough simply to define our terms. Definition is so important that we also need to have a clear idea of just what *it* is, its own nature and purpose. As Irving Babbitt said, we need "to define the limits of definition itself."

To Aristotle, definition was not merely a verbal process or a useful tool of thought; it was the essence of knowledge. It was the cognitive grasp of the eternal essences of Nature, a fixed, necessary form of knowing because an expression of the fixed, necessary forms of Being. These eternal essences and species have turned out to be pretty perishable, or at least have been brought into disrepute by evolutionary theory. Aristotle's logic, however, is still lusty. His forms of knowing have outlived the Being they were designed to express. For men continue to talk and think in terms of essences. They seek definitions on the assumption that a single or absolute quality is involved. They give or report meanings as if they were telling what something really and truly *is*. "Religion," somebody has said, "is a device for keeping people quiet while skinning them." Somebody else has said that it is "the sum total of man's impulses toward good," and still another that it is "the sum of the scruples that interfere with the free exercise of human faculties." They would all be contributing something to understanding—except that they usually mean "Religion *is* so-and-so," not "I am defining religion as so-and-so." When a mathematician declares that *x* equals something, he is consciously assigning an arbitrary value, and can proceed to carry out useful operations. When a critic defines poetry or romanticism or naturalism, he usually assigns an absolute value, believes that he has uttered an eternal truth, and then begins to fight with other critics. Similarly men still have the primitive faith in the magical efficacy of the right name: once you give something a name you have it by the throat. The man on the street believes that he has explained behavior when he labels it "inferiority complex." The sophisticate coins fancier paraphrases that smack even more of mumbo jumbo. The intellectual above all is apt to manipulate verbal symbols in the belief that he is dealing directly with facts.

Now words may heighten or amplify consciousness in subtle ways, apart from their official value in the currency of communication or even their sound effects. To specify and name a quality of experience is often to *feel* it, to possess more fully as well as to see more clearly. Especially with the youthful mind, vocabulary building is an extension of consciousness; once a youngster has really got hold of such words as vulgarity, sentimentality, magnanimity, his perceptions are apt to be finer and his judgments sounder. Any clear definition, moreover, is useful. Among the most useful, in fact, are the purely verbal inventions that have no objective referents. The head-in-the-sand ostrich, Stefansson remarks—the ostrich-by-definition, comparable to the mathematician's triangle—is in many ways more serviceable than the real bird, and in much less danger of extinction. In the last analysis, all scientific definitions are of this kind, involving some imaginary or strictly unreal terms. But the scientist knows that they are arbitrary. He does not mistake the hypothetical for the real bird.

In short, definitions are properly means of knowing, not ends of knowledge. If they are the end products of a given inquiry, they are nevertheless simply convenient formulations, the means to further inquiry; they do not solve a problem but set it. The literary critic above all must remember that they are merely instrumental. His business is to get at the individual work of art, which is a unique combination of concrete particulars; for him the particular is indeed the thing. Hence he must remember as well that no definition can fully comprehend the real bird. Hence he must be on guard against the severely formal definitions that are so efficient in science; if criticism has notoriously suffered from loose talk, it has suffered even more from narrowness and rigidity. Altogether, the critic's terms can never be exact duplicates or complete inventories of the experience he deals with, and they serve him best as they simply lead him to this experience, give general directions for dealing with it. He wants suppleness and sensitivity, ease and sureness in finding his way around. He therefore does well to travel light, with a few guiding principles but without a complete set of fixed categories.

The last word about the whole process of definition is that there can be no last word. Words generate words, definitions inevitably involve other undefined terms, and thought ends where it begins, in the undemonstrable, the unthinkable, the literally unspeakable. Modern scientists are consciously setting out from the assumption that their basic terms—"order," "structure," "relation"—cannot be defined; or what amounts to the same thing, that the indefinable can *only* be defined. Alfred Korzybski therefore maintains that the first demand upon a thinker is not "Define your terms" but "State your undefined terms"—which is another way of saying, "State your assumptions."

Helen Nowlis

What Is a Drug?

The term "drug" has many meanings. The two which are most frequently used by the layman are derived from the medical approach and from the legal approach to drugs. The one equates a drug with a medicine pre-scribed by the physician for specified and limited use in the treatment and prevention of disease, in the relief of pain, and in restoration of a feeling of well-being. The other equates it with a habit-forming narcotic which is widely believed to be so dangerous to the individual and to society that it must be controlled by governmental agencies. Influenced by these two limited definitions, our first impulse is to consider a campus drug problem as either a medical or a legal problem or both and to engage students in discussions about the health and legal risks of drug use. But we find that the students are less interested in talking about risks than about aspects of drug use not wholly encompassed by the medical and legal approaches. Their current interest in drugs grew as they read and learned that others were using certain drugs for such bona fide or illusory purposes as discover-ing more about one's self, exploring the mind, and searching for new mean-ings in personal relationships and in the universe itself—or for expressing disapproval for society and some of the laws they believe to be unjust or idiotic. They also became interested in the right to use drugs for such very personal and seemingly important purposes. Such interests require that drug use be considered in relation to ethical, religious, philosophical and social values as well as in relation to medical and legal facts. To be pre-pared for dialogue at this level, we must find a broad and objective defini-tion of the term "drug."

WHAT IS A DRUG? From *Drugs on the College Campus*, National Association of Student Personnel Administrators, 1967. Reprinted by permission. Available in a paperbound Anchor edition (1969) from Doubleday & Company, Inc., New York.

Defining a drug?

The pharmacological definition of a drug offered by Modell is both broad and objective: "Any substance that by its chemical nature alters structure or function in the living organism is a drug."[1] Its breadth is shown by the list of substances which alter structure or function: "Foods, vitamins, hormones, microbial metabolites, plants, snake venoms, stings, products of decay, air pollutants, pesticides, minerals, synthetic chemicals, virtually all foreign materials (very few are completely inert) and many materials normally in the body."[2] Its objectivity rests in its being descriptive rather than evaluative. Other more limited definitions of the term "drug" may be more useful depending on the kinds of substances and the kinds of short-term and long-term effects, both organismic and social, one wishes to discuss. These more limited definitions are usually based on assumptions about certain kinds of effects. For example, in formulating a definition useful in writing a good popularized book about drugs of current interest, Laurie[3] says, "For the purposes of this book, a 'drug' is any chemical substance that alters mood, perception or consciousness and is misused, to the apparent detriment of society." This is helpful, since the two limiting assumptions are made explicit: (1) There are effects on mood, perception, or consciousness, and (2) there is potential for misuse defined as apparently detrimental to society. Thus in reading this book, we know the special meaning to attribute to the term "drug" whenever it appears. On the other hand, in reading about drugs in other discourse, especially popular and journalistic discourse, we find that the term "drug" may mean many different things and that the assumptions of the writer may be unstated or vague or even erroneous (e.g., all psychoactive drugs are addictive, provide an escape to nowhere or lead inevitably to the use of heroin), going far beyond what is scientifically known about drugs. Such assumptions, when implicit, erroneous or dogmatic, interfere with clear thinking and effective communication.

Pharmacologists classify these drugs in many different ways; some classifications are based on the chemical structure of the substance, others on the effects of the substance on cellular functions, on physiological and biochemical systems, or on behavior and experience. Different modes or levels of classification are necessary because two drugs with similar chem-

[1] Modell, W., "Mass drug catastrophes and the roles of science and technology." *Science,* 1967, 156, p. 346.

[2] Ibid., p. 346.

[3] Laurie, P., *Drugs: Medical, Psychological and Social Facts.* Baltimore: Penquin (S249), 1967, p. 11.

ical structure may produce very different patterns of drug action; or two with very dissimilar chemical structures may produce similar physiological or behavioral effects.

The physician thinks of drugs on the basis of their pharmacological classification, but he also has to be particularly interested in such criteria as: (1) the usefulness of the drug in the diagnosis, treatment, and prevention of disease, in the relief of pain and in the improvement and preservation of health, (2) the side effects of the drugs, (3) the toxicity of the drug in both acute and chronic use, (4) the purity and potency of the drug in the form available to the patient. Essentially these are criteria of therapeutic effectiveness and of safety. New drugs are developed and evaluated according to strict regulations based on the above criteria and administered by the Food and Drug Administration (FDA). Still other substances are of concern to the physician not because of their therapeutic efficacy but because of their toxicity; examples are the household, agricultural, and industrial poisonous chemicals which may be accidentally, involuntarily, or deliberately absorbed by the individual.

Drugs may also be classified in other ways. A drug may have originally been available only as an unknown active agent in a plant product, like coffee, tobacco, marihuana. The active ingredient was then identified, isolated and made available as a derivative from the plant or synthesized from other substances. Drugs also vary in legal status, depending on the nature of the controls on their production, evaluation, distribution, sale, and possession, as established by law. Drugs may also be classified according to social usage. Alcohol and tobacco have for centuries been so widely accepted for general use that governmental controls are now limited to what is acceptable to the public. Peyote is officially classed as a drug with potential for abuse but is legally available to the Native American Church, since this group has for some time used the substance ritually and has what are considered appropriate social controls on its use.

Interesting and sometimes paradoxical attitudes and beliefs about specific drugs emerge out of these complex classification systems, sets of criteria and patterns of use. Ethyl alcohol and diluted ethyl alcohol are currently listed as official preparations in the "United States Pharmacopeia" (U.S.P.). Whiskey, brandy, and sherry wine were formerly official preparations but are no longer so. Society prefers to think of alcohol as a beverage rather than as a drug. Marihuana, a term which has come to refer to all preparations containing parts of the common hemp plant or extracts from the plant, was formerly listed as an official preparation but has now been removed. Its production, distribution, and possession are legally severely restricted in this and many other countries. Although it is not a narcotic drug, the laws for controlling it are similar to those for the control of narcotics. Some States have arbitrarily defined it as a narcotic, and most laymen thus consider marihuana to be a narcotic; others regard it as a social drug similar to alcohol. Nicotine, an active substance in tobacco smoke, is not generally used for therapeutic purposes. It and other substances found in tobacco smoke (like those found in airplane glue) can be generally classed with the many toxic substances which are of interest to the physician primarily because of the injury done to the individual who inadvertently or deliberately absorbs them. The present controversy over the presence or absence of injurious effects from chronic smoking of cigarettes emphasizes the importance of and difficulties inherent in the statistical validation of drug effects.

We return, then, to our original definition of a drug as *any substance which by its chemical nature alters structure or function in the living organism.* Any of these substances may become relevant to the drug problem as man increases his exposure to or involvement with the substance.

Hans Selye

What Is Stress?

Everybody has it, everybody talks about it, yet few people have taken the trouble to find out what stress really is. Many words have become fashionable when scientific research revealed a new concept likely to influence our way of thinking about major issues of life or to affect our everyday conduct. Such terms as "Darwinian evolution," "allergy," and "psychoanalysis" have all had their peaks of popularity in drawing-room or cocktail-party conversations; but rarely are the opinions about them based on a study of technical works written by the scientists who established these concepts.

Nowadays, we hear a great deal at social gatherings about the stress of executive life, retirement, exercise, family problems, pollution, air traffic control, or the death of a relative. But how many of those defending their strong convictions about these matters with heated arguments have bothered to learn the scientific meaning of stress and the mechanism of its workings? Most people have never even wondered whether there is a difference between stress and distress!

The word "stress," like "success," "failure," or "happiness," means different things to different people, so that defining it is extremely difficult although it has become part of our daily vocabulary. Is stress merely a synonym for distress? Is it effort, fatigue, pain, fear, the need for concentration, the humiliation of censure, the loss of blood, or even an unexpected great success which requires complete reformulation of one's entire life? The answer is yes and no. That is what makes the definition of stress so difficult. Every one of these conditions produces stress, but none of them can be singled out as being "it," since the word applies equally to all the others.

Yet, how are we to cope with the stress of life if we cannot even define it? The businessman who is under constant pressure from his clients and employees alike, the air-traffic controller who knows that a moment of distraction may mean death to hundreds of people, the athlete who desperately wants to win a race, and the husband who helplessly watches his wife slowly and painfully dying of cancer, all suffer from stress. The problems they face are totally different, but medical research has shown that in many respects the body responds in a stereotyped manner, with identical biochemical changes, essentially meant to cope with any type of increased demand upon the human machinery. The stress-producing factors—technically called *stressors*—are different, yet they all elicit essentially the same biological stress response. This distinction between stressor and stress was perhaps the first important step in the scientific analysis of that most common biological phenomenon that we all know only too well from personal experience.

But if we want to use what the laboratory has taught us about stress in formulating our own philosophy of life, if we want to avoid its bad effects and yet be able to enjoy the pleasures of accomplishment, we have to learn more about the nature and mechanism of stress. In order to succeed in this, in order to arrive at a basis for a scientific philosophy of conduct—a rational prophylactic and therapeutic science of human behavior—we must concentrate in this somewhat difficult first chapter on the fundamental technical data which the laboratory has given us.

In writing this book, it seemed logical to begin with what the physician means by the term *stress*, at the same time familiarizing the reader with the few technical expressions that are essential.

Stress is the nonspecific response of the body to any demand made upon it. To understand this definition we must first explain what we mean by *nonspecific.* Each demand made upon our body is in a sense unique, that is, *specific.* When exposed to cold, we shiver to produce more heat, and the blood vessels in our skin contract to diminish the loss of heat from the body surfaces. When exposed to heat, we sweat because the evaporation of perspiration from the surface of our skin has a cooling effect. When we eat too much sugar and the blood-sugar level rises above normal, we excrete some of it and burn up the rest so that the blood sugar returns to normal. A great muscular effort, such as running up many flights of stairs at full speed, makes increased demands upon our musculature and cardiovascular system. The muscles will need supplemental energy to perform this unusual work; hence, the heart will beat more rapidly and strongly, and the blood pressure will rise to dilate the vessels, thereby increasing the flow of blood to the muscles.

Each drug or hormone has such specific actions: diuretic drugs increase the production of urine; the hormone adrenalin augments the pulse rate and blood pressure, simultaneously raising blood sugar, whereas the hormone insulin decreases blood sugar. Yet, no matter what kind of derangement is produced, all these agents have one thing in common; they also increase the demand for readjustment. This demand is nonspecific; it requires adaptation to a problem, irrespective of what that problem may be.

In other words, in addition to their specific actions, all agents to which we are exposed also produce a nonspecific increase in the need to perform adaptive functions and thereby to re-establish normalcy. This is independent of the specific activity that caused the rise in requirements. The nonspecific demand for activity as such is the essence of stress.

From the point of view of its stress-producing or stressor activity, *it is immaterial whether the agent or situation we face is pleasant or unpleasant;* all that counts is the intensity of the demand for readjustment or adaptation. The mother who is suddenly told that her only son died in battle suffers a terrible mental shock; if years later it turns out that the news was false and the son unexpectedly walks into her room alive and well, she experiences extreme joy. The specific results of the two events, sorrow and joy, are completely different, in fact, opposite to each other, yet their stressor effect—the nonspecific demand to readjust herself to an entirely new situation—may be the same.

It is difficult to see how such essentially different things as cold, heat, drugs, hormones, sorrow, and joy could provoke an identical biochemical reaction in the body. Nevertheless, this is the case; it can now be demonstrated, by highly objective quantitative biochemical determinations, that certain reactions are totally nonspecific, and common to all types of exposure.

It has taken medicine a long time to accept the existence of such a stereotyped response. It did not seem logical that different tasks, in fact any task, should require the same response. Yet, if you come to think of it, there are many analogies in everyday life in which highly specific things or events share the same nonspecific feature. At first sight it is difficult to see what could be the common denominator between a man, a table, and a tree, yet they all have weight. There is no object completely devoid of weight; the pressure exerted on the scale balance does not depend upon such a specific feature as temperature, color, or shape, any more than the stressor effect of a demand upon the body depends on the kind of adaptive reaction that is required to meet it.

Or consider the appliances in a house that has heaters, refrigerators, bells, and light bulbs, which respectively produce heat, cold, sound, or light, in a most specific manner; yet to function they all depend upon one common factor—electricity. A member of a primitive tribe who never heard of electricity would find it very difficult to accept that all the manifold phenomena just mentioned depend upon the satisfaction of a common demand: the provision of electrical energy.

What Stress Is Not

Since the term "stress" is often used quite loosely, many confusing and contradictory definitions of it have been formulated; hence, it will be useful to add a few remarks stating clearly what it is not.

Stress is not merely nervous tension. This fact must be especially emphasized, since most laymen and even many scientists tend to identify biological stress with nervous exhaustion or intense emotional arousal. Indeed, quite recently, Dr. John W. Mason, a former president of the American Psychosomatic Society and one of the most distinguished investigators of the psychologic and psychiatric aspects of biological stress, devoted an excellent essay to an analysis of my stress theory. He suggested that the common denominator of stressors may simply be activation of "the physiological apparatus involved in emotional or arousal reactions to threatening or unpleasant factors in the life situation as a whole." In man, with his highly developed nervous system, emotional stimuli are in fact the most common stressors—and, of course, these would be encountered most frequently in psychiatric patients.

It must not be forgotten, however, that stress reactions do occur in lower animals that have no nervous system, and even in plants. Furthermore, the so-called stress of anesthesia is a well-recognized phenomenon in

surgery, and numerous investigators have tried to eliminate this undesirable complication of the loss of consciousness.

Stress is not always the nonspecific result of damage. We have seen
that it is immaterial whether a stressor is pleasant or unpleasant; its
stressor effect depends merely on the intensity of the demand made upon
the adaptive capacity of the body. Any kind of normal activity—a game of
chess or even a passionate embrace—can produce considerable stress without causing harmful effects. Damaging or unpleasant stress is "distress."

The word "stress" allegedly came into common English usage, via
Old French and Middle English, as "distress." The first syllable eventually
was lost through slurring, as children turn "because" into " 'cause." In the
light of our investigations, the true meaning of the two words became
totally different despite their common ancestry, just as in correct usage we
distinguish between "because" (since) and "cause" (reason). Activity associated with stress may be pleasant or unpleasant; distress is always disagreeable.

Stress is not something to be avoided. In fact, it is evident from the
definition given at the beginning of this chapter that it cannot be
avoided.

In common parlance, when we say someone is "under stress," we actually mean under excessive stress or distress, just as the statement "he is
running a temperature" refers to an abnormally high temperature, that is,
fever. Some heat production is essential to life.

Similarly, no matter what you do or what happens to you, there
arises a demand for the necessary energy required to maintain life, to
resist aggression and to adapt to constantly changing external influences.
Even while fully relaxed and asleep, you are under some stress. Your heart
must continue to pump blood, your intestines to digest last night's dinner,
and your muscles to move your chest for respiration. Even your brain is
not at rest while you are dreaming. *Complete freedom from stress is death.*

F. L. Lucas

What Is Style?

When it was suggested to Walt Whitman that one of his works should be bound in vellum, he was outraged—"Pshaw!" he snorted, "—hangings, curtains, finger bowls, china ware, Matthew Arnold!" And he might have been equally irritated by talk of style; for he boasted of "my barbaric yawp"—he would *not* be literary; his readers should touch not a book but a man. Yet Whitman took the pains to rewrite *Leaves of Grass* four times, and his style is unmistakable. Samuel Butler maintained that writers who bothered about their style became unreadable but he bothered about his own. "Style" has got a bad name by growing associated with precious and superior persons who, like Oscar Wilde, spent a morning putting in a comma, and the afternoon (so he said) taking it out again. But such abuse of "style" is misuse of English. For the word means merely "a way of expressing oneself, in language, manner, or appearance"; or, secondly, "a good way of so expressing oneself"—as when one says, "Her behavior never lacked style."

Now there is no crime in expressing oneself (though to try to *im*press oneself on others easily grows revolting or ridiculous). Indeed one cannot help expressing oneself, unless one passes one's life in a cupboard. Even the most rigid Communist, or Organization-man, is compelled by Nature to have a unique voice, unique fingerprints, unique handwriting. Even the signatures of the letters on your breakfast table may reveal more than their writers guess. There are blustering signatures that swish across the page like cornstalks bowed before a tempest. There are cryptic signatures, like a scrabble of lightning across a cloud, suggesting that behind is a lofty divinity whom all must know, or an aloof divinity whom none is worthy to know (though, as this might be highly inconvenient, a docile typist

WHAT IS STYLE? From *Holiday*, March 1960. Originally titled "On the Fascination of Style." Reprinted by permission of the Executors of F. L. Lucas deceased.

sometimes interprets the mystery in a bracket underneath). There are impetuous squiggles implying that the author is a sort of strenuous Sputnik streaking round the globe every eighty minutes. There are florid signatures, all curlicues and danglements and flamboyance, like the youthful Disraeli (though these seem rather out of fashion). There are humble, humdrum signatures. And there are also, sometimes, signatures that are courteously clear, yet mindful of a certain simple grace and artistic economy—in short, of style.

Since, then, not one of us can put pen to paper, or even open his mouth, without giving something of himself away to shrewd observers, it seems mere common sense to give the matter a little thought. Yet it does not seem very common. Ladies may take infinite pains about having style in their clothes, but many of us remain curiously indifferent about having it in our words. How many women would dream of polishing not only their nails but also their tongues? They may play freely on that perilous little organ, but they cannot often be bothered to tune it. And how many men think of improving their talk as well as their golf handicap?

No doubt strong silent men, speaking only in gruff monosyllables, may despise "mere words." No doubt the world does suffer from an endemic plague of verbal dysentery. But that, precisely, is bad style. And consider the amazing power of mere words. Adolf Hitler was a bad artist, bad statesman, bad general, and bad man. But largely because he could tune his rant, with psychological nicety, to the exact wave length of his audiences and make millions quarrelsome-drunk all at the same time by his command of windy nonsense, skilled statesmen, soldiers, scientists were blown away like chaff, and he came near to rule the world. If Sir Winston Churchill had been a mere speechifier, we might well have lost the war; yet his speeches did quite a lot to win it.

No man was less of a literary aesthete than Benjamin Franklin; yet this tallow-chandler's son, who changed world history, regarded as "a principal means of my advancement" that pungent style which he acquired partly by working in youth over old *Spectators*; but mainly by being Benjamin Franklin. The squinting demagogue, John Wilkes, as ugly as his many sins, had yet a tongue so winning that he asked only half an hour's start (to counteract his face) against any rival for a woman's favor. "Vote for you!" growled a surly elector in his constituency. "I'd sooner vote for the devil!" "But in case your friend should not stand . . . ?" Cleopatra, that ensnarer of world conquerors, owed less to the shape of her nose than to the charm of her tongue. Shakespeare himself has often poor plots and thin ideas; even his mastery of character has been questioned; what does remain unchallenged is his verbal magic. Men are often taken, like rabbits, by the ears. And though the tongue has no bones, it can sometimes break millions of them.

"But," the reader may grumble, "I am neither Hitler, Cleopatra, nor Shakespeare. What is all this to me?" Yet we all talk—often too much; we all have to write letters—often too many. We live not by bread alone but also by words. And not always with remarkable efficiency. Strikes, lawsuits, divorces, all sorts of public nuisance and private misery, often come just from the gaggling incompetence with which we express ourselves. Americans and British get at cross-purposes because they use the same words with different meanings. Men have been hanged on a comma in a statute. And in the valley of Balaclava a mere verbal ambiguity, about *which* guns were to be captured, sent the whole Light Brigade to futile annihilation.

Words can be more powerful, and more treacherous, than we sometimes suspect; communication more difficult than we may think. We are all serving life sentences of solitary confinement within our own bodies; like prisoners, we have, as it were, to tap in awkward code to our fellow men in their neighboring cells. Further, when A and B converse, there take part in their dialogue not two characters, as they suppose, but six. For there is A's real self—call it A_1; there is also A's picture of himself—A_2; there is also B's picture of A—A_3. And there are three corresponding personalities of B. With six characters involved even in a simple tête-à-tête, no wonder we fall into muddles and misunderstandings.

Perhaps, then, there are five main reasons for trying to gain some mastery of language:

We have no other way of understanding, informing, misinforming, or persuading one another.

Even alone, we think mainly in words; if our language is muddy, so will our thinking be.

By our handling of words we are often revealed and judged. "Has he written anything?" said Napoleon of a candidate for an appointment. "Let me see his *style*."

Without a feeling for language one remains half-blind and deaf to literature.

Our mother tongue is bettered or worsened by the way each generation uses it. Languages evolve like species. They can degenerate; just as oysters and barnacles have lost their heads. Compare ancient Greek with modern. A heavy responsibility, though often forgotten.

Why and how did I become interested in style? The main answer, I suppose, is that I was born that way. Then I was, till ten, an only child running loose in a house packed with books, and in a world (thank goodness) still undistracted by radio and television. So at three I groaned to my mother, "Oh, I *wish* I could read," and at four I read. Now travel among books is the best travel of all, and the easiest, and the cheapest. (Not that I belittle ordinary travel—which I regard as one of the three main pleasures in life.) One learns to write by reading good books, as one learns to talk by hearing good talkers. And if I have learned anything of writing, it is largely from writers like Montaigne, Dorothy Osborne, Horace Walpole, Johnson, Goldsmith, Montesquieu, Voltaire, Flaubert and Anatole France. Again, I was reared on Greek and Latin, and one can learn much from translating Homer or the Greek Anthology, Horace or Tacitus, if one is thrilled by the originals and tries, however vainly, to recapture some of that thrill in English.

But at Rugby I could *not* write English essays. I believe it stupid to torment boys to write on topics that they know and care nothing about. I used to rush to the school library and cram the subject, like a python swallowing rabbits; then, still replete as a postprandial python, I would tie myself in clumsy knots to embrace those accursed themes. Bacon was wise in saying that reading makes a full man; talking, a ready one; writing, an exact one. But writing from an empty head is futile anguish.

At Cambridge, my head having grown a little fuller, I suddenly found I *could* write—not with enjoyment (it is always tearing oneself in pieces)— but fairly fluently. Then came the War of 1914–18; and though soldiers have other things than pens to handle, they learn painfully to be clear and brief. Then the late Sir Desmond MacCarthy invited me to review for the *New Statesman*; it was a useful apprenticeship, and he was delightful to work for. But I think it was well after a few years to stop; reviewers remain essential, but there are too many books one *cannot* praise, and only the pugnacious enjoy amassing enemies. By then I was an ink-addict—not because writing is much pleasure, but because not to write is pain; just as some smokers do not so much enjoy tobacco as suffer without it. The positive happiness of writing comes, I think, from work when done—decently, one hopes, and not without use—and from the letters of readers which help to reassure, or delude, one that so it is.

But one of my most vivid lessons came, I think, from service in a war department during the Second War. Then, if the matter one sent out was too wordy, the communication channels might choke; yet if it was not absolutely clear, the results might be serious. So I emerged, after six years of it, with more passion than ever for clarity and brevity, more loathing than ever for the obscure and the verbose.

For forty years at Cambridge I have tried to teach young men to write well, and have come to think it impossible. To write really well is a gift inborn; those who have it teach themselves; one can only try to help and hasten the process. After all, the uneducated sometimes express themselves far better than their "betters." In language, as in life, it is possible to be perfectly correct—and yet perfectly tedious, or odious. The illiterate last letter of the doomed Vanzetti was more moving than most professional orators; 18th Century ladies, who should have been spanked for their spelling, could yet write far better letters than most professors of English; and the talk of Synge's Irish peasants seems to me vastly more vivid than the later style of Henry James. Yet Synge averred that his characters owed far less of their eloquence to what he invented for them than to what he had overheard in the cottages of Wicklow and Kerry:

> CHRISTY   It's little you'll think if my love's a poacher's, or an earl's itself, when you'll feel my two hands stretched around you, and I squeezing kisses on your puckered lips, till I'd feel a kind of pity for the Lord God in all ages sitting lonesome in His golden chair.
>
> PEGEEN   That'll be right fun, Christy Mahon, and any girl would walk her heart out before she'd meet a young man was your like for eloquence, or talk at all.

Well she might! It's not like that they talk in universities—more's the pity.

But though one cannot teach people to write well, one can sometimes teach them to write rather better. One can give a certain number of hints, which often seem boringly obvious—only experience shows they are not.

One can say: Beware of pronouns—they are devils. Look at even Addison, describing the type of pedant who chatters of style without having any: "Upon enquiry I found my learned friend had dined that day with Mr. Swan, the famous punster; and desiring *him* to give me some account of Mr. Swan's conversation, *he* told me that *he* generally talked in the Paronomasia, that *he* sometimes gave in to the Plocé, but that in *his* humble opinion *he* shone most in the Antanaclasis." What a sluttish muddle of *he* and *him* and *his!* It all needs rewording. Far better repeat a noun, or a name, than puzzle the reader, even for a moment, with ambiguous pronouns. Thou shalt not puzzle thy reader.

Or one can say: Avoid jingles. The B.B.C. news bulletins seem compiled by earless persons, capable of crying round the globe: "The enemy is re*port*ed to have seized this im*port*ant *port*, and reinforcements are hurrying up in sup*port*." Any fool, once told, can hear such things to be insupportable.

Or one can say: Be sparing with relative clauses. Don't string them together like sausages, or jam them inside one another like Chinese boxes or the receptacles of Buddha's tooth. Or one can say: Don't flaunt jargon, like Addison's Mr. Swan, or the type of modern critic who gurgles more technical terms in a page than Johnson used in all his *Lives* or Sainte-Beuve in thirty volumes. But dozens of such snippety precepts, though they may sometimes save people from writing badly, will help them little toward writing well. Are there no general rules of a more positive kind, and of more positive use?

Perhaps. There *are* certain basic principles which seem to me observed by many authors I admire, which I think have served me and which may serve others. I am not talking of geniuses, who are a law to themselves (and do not always write a very good style, either); nor of poetry, which has different laws from prose; nor of poetic prose, like Sir Thomas Browne's or De Quincey's, which is often more akin to poetry; but of the plain prose of ordinary books and documents, letters and talk.

The writer should respect truth and himself; therefore honesty. He should respect his readers; therefore courtesy. These are two of the corner-stones of style. Confucius saw it, twenty-five centuries ago: "The Master said, The gentleman is courteous, but not pliable: common men are pliable, but not courteous."

First, honesty. In literature, as in life, one of the fundamentals is to find, and be, one's true self. One's true self may indeed be unpleasant (though one can try to better it); but a false self, sooner or later, becomes disgusting—just as a nice plain woman, painted to the eyebrows, can become horrid. In writing, in the long run, pretense does not work. As the police put it, anything you say may be used as evidence against you. If handwriting reveals character, writing reveals it still more. You cannot fool *all* your judges *all* the time.

Most style is not honest enough. Easy to say, but hard to practice. A writer may take to long words, as young men to beards—to impress. But long words, like long beards, are often the badge of charlatans. Or a writer may cultivate the obscure, to seem profound. But even carefully muddied puddles are soon fathomed. Or he may cultivate eccentricity, to seem original. But really original people do not have to think about being original—they can no more help it than they can help breathing. They do not need to dye their hair green. The fame of Meredith, Wilde or Bernard Shaw might now shine brighter, had they struggled less to be brilliant; whereas Johnson remains great, not merely because his gifts were formidable but also because, with all his prejudice and passion, he fought no less passionately to "clear his mind of cant."

Secondly, courtesy—respect for the reader. From this follow several other basic principles of style. Clarity is one. For it is boorish to make your reader rack his brains to understand. One should aim at being impossible to misunderstand—though men's capacity for misunderstanding approaches infinity. Hence Molière and Po Chu-i tried their work on their cooks; and Swift his on his menservants—"which, if they did not comprehend, he would alter and amend, until they understood it perfectly." Our bureaucrats and pundits, unfortunately, are less considerate.

Brevity is another basic principle. For it is boorish, also, to waste your reader's time. People who would not dream of stealing a penny of one's money turn not a hair at stealing hours of one's life. But that does not make them less exasperating. Therefore there is no excuse for the sort of writer who takes as long as a marching army corps to pass a given point. Besides, brevity is often more effective; the half can say more than the whole, and to imply things may strike far deeper than to state them at length. And because one is particularly apt to waste words on preambles before coming to the substance, there was sense in the Scots professor who always asked his pupils—"Did ye remember to tear up that fir-r-st page?"

Here are some instances that would only lose by lengthening:

> It is useless to go to bed to save the light, if the result is twins.
> (*Chinese proverb.*)
>
> My barn is burnt down—
> Nothing hides the moon.
> (*Complete Japanese poem.*)
>
> Je me regrette.
> (*Dying words of the gay* Vicomtesse d'Houdetot.)
>
> I have seen their backs before.
> (*Wellington, when French marshals turned their backs on him at a reception.*)
>
> Continue until the tanks stop, then get out and walk.
> (*Patton to the Twelfth Corps, halted for fuel supplies at St. Dizier, 8/30/44.*)

Or there is the most laconic diplomatic note on record: when Philip of Macedon wrote to the Spartans that, if he came within their borders, he would leave not one stone of their city, they wrote back the one word—"If."

Clarity comes before even brevity. But it is a fallacy that wordiness is necessarily clearer. Metternich when he thought something he had written was obscure would simply go through it crossing out everything irrelevant. What remained, he found, often became clear. Wellington, asked to recommend three names for the post of Commander-in-Chief, India, took a piece of paper and wrote three times—"Napier." Pages could not have been clearer—or as forcible. On the other hand the lectures, and the sentences, of Coleridge became at times bewildering because his mind was often "wiggle-waggle"; just as he could not even walk straight on a path.

But clarity and brevity, though a good beginning, are only a beginning. By themselves, they may remain bare and bleak. When Calvin Coolidge, asked by his wife what the preacher had preached on, replied "Sin," and, asked what the preacher had said, replied, "He was against it," he was brief enough. But one hardly envies Mrs. Coolidge.

An attractive style requires, of course, all kinds of further gifts—such as variety, good humor, good sense, vitality, imagination. Variety means avoiding monotony of rhythm, of language, of mood. One needs to vary one's sentence length (this present article has too many short sentences; but so vast a subject grows here as cramped as a djin in a bottle); to amplify one's vocabulary; to diversify one's tone. There are books that petrify one throughout, with the rigidly pompous solemnity of an owl perched on a leafless tree. But ceaseless facetiousness can be as bad; or perpetual irony. Even the smile of Voltaire can seem at times a fixed grin, a disagreeable wrinkle. Constant peevishness is far worse, as often in Swift; even on the stage too much irritable dialogue may irritate an audience, without its knowing why.

Still more are vitality, energy, imagination—gifts that must be inborn before they can be cultivated. But under the head of imagination two common devices may be mentioned that have been the making of many a style—metaphor and simile. Why such magic power should reside in simply saying, or implying, that A is like B remains a little mysterious. But even our unconsciousness seems to love symbols; again, language often tends to lose itself in clouds of vaporous abstraction, and simile or metaphor can bring it back to concrete solidity; and, again, such imagery can gild the gray flats of prose with sudden sun-glints of poetry.

If a foreigner may for a moment be impertinent, I admire the native gift of Americans for imagery as much as I wince at their fondness for slang. (Slang seems to me a kind of linguistic fungus; as poisonous, and as short-lived, as toadstools.) When Matthew Arnold lectured in the United States, he was likened by one newspaper to "an elderly macaw pecking at a trellis of grapes"; he observed, very justly, "How lively journalistic fancy is among the Americans!" General Grant, again, unable to hear him, remarked: "Well, wife, we've paid to see the British lion, but as we can't hear him roar, we'd better go home." By simile and metaphor, these two quotations bring before us the slightly pompous, fastidious, inaudible Arnold as no direct description could have done.

Or consider how language comes alive in the Chinese saying that lending to the feckless is "like pelting a stray dog with dumplings," or in the Arab proverb: "They came to shoe the pasha's horse, and the beetle stretched forth his leg"; in the Greek phrase for a perilous cape—"step-mother of ships"; or the Hebrew adage that "as the climbing up a sandy way is to the feet of the aged, so is a wife full of words to a quiet man"; in Shakespeare's phrase for a little England lost in the world's vastness—"in a great Poole, a Swan's nest"; or Fuller's libel on tall men—"Ofttimes such who are built four stories high are observed to have little in their cockloft"; in Chateaubriand's "I go yawning my life"; or in Jules Renard's portrait of a cat, "well buttoned in her fur." Or, to take a modern instance, there is Churchill on dealings with Russia: "Trying to maintain good relations with a Communist is like wooing a crocodile. You do not know whether to tickle it under the chin or beat it over the head. When it opens its mouth, you cannot tell whether it is trying to smile or preparing to eat you up." What a miracle human speech can be, and how dull is most that one hears! Would one hold one's hearers, it is far less help, I suspect, to read manuals on style than to cultivate one's own imagination and imagery.

I will end with two remarks by two wise old women of the civilized 18th Century.

The first is from the blind Mme. du Deffand (the friend of Horace Walpole) to that Mlle. de Lespinasse with whom, alas, she was to quarrel so unwisely: "You must make up your mind, my queen, to live with me in the greatest truth and sincerity. You will be charming so long as you let yourself be natural, and remain without pretension and without artifice." The second is from Mme. de Charrière, the Zélide whom Boswell had once loved at Utrecht in vain, to a Swiss girl friend: "Lucinde, my clever Lucinde, while you wait for the Romeos to arrive, you have nothing better to do than become perfect. Have ideas that are clear, and expressions that are simple." ("*Ayez des idées nettes et des expressions simples.*") More than half the bad writing in the world, I believe, comes from neglecting those two very simple pieces of advice.

In many ways, no doubt, our world grows more and more complex; sputniks cannot be simple; yet how many of our complexities remain futile, how many of our artificialities false. Simplicity too can be subtle—as the straight lines of a Greek temple, like the Parthenon at Athens, are delicately curved, in order to look straighter still.

Questions

Diction and Structure

1. The definitions of *prose* on page 8 are taken from *The Oxford English Dictionary*, which records changes in usage and meaning of words, and dates the earliest known occurrence of a given meaning. Examine the meanings of *prose* in 1449, 1561, 1589, 1668, 1711, 1805, and 1818. Can you see how and why the word shifted meanings as it did?

2. Look closely at the outline format of the OED definitions of *prose* with the lettered and numbered headings and subheadings. What principle of organization does the paragraph on prose observe? Is the material arranged clearly and usefully for the reader? How else might it have been arranged?

3. Notice the illustrations from Chaucer and other sources for the use of *prose* as a verb. Are the editors of the OED honoring Kemp Malone's etymological principles as stated on page 5 above?

4. Look up the following words in the *Oxford English Dictionary* and see how their meanings have changed: genius, drug, style, nice, livid, husband, school. Are the present meanings sufficiently close to the root meanings to make the latter a useful method of definition?

5. Compare the dictionary definitions of *style* in the OED and a lexicon of current usage (*The American College Dictionary, Funk and Wagnalls, The American Heritage Dictionary*) with the definition given by F. L. Lucas. Which meanings are clearly dependent on usage and which on the stipulative meanings given by an authority? Which give you the most insight into the meaning of *style?*

6. The writer's choice of words depends to a large degree on the kinds of readers he or she has in mind. Judging from his subject and his vocabulary, for what audience is Herbert J. Muller writing: popular or specialized, trained or untrained, moderately or highly educated?

7. Look up the meanings of these words used by Muller: *exegesis, metaphysic, assumption, cognitive.* Does Muller use them accurately when judged by the dictionary definitions? Does he redefine any of them by stipulating meanings not to be found in the dictionary?

8. Muller's point in "A Note on Definitions" might be stated as: definitions are assumptions put into words. Does this definition

of "definition" aptly describe the meanings of *prose* given by the *OED?*

9. Muller's "Note" is a small section from a full length book. Is the "Note" self-contained as a piece of thought and writing? Explain. In what sense is it a definition itself? To what extent is it a statement of Muller's own assumptions?

10. The introductory paragraph to Helen Nowlis' "What Is a Drug" names two specialized ways of defining the term—the medical and the legal—and the body of her essay gives examples of still other definitions. What are these? Are there basic contradictions between the assumptions underlying these definitions? If so, what are they, and how does Nowlis reconcile them?

11. What methods of definition appear in Nowlis' essay? What method is used in the summarizing definition?

12. Some of the definitions of *drug* cited by Nowlis are quite broad and inclusive, covering such things as snake venom, air pollutants, and even food. Others are very narrow and exclude things with the properties attributed to drugs; for instance, whiskey and tobacco. Is her final definition too inclusive or too exclusive? Why does she choose it?

13. Since Nowlis begins her definition with Modell's term and concludes with it, could she just as well have stated it and accepted it for future use without going into alternative definitions? What would she have lost or gained by doing so?

14. Identify the forms of definition used by Hans Selye in his essay on stress. Which form is the most important?

15. Selye traces the origins of the word *stress* back to Old French and Middle English words for *distress*. Sometimes defining by giving the root meaning of the word is cited as the basic form of definition. How does Selye suggest the limitations of defining a word by its original meaning?

16. Many of Selye's definitions are based on the principle of opposites: of defining by telling what a word does *not* signify. Locate examples of this technique in Selye's essay. How is the principle of negation related to the other forms of definition?

17. Make an outline of Selye's essay. Do his successive definitions follow any logical principle of development; that is, does the first attempt to define *stress* lead to the second, third, and so forth? How is the final italicized sentence in the essay related to the earlier definitions?

18. Does F. L. Lucas ever give a definition of *style* in a concise phrase or two in his essay "What Is Style?" Can you define *style* briefly, using Lucas' opinions about it?

19. To what extent does Lucas intend his essay to be a definition by example? Justify your answer.

20. "Style is the man himself," goes the French aphorism. Does Lucas agree with this definition? Is the statement a truly satisfactory definition? Why or why not?

Style and Rhetoric

1. The *OED* section on "Prose" is a succinct, dictionary definition; Nowlis' essay on drugs cites a number of definitions and concludes by stipulating a working definition; Hans Selye also gives various definitions, then expands the encyclopedia definition into a longer version; Lucas writes a long or extended definition of "style" that elaborates upon his own assumptions. Compare and contrast in each instance the ways in which the writer's use of definitions reflects his or her assumptions and purposes.

2. Using Selye and Lucas as a case in point, why is the use of extended definitions instead of dictionary meanings sometimes necessary? Which kinds of terms are more likely to require extended definitions; words indicating tangible things (prose, drugs) or intangible qualities (stress, style)? Could the Muller and Nowlis essays have been profitably extended or the Selye and Lucas essays profitably condensed? Justify your opinion.

3. Compare the kinds of sentences used by Muller, Nowlis, and Lucas. Who writes the shortest, most syntactically simple sentences and who, the most complex and lengthy? Whose prose style is the most colorful and whose, the least colorful? Are the kinds of writing illustrated in these essays appropriate for the different natures of the subjects treated? Explain why or why not.

4. In her essay "What Is a Drug?" Nowlis often lists information, numbering the points supporting a general statement. Point out examples of this technique and identify its advantages and disadvantages. Is it necessary to the writer's purpose in the essay? Does it help or distract the reader?

5. In her essay, Nowlis uses a fairly large number of technical or specialized terms: "pharmacological," "organismic," "toxicity," and so on. Must the reader have a precise knowledge of their meaning in order to understand the author's point? In general, would you call Nowlis' style "formal," "technical," or "informal"? Justify your answer.

6. From their essays, do you develop any sense of the "person-

ality" of Muller or Nowlis? Of Selye or Lucas? Does the presence (or absence) of the personality of a writer in any way affect the quality or authority or effectiveness of an essay?

7. Selye begins his essay on stress with a statement about the difficulty of defining such common terms as "happiness." Does he confirm the views of Muller or deny them? Do Selye's definitions avoid the pitfalls he indicates?

8. For what audience is Selye writing, if his diction and tone are any evidence: a specialized, educated one; a general, "common" reader; neither, or both? What problems with word choice does Selye's choice of an audience involve? How does he meet these problems?

9. Notice the final statement of Selye's essay. Is his concluding point one the essay has prepared the reader for? Which previous portions have foreshadowed the concluding statement? Could the final sentence serve as a topical sentence for another section to follow? What points might such an additional section add to the essay as it is given here?

10. Summarize succinctly Lucas' standards for a "good style" and apply them to Lucas' own essay. How does his style rate, by his criteria? How do the other definition essays in this section rate?

11. What does Lucas' remark about the length of his own sentences (p. 27) suggest about the relationship of sentence structure to overall style?

12. How would you characterize the tone of "What Is Style?" What does it suggest about Lucas' views of language and its relationship to intelligence (or creativity or genius)?

Theme and Viewpoint

1. In "A Note on Definitions," Muller contrasts the scientific use of definitions with the literary or critical use. What are the differences, according to him? If he is correct in making a distinction between scientific language and literary language, would the *prose* written by a scientist differ importantly from that written by a poet? (Compare Graham Hough's views on prose, verse, and poetry in the section immediately following.)

2. *Drug* is a word that has many associations today: some people react violently against it and others react favorably. Compare the associations of *drug* with *druggist, drugstore, pharmacy,* and *pharmacist.* Which words have the most emotional impact

and which the least? Is the difference a matter of changing meanings, word usage, or something else?

3. Compare the various definitions of *drug* in Nowlis' essay. Which are the most detached in tone and attitude? What is Nowlis' own attitude toward drugs? How does her purpose in writing the essay affect her tone?

4. No matter how impersonally he or she writes, the essayist nevertheless provides indications of personal feelings about the topic. These attitudes—or "points of view"—may be found even in the most objective and detached factual essay: perhaps in the form of a punctuation mark or the choice of an adjective. Read carefully the essays of Muller and Nowlis and suggest ways in which each reveals some personal bias, implicitly or explicitly, toward his or her subject. Are any hints of a personal attitude present in the OED entry on *prose*, which was of course written by a human being with human feelings?

5. In discussing stress, Selye mentions the effects of drugs on the body and the mind in several places. Does he agree with Nowlis' definition of *drug*, either openly or covertly? Are the Nowlis and Selye essays interested in some of the same subjects or in quite different subjects? Do the two essays complement, contradict, or qualify each other in their themes and points of view toward drugs?

6. Lucas derides the writer who tries for a unique or individualistic "style" as an "eccentric." Read Louis Kronenberger's essay on page 47. Are Lucas and Kronenberger in agreement about cranks and eccentrics and their ways of expressing themselves? Would Lucas' "good stylist" be Kronenberger's "individualist"?

Classifying

To many people, classification, or the placing of things into categories, may suggest merely what the United States Civil Service does to government employees or what newspaper printers do to want ads. However, classifying is one of the most constant activities of human beings. Soldiers are given "ranks"; school children are "graded"; taxpayers are put into taxable "categories"; and questionnaires collect data that will ultimately be used to classify us as male or female, children or adults, Democrats or Republicans or Liberals or Conservatives, and so forth. Even in conversation we tend to classify: "Today is Friday, August the 15th"; "He lives in the suburbs"; "That piece of steak is tough." Some grammarians claim that every sentence in English is actually a kind of classification, with the subject being the object to be classified and the predicate the category into which it is placed. Even questions and exclamations are forms of classification. When you yell, "Help!" you indicate that you belong in the category of helpless persons!

Even if every English sentence is not a version of classifying, many of them are—including this one. Indeed, if the basic technique of defining words is to place them into a category (*genus* or family) and then distinguish them from other members of that family, it seems natural for the sentences that are made of words to be extended versions of classification.

Take a simple instance of two words: your own name or someone else's. It is a classification. George Washington is that member of the family of Washingtons who is designated as "George." He is a member of the category of Washingtons, a family that is an identifiable group. Human families are identified by a theoretical blood relationship, although in fact a human family includes members by marriage and adoption, and every family contains members whose blood types differ widely. Perhaps the idea of blood as the principle by which a family is identified does not operate at all: a family is actually a category based on certain assumed principles of biological and legal relationship. If people are categorized by blood chemistry, they are O, A, B, or AB and not Washingtons, Adamses, Cohens, Kovaks, Kims, Gonzalezes, and so on. Thus if the three billion people on earth are classified by blood types, they may be put in four categories or classes; whereas if they are placed in families of legal relationships, there are literally thousands of categories and every one of us belongs in several dozen or more of them through maternal and paternal relationships.

What is the purpose of classifying? There are a great many purposes, from knowing what kind of blood to give in a transfusion to making legal decisions to voting in an election. In fact, to make sense of a world filled with billions of objects, we must have some way of forming a workable general notion of larger categories to which many given examples belong. Think of the many makes and models of automobiles, for example—there are several hundred. But the general term *automobile* covers them all and is both necessary and useful. Imagine the trouble and time involved if, instead of having the general term to use, you had to refer to the specific object by its many physical properties! "This red 1967 Volkswagen VW 1600, License number MV 9006, of mine has a leaky carburetor." No, we need general words, categorical terms that will cover many different kinds of individual items; words like *animal, mammal, tree, nation, teacher, structure, system, phenomenon,* and so on. Thus, the very nature of words— general and specific, abstract and concrete—depends upon the principle of classification. Similarly, much written prose depends upon classification for developing and organizing the writer's ideas, and classification becomes one of the basic techniques for developing an essay.

The essential technique of classification is grouping like objects on the principle of their similarity. The objects we call *rocks* may vary from soft pumice to glassy obsidian but the class of rocks shares common qualities or *rockness*. Rocks not only share qualities but differ, from one subgroup to another. Geologists thus subdivide the category of rocks into three subclasses according to the way in which they were formed: sedimentary, igneous, and metamorphic. And these subclasses may in turn be subdivided until a single piece of malachite occupies a unique category of shape, size, color, and location. If one general class is subdivided once—say, *igneous* into *intrusive* and *extrusive,* according to whether they stick out of the ground or not—this is called *horizontal classification.* If a large group is subdivided then subdivided again (and so on), this is called *vertical classification.* Horizontal classification is useful in understanding the characteristics of entire categories; vertical classification aids in showing the relationship of smaller categories or individual objects to a larger body of similar objects.

If you wish to know something about the tarantula, for example, you may go to a dictionary or encyclopedia and look up *tarantula,* only to find a brief definition of it and a cross reference: See *arachnids. Arachnids* is the categorical term for several families or *genera* of creatures that are basically alike but also have significant differences. Arachnids include scorpions, daddy-longlegs, ticks, and mites, as well as spiders: categories that are an example of horizontal classification. By learning the characteristics of the larger category to which spiders as a group belong, you will be able to understand better the nature of the kind of spider called a tarantula; and if you go on to study the varieties of tarantula, you can relate them to tarantulas, spiders, and arachnids in a use of vertical classification that illuminates the distinctive nature of your particular specimen of "wolf spider."

Being arbitrary and academic, the classifications of the natural or social scientist (chemist, botanist, zoologist, etc.) have a definiteness that other kinds of classification do not. A rock is a rock and a spider is a spider, by definition; but to how many classifications do people and ideas lend themselves? If you think of the many ways to categorize human beings—by race, nationality, geographical location, political alliances, religious preference, style of dress, diet, family connections, educational level, amount and nature of income, and so on— you will see that the principle of classification depends upon the particular interests and aims of the classifier. The politician will be interested in one set of principles; the physician in another; the public health official in another; as will the school principal, the traffic director, the city planner, and the fund raiser. Each will want to see the larger body of the population classified according to a different principle.

The usefulness of classification depends on how valid and how inclusive the chosen categorical principle is. It is not very helpful to classify people as "living" or "dead" when you want to know something about their relationships to each other or their political systems. Also, it is not particularly useful to set up categories of illnesses in the United States and forget about a minority group, such as albinos or children. Limited classifications, however, may still be interesting and helpful, providing they are properly limited. It is futile to write a study entitled "Food Preferences in the Human Race" if your findings are based on you, twelve members of your immediate family, fifty friends, and a stranger you observed eating in the local delicatessen. A good classification sheds some light on the things it classifies; and it must apply to every object that belongs to its chosen class.

Graham Hough

Prose, Verse and Poetry

[102] Up to now we have been inclined to use the word poetry in the extended sense, as synonymous with imaginative literature in general. But in common speech poetry is distinguished from prose; and we must now consider this distinction.

If we consult the dictionary under the article 'poetry' we find among other special senses two definitions that contradict each other.

(a) 'Any composition in verse, or what is intended as such, irrespective of whether it possesses any true poetic quality or not.'

PROSE, VERSE AND POETRY Reprinted from *An Essay on Criticism* by Graham Hough. By permission of W. W. Norton & Company, Inc., and Gerald Duckworth & Co., Ltd. Copyright © 1966 by Graham Hough.

(b) 'Thoughts, ideas, in themselves possessing some poetic quality, expressed not in verse but in prose.'[1]

If we enquire further what 'true poetic quality' is, the dictionary discreetly falls silent.

Evidently we have three terms to consider, poetry, verse and prose. Verse and prose are mutually exclusive (or can be considered so for the present); and poetry occupies an undefined area which overlaps the prose-verse distinction.

Jeremy Bentham said he knew the difference between poetry and prose because in prose the lines go to the edge of the page and in poetry they do not. Obviously he was distinguishing between *verse* and prose—besides slyly implying that any other distinction of poetry was unreal. So long as this confusion is merely semantic it does not cause much difficulty. The context is usually enough to keep us straight. However, there is a matter of substance involved. What we actually feel, and what is expressed somewhat vaguely in our common usage, is that there is a distinguishable quality of discourse, associated particularly with verse form but not exclusively confined to verse form, that we call poetry.

[103]   This sense of the word poetry is midway between the most extensive sense (poetry = imaginative literature) and the narrowest sense (poetry = verse). Since this sense indicates something that we feel really to exist we should try to describe it more closely. Honorific and rhetorical definitions abound (poetry is the breath and finer spirit of all knowledge, etc.), but they are not useful for our purpose. Here we slip over easily into metaphysics, epistemology or the psychology of the creative process; but we want to delimit a kind of discourse.

Prose tends to specialize in the direction of the factual, the descriptive and the analytical; and it is sometimes said that the special province of poetry is the emotional, the expression of feeling. But this will not do. The hortatory and the rhetorical, 'emotive' in purpose and strongly charged with feeling, are largely the domain of prose. No one would be tempted to describe the speeches of Demosthenes or Cicero or Burke as poetry. And poetry may be descriptive. No one would be tempted to describe the *Georgics* as prose.

Let us try again. Prose tends to point to an end beyond itself—to indicate or to describe a state of affairs (real or imagined); to exhort to, to prescribe, or to give instructions for, a course of action.

Poetry may do these things too. It is idle to deny that it does so, and attempts to make poetry exclusively autotelic, to isolate a 'pure' poetry,

---

[1] H. C. Wyld, *Universal Dictionary of the English Language*.

always break down against the facts. But though poetry does not deprive the word of transitive significance, the primary aim of poetry is not to use words transitively, but to make a structure of words on which the imagination rests. Poetry, like prose, uses words. But it does not use them in the same way. 'It can even be said that it does not *use* them at all; one would rather say that they use it. Poets are men who refuse to *utilise* language.' For prose discourse words are useful tools, to effect a purpose; for poetry they are ends in themselves. This view is brilliantly and profoundly stated by Sartre, a writer who is commonly thought to be little sympathetic to poetry. The passage (from which the quotation above is taken) is unfortunately too long to reproduce here, but the reader must be referred to it,[2] for it defines the quality of poetry in the sense we are considering better than any other piece of criticism known to me.

[104]   Poetry then makes its own verbal organization in some sense an absolute, though it may do other things besides. Prose uses its verbal organization for ulterior ends—expressive, descriptive, analytical. To use the terminology in 16, poetry is that kind of discourse, whether in prose or verse, that makes *radiance* its dominant aim.[*]

Since verbal radiance is to some degree present in all literature, and since *verbal* radiance is present in literature alone and not in any of the other arts, it is easy for the term poetry to become extended, as we have seen, to cover imaginative literature in general. This suggests what Sartre would not, that poetry is at the centre of imaginative literature as a whole; that however unevenly it may be distributed through the whole, it is the vital essence of imaginative literature.

[105]   The fact that this distinction between poetry and prose is clear in principle does not mean that it is easy to draw. Nor is it important to draw it exactly. Individual cases may be felt differently by different readers; but it does not matter.

Some obvious 'prose poems' come to mind—De Quincey's *Suspiria*, Maurice de Guerin's *Le Centaure* (with its sentence that so enchanted the young Matthew Arnold). And we can see places in writers as different as Sir Thomas Browne, Ruskin, Joyce, Hemingway, where the aim of

---

[2] 'Qu'est-ce que la littérature?', *Situations*, II, 1948, pp. 63–71. Passage quoted in my translation.

[*] In 16, Hough defines *radiance* as: "all that gets lost in translation; all that is comprised in the aesthetic organization of the linguistic surface; all that goes beyond a utilitarian or simply expressive use of words. Literature must have *radiance* in order to satisfy and illuminate by its verbal surface . . . its texture." [editor's note]

verbal radiance suddenly takes over from the prevailing hortatory, descriptive, or narrative purpose, and we are in the presence of poetry:

'Yes, the newspapers were right: snow was general all over Ireland. It was falling on every part of the dark central plain, on the treeless hills, falling softly upon the bog of Allen, and further westward, softly falling into the dark mutinous Shannon waves. . . .'[3]

[106]   This does something to clarify common terminology, but the critical distinction arrived at is not of great importance. We do not in fact often want to distinguish between 'prose' and 'poetry' in this way; we more often want to see them working in collaboration.

There remains the distinction between prose and verse; and this is easier. Bentham was on the right track; verse is discourse divided into more or less regular formal units by a principle other than the meaning. The formal organization of prose arises directly out of its meaning; verse has a formal organization independent of its meaning.

Attempts have been made by free-verse theorists, and notably by Sir Herbert Read,[4] to see the formal organization of verse as arising directly out of its meaning. But though this way of thinking has its local applications, as a generalization about verse form it is radically mistaken. However they may come to subserve meaning, the hexameter, the Alexandrine, the English heroic line are formal structures logically anterior to any particular meaning that may find its way into them.

[107]   The distinction of verse from meaning may be seen by considering its origin. Meaning arises from the need to express, or to describe, or to persuade. Verse form arises from a delight in rhythm, that has nothing to do with expressing, describing or persuading. The delight in rhythm, first noted as natural to man by Aristotle, is also, according to Darwin, natural to animals. It can be observed in the play of small children (rhythmical bangings, cries, etc.), in the drum-beating of primitive peoples, and in the dance. It is of course physiological in origin, related to the rhythms of bodily life, of which the beat of the heart and the rhythm of breathing are the most important. The smaller rhythmical units, metrical 'feet', marked in English verse by the ictus or stress, correspond roughly to the beat of the heart. The next larger units, the individual lines of verse, correspond roughly to the rhythm of breathing.

The beating of the heart, the act of breathing, are vital movements

---

[3] Joyce, last paragraph of 'The Dead', the last story in *Dubliners*.

[4] *Form in Modern Poetry*, 1932 and 1948. Reprinted in *The True Voice of Feeling*, 1953.

of which we are normally unaware. To stress or reinforce them consciously by sound or movement gives an enhanced sense of life. Here we have a fundamental cause of pleasure in verse entirely independent of meaning. This independence persists. Children often delight in verse as jingle without any understanding of the meaning. Many adults on occasion do so too; and it is to be suspected those who are most sensitive to poetry are among them.

[108]   Rhythm as an independent source of pleasure is soon taken over for expressive purposes; but only taken over in part. An element of independence remains. Those like Coleridge who would discover the origin of the regular rhythm of verse in emotion, or the effort to keep emotion in check,[5] are not taking their enquiry far enough back. Rhythm does become a means of expressing and controlling emotion; but it is an independent source of satisfaction first.

It is easy to see how the sense of rhythm becomes the agent of emotional expression. For obvious physical reasons rhythms faster than the normal, (faster, that is, than the normal beat of the heart) suggest gaiety, activity or urgency; rhythms slower than the normal suggest melancholy, pensiveness or exhaustion. The development, the elaboration, the subtilizing, of these crude rhythmical effects form a considerable part of the technical history of verse. With the passage of time certain rhythms become conventional and acquire set forms. We then call them metres; and what began as spontaneous gesture does in the end become a matter of conscious measurement. The standard metres become paradigms within which poetry develops its meaning.

It is as well to remove the vulgar error that this formalizing of rhythmic organization has been the affair solely of grammarians and pedants. The poets themselves have been closely and technically interested in metrics. Among the English poets we may instance Spenser, Sidney, Milton, Dryden, Pope, Coleridge, Tennyson, Patmore, Hopkins, Bridges, Eliot, Pound.

The particular phonetic features used to constitute verse-rhythm vary, naturally, in different languages—quantity in Greek and Latin, stress in English and German, etc. Alliteration is part of the formal structure of Anglo-Saxon verse and pitch a part of the formal structure of Chinese verse; while in English verse both these features are expressive variables, but are no part of the formal pattern.

No more can be said here about formal prosody or the expressive value of particular rhythmic devices. These things belong not to the principles

---

[5] *Biog. Lit.*, chap. XVIII.

but to the practice of criticism, and to a special technical branch of it at that.

[109]   The important matter of principle that has emerged so far is that we have two branches of literature, one (prose) with a loose formal organization arising out of meaning; the other (vĕrse) with a much stricter formal organization independent of meaning.

We next want to ask whether this difference brings other differences in its wake. This we have partly answered already. Verse with its strict formal organization tends to attract into its sphere most poetry—most, that is to say, of the literature that makes verbal radiance its prime end. (Most but not all: 102–4 above.) The reason for this is suggested by Coleridge: the 'exact correspondent recurrence of accent and sound' that we find in verse is calculated to excite a 'perpetual and distinct attention to each part' of the discourse.[6] Discourse in verse therefore is required to be of finer verbal texture than that in prose which is read with a more general attention. And it is in part enabled to fulfil this requirement by subtleties of stress and intonation that verse alone can control.

Take Pope's line to the Goddess of Dullness: 'Light dies before thy uncreating word.' How much metaphysics and cosmology is concentrated in the single syllable un-; the whole idea of a destructive logos, the anti-thesis of all that has made our world. And how much of this vista is opened up by the fact that this unimpressive syllable is the subject of a metrical stress.

Close verbal criticism of poetry has in consequence always seemed natural and appropriate. Prose is taken in larger draughts; and to subject it to similar analysis has always seemed somewhat of a pedantry, or the purpose of some special kind of scholarship.

[110]   Until recent times, however uncertain the boundary between prose and poetry, the boundary between prose and verse was clear and undis-puted. Since Whitman there have been continual formal experiments of several different kinds that have tended to obscure this boundary. 'Free verse', in its numerous manifestations, is not strictly metrical in the old sense; i.e. it is not 'measured'. There have been some, though fewer, experiments in self-consciously rhythmical prose. This has led to the ques-tion whether the old prose-verse distinction is as absolute as it seemed; and to one notable attempt at obliterating it.

This is Mallarmé's essay 'Crise de vers',[7] which suggests that the real

6 *Biog. Lit.*, chap. XIV.
7 *Œuvres,* Pléiade edn., p. 361. Cf. 16 (c).

distinction is not between verse and prose but between language used with an aesthetic purpose and language used without any such intention. Verse, to this way of thinking, begins as soon as there is any conscious aesthetic organization of language. Mallarmé hails the rise of a *majestueuse idée inconsciente*, to wit, that verse is present as soon as diction is accentuated, rhythm as soon as style. This is a radical and attractive notion, and one that would effect a considerable alteration in our ordinary critical habits. It has obvious applications to the highly-wrought and specialized literature of the Symbolist movement and its aftermath. But its application to our general literary experience is less obvious. We return to the customary concepts of prose and verse simply because over most of the literary field they are more useful. And Mallarmé's *majestueuse idée* had better remain a seductive and delicate tool, used only for special purposes.

George R. Bach & Peter Wyden

The Ways Lovers Fight

Most marriages are chronic complaint societies. The husband always leaves his socks on the living-room floor. The wife always turns the bathroom into a laundry. He always forgets to put gas in the car. She always messes up the newspaper before he's through with it. He always hogs the conversation at parties. She's always too tired to make love. And so on and on. It doesn't much matter which of the partners complains for the umpteenth time about which source of perpetual annoyance; if the couple is untrained, the ensuing fight drags on approximately as follows:

> PARTNER A (*wearily*): I know, I know. God, how many times have we been through all this before? I know you hate it.

THE WAYS LOVERS FIGHT   Abridged by permission of William Morrow & Co., Inc. from *The Intimate Enemy* by George R. Bach & Peter Wyden. Copyright © 1968, 1969 by George R. Bach & Peter Wyden.

PARTNER B (*exasperated*): So why in hell don't you quit?

A: I've told you and told you! That's just the way I am. Don't you know that by now?

B: Sure, but I'll never get used to it and it's driving me up the wall!

A: Why don't you get off my back about the same old stuff? What's the use? You know I can't change.

B: Well, neither can I . . .

We call such stalemates round-robin fights. Untrained couples can't get off these depressing merry-go-rounds because they subscribe to the notion that "you can't change people." This defeatist attitude couldn't be more unfortunate; it inhibits the enterprise and imagination that partners need to come up with new solutions.

To dislodge trainees from such an impasse we point out that in these fast-changing times the willingness to change oneself, and to be changed by others, is as important as growing to adulthood in the first place. It is a vital sign of maturity and mental health. A noted psychoanalyst, Dr. L. S. Kubie, has explained it like this: "The measure of health is flexibility, the freedom to learn through experience, the freedom to change with changing internal and external circumstances, to be influenced by reasonable argument, admonitions, exhortations, and the appeal to emotions; the freedom to respond appropriately to the stimulus of reward and punishment, and especially the freedom to cease when sated."

Making changes is easier than most people think because the alternatives are just about endless. One can change one's self. Or one's partner. Or one's way of dealing with the other. Or one's environment (perhaps by making new friends, moving to a new neighborhood, or visiting the in-laws less often).

Perhaps the partner who is annoying his spouse simply needs to be more careful to go into action at times when the spouse is in a good mood and better able to "take it." Or the annoyed partner should demand some improvement in living conditions or some other compensation for putting up with the annoyance. Or the annoying partner might try to persuade the other to join in the very activity that's considered annoying (drinking, golf, swearing, smoking, going to church, making love in a certain way, or whatever).

There are times when round-robin rituals can be inoffensive or even useful. If partners decide, after candid negotiations, that a particular chronic fight issue is, in fact, unimportant as long as they are getting along otherwise, they may choose to adopt such an annoyance as a family pet and trot it out for a quick fight round whenever they feel the urge to uncork some pent-up hostile feelings. But in our experience the best way to handle a chain of round robins is to break it up.

Another brand of unguided hostility that can lead to dreadful trouble is the volcanic eruption that we call the Vesuvius. This is just blowing off steam—a spontaneous irrelevant sounding-off of free-floating hostility. It is an adult temper tantrum that does not involve a partner directly, although it is advisable to have an intimate on hand as an audience. A Vesuvius unleashed against no one and on the open street would lead to curious glances and conceivably to arrest on charges of disturbing the peace.

A beautiful Vesuvius was delivered by one husband who came home from work and yelled at his wife, *à propos* of nothing in particular, "If that S. O. B. Jones does it just once more, I'll punch him in the nose and that goes for your Uncle Max, too!" (Nobody had mentioned Uncle Max for weeks; he functioned here only as a free-floating kitchen sink handy for throwing into the Vesuvius.)

The Vesuvius is never directed at anybody who is at the scene of the explosion or nearby. It never involves issues that are pending between partners. It doesn't deal with anything that the partner who is witnessing the Vesuvius could be expected to do anything about. And it evaporates as quickly as a puff of smoke. The best way to make certain that a Vesuvius is not, in fact, a bugle call to a serious fight about some brand-new issue is to listen sympathetically to a partner's outburst and to wait a bit for what happens next. In an authentic Vesuvius, nothing does.

There are, on the other hand, clues that crop up in the most peaceful marriages and should never be ignored (although they usually are). They may just signal minor annoyances. More likely, they are flashing yellow danger signals indicating that the partner who is doing the clue-dropping is toting a dangerously ballooning gunny sack full of grievances. At any rate, these clues should be investigated for what's behind them. Here are some examples of clues that should never be met by silence or indifference:

"I wish you wouldn't *do* that!" Or: "You've got to stop ignoring me!" Or: "Don't push me too far!" Or: "I wish you'd take a stand!" Or: "It drives me batty when you feed the dog after I've already fed him!"

Unlike the Vesuvius, such a danger signal is intensely personal. It is a direct demand upon a loved one to stop being unlovable. It is smoke before a fire; and it deals with something that the signal's recipient is equipped to do something about.

This is the time to start the process we call leveling. Its superficial meaning is clear enough. It means that one should be transparent in communicating where one stands and candid in signaling where one wants to go. It is a special preserve of intimates and should run like a red thread through all their conflicts. With a casual acquaintance or a business associate, leveling is rarely worth the trouble. It may even be unwise. With a loved one, the art of aggressive leveling calls for careful cultivation. By "hooking in" to a partner's complaints or his hurt looks or stony silence intimates can find out "where they're at," and can then go on to fight for better mutual understanding.

A truly intimate aggressor will try not to start a fight until she has conducted a warm-up encounter within herself to clarify in her own mind what's at stake and how far she should go to press her point, for the truth is that one cannot competently level with one's partner until one has leveled with oneself.

An inner dialogue can expose crucial information—nuggets of intelligence which untrained fighters, much to their disadvantage, rarely develop for themselves before opening up on a spouse. Here are some questions that we recommend our trainees ask themselves before doing battle:

"Is this really my fight or somebody else's? Maybe my mother's? Or the President's?"

"Do I really have a legitimate bone to pick with my partner? Or do I just want to put him down and hurt him for the sake of a sadistic kick?"

"Am I really convinced that my partner's action or attitude is bad for our relationship?"

"What's at stake here? What does this fight really mean to me? Am I approaching it with realistic arguments and weapons or am I overreacting and getting ready to 'drop the bomb on Luxembourg'?"

Trainees often tell us that their fights begin with Pearl Harbor-type surprise attacks that leave no time for inner dialogues. "How can I go around talking to myself?" one hawk said. "When I get angry, I just blow up."

This is just another price of gunny-sacking one's grievances. True intimates who have real beefs against their partners don't wait for provocations and risk no Pearl Harbors. They balance their books on their aggressions as soon as practical.

Whether or not there is time for an inner dialogue before a fight, a wise aggressor will make sure that his opponent knows the real nature of the fight they're fighting. The steps to convey this intelligence are a vital part of leveling. We suggest that, as a fight proceeds, the aggressor make as clear a statement as possible of his demands or expectations; of the rational basis for his goals; and of realistic ways for his opponent to meet these demands. The aggressor should specify precisely what's at stake, what it would mean to him to lose the fight, and how the changes that he seeks will benefit both fighters.

When a wife says, "You'll really ruin my whole vacation if we don't go to the antique stores at least one afternoon," she places her husband on notice that he'd better give in if he doesn't want his own vacation ruined by her grousing.

When aims and proposed solutions are logically presented, most intimates can be gradually induced to absorb far more aggression than people usually think. But everybody maintains limits of tolerance—inner fortresses that one will not give up and whose inviolability is nonnegotiable. We suggest that partners acquaint themselves with their own nonnegotiable limits, preferably by way of an inner dialogue on each fight issue as it comes up. Once a partner is sure what his own limits are, he should level with the other and tell him the point beyond which there is no room for negotiation—at least not until further notice.

Louis Kronenberger

The Crank, the Eccentric, and the Individualist

Our well-founded distaste for cranks has . . . rather blurred our ability to tell a crank from a mere eccentric, or even an eccentric from an individual. On a very rough-and-ready basis we might define an eccentric as a man who is a law unto himself, and a crank as one who, having determined what the law is, insists on laying it down to others. An eccentric[1] puts ice cream on steak simply because he likes it; should a crank do so, he would endow the act with moral grandeur and straightway denounce as sinners (or reactionaries) all who failed to follow suit. The crank, however, seldom deals in anything so agreeable as steak or ice cream; the crank prefers the glories of health bread or the splendors of soybeans. Cranks, at their most familiar, are a sort of peevish prophets, and it's not enough that they should be in the right; others must also be in the wrong. They are by definition obsessed, and, by connotation, obsessed with something odd. They mistake the part for the whole, the props for the play, the in-

THE CRANK, THE ECCENTRIC, AND THE INDIVIDUALIST From *Company Manners*, copyright © 1951, 1953, 1954, by Louis Kronenberger, reprinted by permission of the publishers, The Bobbs-Merrill Company, Inc.
1 Many "eccentrics" are, of course, mere poseurs and publicity seekers. But many are real, and I speak here only of such.

convenience for the efficacy; they are spoil-sport humanitarians, full of the sour milk of human kindness.[2]

The crank is for several reasons a fairly common figure in American life. To begin with, our reaction against cranks has helped breed more of them. A society that worships good-guyism brands the mere dissenter a misfit, and people who are shunned as square pegs will soon find something deeply immoral about round holes. A society, again, that runs to fads and crazes, that has a natural turn for the ingenious and inventive, will encourage some of its members to be cranks and will doom others. There must be, so to speak, lots of factory-damaged human products that, from being looked upon as rejects, come to crankhood rather than true creativity. Careerwise, there is frequently a missed-the-boat quality in cranks, a psychological origin for their moral obsessiveness; and their "flourishing" off failure is tied up with their having failed at the outset. The crank not only increasingly harangues his audience, but the audience increasingly yawns at, and even walks out on, the crank.[3]

Where a crank is either a moral crusader by nature or a man at war with his surroundings, an eccentric is neither given to crusading nor oppressed by the world. Perhaps a certain amount of enjoyment is essential to the eccentric—his life is satisfactory *because* it is pleasant—as a certain lack of enjoyment is essential to the crank. The great blessing of eccentricity is that, since it is a law unto itself, one isn't constantly torn between what is expedient on the one side and what is personally desirable on the other. Something of an anarchist (as your crank is something of a bigot), the eccentric will often display very unsound, or unsocial, habits and beliefs. But there is nothing self-righteous about his wrongheadedness; he doesn't drag God into keeping a pet leopard in his back yard, or Americanism into going in for rifle practice at 2:00 A.M.

True eccentrics, I would think, are fairly rare, for they must not only differ from other people but be quite indifferent to other people's ways:

---

[2] They can be useful, at moments even invaluable, goads; but they fail of love no less than of humor, and seem most ready to plow the earth where they can spoil the lawn. John the Baptist *requires* the wilderness, and even a man of the critical excellence of Mr. F. R. Leavis evokes the workhouse. After all the gush of the Janeites, Mr. and Mrs. Leavis are well worth hearing on Jane Austen; but they, in the end, misrepresent her no less. They are the sort of people who, in assessing champagne, would give no consideration to the fizz.

[3] Just as many eccentrics are poseurs, so many cranks are charlatans. The charlatan shrewdly exploits human weakness where the true crank rails against it; the charlatan, preaching some form of nudism or trial marriage, some "holy" brand of licentiousness or God-sent type of laxative, may end up a millionaire. But the true crank has only a chip on his shoulder or bee in his bonnet, not a card up his sleeve.

they must, in other words, be as well adjusted as they are odd. So soon as maladjustment enters in, they cease to be characters and turn into cases. On the other hand, many people who with a little encouragement might emerge as eccentrics are, from childhood on, judged—and hence turned into—misfits. Where their peculiarities are mocked, and certainly where they are penalized, the results can be very unhappy. In America, where even the slightest individualist must resist great pressure, the true eccentric is never free from it. In England there is a proud tradition of eccentricity: the English are far more given than we are to keeping strange pets, collecting strange objects, pursuing strange hobbies, adopting strange careers; even where they most conform, as in their club life, they will behave toward one another with what, to other races, seems a wild and splendid strangeness. This is so true that England's—and sometimes New England's —eccentrics have often a great air about them, possess style rather than mere singularity. Consider how Julia Margaret Cameron would walk the two miles from her house to the railway station stirring a cup of tea as she went. In England and New England on the one hand, and in most of America on the other, there may be a quite opposite basis for eccentricity: in the one case, the law unto oneself born of social privilege; in the other, the self-made born of being left out of things. The English eccentric suggests a grande dame, the American a spinster.

The individualist is by no means an eccentric. He is for one thing aware of alternatives; he chooses—for the most part consciously—between the expedient and the self-satisfying; he refuses to play ball rather than doesn't know a game is in progress; and he will seldom seem freakish or even picturesque. Yet, more and more, the individualist is being looked on as an eccentric and perhaps even a crank; though this attitude is scarcely deliberate on the public's part, it yet subconsciously—or by force of repetition—constitutes a gimmick, a pressure to make people conform. The other method of diminishing individualism in America has been to foster and develop "personality." Though the difference between "personality" and individuality is vast, there exists a strong, however thoughtless, tendency to identify the one with the other. So greatly has conformity triumphed that, no matter how orthodox a man's opinions or conventional his behavior, if he happens to express or conduct himself with the slightest vividness or briskness, he is rated and touted a "person"—what might be supposed an individual! Actually, he may not even have an iota of real personality, may just possess a breezy, adaptable, quick-on-the-trigger manner that enables him to be the life of the party or the spark plug of the conference. In the same way, a woman with a gift for dinner-party chatter and a feminine, discreetly flirtatious air will be thought to have enormous personality.

And though such mere types must be written off, there yet *are* a great many Americans with true personality—with an easy charm, a distinctive way of doing and saying things, a regional tang, a surviving girlishness or small-boy quality. They have the appeal, at the very least, of not being like everyone else. But that, in the cliché sense, they are "real persons" is to be doubted. One may go a year without hearing them utter an original, not to say controversial, remark, or seeing them perform a striking, not to say truly unorthodox, act. The centrifugal and extrovert charm of personality is in many ways hostile to individualism, which more naturally manifests itself in withdrawal than in contact, in quiet dissent than in eager acquiescence. Personality and individuality are by no means mutually exclusive, nor is genuine personality necessarily engaging nor genuine individuality necessarily difficult. But the fact remains that we regard personality as a decided blessing, as something a man can't have too much of, and individuality as, oftener than not, a handicap. Individuality is almost by definition antisocial; and the sound "social" maneuver—or it were perhaps better called instinct—is to discredit individuality and eventually outlaw it through enabling people to live *colorfully* alike. As for "personality," it has passed from having great social to acquiring great economic importance: it is the prime mark, and prize asset, of the salesman. And ours is the country where, in order to sell your product, you don't so much point out its merits as you first work like hell to sell yourself.

Erich Fromm

Symbolic Language

One of the current definitions of a symbol is that it is "something that stands for something else." The definition is too general to be useful, un-

SYMBOLIC LANGUAGE   From pp. 188–93 of "Symbolic Language of Dreams" by Erich Fromm in *Language: An Enquiry into Its Meaning and Function,* edited by Ruth Nanda Anshen. Copyright © 1957 by Harper & Row, Publishers, Inc. Reprinted by permission of Harper & Row, Publishers.

less we can be more specific with regard to the crucial question concerning the nature of the connection between symbol and that which it symbolizes. . . .

We can differentiate between three kinds of symbols: the *conventional*, the *accidental*, and the *universal* symbol.

The *conventional* symbol is the best known of the three, since we employ it in everyday language. If we see the word "table" or hear the sound "table," the letters *t-a-b-l-e* stand for something else. They stand for the thing "table" that we see, touch, and use. What is the connection between the *word* "table" and the *thing* "table"? Is there any inherent relationship between them? Obviously not. The *thing* table has nothing to do with the *sound* table, and the only reason the word symbolizes the thing is the convention of calling this particular thing by a name. We learn this connection as children by the repeated experience of hearing the word in reference to the thing until a lasting association is formed so that we don't have to think to find the right word.

There are some words, however, in which the association is not only conventional. When we say "phooey," for instance, we make with our lips a movement of dispelling the air quickly. By this quick expulsion of air we imitate and thus express our intention to expel something, to get it out of our system. In this case, as in some others, the symbol has an inherent connection with the feeling it symbolizes. But even if we assume that originally many or even all words had their origins in some such inherent connection between symbol and the symbolized, most words no longer have this meaning for us when we learn a language.

Words are not the only illustration for conventional symbols, although they are the most frequent and best-known ones. Pictures also can be conventional symbols. A flag, for instance, may stand for a specific country, and yet there is no intrinsic connection between the specific colors and the country for which they stand. They have been accepted as denoting that particular country, and we translate the visual impression of the flag into the concept of that country, again on conventional grounds. Some pictorial symbols are not entirely conventional; for example, the cross. The cross can be merely a conventional symbol of the Christian Church and in that respect no different from a flag. But the specific content of the cross referring to Jesus' death or, beyond that, to the interpenetration of the material and spiritual planes, puts the connection between the symbol and what it symbolizes beyond the level of mere conventional symbols.

The opposite to the conventional symbol is the *accidental* symbol, although they have one thing in common: there is no intrinsic relationship between the symbol and that which it symbolizes. Let us assume that someone has had a saddening experience in a certain city; when he hears the name of that city, he will easily connect the name with a mood of sadness, just as he would connect it with a mood of joy had his experience been a happy one. Quite obviously there is nothing in the nature of the city that is either sad or joyful. It is the individual experience connected with the city that makes it a symbol of a mood. The same reaction could occur in connection with a house, a street, a certain dress, certain scenery, or anything once connected with a specific mood. . . . The connection between the symbol and the experience symbolized is entirely accidental.

In contrast to the conventional symbol, the accidental symbol cannot be shared by anyone else except as we relate the events connected with the symbol. For this reason accidental symbols are rarely used in myths, fairy tales, or works of art written in symbolic language because they are not communicable unless the writer adds a lengthy comment to each symbol he uses. In dreams, however, accidental symbols are frequent, and Freud by his method of free association devised a method for understanding their meaning.

The *universal* symbol is one in which there is an intrinsic relationship between the symbol and that which it represents. Take, for instance, the symbol of fire. We are fascinated by certain qualities of fire in a fireplace. First of all, by its aliveness. It changes continuously, it moves all the time, and yet there is constancy in it. It remains the same without being the same. It gives the impression of power, of energy, of grace and lightness. It is as if it were dancing, and had an inexhaustible source of energy. When we use fire as a symbol, we describe the *inner experience* characterized by the same elements which we notice in the sensory experience of fire—the mood of energy, lightness, movement, grace, gaiety, sometimes one, sometimes another of these elements being predominant in the feeling.

Similar in some ways and different in others is the symbol of water— of the ocean or of the stream. Here, too, we find the blending of change and constant movement and yet of permanence. We also feel the quality of aliveness, continuity, and energy. But there is a difference; where fire is adventurous, quick, exciting, water is quiet, slow, and steady. Fire has an element of surprise; water an element of predictability. Water symbolizes the mood of aliveness, too, but one which is "heavier," "slower," and more comforting than exciting. . . .

The universal symbol is the only one in which the relationship between the symbol and that which is symbolized is not coincidental but intrinsic. It is rooted in the experience of the affinity between an emotion or thought, on the one hand, and a sensory experience, on the other. It can be called universal because it is shared by all men, in contrast not only to the accidental symbol, which is by its very nature entirely personal, but also to the conventional symbol, which is restricted to a group of people sharing the same convention. The universal symbol is rooted in the properties of our body, our senses, and our mind, which are common to all men and, therefore, not restricted to individuals or to specific groups. Indeed, *the language of the universal symbol is the one common tongue developed by the human race,* a language which it forgot before it succeeded in developing a universal conventional language.

There is no need to speak of a racial inheritance in order to explain the universal character of symbols. Every human being sharing the essential features of bodily and mental equipment with the rest of mankind is capable of speaking and understanding the symbolic language that is based upon these common properties. Just as we do not need to learn to cry when we are sad or to get red in the face when we are angry, and just as these reactions are not restricted to any particular race or group of people, symbolic language does not have to be learned and is not restricted to any segment of the human race. Evidence for this is to be found in the fact that symbolic language as it is employed in myths and dreams is found in all cultures, in the so-called primitive as well as such developed cultures as those of Egypt and Greece. Furthermore, the symbols used in these various cultures are strikingly similar since they all go back to the basic sensory as well as emotional experiences shared by men of all cultures. Dreams of people living in the United States, India, or China today, as well as those which are reported to us from Greece, Palestine, or Egypt 3000 years ago, are essentially the same in contents and structure.

The foregoing statement needs qualification, however. Some symbols differ in meaning according to the difference in their realistic significance in various cultures. For instance, the function and consequently the meaning of the sun is different in northern countries and in tropical countries. In northern countries, where water is plentiful, all growth depends on sufficient sunshine. The sun is the warm, life-giving, protecting, loving power. In the Near East, where the heat of the sun is much more powerful, the sun is a dangerous and even threatening power from which man must protect himself, while water is felt to be the source of all life and the main condition for growth. We may speak of *dialects of universal symbolic language,* which are determined by those differences in natural conditions which cause certain symbols to have a different meaning in different regions of the earth.

Different from these "symbolic dialects" is the fact that many symbols have more than one meaning in accordance with various kinds of experiences which can be connected with one and the same natural phenomenon. Let us take the symbol of fire again. If we watch fire in the fireplace, which is a source of pleasure and comfort, it is expressive of a mood of aliveness, warmth, and pleasure. But if we see a building or forest on fire, it conveys to us an experience of threat and terror, of the powerlessness of man against the elements of nature. Fire, then, can be the symbolic representation of inner aliveness and happiness as well as of fear, powerlessness, or of one's own destructive tendencies. The same holds true of the symbol of water. Water can be a most destructive force when it is whipped up by a storm or when a swollen river floods its banks. Therefore, it can be the symbolic expression of horror and chaos as well as of comfort and peace.

Another illustration of the same principle is a symbol of a valley. The valley enclosed between mountains can arouse in us the feeling of security and comfort, of protection against all dangers from the outside. But the protecting mountains can also mean isolating walls which do not permit us to get out of the valley and thus the valley can become a symbol of imprisonment.

The particular meaning of the symbol in any given place can only be determined from the whole context in which the symbol appears, and in terms of the predominant experiences of the person using the symbol. . . .

Questions

Diction and Structure

1. How does Graham Hough make use of definition, directly and indirectly, in "Prose, Verse and Poetry"? Is his essay an extended definition?

2. What specific criticism does he make of the dictionary definition of *prose, verse,* and *poetry?* Are his own definitions free from this criticism?

3. Does Hough make clear the meanings he intends for these words in his essay: *semantic, discourse, utilize, ulterior, imaginative, prosody?* Look up the meaning of these terms: *hortatory, epistemology, autotelic.* Does Hough use them conventionally?

4. The paragraphs of Hough's chapter from a longer critical study are numbered. From evidence within this section, why do you suppose he chose to break up his essay and to number the parts? Is the device one that makes Hough's ideas more apparent? Does it aid the logical development of the essay?

5. In section 104, Hough refers to an earlier section (16) for a definition of *radiance.* Is the meaning of the term clear without

consulting the earlier section? Look up *radiance* in a dictionary; what meaning(s) would be appropriate to Hough's stipulative use of the word as you understand it in the present essay?

6. George R. Bach and Peter Wyden, in their essay on lovers' fights, appear to use what definition of *fight?* Is this use a commonly understood one?

7. Are the ways of fighting described by Bach and Wyden "good," "bad," or both? What unifying principle holds the essay together?

8. Look up the term *colloquialism* in the dictionary. How do Bach and Wyden utilize colloquialisms in their essay? Why do they do so?

9. Louis Kronenberger also uses definition to augment his classification; what techniques of definition do you find in his essay?

10. Exactly what group of things is Kronenberger classifying? Is he dealing with human beings as a whole? Americans as a national group? Some minority group or groups? Justify your answer.

11. How precise are the distinctions between a crank, an eccentric, and an individualist, as Kronenberger draws them? What is their relationship to a "personality"?

12. In Kronenberger's terms, are the ways of behavior described by Bach and Wyden "eccentric"? "cranky"? "individualistic"? Explain.

13. Look up the meaning of *eccentric* in the OED or some other dictionary. How does the root meaning relate to the meaning assigned to the word by Kronenberger?

14. Erich Fromm begins his essay "Symbolic Language" by rejecting one definition of *symbol;* with what definition, stated or understood, does he replace it?

15. What, exactly, is Fromm classifying in his essay: words, symbols, objects, or feelings? What principle of classification does he use?

16. Fromm uses many of the same examples—fire, water, the sun—for more than one of his categories of symbol. Does this mean that his categories are poor ones, unable to divide the members of a group significantly?

17. Look up the meaning of *denotation* and *connotation* and relate them to Fromm's classes of verbal symbols.

Style and Rhetoric

1. What principle(s) of classification does Hough reject in establishing his categories of poetry, prose, and verse? What

principle does he settle upon in making his own classification?

2. What is the relationship of poetry to prose, as Hough establishes it? To verse? Are there basically two or three categories?

3. If Hough's classes of prose and verse are used, could any single example be placed into both categories? Are they mutually exclusive?

4. Reread the final paragraph in Hough's essay. Does it threaten to destroy the classification he has made? Explain.

5. Unlike Hough, who gives almost no examples of items to be put into his theoretical classes, Bach and Wyden give specific examples of fights. Are their categories therefore better or more firmly "proved" than Hough's categories?

6. Why did Bach choose "Vesuvius," "Pearl Harbor," etc., as headings for his classifications?

7. How would you classify Bach's prose style in his essay: formal, informal, or technical? Or none of these? For what audience is he apparently writing?

8. Is the prose used in the fight "dialogues" very different from the essay text itself? Is the essay as a whole "formal" or "informal"?

9. Compare the use of footnotes in the essays by Nowlis and Hough with Kronenberger's footnotes. How are Kronenberger's notes different from the customary usage typified by the other writers? How do they affect the style and tone of Kronenberger's essay?

10. Look up these terms: *idiom, colloquialism, vulgarism.* Is Kronenberger writing in an idiomatic, colloquial, or vulgar style — or none of these? Can an essay on formal classification be written in an informal manner?

11. Erich Fromm's essay on symbolic language, by its very nature, deals with abstractions: sounds, words, thoughts, feelings. How does he keep his treatment of an abstract subject from becoming overly abstract and vague itself? Notice the diction of the essay: are the words abstract or concrete, general or specific, denotative or connotative?

12. Test the accuracy of Fromm's statements about verbal symbols being conventional, accidental, and universal by formulating your responses to the following terms, then placing them into one or another of Fromm's categories: blood . . . the Eiffel Tower . . . Dallas, Texas . . . the moon . . . the Statue of Liberty . . . X . . . bread . . . Hollywood . . . C+ . . . skull and bones . . . salt . . . ashes . . . mistletoe. Why did Fromm avoid giving numerous examples for his classes?

13. By Lucas' standards for style, are the essays on classification

in this section well written or not? Is there anything inherently difficult about organizing and writing a classification essay?

Theme and Viewpoint

1. Are the kinds of marital fights enumerated by Bach and Wyden instances of Selye's "stress" or not? Would Bach accept the idea that quarreling and fighting between intimates is a necessary aspect of "stress" as "life"? How so?

2. Do Wyden and Bach actually define the headings for their fight classifications: "Drop the Bomb on Luxembourg," "Vesuvius," etc. Do they need to? Explain.

3. Do the classifying terms of Bach and Wyden fit into Fromm's categories of symbolic language? Is "Pearl Harbor" a "universal" term? An "accidental" one? What about "Vesuvius" and "Round Robin"?

4. Is the language in Bach's and Wyden's essay "poetic" in any sense as Hough defines poetry? Is it exclusively prose? Justify your opinion.

5. Does Fromm's discussion of the ambiguous symbolism of such objects as fire and water help to explain why "drug" has both positive and negative associations today? Which definitions given by Nowlis serve to illustrate the positive and negative associations that Fromm identifies?

6. Compare and contrast the ways that Hough, Bach and Wyden, Kronenberger, and Fromm use arbitrary or stipulative definitions as headings for their classifications. Are any of the classifications in this section "scientific" in the sense of physical fact? Would that affect the need for arbitrary as compared with "established" definitions? How?

7. Do Fromm's theories of symbolic language pertain to Lucas' assumptions about style or to Hough's idea of radiance? Elaborate upon your opinion.

Comparing
and contrasting

"What is it like?" How often this question crops up in conversation! And, whether stated or not, it frequently underlies the essay which explains or presents information. What is it like? The word "like" indicates the basic technique of the expected answer: it is like this thing or that; it is similar to one object in this characteristic or quality and dissimilar in other qualities.

Explaining an unknown person, place, thing, or idea in terms of something familiar by identifying their shared qualities is the method of comparison. To compare is to point out similarities, usually by employing words such as "like," "as," "similar," and their compounds, "likewise," "similarly," and so forth. The Latin word *similis* means "like" or "as"; and the figure of speech called a *simile* is a direct comparison between two things. In this way, the distinctive qualities of something—say, a zircon—can be identified by listing better known objects that share these qualities; it has a shining surface like glass, can be cut like a diamond, reflects light as a diamond or prism does, and so on. Or a ziggurat is a tower that looks like an inverted cone with a spiralling, snakelike ramp around it. Comparison is also a basic way of conceiving abstract or intangible qualities—for instance, radio "waves," or "dirty" jokes. In this condensed, covert form, the comparison becomes a *metaphor*.

The reverse of comparison is contrast, which is really negative comparison. "My mistress's eyes are nothing like the sun," Shakespeare wrote, thereby making fun of the poetically worn-out comparison of other, trite writers; "If hair be wires, black wires grow on her head." By listing all the qualities his beloved does *not* have, he manages to show her as a real woman and not a gaggle of clichés.

As intellectual and literary devices, comparison and contrast are found everywhere. Their importance to defining— where the term is grouped according to a principle of similarity and then distinguished from the rest of the group by its differences—is obvious. Classification is the result of systematically comparing and contrasting numbers of things. Unlike definition or classification, however, comparisons may be made between seemingly quite unlike objects—perhaps a thermometer and a bicycle pump. Comparisons and contrasts may be based on a number of different criteria: shape, color, and size; cost, value, use; principle of operation; method of manufacture or development; or various others. Selecting a really significant basis of comparison or contrast is the key to using the method to best advantage, just as selecting a principle of categorization is the essence of useful classification.

Comparing and contrasting may perform many functions: making the unknown familiar or simply understandable; revealing the essence of something by showing how it resembles or differs from something else; disclosing operative principles that apparently unlike objects share; helping to define and classify. Measuring the subject's ability to compare and contrast is one of the chief ways by which psychologists determine intelligence: remember those I.Q. tests which show five geometric shapes and ask you to identify the one that is unlike the rest? Or the word-lists in which one word does not apply to the key term provided? Whether you match buttons or screws in a store, pick out your own automobile among five hundred others in a parking lot, or try on several outfits of clothes before buying one, you are comparing and contrasting. This procedure extends to a large part of the range of human activities; it is, therefore, little wonder that it should be so widespread a literary method.

Margaret Mead

New Year's—A Universal Birthday

Just before midnight an expectant hush falls on the party gaiety. Someone throws open a window. In the moment of waiting silence the thoughts of some turn to the past, while others, making a half-serious wish or resolution, look to the future. And some only wait impatiently. Then suddenly the spell is broken as bells ring out, whistles and sirens blow and the holiday-makers join in the din with their horns and shouts of "Happy New Year!"

New Year is a festival of transition, the point where end meets beginning. It is a celebration of the idea of time, an idea that has captured man's imagination for millenniums. Traditional celebrations, however they varied over the centuries and in different cultures, gave formal and public expression to feelings of awe and wonder, mourning and rejoicing, repentance and hope and purpose, the sense of men's relations to one another and to the whole universe.

But New Year's today has become for most people the mere shell of a celebration, without content or focus. Everywhere there are parties: office parties, parties in homes, country-club dances, crowds in hotels and night spots, pushing and raucous crowds in the streets, moody crowds in bars—and the lonely feel doubly alone. There is incessant talking and noise and almost everywhere there is too much to drink—too often the prelude to louder noise, accidents on the road and hangover headaches on New Year's Day.

We treat the New Year casually. In our time it has become a wholly secular holiday. Only a few tag ends remain of old beliefs. There is the modern Mummers Parade in Philadelphia, but no one now connects this with the old idea that at New Year the world is turned topsy-turvy. We at-

NEW YEAR'S —A UNIVERSAL BIRTHDAY   Reprinted from *A Way of Seeing* by Margaret Mead and Rhoda Metraux, by permission of The McCall Publishing Company. Copyright © 1967 by Margaret Mead and Rhoda Metraux.

tribute no magical power to our resolutions and no one treats the events of the day as omens for the year. No one waits to see who will be the first to step over the doorsill (a dark man, good luck; a fair man, bad luck; a woman, death).

Few of us remember that the decrepit Old Year, whom we picture in cartoons as a bowed and bald Father Time with his sickle, is also a figure of death; or that the baby New Year, chubby and smiling as a cupid, is also a symbol of love and light. These two figures survive, often as figures of fun, but we barely acknowledge their older meaning. And almost no one now realizes that in our own tradition the pealing of bells, not only at the New Year but also at births and weddings and on other occasions marking a transition, once was intended to drive out evil and all that might endanger what was so newly begun. Instead, our noisemaking has become a very slightly ritualized salute to the future.

But noise is only one way of marking a transition.

In Bali, once every 400 days quiet descends. On this day nothing stirs on the whole densely populated island. People speak of it as "the Silence," the Balinese New Year. On every other day the roads are crowded with hawkers, people going to and from market, small boys driving oxen or water buffalo and people hurrying lightly under heavy loads. On feast days there also are gaudy processions walking behind their orchestras and theatrical troupes traveling to the villages where they will perform.

The air on every other day is loud with the sound of voices, the shouts of vendors, laughter at jokes, the squalling of babies carried on the hips of their child nurses, the yapping of dogs and the music of practicing orchestras. Even in the deepest night the quiet is broken by shrill cockcrowing, dogs barking and lonely peasants out in the fields playing bamboo xylophones softly to themselves. But on New Year no one moves about and every sound is hushed. Each family, its fires out and offerings arranged in the house temple, stays at home to observe the Silence.

Looking the world over, one very striking thing is the limited number of ways in which men have regarded the progress of time. Many peoples treat time as we do, as a stream that flows forever onward, never passing the same point twice. What is passed cannot come again.

Other peoples, such as the Balinese, think of time as a cyclical process, as if time were a wheel that periodically turned on itself. And some peoples have regarded man's life as part of a cycle—the individual is born and dies and eventually is born again. Very often, just at the turning point—at the end of each year or of a set of years—people have believed that this was potentially a period of great danger when the sun might never rise again or the earth might cease to be fertile or all human life might be destroyed in some great disaster. To avert the danger many peoples have ritually fasted and organized their affairs—paying their debts, ending their quarrels, cleaning their houses, rebuilding their temples and in other ways straightening out their own and the world's affairs. Then, when the new time has come, they have celebrated its arrival with other rituals, some expressing joy at danger overcome, some interpreting omens for the future and others designed to make the new time safe and fruitful.

Our own feeling that the turn of the century has a special quality carries with it something of this sense of precarious balance at the end of a cycle. Already, at the end of the 1960s, we are engaged in predicting what life will be like for our children in the year 2000, and we are concerned with preparing the world for the millennial shift to a new 1,000-year cycle. But we have no rituals to focus our activities, only a diffuse sense of concern that shapes our discussions of the year 2000, as deeper emotions once gave meaning to ceremonies of transition.

To a certain extent the heightened sense of the meaning of time at New Year is related to the invention of calendars, and peoples who have no script and no calendar for measuring regular intervals over a very long span have a more limited conception of time. For them time stretches back only as far as memory does and forward into the lives of their grandchildren, and it is only the seasons that come and come again. Very indefinitely, also, time goes back to the beginning, when they as a people came into being.

This beginning may be only four or five generations ago, just beyond the reach of the memory of living men, as it was for some of the peoples of the New Guinea highlands. Or it may have been long, long ago, its extent unmeasured and unmeasurable, as the Iatmul people of the Sepik River in New Guinea believed. And memory can be extraordinarily stretched out, as it was among Polynesian islanders who kept track of the names and adventures of important ancestors in strings of genealogies that went back sometimes to mythological beginnings.

Even so, without the idea of a calendar it is impossible to conceptualize great spans of time. In the past 100 years we have stretched out time over millions of years in reading the history of the earth. Today we also have the means of dividing time into milliseconds for fine measurements. All this has depended on complex inventions.

But for primitive peoples, day and night, the shifting patterns of the night sky, seasonal changes in winds and weather, seedtime and harvesttime, the waxing and waning of the moon, the changing position of the sun and, of course, the birth, maturation and death of human beings—all these changing and recurrent aspects of the natural world have given men ways of punctuating time and marking transitions.

Some peoples have made very little even of these ways of marking time. When I was working among the Arapesh of New Guinea, I myself began to wonder what the date was. They had names for moons, such as "the moon when we get bananas from the deserted yam gardens." But as each family planted its garden with yams and bananas at a different time, they called the same moon by different terms. They said to me: "You count the moons, but we just know their names." And all they really knew was some names that could be appropriately used, and no two families followed the same calendar. They even thought it was odd that anyone should expect a moon to have only one fixed name.

Other peoples had a much more definite sense of cycles. In the past the Manus of the Admiralty Islands spoke of days and nights (measuring the length of journeys, for example) and moons and then of time expressed in terms of the life span. They would place an event in terms of other significant events, saying "when my father was a child" or "when I make the last marriage payment for my daughter." But they had no way of measuring, as we do, the months that become a year and the years that become a decade or a century.

When the Manus moved into the modern world they seized upon the European calendar, learned every detail about how it works and now talk endlessly in calendar time.

"Today is Sunday, the thirteenth of November, 1966," they would say to me. "It is just six weeks before Christmas."

The Manus write down not only the year and day of the month but even the hour on which a baby is born or a quarrel is ended. At home or away from home they know exactly the date on which their children will be taking final examinations and they plan for the future, setting their goals as we do by dates. With one leap they have taken over the conception of time that moves onward and its modern handling.

Heirs as we are to so many traditions, we have relegated all the solemn beliefs and celebrations connected with the turning of the seasons and the year to our different religious calendars. For a time in Western Europe, this meant that people lived by different calendars and celebrated the New Year at different seasons. In 1582, when Pope Gregory XIII modified the old Julian calendar and decided that the secular New Year should come (as it had for the Romans) on January 1st, Catholic countries made the change quickly; but Protestant countries continued to use Old Style dates for a long time and to celebrate the New Year as a spring festival, on March 25th, as medieval Christians had. England (and so England's colonies) made the change only in 1752. Few people today think of this, though there is an echo in a New Year's song we have assimilated into Christmas carols:

> Here we come a-wassailing
> Among the leaves so green.

The Jewish religious calendar, by contrast, has been stable for a much longer period, and the ceremonies ushered in by Rosh Hashana, which comes at the beginning of the first month of the year (the autumn of the secular year), still carry the symbolism of beginning and ending, repentance and rejoicing, death and life, darkness and light, that is the central expression of our human sense of transition.

In spite of our heritage, we make very little of the turn of the year. All that remains is the vague feeling that it is an occasion to be remarked, the sense that it is a time when people should come together, as families do to celebrate a birthday. And perhaps, just because it is a holiday that once focused men's deep emotions about the past and the future and the continuity of time, the New Year may again become infused with meaning. A world society that must take into account the lingering traditions of all peoples may come to observe it as a day in which humanity can celebrate a common birthday in time.

John H. Steele

The Fiction of Science

People often talk about science being objective. They think of it as something logical and rather inhuman, with an attitude to life symbolised by the cold neutral colours of its apparatus. I sometimes wonder how true this is. I work in a laboratory. There is chemical apparatus on my bench and a calculating machine on my desk. The scientific journals are prepared to publish my results, so I suppose I can call myself a scientist. But does this job of mine deserve these attributes which people give to 'science'? For example, Kathleen Nott says 'progress for the whole human race would be, if not inevitable, at least highly probable, if a sufficient majority of people were trained to use their reasoning power on their general experience as a scientist is trained to use his reasoning power on his special experiences'.

THE FICTION OF SCIENCE   From *The Listener,* June 13, 1957. Reprinted by permission.

This blunt instrument of the analogy with science is also used frequently by literary men. Irving Singer wrote:

> Science is based on observations that are not affected by the idio-
> syncrasies of time and space, but critical evaluation depends on
> interpretations which vary from observer to observer; scientific
> statements are true or false, but statements in art criticism are
> neither one nor the other and can only be accepted or rejected.

It is this sort of thing that worries me. Is science—or, to put it simply, am I—'not affected by the idiosyncrasies of time and space'? Am I a machine with observations going in one end and scientific papers coming out the other; an automatically recording angel in a white coat? If that is science, then I must find another name for my job. What I know as science is not so objective, so neutral, nor so inhuman as these descriptions suggest. What are these supposedly neutral, objective 'facts' and 'observations'? Probably the commonest image is a young man noting the reading on a dial. In photographs he wears a laboratory coat and spectacles and looks suitably anonymous. He could be anyone; it is the foreground which counts.

Yet it need not be as simple as that. Niko Tinbergen has worked for many years on the instinctive acts of animals. He believes that the patterns of behaviour which an animal inherits are much more complex than was once thought possible. To prove this he has watched the reactions of different animals in widely varying situations, natural and artificial. But what are his observations? Which movements of a continuously moving animal are to be considered relevant to his theory? There is a film taken by Dr. Tinbergen of a colony of herring gulls showing how impossible it is for a casual observer to separate particular recurrent gestures from all the other acts which the birds make. But Dr. Tinbergen has watched gulls for many years and his facts, his observations, are chosen typical gestures which he considers relevant to his theories. The whole complex pattern of such a piece of work is highly individual; it is reasonable to say that it could not have been done by anyone else.

Yet it is not only in the biological sciences that this kind of individual judgement is required. It occurs in any study of natural events. Often it is impossible to ensure that every observation is correctly made and often they cannot be repeated—we must decide which to accept. In physical oceanography, for example, the data are collected at sea in difficult circumstances and not until later will it be noticed that certain observations 'look wrong'. It is possible to think of explanations of these in terms of faulty equipment. It is possible to make special experiments to show that such things occasionally happen. But, finally, for the routine data, the scientist has to make his own decision to ignore certain values, to interpret a curve in a certain way.

These, then, are the situations in which the facts themselves are difficult, where the scientist is forced to make his own judgements on what is important or unimportant, right or wrong. Like all judgements they are based on experience, but also like all judgements they have no final justification. The answer is that these difficulties merely illustrate the shortcomings of this type of scientific work. They show how far it is from the ideal of science; an ideal more closely approached by theoretical physics. It is for this reason that physics is so often taken as the example by all the writers who wish to compare science with their own bit of the world.

Yet even if this were true, physics does not necessarily make the best model for comparison with, say, the criticism of poetry. Surely it would be better, if rather less imposing, to compare the critic Dr. Leavis studying a group of poems with Dr. Tinbergen watching a colony of herring gulls. There are differences but the similarities are just as interesting. Both must continuously decide what is important and what is unimportant, and they must convince us that their decisions are the right ones. But the main thing which they have in common is their strong individuality separating them from other critics or other scientists. Still the hankering after the ideal remains. There is the criticism of criticism; no longer the struggle with detail, the problems in one stanza; the concern now is with poetry itself, so now surely the comparison is with what science ought to be.

But what is this world of physics like, this place of controlled observation, of tame facts? It is the world of theory. A hypothesis is set up and it is deduced from it that a certain event should occur in certain circumstances. An experiment is performed to see if this happens. If it does not, then the hypothesis is disproved; if it does, then it is evidence in its favour. But how decisive is the experiment? To what extent does it help to establish the hypothesis? Is it possible there are other unthought-of explanations of this result?

The more general, and thus the more important, the theory is, the more it tries to explain. But this means there are more possibilities to be considered, more chance of something being neglected, a greater need for further experiment. It is here that we have arguments and disagreements; people have ideas which they cannot see how to prove; or they disagree about the interpretations of experiments. Now where are we with the statement, 'scientific laws are true or false but literary criticism is only a matter of emotion or opinion'? Surely it is obvious that while it is science, while the experiments are being made, it is only the results of these experiments which exist. They are part of the world just as a poem is. We argue about them, we interpret them and disagree about our interpretations. Afterwards when we have made a number of experiments we have learned something. We can make 'planes fly faster than sound and we can stop them with guided missiles that have atomic warheads. But this is no longer science, it is engineering or technology. The scientists are arguing now about something else, the theory of the 'heat barrier', perhaps, or the possibility of a new bomb. The usefulness is a by-product of science. It provides money to go further, just as a packed theatre or a third edition helps the writer. But these, so we are told, are not the definition of art.

How has this illusion come about? How is it that science is considered an impersonal activity, a kind of automation? Perhaps scientists themselves are to blame. In conversation one of them might say: 'I felt such-and-such might be the right way of looking at things, so I did this experiment. I was unlucky though, it turned out to be quite the opposite to what I had expected, but I made a better guess the next time'. However when he comes to make it public, he will write up his second guess (the first being quietly ignored) in this way: 'It can be deduced mathematically from this theory that an experiment should show . . .', and you may be sure it does. It is all done in the traditional manner; the personality, if there were any signs of it, has been removed by the editor. Sometimes a little emotion may creep in among the letters at the back of a journal; an opponent's arguments considered to be 'as violent as they are empty'. It could almost be a literary magazine—but it is soon hushed up.

Have I been exaggerating? I suppose so. Being a scientist is very different from being a literary critic, and both are unlike the job of a stockbroker. It is unusual to be successful at any two of these but it is not *a priori* impossible, for they are all ways of living. Stockbrokers would not try to prove that their job was not worldly, and the same attempt with literature has never been noticeably successful. It is only with science that the illusion exists; the illusion of a neutral, inhuman activity separate from the world of 'telegrams and anger'. Perhaps scientists are to blame for their part in creating it, but it would not last if it were not bolstered up by every writer who wishes to use this 'objectivity' to beat up his opponents for being emotional and opinionated.

Does it matter, though, if the illusion is so widespread that both the public and the scientists themselves believe it? Perhaps it does no harm beyond creating confusion in the literary journals. I think its effects are more serious. If people believe that science is something objective, then they will try to use it like a term in an equation—such an equation as 'science plus money equals bigger bombs'. When, for a time, this equation did not work for the hydrogen bomb, they looked for a simple logical explanation, and investigated the loyalty of the scientist in charge, Robert

Oppenheimer. But it is not as simple as that. The fallacy in the equation was not logical, it was human.

The problem of making a hydrogen bomb seemed purely technical. One man thought it could be made; another, Oppenheimer, thought it could not. The evidence which they had was not decisive. It was one of these occasions when there can be arguments, interpretations, opinions; just as there can be with the moral problems of creating such a weapon. These problems are different but they are not separate. They are linked by the fact that they both have to be worked out in the mind of one man, and in the attempt to understand them they become connected; connected, not by logic, but because they are both human activities. And the greater that man's mind the more important and more subtle are those connections.

To pretend that they can be kept separate, one in a world of facts, the other in a world of opinion, can lead to tragedy; to the tragedy of Robert Oppenheimer who tried to keep them apart. When he was cross-examined at the public enquiry into his loyalty, he said: 'I have always thought the hydrogen bomb was a dreadful weapon. Even though from a technical point of view it was a sweet and lovely and beautiful job, I have still thought it was a dreadful weapon'.

'But', he was asked, 'did you say so?'

'Yes', said Oppenheimer, 'I would assume that I've said so'.

'You mean that you had a moral revulsion against the production of such a dreadful weapon?'

'Oh that's too strong', replied Oppenheimer.

'What is too strong', said his questioner, 'the weapon or my expression?'

'Your expression', said Oppenheimer. 'I had a grave concern and anxiety'.

'You had moral qualms about it, is *that* accurate?'

'Let us', said Oppenheimer, 'leave the word "moral" out of it'.

Leo Rosten

English, Ameridish, and Yinglish

This is a book about language—more particularly, the English language. It shows how our marvelously resilient tongue has been influenced by another parlance: Yiddish. It illustrates how beautifully a language reflects the variety and vitality of life itself; and how the special culture of the Jews, their distinctive style of thought, their subtleties of feeling, are reflected in Yiddish; and how this in turn has enhanced and enriched the English we use today.

So, this book explores a fascinating aspect of English: those words and phrases from Yiddish (some I call "Yinglish," some "Ameridish") that we today encounter in English books, magazines, newspapers; or hear on television or radio, in movies or nightclubs; or may overhear on the street or in a bus in many a large city in the United States.

By "Yinglish" I mean Yiddish words that are used in colloquial English in both the United States and the United Kingdom: *kibitzer, mishmash, bagel,* etc.

By "Ameridish" I mean words coined by, and indigenous to, Jews in the United States: *kochalayn, utz, shmegegge,* etc.

"Yiddish," "Hebrew," and "Jewish"

For the benefit of innocents, I hasten to add that Yiddish and Hebrew are entirely different languages. A knowledge of one will not give you even a rudimentary understanding of the other. True, Yiddish uses the letters of the Hebrew alphabet, employs a great many Hebrew words, and is written, like Hebrew, from right to left, thusly:

UOY EVOL I ACIREMA

—which should delight any reader under fourteen. But Yiddish and Hebrew are as different from each other as are English and French, which also use a common alphabet, share many words, and together proceed from left to right.

Nor is "Yiddish" a synonym for "Jewish." "Yiddish" is the name of a language. Technically speaking, there is no language called "Jewish." Strictly speaking, Jews do not speak "Jewish" any more than Canadians speak Canadian, or Baptists read Baptist. But it would be foolish to deny that in popular English usage, "Jewish" *is* used as a synonym for "Yiddish." After all, "Yiddish" comes from the German *Jüdisch*, meaning "Jewish," and in the Yiddish language itself *Yiddish* means "Jewish." We may as well accept reality.*

The Scope of This Wordbook

This book, accordingly, is a lexicon of certain foreign-born words that:

(1) are already part of everyday English (*shmaltz, gonif, shlemiel*);

(2) are rapidly becoming part of English (*chutzpa, megillah, shlep, yenta*);

(3) should be part of our noble language, in my opinion, because no English words so exactly, subtly, pungently, or picturesquely convey their meaning (*shmoos, kvetch, shlimazl, tchotchke,* etc.)

Were I writing all this in the style and with the impudent imagery so characteristic of Jewish humor, I would say: "This book is a collection of three kinds of simply *delicious* words: those which are naturalized citizens; those which have taken out their first papers; and those which should be drafted into our army just as soon as possible."

The Influence of Yiddish on English

It is a remarkable fact that never in its history has Yiddish been so influential—among Gentiles. (Among Jews, alas, the tongue is running dry.) We are clearly witnessing a revolution in values when a Pentagon officer, describing the air-bombardment pattern used around Haiphong, informs

---

* The distinction between "Jewish" and "Yiddish" is, I may say, ignored by many Jews: those who do not know there is a difference, and those (especially third-generation, or of German descent) who dislike and deliberately avoid the word "Yiddish."

the press: "You might call it the bagel strategy." Or when a Christmas (1966) issue of *Better Homes and Gardens* features: "The Season's Delightful Jewish Traditions and Foods." Or when the London *Economist* captions a fuss over mortgage rates: HOME LOAN HOO-HA. Or when the *Wall Street Journal* headlines a feature on student movements: "REVOLUTION, SHMEVOLUTION." Or when a wall in New York bears this eloquent legend, chalked there, I suppose, by some derisive English major:

> MARCEL PROUST
> IS A
> YENTA

Or when England's illustrious *Times Literary Supplement,* discussing the modern novel, interjects this startling sentence: "Should, schmould, shouldn't, schmouldn't." Or when a musical play about the Jews in the Polish *shtetl* of fifty years ago, *Fiddler on the Roof,* scores so phenomenal a success.

Yiddish phrasing and overtones are found in, say, the way an Irish whiskey advertises itself:

> "Scotch is a fine beverage and deserves its popularity.
> But enough is enough already."

Or in an advertisement for a satirical English movie, *Agent 8¾*:

> "By Papa he's a spy,
> By Mama he's a spy,
> But from spies he's no spy!"*

I can cite dozens of similar uses of Yinglish idiom.

Yiddish Words and Phrases in English

Every so often I run across the statement that *Webster's Unabridged Dictionary* contains 500 Yiddish words. I do not know if this is true, and I certainly doubt that anyone actually counted them. For my part, I am

---

* This ploy of deflation originally involved the playwright Samson Raphaelson and his mother. Mr. Raphaelson, having scored a considerable success on Broadway and in Hollywood, bought himself a yacht—and a nautical cap, on which "Captain" was embroidered. Old Mrs. Raphaelson studied the cap on her proud son's head and won immortality by saying, "By you you're a captain, and by me you're a captain; but tell me, Sammy, by a *captain* are you a captain?"

surprised by the number of Yiddish words, thriving beautifully in everyday English, that are *not* in *Webster's,* nor in other dictionaries of the English language—including the incomparable thirteen-volume *Oxford English Dictionary.* You will find many of these lamentably unrecognized words in the volume you now hold in your hands.

Many a scholar has commented on the growing number of Yiddish words and idioms that "invade" English. But English, far from being a supine language, has zestfully borrowed a marvelous gallimaufry of foreign locutions, including many from Yiddish; and who will deny that such brigandage has vastly enriched our cherished tongue?*

Take the popular usage of the suffix, *-nik,* to convert a word into a label for an ardent practitioner or devotee of something: How could we manage without such priceless coinages as *beatnik* and *peacenik? The New York Times* recently dubbed Johann Sebastian's acolytes "Bachniks"; some homosexuals dismiss nonhomosexuals as *straightniks;* the comic strip *Mary Worth* has employed *no-goodnik;* and a newspaper advertisement even employed Yiddish-in-tandem to get "NOSHNIKS OF THE WORLD, UNITE!"

Many a student of contemporary mores has discovered the degree to which novelists, playwrights, joke writers, comedians, have poured Jewish wit and humor into the great, flowing river of English. This is also an indication of the extraordinary role of Jewish intellectuals, and their remarkable increase during the past forty years, in the United States and England.

Who has not heard or used phrases such as the following, which, whatever their origin, probably owe their presence in English to Jewish influence?

> Get lost.
> You should live so long.
> My son, the physicist.
> I need it like a hole in the head.
> Who *needs* it?
> So why do you?
> Al*right* already.
> It shouldn't happen to a dog.
> O.K. by me.
> He knows from nothing.
> From that he makes a *living?*

---

* I have elsewhere pointed out that a sentence like "The pistol in our bungalow is stuffed with taffy" contains words from six languages (Slovak, Czech, Hindustani, Tagalog, Old French, English—via Old Frisian), and that an utterance such as "Oh, bosh! Some nitwit has put alcohol in the ketchup!" entails the uncopyrighted use of Turkish, Dutch, Arabic, French, Malay, Chinese, and pidgin Japanese.

How come only five?
Do him something.
This I need yet?
A person could bust.
He's a regular genius.
Go hit your head against the wall.
You want it should sing, too?
Plain talk: He's crazy.
Excuse the expression.
With sense, he's loaded.
Go fight City Hall.
I should have such luck.
It's a nothing of a dress.
You should live to a hundred and twenty.
On him it looks good.
It's time, it's time.
Wear it in good health.
Listen, *bubele* . . . ?

What other language is fraught with such exuberant fraughtage?

Colloquial Uses in English of Yiddish Linguistic Devices

But words and phrases are not the chief "invasionary" forces Yiddish has sent into the hallowed terrain of English. Much more significant, I think, is the adoption by English of linguistic *devices*, Yiddish in origin, to convey nuances of affection, compassion, displeasure, emphasis, disbelief, skepticism, ridicule, sarcasm, scorn. Examples abound:

1. Blithe dismissal via repetition with an *sh* play-on-the-first-sound: "Fat-shmat, as long as she's happy."
2. Mordant syntax: "Smart, he isn't."
3. Sarcasm via innocuous diction: "He only tried to shoot himself."
4. Scorn through reversed word order: "Already you're discouraged?"
5. Contempt via affirmation: "My *son*-in-law he wants to be."
6. Fearful curses sanctioned by nominal cancellation: "A fire should burn in his heart, God forbid!"
7. Politeness expedited by truncated verbs and eliminated prepositions: "You want a cup coffee?"
8. Derisive dismissal disguised as innocent interrogation: "I should pay him for such devoted service?"
9. The use of a question to answer a question to which the answer is so self-evident that the use of the first question (by you) constitutes an

affront (to me) best erased either by (a) repeating the original question or (b) retorting with a question of comparably asinine self-answeringness. Thus:

[A]

Q. "Did you write your mother?"

A. "Did I write my mother!" (Scornful, for "Of course I did!")

[B]

Q. "Have you visited your father in the hospital?"

A. "Have I visited my father in the *hospital?*" (Indignant, for "What kind of a monster do you think I am?")

[C]

Q. "Would you like some chicken soup?"

A. "Would I like some *chicken* soup?" (Emphatically concurring, for "What a stupid thing to ask.")

[D]

Q. "Will a hundred dollars be enough?"

A. "Will a hundred dollars be enough?" (Incredulously offended, for "Do you think I'm crazy to accept so ridiculous a sum?")

[E]

Q. "Will a thousand dollars be enough?"

A. "Will a *thousand* dollars be enough?" (Incredulously delighted, for "Man, will it!")

[F]

Q. "Will you marry me?"

A. "Will I *marry* you?" (On a note of overdue triumph, for "Yes, yes, right away!")

Or consider the growing effect on English of those exquisite shadings of meaning, and those priceless nuances of contempt, that are achieved in Yiddish simply by shifting the stress in a sentence from one word to another. "Him you *trust?*" is entirely different, and worlds removed, from "*Him* you trust?" The first merely questions your judgment; the second vilipends the character of the scoundrel anyone must be an idiot to repose faith in.

Or consider the Ashkenazic panoply in which insult and innuendo may be arrayed. Problem: Whether to attend a concert to be given by a neighbor, niece, or friend of your wife. The same sentence may be put through maneuvers of matchless versatility:

(1) "*Two* tickets for her concert I should buy?" (Meaning: "I'm having enough trouble deciding if it's worth one.")

(2) "Two *tickets* for her concert I should buy?" ("You mean to say she isn't distributing free passes? The hall will be empty!")

(3) "Two tickets for *her* concert I should buy?" ("Did she buy tickets to *my* daughter's recital?")

(4) "Two tickets for her *concert* I should buy?" ("You mean to say they call what she does a 'concert'?!")

(5) "Two tickets for her concert *I* should buy?" ("After what she did to me?")

(6) "Two tickets for her concert I *should* buy?" ("Are you giving me lessons in ethics?")

(7) "Two tickets for her concert I should *buy*?" ("I wouldn't go even if she gave me a complimentary!")

Each of the above formulations suggests a different prior history, offers the speaker a different catharsis, and lets fly different arrows of contumely. And if all emphasis is removed from the sentence, which is then uttered with mock neutrality, the very unstressedness becomes sardonic, and—if accompanied by a sigh, snort, cluck, or frown—lethal.

Ian Stevenson

People Aren't Born Prejudiced

What is prejudice? Its characteristics and origins have by now been carefully studied by psychologists and sociologists so that today we know a good deal about how it is transmitted from one person to another.

PEOPLE AREN'T BORN PREJUDICED From *Parents' Magazine*, February 1960. Reprinted by permission.

Prejudice is a false generalization about a group of people—or things —which is held onto despite all facts to the contrary. Some generalizations, of course, are true and useful—often needed to put people and things into categories. The statement that Negroes have darkly pigmented skin and nearly always curly hair, isn't a prejudice but a correct generalization about Negroes.

Ignorance isn't the same as prejudice, either. Many people believe that Negroes are basically less intelligent than white people because they've heard this and never have been told otherwise. These people would be prejudiced only if they persisted in this belief after they knew the facts! Well documented studies show that when Negroes and whites are properly matched in comparable groups, they have the same intelligence.

Prejudiced thinking is rarely, probably never, confined to any one subject. Those prejudiced against one group of people are nearly always prejudiced against others. Prejudice, then, could be said to be a disorder of thinking: a prejudiced person makes faulty generalizations by applying to a whole group what he has learned from one or a few of its members. Sometimes, he doesn't even draw on his own experiences but bases his attitudes on what he has heard from others. Then he behaves toward a whole group as if there were no individual differences among its members. Few people would throw out a whole box of strawberries because they found one or two bad berries at the top—yet this is the way prejudiced people think and act.

There are different kinds of prejudice, and two of these deserve separate consideration. First there is that loosely spoken, loosely held opinion that can be called conforming prejudice: people make prejudiced remarks about other races, nations, religions or groups because they want to conform to what they think are the conventions of their own group. Attacking or deriding members of another group who "don't belong" gives them a sense of solidarity with their own group. It's rather sad but also fortunate that most prejudice is probably this conforming kind. Fortunate, because this type of prejudice is easily given up when a new situation demands it.

A number of studies have shown that while people may protest about some social change, when the change actually takes place most will fall silently and willingly into line. It's the rare examples of change being resisted with violence that unfortunately receive most publicity. A psychologist interested in this phenomenon once made an amusing study of the differences between what people say they'll do and what they really do in a particular situation that evokes prejudice. Traveling across the country with a Chinese couple, he found that the three of them were received in 250 hotels and restaurants with great hospitality—and only once were refused service. When the trip was over, he wrote to each of the hotels and restaurants and asked if they would serve Chinese people. Ninety-two percent of those who had actually served them said they would not do so!

The second kind of prejudice is less easily relinquished than the conforming type, for this second kind stems from a more deep-rooted sense of personal insecurity. A prejudiced person of this kind usually has a feeling of failure or guilt about his own accomplishments and, to avoid the pain of blaming himself, he turns the blame on others. Just as the Jews once symbolically piled all their guilt on a goat and drove it into the wilderness, so these prejudiced people make scapegoats out of Negroes, Southerners, Jews, Russians or whoever else fits their need. Moreover, insecure people like these are anxious, too, and anxious people can't discriminate among the small but important differences between people who seem alike. So, on the one hand they often can't think clearly about other people; and on the other, they need to blame scapegoats in order to feel more comfortable. Both these mechanisms promote faulty generalizations; these people respond to others not as individuals but as Negroes, Russians, women, doctors—as if these groups were all alike.

The first important point about how children learn prejudice is that they do. They aren't born that way, though some people think prejudice is innate and like to quote the old saying, "You can't change human nature." But you can change it. We now know that very small children are free of prejudice. Studies of school children have shown that prejudice is slight or absent among children in the first and second grades. It increases thereafter, building to a peak usually among children in the fourth or fifth grades. After this, it may fall off again in adolescence. Other studies have shown that, on the average, young adults are much freer of prejudice than older ones.

In the early stages of picking up prejudice, children mix it with ignorance which, as I've said, should be distinguished from prejudice. A child as he begins to study the world around him, tries to organize his experiences. Doing this, he begins to classify things and people and begins to form connections—or what psychologists call associations. He needs to do this because he saves time and effort by putting things and people into categories. But unless he classifies correctly, his categories will mislead rather than guide him. For example, if a child learns that "all fires are hot and dangerous," fires have been put firmly into the category of things to be watched carefully—and thus he can save himself from harm. But if he learns a category like "Negroes are lazy" or "foreigners are fools," he's learned generalizations that mislead because they're unreliable. The thing is that, when we use categories, we need to remember the exceptions and differences, the individual variations that qualify the usefulness of all generalizations. Some fires, for example, are hotter and more dangerous than others. If people had avoided all fires as dangerous, we would never have had central heating.

More importantly, we can ill afford to treat people of any given group as generally alike—even when it's possible to make some accurate generalizations about them. So when a child first begins to group things together, it's advisable that he learn differences as well as similarities. For example, basic among the distinctions he draws is the division into "good" and "bad"—which he makes largely on the grounds of what his parents do and say about things and people. Thus, he may learn that dirt is "bad" because his mother washes him every time he gets dirty. By extension, seeing a Negro child, he might point to him and say, "Bad child," for the Negro child's face is brown, hence unwashed and dirty and so, "bad." We call this prelogical thinking, and all of us go through this phase before we learn to think more effectively.

But some people remain at this stage and never learn that things that seem alike, such as dirt and brown pigment, are really quite different. Whether a child graduates from this stage to correct thinking or to prejudicial thinking, depends to a great extent on his experiences with his parents and teachers.

Generally speaking, a child learns from his parents in two main ways. Each of these may contribute to his development either as a prejudiced personality or a tolerant one. First, a child learns a good deal by direct imitation of his parents. If parents reveal prejudiced attitudes, children will tend to imitate those attitudes. If a mother or father, for example, tells a child, "I don't want you playing with any colored children," they foster in their child's growing mind the connection between "colored" and "bad"—and thus promote the growth of prejudice. If instead of saying "colored children," a mother says "nigger" in a derogatory tone of voice, this makes another harmful connection in a child's mind. Even before he clearly knows to what the words Negro or "nigger" refer, he would know that these words mean something "bad" and hence indicate people for him to avoid. It may be that some colored children, like some white children, are unsuitable playmates. But the prohibition should be made on the grounds of the particular reasons for this unsuitability, not on the basis of skin pigment.

How parents actually behave toward members of other groups in the presence of their children influences children as much or more than what parents say about such people. Still, parents can and do communicate prejudices in subtle ways, by subtle remarks. For example, some parents take pride in belonging to a special group, lay stress on the child's membership in that group, and consequently lead him to believe that other people are inferior because they're outside this group. Sometimes parents are unaware that the pride they take in such membership in a special group can be an insidious form of prejudice against other groups. This isn't always so, because often pride in belonging can be related to the genuine accomplishments of a group. But just as often, pride stems simply from thinking of the group as special and superior because of its selectivity, not because of its accomplishments. However, this kind of direct transmission of prejudice from parents to children is the conforming type, and so can usually be modified by later experience if the child comes into contact with other unprejudiced people or if he has the opportunity to get to know members of the group toward which he has had prejudiced attitudes. For example, during the Second World War and the Korean War, many white soldiers of both North and South fought with Negro troops; knowing Negroes as people, they lost their old prejudices.

Unfortunately, however, parents tend to restrict their children's experiences with different kinds of people, for fear that the children might be harmfully influenced. This naturally prevents the children from unlearning prejudices. Unfortunately, these children who most need broadening and correcting experiences are often deprived of them.

Parents promote prejudice in a second, more subtle and harmful way by their own treatment of their children. Studies of markedly prejudiced persons show that they usually come from families in which they were treated harshly, authoritatively and unfairly—in other words, they were themselves the objects of prejudice. This parental behavior promotes prejudice in the children—apart from their imitation of it—in two ways. First, if parents treat a child harshly and punish him unfairly, they are relating to the child in terms of power instead of love. Treated as if he were always bad, the child will respond to his parents as if they were always dangerous. Growing skilled in the quick detection of threats or possible injury, he becomes sensitive to danger not only from parents but from other people as well. He makes quick judgments in order not to be caught unaware. Quick judgments are a facet of prejudiced thinking. An insecure and easily frightened person makes sweeping judgments about whole groups, finding it safer to treat the whole group as if it might be harmful to him. He thinks, often unconsciously and always incorrectly, that then he can never be hurt.

Secondly, when parents relate to a child in terms of power, when they punish him, say, with equal severity for accidentally knocking over a dish or for biting his baby brother, he not only thinks of his parents as dangerous people but he thinks of himself as dangerous, too. He must be bad, otherwise why would he be punished so often? Given this low opinion of himself, he will often try to raise it by putting the blame on others—using the old unconscious scapegoat mechanism. Here again, psychological studies have shown that people who are able to blame themselves when they're responsible for things going wrong tend to be much less prejudiced than people who blame others when things go wrong. But a child can only learn to accept blame fairly if his parents attribute blame fairly to him. If he is blamed for everything, he may—in his own defense—grow up unable to accept the blame for anything. If he cannot blame himself he has to blame others—he has to see them as more deficient and blameworthy than they are—which means making prejudiced judgments about them.

School can help undo the damage. Actual personal experience with children of other groups can show a child directly, immediately and concretely that not all members of a group are blameworthy, stupid, dirty or dishonest. In addition, unprejudiced teachers can instruct children in the ways of clear thinking that underlie tolerance. There is definite evidence that education reduces prejudices. It's been found, for example, that college graduates are less prejudiced on the whole than people with less education. Direct instruction about different groups and cultures, another study shows, reduced prejudice in those who were taught.

Fortunately, we seem today to be making progress in the direction of less prejudiced belief and behavior. Today, parents treat children with greater respect for them as individuals—in short, with less prejudice. This will continue to exert a healthy influence on the next generation. In fact, one survey has shown that it already has! College students of our generation, it demonstrates, are less prejudiced than college students of the last generation.

But since prejudice against members of a minority group or the peoples of other countries is a luxury we can increasingly ill afford—no parent should relax his vigilance in guarding against sowing the seeds of intolerance.

Questions

Diction and Structure

1. Dr. Margaret Mead is a famous social scientist, specifically a cultural anthropologist. Her essay "New Year's —A Universal Birthday" was written for a nonprofessional magazine, however.

Is her diction in the essay formal or informal? Is it technical or scientific?

2. Mead's essay deals in part with humanity's sense of time. Is "time" defined anywhere? Can you explain why?

3. What is the chief purpose of Mead's essay, judging from the way it is developed and the emphasis on its various groups of data? What is the reason for comparing and contrasting the facts that Mead has amassed?

4. To what extent is John H. Steele's "The Fiction of Science" an extended definition? What is he defining and how does he go about it?

5. Steele uses a great many rhetorical questions; in fact, almost every paragraph in his essay begins with one or contains two or more. How are they related to the author's central topic? What is their effect on the tone of the essay?

6. Although he is a scientist (i.e., a chemist), Steele avoids almost all obviously scientific language in his essay. Can you explain why? Is this an effective method for getting his point across or not?

7. The words in the title of Leo Rosten's "English, Ameridish, and Yinglish," are neologisms. What are neologisms and what purpose(s) do they serve, if any? What restrictions prevent all of us from inventing neologisms whenever we feel like it?

8. In his *The Joys of Yiddish*, Rosten defines the terms used in this essay. *Megillah* is a scroll, a long, prolix account full of details; *yenta* is a gossipy woman, a scandal-spreader; *shmegegge* is a dope, whiner or drip; *utz* is to tease or fool. If these Yiddish words can be defined in proper English, of what use are they as Yiddish? How does Rosten justify the Yiddish rather than the English terms?

9. Rosten mingles some erudite polysyllables—"vilipends," "panoply," "gallimaufry," "catharsis"—with slang and Yiddish idioms in his essay. Why does he do this? What is the effect of the mixture?

10. Rosten's essay begins with stipulative definitions. Are they necessary or useful? Do they clarify or merely serve to provoke interest in the subject?

11. Ian Stevenson begins his essay "People Aren't Born Prejudiced" with a rhetorical question about definition. Does he answer the question satisfactorily? Is his definition a successful working one upon which to build the essay?

12. Notice Stevenson's discussion of the associations carried by the terms "colored," "Negro," and "nigger." Do these terms

belong to different levels of diction? Are words "formal," "informal," "vulgar," "obscene," or "profane," entirely because we are emotionally conditioned as children to consider them so?

13. To what extent does Stevenson think prejudice is a matter of verbal clichés ("You can't change human nature!")? If the prejudice of ignorance is largely verbal, does Stevenson's theory that education erases prejudice logically follow?

Style and Rhetoric

1. Mead's essay begins with a description of a New Year's Eve party in the United States, and then goes on to state the central idea of the essay. How are these related? How is the description of the Balinese Silence connected to the opening sections? How does the final paragraph of the essay tie together these opening ideas?

2. "New Year's—A Universal Birthday" makes a number of comparisons and contrasts: the American celebration and the Balinese; the average Balinese day and the day of Silence; different ideas of time. Identify the various sets of comparison and contrast in the essay. What principle unites them all into a coherent essay?

3. Compare and contrast Mead's discussion of the Manus' use of symbolic language with Fromm's treatment of symbolic language (p. 50 above).

4. What aspects of the scientist and the literary critic does Steele compare and contrast: their mental equipment, operational procedures, physical apparatus, their purposes and effects, or something other than these?

5. How does Steele use the stockbroker, the technician, and the engineer to assist his comparisons and contrasts? Are the comparisons and contrasts clear? Are they accurate?

6. Identify the ways Steele uses comparisons and contrasts in his treatment of the sciences—e.g., ornithology, botany, physics. Do these show that each science resembles another science less than it resembles literary activity? What do the comparisons and contrasts show?

7. Rosten's "English, Ameridish, and Yinglish" uses several methods of rhetorical development in addition to comparison and contrast. What are they and how do they prepare for the central sections using comparison as an extended technique?

8. How does Rosten's title suggest the methods and tone of his exercise in comparison and contrast? Are the things being com-

pared and contrasted tangible or intangible or both? If you think they are intangible, explain how Rosten's rhetorical approach helps to make them concrete and vivid.

9. Examine the final section of Rosten's essay carefully. Just what is he comparing and contrasting?

10. What is being compared and contrasted in Stevenson's article "People Aren't Born Prejudiced"? Does the author use any of the techniques of classification?

11. How is prejudice related to errors of classification, according to Stevenson? Are errors of classification errors of ignorance, conforming prejudice, or "scapegoat" thinking? In his discussion of "a child," "a Negro child," and "a bad child" on page 78, does Stevenson himself slip into any of these errors of classification? Explain.

12. Outline Stevenson's essay. In your outline, show how the author divides and subdivides his topic.

Theme and Viewpoint

1. Rosten's discussion of the origins of "Ameridish" and "Yinglish" bears comparison with Morton Bloomfield's methods and interests in "A Brief History of the English Language" on page 331 below. Read Bloomfield's essay. How do his approach and style differ from Rosten's? May Rosten's essay on the contribution of Yiddish to the English language be considered a legitimate addition to Bloomfield's "Short History" or not?

2. Compare and contrast the format and tone of the definitions given by the *Oxford English Dictionary* with Rosten's. Can the two approaches be fully described by the terms "formal" and "informal"? What words best describe the two methods? Is there any reason a "dictionary" must be "formal" and "dignified" rather than cheerful and breezy like Rosten? Discuss.

3. Are the examples of Yiddish words and usages given by Rosten an example of the way prejudiced attitudes may be embodied in language? Do Stevenson's comments about prejudice apply to the Yiddish dialect in any way? How so?

4. Has Yiddish any of the qualities of "symbolic language" as Fromm described it?

5. Are the distinctive elements of Yiddish "poetic" in Graham Hough's sense of the word? Does Rosten imply that Yiddish has "radiance"? Is so, where and in what terms?

6. Steele is a scientist who compares and contrasts scientists and literary critics. Herbert Muller is a literary critic who makes

the same comparison. How do their conclusions differ? Are they alike in any way? Do Steele and Muller work out of the same or different assumptions? Do they define their terms differently?

7. Steele's essay tries to destroy the stereotyped idea of the Objective Scientist. How does this stereotype resemble prejudice of the favorable variety? In Fromm's terms, is the stereotype of the Objective Scientist a form of the "conventional symbol"? How did it develop?

8. Are Kronenberger's categories of crank, eccentric, and individualist pertinent to the Steele essay in any way?

9. Do Kronenberger's descriptions of the crank and the eccentric smack of prejudice to any degree? Is he favorably prejudiced toward the individualist or not?

10. Which do you find most provocative among the titles of the essays read so far? Are any of your responses due to favorable or negative prejudices you have been nurturing in the past? Can you explain how you might have acquired any such prejudices?

Analyzing

The word "analysis" comes from two Greek words, *ana* —"throughout" or "completely," and *lyein*—"to loose" or "to set free," that is, to separate something into its parts for the purpose of seeing how it is constituted. In a sense, the physicist carries on a kind of violent analysis when he or she splits atoms into their component parts: electrons, protons, neutrons, neutrinos, and so forth. But ordinarily we think of analysis as a less forceful and more deliberate procedure, whether it is the chemist's separation of a compound into its elements, the Madison Avenue researcher's "breakdown" of cereal consumption in New England, or the English teacher's taking apart of a Shakespearean sonnet to show how it is a structure of ideas and words.

The impulse to take things apart can be observed in all human beings: from the little girl with a screwdriver and her mother's toaster to the irate husband who disassembles the television set when it flashes off in the middle of a triple play during the Sunday ball game. Curiosity may kill cats but it motivates people to analyze for the sake of understanding something, perhaps changing and improving it, or restructuring it to suit another purpose. The atom theory has proved to us that virtually everything is made up of lesser parts, even the atom itself (which the Greeks called *a tom*, "without parts," because they thought it was irreducible matter). Nowadays, the desire for knowing what things are and how they operate often takes the form of analyzing.

Analyzing may be a mechanical process, the systematic separation of tangible objects (plants, minerals, chemical compounds, machines) into their constituent parts. Electrolysis and stripping a radio chassis are examples. Analysis may be a logical procedure in which a set of figures (stock market prices, mortality rates, results of interviews) are "broken down" into their significant elements and relationships (the rise in steel prices is directly related to the price rise for automobiles; the incidence of heart disease is less than cancer; 68 percent of all married men have at least one extramarital affair). Or analysis may be an intellectual or intuitive way of viewing something—a written composition, a recurrent event, a style of behavior—and systematically explicating its operative principles and connections. The social critic who examines the attitudes that underlie jokes about women is analyzing in this fashion. So is the psychologist who dissects human emotions and their subconscious connections to show how love and lust are differently constituted. And so is the T.V. critic who looks into the workings of the Disney industry in a Florida wonderland.

Analyzing occasionally uses the techniques of definition, classification, and comparison and contrast for its own ends. At times, it may appear to be indistinguishable from these, especially from classification. Classification, however, deals with groups of things that are related by their surface similarities or some organic principle. The relationship between hundreds of rocks or thousands of spiders that is expressed in classification actually is an artificial one that people arbitrarily create for the sake of convenience. A tarantula in Tasmania and one in the Galapagos possess like qualities but there is no real connection or tangible relationship between them. They do not function in concert or share some cohesive role. The single tarantula can be dissected by an entomologist and its physiology analyzed; but this kind of internal analysis is quite different from the classification of the spider by family or *genus*.

Analysis does not have to be of physical objects, however. So long as the phenomenon under observation is a coherent, unified entity—a body of verbal humor, the national food supply, a branch of the entertainment industry—it is susceptible to the techniques of the analyst, who views the corporate phenomenon as a whole made up of functioning and related parts and who then separately examines these parts and their connections for the sake of comprehending the vital and total nature of the subject under examination. Thus Elizabeth Janeway observes the overall assumption that women's liberationists have no sense of humor, then defines humor, and dissects the attitudes inherent in jokes that men tell about women. She is analyzing a truism and the evidence upon which it is founded. Michael Jacobson similarly views the overall pattern of food consumption in the United States, contrasts the modern diet with those of the past, and analyzes the synthetic ingredients that constitute modern processed foods. He is analyzing the chemical components of American food. Sedulus looks at the constituent elements in the Florida Disneyland: the entertainment process, its agents, and the emotional and intellectual expectations of the audience. He is analyzing a "typical" American form of amusement and the business assumptions that govern it. Theodor Reik separates a complex of sensations and emotions, open and hidden, to show what love is made of; he is "psychoanalyzing," identifying a psychological state or process.

Analytical writing ranges from instruction manuals that tell how to disassemble and reassemble toy trucks to philosophical treatises that dissect the component premises of Aristotelian ethics. Most prose analysis, however, falls somewhere between these mechanical and speculative extremes. The "news analysis" in the daily paper, the book or movie "review," the student's lab reports, are all versions of analytical writing. Analysis sees the whole in terms of its component parts and explicates the parts as contributing to the nature and meaning of the whole.

Elizabeth Janeway

Why Does the Women's Movement Have No Sense of Humor?

What a good question! I'm glad you asked me that since I believe (perhaps too optimistically) that inside every Male Chauvinist Pig there's a human being struggling to get out. Maybe a candid reply will inspire those striving humans to struggle harder.

In the first place, why *should* the Women's Movement have a sense of humor? Do you burst into peals of laughter reading Malcolm X or *The Thoughts of Chairman Mao?* Who played that smash week in Moscow in 1917—Smith and Dale, or Lenin and Trotsky? The Women's Movement is *serious*. Some of it, not all of it, is revolutionary. I think myself that a revolution in technology, economics and the underpinnings of social relations has already happened, and that we all would do well to face up to it and adjust our minds and our myths to the data of existence. But revolutionary or no, and the Movement is anything but monolithic, it is serious about its aims; especially so because one of the severest limitations on women's ambitions and activities has been the male view that their work and their goals are secondary if not actually frivolous. A good way to support this view and hold down rising feminine confidence is to describe Movement actions as jokes. Thus, the drive for equal opportunity and access to male prerogatives is often presented as those pickets around McSorley's Bar. What's serious, men ask, about *them?*

Well, what's serious about a business lunch? The IRS assumes you do business at one, so I will too. If women can't attend them because restaurants are permitted to practice sex segregation, that's a serious invasion of their rights. And believe me, in many professions the lunching, drinking, dining sessions that used to be limited to men (the past tense of course is madly wishful) were (are) places where candidates for promotion are put through their paces, discussed and helped on their way. Excluding women from these gatherings excludes them effectively from easy consideration for jobs, raises and steps up the ladder. In the Old Boys' Network there are few girls. No doubt you can't do away with the Old Boys' Network by legislation, but at least you can stop supporting it by legal segregation.

It isn't the beer at McSorley's that women want, any more than it's the squash courts at the Harvard Club that Radcliffe alumnae have been aiming at. It's a natural place in the natural social life of business, the professions and academia instead of the old "separate but equal" accommodations which operate against women in the same way they operate against Blacks. Picketing McSorley's may have been roundabout as well as symbolic, but it wasn't irrelevant and I even think it was kind of funny. Funnier anyway than being a female full professor who is expected to "join the ladies" when she dines at the President's house while her male colleagues settle down to a discussion of campus affairs.

You say that doesn't happen anymore? I wonder why. Could it be the effect of the Women's Movement and its humorless pursuit of women's rights?

So my first answer to the question about lack of humor in the Women's Movement is: What's so funny, anyway? Unequal wages, unequal opportunities, closed doors and closed minds don't make for hilarity in the people who run into them. Instead these people tend to argue, shout and repeat themselves endlessly, which is certainly irritating and boring to the people who don't run into inequities and so, quite naturally, can't see what the fuss is all about. "Do you think there's something wrong with being a woman?" an agitated young man asked me the other day. Alas, I do, and here's a simple for-instance. In the field of teaching at elementary and secondary school level, where women are a majority and "equal wages" supposedly an enforced obligation—women working full time in 1969 averaged $7,200. Full-time male teachers pulled down $10,000. I'm willing to say with the fabled Frenchman, "*Vive la petite différence!*" But does it have to add up to $2,800, more than a third of the female wage? To me that's not so petite.

Another response, complementary to the first, is also a question: Whose sense of humor, yours or mine? Too often men's jokes about women are put-downs, often sexist and sometimes racist too. A good example is the oldie about the anthropologist who sees a Black woman pushing a baby carriage, looks inside, discovers the baby has red hair and says, "How interesting! Did the father have red hair too?"

To which the woman replies, "I don't know, Boss, he didn't take his hat off."

The funniest thing about that joke has got to be the state of mind of the man who told it to me. He clearly wasn't trying to make me laugh, but did he realize what he was doing? The urge to keep women in their place by insulting them breaks over into irrationality so fast that one can't be certain. For instance when two women from NOW went up to Yonkers to speak at the Rotary Club (by invitation), one member addressed them thus: "If my wife said anything about women's lib, I'd leave her. She's got a pocketful of credit cards. What more freedom does she need?" This genial assessment of his wife's interests and aspirations came from a retired admiral who had served as City Tax Commissioner. Isn't it odd that a man intelligent and responsible enough to hold those posts should *unhesitatingly* reveal how meanly he thinks of the woman he courted and wed? I mean, if we're going to laugh, this kind of self-exposure strikes me as funny.

Indeed there are magic moments when failure of imagination is so complete that these put-downs attain a grotesque charm. The *Sunday Times* of London has been publishing a series of them recently, under the title "Woman's Role." Here's a snatch of conversation from an audience participation program on radio:

"Good morning, Mrs. ———. It's very nice to hear from you."

"Good morning, Jimmy. Thank you."

"Tell me something about yourself. What does your husband do?"

Once alerted to this kind of unconscious male humor one finds examples everywhere. How about those two late papers on women where Freud repeatedly refers to "the fact of female castration?" What kind of a fact can that be? So far as I know, no woman in Western society has suffered even the trauma of circumcision. How about the up-to-date advice offered by Dr. Alex Comfort in *The Joy of Sex* to women about to be raped? Dr. Comfort is inclined to think that they must have done something to provoke this behavior, a well-known male view, but he suggests a way to put the rapist off if the provocateuse subsequently changes her mind: Let her have a bowel movement. Unfortunately he doesn't say how to do this.

Men, in fact, are funny people. So are women. Both often deserve to be laughed at—as people. But to laugh at people in groups is to deny them their full humanity because it denies their individual diversity. Jokes about Italians or Swedes or Chinese are intended to set these folk off in categories separate from the fun-loving human rest of us. It makes them lesser breeds without the law, whose opinions we can ignore. And so, when I pick up *A Treasury of Humorous Quotations for Speakers, Writers and Home Reference,* I am not astounded to discover that there are 105 funny things to say about women, and only 6 about men. It appears that dominant males, like Sam Goldwyn's comedies, are not to be laughed at. Which is all right with me, for I don't want to group them either. Some of them are quite nice, though even the nicest find it a bit hard to laugh at themselves.

It is this ability to laugh at oneself that is usually meant by "having a sense of humor," and I agree that it isn't a striking attribute of the Women's Movement qua Movement. One more reason, then, and that out of history. To laugh at yourself when you're top dog is appealing and humanizing. When underdogs laugh at themselves, it's different. It's a way to ease the pain of being stuck in a life situation you can't control: the sort of gallows humor which prompts Jews to tell anti-Semitic jokes. Lately a lot of underdogs have decided they don't need to be stuck. Black comics aren't telling Stepin Fetchit jokes any more, and women are laughing less at those familiar quips about women drivers, mothers-in-law and dumb blondes. Fewer and fewer are even laughing, as Dorothy Parker did, at the "normal" pain of loving a man who cheats or walks out, in the old grin-and-bear-it syndrome. The "grin" used to be part of the "bearing it"; but if you can walk out yourself, you really don't need to do either. Which doesn't necessarily mean that you'll grin less, simply that you'll enjoy it more because you'll be grinning at the oddities of the whole human condition.

Like the fascinating fact that the most popular speaker at Yale University in 1972 was a woman who was talking about chimpanzees. I'm not sure whether that's a triumph for men, women or apes (though it's certainly a tribute to an individual named Jane Goodall). Who knows? Perhaps there will come a day when the life-style of primates called women will seem as relevant to Yale men as that of chimpanzees; a day when group think and group jokes will be over, and we can sit down in all our individual differences and laugh together at the same things.

Michael Jacobson

Our Diets Have Changed, but Not for the Best

If the bromide, "You are what you eat," is true, we could all end up being very different people from our ancestors. Modern science and agriculture have freed the United States and many other nations from traditional diets based largely on natural farm products. New varieties of crops, transcontinental shipping, a wide spectrum of food additives, and new food-processing techniques have led, for better or worse, to diets different from any previously consumed by human populations. But these dietary changes reflect the decisions of business executives and investors, rather than nutritionists and public health officials.

The United States, not surprisingly, has been the leader in the genetic engineering of food crops and in the laboratory creation of new foods. Benjamin Franklin and Abraham Lincoln, if they could visit us, would probably have some difficulty distinguishing between a toy store and a supermarket. They would not even recognize as foods such products as artificial whipped cream in its pressurized can, or some of the breakfast "cereals" that are almost half sugar and bear little resemblance to cereal grains. Franklin and Lincoln would probably feel much more at home in the homey "natural foods" stores that are popping up everywhere than they would in the 10,000-item supermarkets. Many of the new foods do save us time and trouble, but they are often costly, in terms of both dollars and, ultimately, health.

"Modern" eating practices start young, often with the tiny infant. Most pediatricians agree that good old-fashioned breast-feeding is the best way to feed a baby, but all too often mothers are persuaded by cultural and commercial pressures—or because of their work schedule—to bottle-feed with canned baby formula. Only about one in four infants enjoys the nutritional (and psychological) benefits of breast-feeding.

Until the 1930s solid baby food was prepared at home by the mother. Now, however, commercially prepared strained baby foods are the rule and are being introduced into a baby's diet at an increasingly early age. Mothers often compete with one another on the basis of how early little Johnny or Susie starts to eat solid food. Many researchers believe that feeding a baby solid foods too early can lead to both over-feeding and allergic reactions.

Some pediatricians and researchers worry about the health consequences of commercial baby foods. In the past 20 years canned formula has become the most popular food for infants. Although this is probably superior to the old-fashioned formulas based on evaporated milk and corn syrup, it is still a pale imitation of human breast milk. For instance, it lacks the antibodies and enzymes that help ward off disease and the "bifidus factor" that promotes the growth of favorable intestinal bacteria. Because it is based on cow's milk, infants may have allergic reactions. Differences include higher levels of sodium and unsaturated fats and lower levels of cholesterol as compared to breast milk.

A researcher at the University of Iowa, Dr. Samuel J. Fomon, suggests that formula feeding may be more likely than breast-feeding to lead to obesity in later life. He reasons that the formula-fed infant is expected to finish the last drop in the bottle, while the breast-fed baby stops when he has had enough. Fomon and his colleague, Dr. Thomas A. Anderson (who once worked for Heinz, a major baby food manufacturer), have also suggested that early introduction of solid foods may lead to overfeeding—the infant often is expected to finish the last spoonful in the dish.

Pediatricians also wonder about strained baby foods. Although as yet they have little solid evidence, some fear that the salt and sugar used so freely as flavorings establish taste patterns that remain with a person throughout life.

In 1969 a Congressional committee held hearings that focused on the high salt content of baby food. This attention led the manufacturers to reduce voluntarily the salt levels in baby foods, but many products still contain up to ten times as much sodium (mainly from added salt) as does breast milk. Salt is of great concern to doctors and nutritionists because too much of it in the diet of adults contributes to high blood pressure (hypertension), which is the primary cause of about 20,000 deaths a year and is the major underlying factor in some 900,000 deaths a year from stroke and cardiovascular disease. Dr. Jean Mayer, Professor of Nutrition at Harvard University and probably the most influential nutritionist in the country, has said that "preventing hypertension would be much better than finding it and treating it—and a critical step in prevention is so easy: Just eat less salt."

For a child whose taste buds were initiated on blueberry buckle, raspberry cobbler and other sweetened and salted baby foods, the step to artificially colored and flavored sugar-coated breakfast "cereals" is a small and natural one. Many of these products, which could be called candies, are 30 to 50 percent sugar. One widely known children's cereal, for instance, contains a higher percentage of sugar (approximately 50 percent) than a chocolate bar (40 percent).

Highly sweetened foods encourage young children to develop a taste for sugar, of which the average American consumes approximately 100 pounds per year. Dental researchers have proved that sugar is a major cause of tooth decay. In addition, sugar's "empty calories" displace nutritious foods and contribute to obesity, diabetes and heart disease.

While the Food and Drug Administration has not taken any action on the high sugar content of some cereals, Dr. Lloyd Tepper, Associate Commissioner for Science at FDA, said this at a 1973 Senate hearing on nutrition:

"I don't think you have to be a great scientist to appreciate the fact that a highly sweetened, sucrose-containing material, which is naturally tacky when it gets wet, is going to be a troublemaker. And I would not prescribe this particular food component for my own children, not on the basis of scientific studies, but because I do not believe that prolonged exposure of tooth surfaces to a sucrose-containing material is beneficial."

While tooth decay is certainly not a deadly disease, it can be both painful and costly. Army surveys indicate that, on the average, every 100 inductees require 600 fillings, 112 extractions, 40 bridges, 21 crowns, 18 partial dentures and one full denture. Although Americans currently pay dentists about $2 billion a year for treating decayed teeth, Dr. Abraham E. Nizel, of the Tufts University School of Dental Medicine, has estimated that we would be paying $8 billion a year if everyone went to the dentist and had all his dental needs taken care of. It is Dr. Nizel's impression that tooth decay is so rampant that even "if all the 100,000 dentists in the United States restored decayed teeth day and night, 365 days a year, as many new cavities would have formed at the end of the year as were just restored during the previous year."

As children grow older and more independent, most of the messages they get from the adult world encourage them to eat food that is not best for their health. School cafeterias frequently serve meals rich in fat and low in whole grains. Television commercials employ the latest ad agency techniques to promote sugar-coated cereals and snack foods. The U.S. Department of Agriculture—over the objection of many nutritionists—allows schools to serve children nutrient-fortified cupcakes for breakfast in place of cereal and orange juice. Vending machines invite children (and adults) to buy soda pop, candy and gum. Fast-food outlets specialize in meals that are almost devoid of vitamins A and C, two of the vitamins that many Americans consume too little of. Living in this kind of environment, children may be confused when their health teacher admonishes them to "eat good foods."

America's eating habits are epitomized by what is served at our standard celebrations: baseball games, carnivals and picnics. What child would be caught at one of those affairs without a hot dog and soda pop? The child does not realize (and is not told), of course, that a diet with too high a fat content (including, for example, too many hot dogs) can contribute to the epidemic of heart disease and obesity with which this country is saddled.

Obesity is a serious medical problem. Dr. Ogden Johnson, former Director of Nutrition at FDA, has estimated that 40 million Americans are overweight or obese. In addition to being a severe social and psychological handicap, obesity is a major factor in cardiovascular diseases, mentioned earlier.

The fluffy white bun in which the hot dog is served is made from white flour, which lacks some of the nutrients that are present in whole wheat flour. Fiber is one substance that is almost entirely eliminated when the flour is refined. For several decades most researchers ignored this indigestible carbohydrate, disdaining it as mere "roughage." But evidence is mounting rapidly that fiber plays a crucial role in maintaining the health of the gastrointestinal tract (particularly the large intestine), in controlling calorie intake and in excreting cholesterol.

British physicians, notably Drs. Denis Burkitt, Thomas Cleave, G. D. Campbell and Hubert Trowell, have led the campaign to awaken the medical world to the importance of fiber. On the basis of field experience and laboratory studies, they maintain that people who consume too little fiber—and too much sugar—stand a high risk of developing obesity, diverticulosis, appendicitis, hemorrhoids, constipation, peptic ulcer, diabetes, heart disease and cancer of the colon.

Although Americans do get a substantial amount of fiber from fruits and vegetables, Burkitt and Trowell believe that this fiber is not nearly as effective in maintaining health as that found in whole grains and legumes. Many physicians and nutritionists in the United States are now urging Americans to base a larger part of their diet on whole grains, nuts, bran and other fiber-rich foods.

In their middle years, most Americans consume a diet that is reasonably complete as far as vitamins, minerals and protein are concerned. The typical diet usually reflects eating habits formed in childhood, however, and is hazardously high in calories, sugar, fat, cholesterol and salt, and hazardously low in fiber. Still, aside from dental problems and obesity, this diet usually causes no overt problems during the middle 20 or 30 years of most people's lives. Scurvy, pellagra, beri-beri and other nutritional-deficiency diseases are almost unknown in the United States. After about age 40 or 50, however, the changes within the body that have been gradually and silently occurring over the decades begin to make themselves felt.

A heart attack or stroke is often the first sign that something is wrong. After the fact, physicians often urge dietary (and other) changes to prevent recurrences. The patient is ordered to lose weight and eat less cholesterol and less fat—especially the saturated fat found in meat and dairy products. The person who is around to make these changes in eating habits should consider himself lucky. The American Heart Association recommends reducing fat consumption and body weight *before* a heart attack drives home the message.

As old age approaches, signs frequently show up first—and painfully —in the large intestine. Every television watcher who suffers through the incessant commercials for laxatives surely knows that constipation or, euphemistically, "irregularity" affects millions of people. The commercials push brand-name panaceas, but vegetables, whole grain breads and cereals, and fiber-rich bran (which you can get in bulk from health food stores or as one of the all-bran cereals) can do the trick equally well. Of course, eating an adequate amount of fiber-containing foods all along would have helped prevent constipation from developing.

Many elderly Americans suffer from diverticulosis of the colon, and every year approximately 170,000 people are hospitalized for treatment. This often painful illness develops when pressure builds up within the large intestine, causing outpouchings, which frequently become infected. The prescription for prevention or treatment is the same: a diet high in fiber-rich foods.

To complete our description of a lifetime of eating, we return to baby food. This time around, though, the consumers are not infants, but the elderly who have lost their teeth as a result of decay and gum disease and can eat only semisolid strained foods. About 18 percent of all American adults have no teeth.

Ironically, some of the same companies that manufacture the foods that contribute to heart disease, constipation, and other illnesses of middle and old age have special lines catering to the sufferers of these illnesses. Individuals who have become constipated partly through eating sugar-coated flakes can switch to all-bran. Did high blood pressure result partly from heavily salted soups? The hypertensive patient can turn to dietetic low-salt soups (and pay a little extra for *not* having salt). Diabetics who once loved fruit canned in heavy sugar syrup must pay a premium price for fruit packed in water.

Despite the close relationship between diet and disease, no person, governmental agency or private organization in the United States has had the mission or authority to develop a broad national food policy that would consider nutritional value as a top priority in the way our food is grown, processed and distributed. As it is, our agricultural practices and eating habits have developed with little guidance from health professionals.

The importance of developing a coherent national food policy has gained much high-level support in the past year, largely because of rising food prices and an increasing awareness of nutrition. Famine overseas has also awakened many people to the moral obligations of the wealthy nations. The development of a food policy was given a boost last June, when the Senate Select Committee on Nutrition and Human Needs held a hearing on a national nutrition policy.

Heard time and time again at the Senate hearing was the need for us to base a larger part of our diet on vegetables than we now do. As Frances Moore Lappé explained so eloquently in *Diet for a Small Planet,* growing soybeans and grain to feed livestock and then eating the livestock is a much less efficient way of producing food than eating the vegetable crops (see SMITHSONIAN, January 1975). Huge amounts of fertilizer, energy and food would be saved if Americans ate less grain-fed meat. More food could go to nations in short supply.

Serving as one cornerstone of a food policy should be the vast amount of knowledge that the world's researchers have produced in recent decades. We need to *apply* the findings of this research. One way of facilitating this would be to establish a Federal Nutrition Advocacy Agency, which could disseminate information to the public and professionals, and prod other governmental agencies to employ their resources to encourage better nutrition.

While awaiting the creation of such an agency, we can easily improve our own diets. For most of us, that means eating less fat, sugar, refined flour and salt—and more fiber. In terms of foods, that translates into more whole grain foods, fruits, nuts, beans and vegetables, and less meat and snack foods. A change to this kind of diet would mean better health for Americans and more food for the rest of the world and would give us less cause to worry about becoming what we eat.

Sedulus

Mickey Mouse Slouches Toward Bethlehem

When I was a young, tame radical in college Walt Disney received an honorary degree from that college. The citation, written by a very famous English prof, William Lyon Phelps, contained the line, "he laboured like a mountain and brought forth a mouse," which went over the nation's wires and amused everybody, even radical me. I was not amused, though, by the award itself. I had been brought up on Disney shorts, and had enjoyed them unreservedly like the rest of the world; but at the time of the honorary degree Disney was suffering a change of life, being deep in the production of full-length films—*Bambi, Snow White* and the like—that seemed to me and my radical friends to be wholly decadent, though they were obviously profitable outlets for the Disney entrepreneurial energy. Some French or classical voice in us whispered that a genre had been villainously encouraged to jump its bounds, with the result that a mouse had brought forth a mountain. And *that* was wrong.

Last week my family and I stumbled for the first time through the new Disney World in Florida—we have never been near the California establishment—and my old feelings swept over me again, though my radicalism was asleep. My family agreed. We found the whole show a rip-off. As we saw it the Disney interests had out-Barnumed Barnum; they had figured out a way to persuade half the country to travel tremendous distances to be relieved of significant sums; theirs was a triumph in the converting of people into sheep. We left early without using all our tickets.

Since our visit we have been quizzing citizens on street corners about the merits of Disney World, and the responses have been largely positive, a fact we are trying to live with. True, a garage man acknowledged that though he liked Disney World he liked it for the wrong reasons; that is, he had been privileged to see the "inside," all sorts of operational detail that the sheep miss. But the bulk of affirmation was unquestionably from the happy sheep themselves. They *enjoyed* it.

Now why should I knock pleasure? I shouldn't, I won't, I think pleasure is pleasurable. But I must stand firm and say that I don't think Disney World can be let off as a simple pleasure dome. Just as Walt Disney's original move from shorts to full-length cartoons violated, in the days before World War II, the natural and healthy pleasures of the original cartoon genre, similarly the new Floridian monstrosity violates the simplicities it celebrates; it is much more than a monument to the joys of Mickey, Minnie and Donald; it emerges as a sort of cultural, mebbe spiritual, shrine.

I grant that my first hint at being in the presence of holiness occurred before we actually arrived at Disney World. We spent the night at a clip joint nearby, paying more for minimal accommodations in the middle of a cold nowhere than we had spent each night the previous week for pleasant rooms with kitchenette on the beach at Palm Beach. But hotel gods are minor deities and it was evident that these particular itchy Mammons were clustering in central Florida because there was a higher god, a true determiner of price. Sure enough we came into his august presence in the Mickey Mouse Theater the next morning.

First we were herded into a stand-up auditorium and treated to a short pious history of Mickey Mouse cartoons. Then we were herded into a sitdown puppet theater (the two-auditorium arrangement was a logistical triumph, since it speeded the flow *through* the show), where a concert by characters out of the whole Disney heaven took place for perhaps 20 minutes, with Mickey himself as the orchestra conductor. He and his orchestra rose from the pit at the beginning, and played a tune through in a mock symphonic manner borrowed from *Fantasia*; then the orchestra gave way to specialty numbers by Snow White, Donald Duck and so on for a few minutes, after which the whole cast was exposed for a grand finale that ended with Mickey turning around and bowing to us, the sheep.

Remember, the Disney characters were all presented as puppets. They were in constant motion during the show, doing their respective things, and they were programmed very precisely so that their mouths opened and their arms wiggled for just the right musical notes (I pictured behind the scene a complicated version of an oldtime player-piano roll), so that one could have said of the show—had one been disposed to defend it as pleasure merely—that it was merely a puppet show and a rather good one. But my point is that when Mickey turned to us and bowed, it seemed absolutely plain that he had graduated from his modest "merely" roles; he was no longer a simple fantasy figure from a smart artist's pen, but the central idol of a $400 million church. Certainly as he bowed he gave us sheep a moment of genuine confusion about what we were in the presence of. As a herd we clapped, ever so briefly, then stopped, embarrassed.

After all, what were we applauding? The player-piano machine? The engineers who built it? The entrepreneurs who financed it? Or the great imago, Mickey himself?

The embarrassment came, I think, from the sudden realization that we *were* applauding a puppet, and a computerized puppet at that, a puppet that had gone through its whole performance untouched by human hand. Furthermore it was an absurd puppet, a mouse puppet—nothing with a long beard and high forehead like a sage, but a plump round thing with large round ears that had nonetheless been presented as more than that, with the result that we sheep were confused about what we had experienced, and about the intentions behind the production—justifiably because the confusion was central. If that performance had been originally constructed as a serious satire on the capacity of human sheep to find huge, and hugely ridiculous, imagos for worship, not a single change would have been needed in the "script."

Pieties abound elsewhere at Disney World. Perhaps the central piety —which is behind the imago fascination of Mickey himself but controls as well the mythology propagated by the entire enterprise—is a faith in the simple virtues of children and childhood. But as those virtues get filtered through the American money machine they become, as we all know, drippy sentimental. This they of course do at Disney World. Even the cutie corn of Winnie-the-Pooh has been incorporated. Furthermore many of the peripheral characters and myths that the Disney interests have appropriated over the years have been gimcracked to death, so that they have none of their original integrity. As my wife observed, Mickey Mouse is in some respects the only authentic figure on the grounds. Now I submit, Mr. Bentham, that when half the country is busy flying, driving and pedaling down to Fla. to be infantile—and infantile as well in the worship of gods that are false, and that drip—then there is at work here more than a pleasure principle.

I have just seen this phenomenon, and though I thought I was too old and experienced in the ways of my country to be shocked by anything, the experience did shock me. We are being *taken*, ladies and gentlemen, taken in a big way. We sheep weren't there just for pleasure, just for laughs. We were there for something higher, something ineffably cultural, an important life-experience, and perhaps more than that, an *ultimate* experience; at any rate something to fill the vacuums of our lives. The mouse knew our need.

And TV? (I have not forgotten that this is a TV column.) The precedent at Disney World shows us how far a country that lives in a social and ideological vacuum can be betrayed by a vacuum-ideology. I doubt if we can find in the history of the world a better example of the worship of a false god than now, west of Orlando; in our national emptiness we are, it has been convincingly demonstrated, open to *anything*. So the question immediately comes up: what will the next anything be?

If *The Wizard of Oz* were not a teensie weensie bit passé I would suggest that somebody build a $500 million empire based upon it in the Arizona desert. For would not the Wizard make another perfect non-god for eventual serious worship? (The film is halfway there already.) Aside from the Wizard my inclination is to look to the tube for the next big imago breakthrough, and while I don't know which tube celebrity to put money on—Lucy in the Everglades? Archie Bunker in the Tetons?—my heart sinks when I contemplate the tube's potential to follow the Disney path.

Yet so far, happily, the big TV money has been devoted to the production of simple pleasure shows, as in the early days of Disney and of the movies as a whole. I see little to fear from Lucy and the like as they now exist, and it seems to me shortsighted of the idealistic reformers of TV to keep proposing that TV perform somehow more significant functions. In a society that can make a god of Mickey Mouse the chief danger is probably not that TV *fail* to raise its sights, but rather that it do so and raise them toward the wrong targets, letting significance be created arbitrarily, created by unscrupulous entrepreneurs.

Do I mean that TV would do best simply to avoid "worthy" social and educational ventures? Of course not. I mean that TV's functions, whatever they are or may become, should be modestly conceived and performed; tube operators with high and churchy notions should be emphatically discouraged. In reverse, the talents of those still devoted to keeping the tube lowbrow and light should not be scorned. We could be in the hands of darker forces, and probably will be.

Theodor Reik

Of Love and Lust

If we are honest with ourselves we must admit that we are rarely satisfied with ourselves, with our physical and mental qualities, with our achievements and our position in life. Beside the person that we really are is a picture in our minds of the person we should like to be. When we look more closely we even see with pitiless clarity how far short of this picture we fall. We call this image the ego-ideal. This expression may perhaps be found more appropriate than the term superego that Freud used. Ego-ideal is a less abstract description than superego, although both words have, if not the same, at least similar connotations. I am also of the opinion that the term ego-ideal cannot be misused in the same way as the other.

We treat this picture of our idealized selves differently at various times. Sometimes we even revolt against it; but most of the time, especially in our youth, we spend many hours looking at it admiringly, fondly, but keeping it as a most precious, secret treasure. On the other hand the image itself seems to look at us with cold and often disapproving eyes. Only rarely do we observe anything like satisfaction and recognition in its attitude toward us. We try to discover in it a similarity in ourselves, but almost always we are disappointed. We pretend sometimes to ourselves that we resemble the image, but we know at the same time that our personality does not correspond to the figure we created. This fictional self is not the man or woman we are, but the one we would like to be.

Every one of us has painted such a picture. It was meant to be a self-portrait but it was not done in a realistic manner. Looking into a mirror while we worked on it, we painted not so much what we saw as what we would like to have seen in ourselves. As a matter of fact we disliked what we really saw, and so we executed a flattering picture. It is not only home-made, but is also meant only for home use. We do not like to show it to our friends; we keep it secret; we are ashamed because it bears so little resemblance to our real looks.

Actually, the ego-image is a physical acquisition of our late childhood, a result of our growing awareness that we are not what we would like to be. Of course this attitude toward ourselves is conditioned by the attitude toward us shown by others. We early learn to look at ourselves through the critical eyes with which grownups regard us. Children feel early enough the contrast between what they do and what they should do. The child wants to conform, to fulfill the demands of his mother, but his will to do so is at desperate odds with his powerful impulses and wishes.

There are times later on, of course, when we lose sight of our ego-ideal, even times when we rebel against it and endeavor to throw it overboard. But we seldom succeed. It accompanies us through most of our life and admonishes us to fulfill its aims—aims that are reduced only as old age approaches. We realize then, at last, that its demands were perhaps too high, that there is not time enough left to pay all debts, and we become resigned. The personality of every individual is determined by his actual qualities, his ego-ideal and his attitude toward the gulf between the two. If you could collect all the different ego-ideals of human beings you would know what humanity wants to be. You would have a complete "ideology" of men. If you could see in one broad view all the efforts of the human race to reach the ego-ideal, so near and yet so far away, you could survey the eternal struggle for recognition and fulfillment, the victories and defeats of mortals.

No phantasy is merely fantastic; no imagination can bring forth images from a void. A child of fancy has parents in reality. A fantastic being like the Sphinx consists of the body of a lioness or lion and the head of a man. The most fanciful pictures of Greek and Indian mythology are composites of different pieces of real life. This image-self, the ego-ideal, also has its patterns in reality. There are the examples of our parents and teachers, the representative men and women whom we admire later on. But more important than they, in those decisive years when the ego-ideal is formed, are the patterns held up before us: patterns of virtue in other children, in brothers and sisters, playmates and strangers, heroes in books or pictures. We looked at them with grudging admiration and envy, because we could never attain these high standards. Faced with them we become painfully aware of our shortcomings. Later on other figures are substituted and become examples of achievement that we would like to attain, of virtues that we wish to possess.

I call these patterns, taken from reality, ego-models, because they have a strong influence on the make-up of the youthful personality. The imprints and impressions that they unconsciously leave on the ego, which is too weak to resist such powerful influences, furnish the material for building the status of the ego-ideal which we erect in ourselves. All these pictures are immortalized in this one gigantic figure which we revere. Some of the ego-models are unconsciously kept intact despite later development, like ancient buildings that excavators dig out of the identical ground upon which modern houses have been erected. They really have an indelible character. What we admired and aspired to in late childhood and in our teens, in our boyhood and girlhood, remains important throughout our whole life.

The figures that are the center of these ego-models are alive, while the ego-model itself is a strange product of reality and phantasy, fact and fancy. In it the qualities of living persons appear very exaggerated, the negative side being removed or neglected and the achievements overestimated. It is like the beginning of the idealization with which we later invest a love-object. The ego-models, those in-between forms of truth and daydream, may be compared to the heroes and heroines of the stories and plays, in whom the realities and potentialities of living models are merged. The adolescent girl imagines that she will be very beautiful, gracious, and kind; the boy, that he will be strong, valiant and heroic, like their chosen models. The figures in these daydreams are certainly not identical with real persons, but neither are they identical with the daydreamer as he or she is. They are his or her wished for ego.

The theory of narcissism, generally accepted by the psychoanalysts, proclaims everybody originally to be in love with himself. The creation of an ego-model would thus be a psychological impossibility. It does not reflect the person as he is but as he would like to be. This phantasy does not spring from an overflowing self-love but from a discontent with oneself, and marks an attempt to assuage this unpleasant feeling by means which the imagination can provide.

The ego-model is an extension of the daydreamer. It is his desired shape, the forerunner of the ego-ideal. The frontiers between the two representations are at first fluid. The ego-model of a boy may be a baseball champion; that of a girl may be a film star. The boy becomes a baseball fan; the girl has a crush on the movie actress. Instead of a film star it may be her teacher or an older girl. Here are the roots of childish love before calf love. The continuation of the ego-models, the stuff of which is shaped from living persons, is the ego-ideal, heightened beyond the realm of reality and more or less deviating from real life. Later there are numerous transitions from one type to the other.

Why do I discuss at such length the creation of the ego-ideal? Because two separate lines lead from this phantom directly to the heart of our problem. The first gives the cause for the discord or the displeasure which, as I said before, runs unconsciously ahead of love. In all cases this discontent is in the nature of a dissatisfaction with oneself. We are now able to say that it is founded on the awareness that we fall far short of our ego-ideal, far below our unfulfilled wishes.

The mood that results from this disappointment—if it is not too desperate—disposes one, more than anything else, to fall in love. Love is a substitute for another desire, for the struggle toward self-fulfillment, for the vain urge to reach one's ego-ideal. The nonrealization of this drive makes love possible, but it also makes love necessary because the tension within the ego increases. The fulfillment of the ego-ideal would make one self-satisfied and self-sufficient and would remove the internal distress. If we could silence forever this persistent voice within us we could perhaps lead a loveless but happy life. But that is hardly possible for cultured people. Thus love is really a second-best, a compensatory way for not obtaining the ego-ideal state. Yet it is not self-love, as the theory of narcissism makes out. As a matter of fact it is nearer to self-hate. It is love for one's own ego-ideal, which will never be reached in oneself.

The second line leads to the transition from the ego-ideal to the loved person. The ego-ideal disappears from the stage of phantasy when the love-object makes its appearance there, like a sentry relieving the guard on duty. As we now know, this phantom-ego was not entirely fantastic. Pieces of the pattern were taken from living persons who become ego-models. Under certain psychological circumstances the development can be reversed. The phantom-ego, this second self, can become alive again. The love-object then takes the place that was filled by the ego-ideal in our soul. In other words, loving means exchanging the ego-ideal for an external object, for a person in whom are joined all the qualities that we once desired for ourselves. The unconscious process by which that is done is in the nature of a projection. As you can cast a picture onto a screen or a reflecting surface, so you can project this ideal image of yourself onto another person. The process relieves the psychical pressure felt by shifting the burden from one's own shoulders. Projection in general means an alleviation of psychical distress, as we can observe in many cases of a different kind. The ascetic in the desert does not feel responsible any longer for the sexual temptations which torment him. It is an outside power, the devil, the evil one, who visits him with lascivious visions. No more is it a conflict within himself. He is fighting Satan. Such is the beneficent effect of projection.

But it is astonishing how seldom people are willing to moderate their inner demands, how insistent they are on achievement. It seems that we have an imperative need to fulfill the secret claims of achievement which have been in us from childhood.

The other day in New York's Central Park I saw a little boy climb up onto a rock. From the modest height which he had reached he shouted triumphantly, "Mother, just look where I am!" On the same walk half an hour later I saw a little girl show her mother how pretty she looked with flowers in her hair. As I walked along it occurred to me that the two children's behavior was a true reflection of all mankind. As the twig is bent, so the tree inclines. We behave like the little boy when we become men. The desire for recognition never dies in us. We all want to be appreciated and admired in these daydreams, in which we secretly polish and shine our ego-ideals. It does not make much difference whether we want to impress our circle of friends, or dream of making the old home town proud of us, or of being praised by posterity. Do we not all think, in grown-up terms of course, "Look where I am!"

It is this very need which is responsible for much, perhaps for most, of our achievements in whatever field we perform them. By achieving something, or even by doing some job well, this inner tension eases up for a time, though not for long. "*L'appétit vient en mangeant,*" and we want to achieve more. Our failure to fulfill the inner claims produces then an increased tension, aggravates the lingering discord in us. We do not know why one person is more inclined to strive for achievement in his work than another who tends to find it in love—which is a physical achievement too. It is likely that our pursuit of happiness goes in both directions.

The first love-object thus is a glorified ego, the phantom-self as we imagined it in our daydreams. The second is the embodiment of this desired image in a real person. The ego-ideal was built up by outside influences, stimulated by living figures. It is a return, by a detour, to the old pattern, if now the original of the ego-ideal is sought and found in the external world, in the love-object. The new ideal, strictly speaking, is only a renewal of an old one in a different form.

At this point we find ourselves faced with a new difficulty. Suppose we tentatively agree to this concept, then that leaves us no place for the most powerful form of love, that between the sexes. You call your sweetheart your better self, it is true, but can it be that in this kind of love also —the most important one for society and civilization—the emotion is a substitute for the desire to fulfill the ideal ego? Is this love, too, a second best? Yes, I think that the concept here sketched also holds good for this case. It is of course modified and complicated by the mighty factor of sex.

Another question must be asked here: Why do we not choose the most natural way when caught in this internal discomfort set up by the nonfulfillment of our concealed ego-ideal? Why do we not become more modest or more tolerant toward ourselves? I shall present an answer to this question later on.

I have stressed the fact that the beloved person is a substitute for the ideal ego. Two people who love each other are interchanging their ego-ideals. That they love each other means they love the ideal of themselves in the other one. There would be no love on earth if this phantom were not there. We fall in love because we cannot attain the image that is our better self and the best of our self. From this concept it is obvious that love itself is only possible on a certain cultural level or after a certain phase in the development of a personality has been reached. The creation of an ego-ideal itself marks human progress. When people are entirely satisfied with their actual selves, love is impossible.

The transfer of the ego-ideal to a person is the most characteristic trait of love. The development thus starts as a striving after self-perfection, which is frustrated. It ends in finding the perfection which we could not reach within ourselves in this second self. The object now becomes the holder of all values. The image becomes flesh in the beloved person. While before we slaved in the strenuous service of an ideal, now we are in bond-age to an actual person.

Is there not another change when we substitute a person for the un-attainable ego-ideal? This ideal was a phantom, and the love object is a real, existing person. But is that so? No. The love-object is also a phantom to a great extent, a peg on which we hang all the illusions of ourselves which we longed to fulfill. The living person is, so to speak, only the ma-terial from which we create a fantastic figure, just as a sculptor shapes a statue out of stone.

While I write these words someone has turned on the radio in the adjoining room. I hear a not unpleasant tenor voice sing a new song: "I shall never know why I love you so." If the singer would be content with a provisional answer we could offer it. He loves her so because she fulfills his secret ego-ideal.

Questions

Diction and Structure

1. Elizabeth Janeway capitalizes several phrases in her essay on the women's movement: Male Chauvinist Pig, Old Boys Net-work, Movement, Blacks. Are the capitals all used for the same or for different reasons? Explain.

2. What is the purpose of the question in the title of the Jane-

way essay? How is it related to the opening paragraph? To whom is the author addressing herself and how does this affect the structure of the essay as a whole?

3. Janeway uses several devices to call the reader's attention to her points: italicized words, foreign phrases, figures, parentheses, words in quotes. Look at some of these devices and suggest why Janeway uses them as she does.

4. How does Janeway use the erroneous use of words by others (men) for humorous purposes? Is she making a covert point about false or sloppy definitions?

5. What is the meaning of these words in Michael Jacobson's essay on the American diet: "bromide," "blueberry buckle," "tacky," "beri-beri," "panaceas"?

6. What organizing principle does Jacobson's essay follow? Is it an effective one or not? Why?

7. Essays like Jacobson's, which use many numbers in order to give statistics, run the risk of losing the reader's interest or interrupting the flow of the author's prose. Does Jacobson handle statistics in such a manner as to avoid these risks or not?

8. "Sedulus" is a pen name used by the T.V. critic of *The New Republic*; it is Latin for "sitting fast" by root meaning and its further meanings are contained in the English word *sedulous*. For what reasons would a television critic choose this *nom de plume?*

9. The title of the Sedulus essay is based on the final line of William Butler Yeats's poem, "The Second Coming." Read the poem and analyze the way Sedulus organizes his article to reflect Yeats's vision of the future.

10. The diction used by Sedulus is varied, ranging from "entrepreneurial" and "imago" to "rip-off" and "mebbe." What is the effect of this mixture? Why does Sedulus use it? For what audience is he writing?

11. How does Sedulus use time as a principle of structuring his essay? How does he use personal information about himself?

12. Theodor Reik is a psychiatrist. Point out instances in which he uses professional terminology in "Of Love and Lust." What evidence is there that he is writing for a nonspecialist audience, in spite of his technical language?

13. Outline Reik's essay. Is the title appropriate? Can you think of a more accurate title?

14. Look up these words: ego, narcissism, fantasy (phantasy), projection, personality. Compare Reik's use of them with their root meanings.

Style and Rhetoric

1. How does the title of the Janeway essay embody all of the elements she goes on to analyze? To what extent does her analysis depend upon definition? On comparison and contrast?

2. In addition to her close examination of single words, Janeway also dissects phrases and entire statements. Why is it necessary for her to pay so much attention to word usage by others? How is it related to her basic purpose in the essay?

3. How are the various sections of the Janeway essay connected with each other? What devices further serve to give the essay its coherence?

4. Is the American diet a single phenomenon or is it a whole that is made of subcategories or classes of foods? Explain. How does Jacobson treat it? What single principle can be found in American food as a whole, according to him?

5. Does Jacobson himself believe the truth of the "bromide" he quotes at the start of his essay? Justify your answer. Why did he write his essay, judging from internal evidence?

6. The style of Jacobson's piece is quite different from that of Janeway. Compare and contrast the two styles and suggest how they are (are not) suited to their subjects. Must "serious" subjects be devoid of humor?

7. What single principle does Sedulus see as holding Disney World together? What evidence does he present to show this principle? Do you accept his analysis of what makes Disney World operate as it does?

8. How does Sedulus define "pleasure"? Does he attempt to analyze the emotions that give pleasure? Why?

9. Look at the passage about the audience applauding the Mickey Mouse puppet. What is Sedulus analyzing? How does he go about it?

10. Are the final paragraphs about T.V. really related to the major portion of Sedulus's essay about Disney World? Show how they are (are not).

11. How many of the following does Theodor Reik analyze in his essay "Of Love and Lust": human nature, an emotional state, a body of attitudes, a myth? Can you think of more topics he analyzes?

12. How useful is Reik's comparison of adult emotions to those of the little boy on top of the rock? Is the analogy emotive rather than logical? Is this appropriate?

13. In dealing with such intangibles as emotions or feelings, Reik makes a number of unprovable assertions: note, for example, the opening sentence. How does he imply a method of proving what he asserts, here and elsewhere? Does this device make his views more or less authoritative?

Theme and Viewpoint

1. In taking his stand against Walt Disney, does Sedulus represent himself as a crank, eccentric, or individualist? How do his views toward conformity compare with those of Louis Kronenberger?

2. Does Reik's discussion of fantasy and the ideal self help to explain why many Americans feel such affection for Mickey Mouse and the other Disney characters? Does Sedulus offer any explanation?

3. If love is really searching for an ego-ideal as Reik says, how do you account for the fact that lovers do and ought to fight each other, as Bach and Wyden describe the fights in their essay?

4. Would Janeway find Ian Stevenson's views on prejudice relative to the attitudes of men toward women? Of women toward men? Does Janeway show herself prejudiced in any way? Explain your opinion.

5. Would any of the ingredients put into American food by manufacturers be classified as "drugs" by Helen Nowlis's definition? Does Jacobson view these additives as having the qualities of drugs in some cases?

6. Would Leo Rosten agree with Janeway's remarks about the relationship between humor and suppression as it may be seen in Jewish jokes? Look at Rosten's humorous examples and compare them with Janeway's; are they similar or different?

7. Are Reik's assumptions about behavior the same as those of Ian Stevenson or not? How would prejudice be related to the ego-ideal, if at all?

8. Can you find in any of the earlier essays in this collection unconscious examples of the sort of male attitudes toward women that Janeway criticizes? (For instance, look at the articles by Lucas and Kronenberger.)

Describing

The terms "describe" and "description" appear at first to be of the sort whose meanings are very far from their roots. The Latin words from which they come mean simply "to write down." Write down what? we wonder; all prose might seem to qualify as description if it is written. Actually, description *is* verbal representation; that is, re-presenting something experienced by the writer—an object, condition, scene, atmosphere, feeling, state of mind—in such a way that the reader can "see" it too. Describing may be called "picturing in words."

The word "pictures" denotes visual images; and many a description—of a country meadow, the Opera House at Covent Garden, a reception at the Kuwait Embassy, a rose garden—uses words to create a corresponding image or series of images in the reader's mind. From the social column that gives details of a bride's dress ("Her veil of illusion was embroidered with seed pearls and crystals . . .") to eyewitness reports of the bombing of Hiroshima ("A yellow flash split the sky and the concrete wall suddenly rose into the air . . ."), the basic rhetorical technique is turning words into images.

In one of his essays for the *Rambler,* Dr. Johnson declared, "Descriptions are definitions of a more lax and fanciful kind." If you think of what a definition does—it identifies a thing by its external, generic qualities and its internal, differential qualities—and compare that with a description, you will readily agree with Johnson that the difference is the degree of imagination involved. A description is not as concerned with producing a concise, formal phrase to *denote* the thing as it is in reproducing the thing through *connotations.* The language of definition, ideally, is a formula or symbol; the language of description is a pattern of associative words and images that evoke an experience in the hearer. Therefore, a description compares its subject to things which may share certain qualities with it but which do not belong to the same *genus,* or category. Fireflies may be described as miniscule fairy lanterns or floating gleams from a cat's eyes, but they do not belong in the family of lighting fixtures or optical reflections. By enumerating a series of shared qualities, the writer may describe something in terms of other things with which it has no intrinsic or logical relationship.

Qualities may be internal as well as superficial, of course, and a description may at times use some of the techniques of analysis. To convey a vivid impression of something, a writer may suggest its innate qualities, physical or nonphysical, by the same use of connotation that he or she employs to reproduce its external qualities or properties. Psychological states—sensations, moods—which are internal and intangible may be suggested by connotative language. "I wandered lonely as a cloud," wrote Wordsworth descriptively. Compare this phrase with the more denotative or definitive statement, "I was melancholy."

Describing is not a mechanical listing of one comparison after another. Nor is it casting frantically about for exotic, lush, or "pretty" figures of speech. Descriptions may be of harsh or terrible or ugly scenes and feelings: automobile wrecks, death in battle, or mad fantasies. Nor is description a great massing of detail upon detail. The writer who wants to describe something may use metaphoric language, to be sure; he or she may give many details or few, use lots of adjectives or none. The only true guiding principle is to identify the significant attributes of the thing he or she wishes to describe, then to select the essential qualities of these attributes, and, by arranging them in some kind of logical or sensual pattern, to reproduce in words personal perceptions as they were experienced in specific or general circumstances. He may have seen ants battling each other or have watched cats for many years; she may nostalgically remember the twilights of her childhood or form a composite picture of a certain kind of person. Whatever the subject, verbal description of it will work only if it successfully reproduces in the reader perceptions like the writer's own; this is the test of descriptive methods.

Henry David Thoreau

The Battle of the Ants

It is remarkable how many creatures live wild and free though secret in the woods, and still sustain themselves in the neighborhood of towns, suspected by hunters only. How retired the otter manages to live here! He grows to be four feet long, as big as a small boy, perhaps without any human being getting a glimpse of him. I formerly saw the raccoon in the woods behind where my house is built, and probably still heard their whinnering at night. Commonly I rested an hour or two in the shade at noon, after planting, and ate my lunch, and read a little by a spring which was the source of a swamp and of a brook, oozing from under Brister's Hill, half a mile from my field. The approach to this was through a succession of descending grassy hollows, full of young pitch-pines, into a larger wood about the swamp. There, in a very secluded and shaded spot, under a spreading white-pine, there was yet a clean firm sward to sit on. I had dug out the spring and made a well of clear gray water, where I could dip up a pailful without roiling it, and thither I went for this purpose almost every day in midsummer, when the pond was warmest. Thither too the woodcock led her brood, to probe the mud for worms, flying but a foot above them down the bank, while they ran in a troop beneath; but at last, spying me, she would leave her young and circle round and round me, nearer and nearer till within four or five feet, pretending broken wings and legs, to attract my attention, and get off her young, who would already

THE BATTLE OF THE ANTS   From *Walden, or Life in the Woods*, 1854.

have taken up their march, with faint wiry peep, single file through the swamp, as she directed. Or I heard the peep of the young when I could not see the parent bird. There too the turtle-doves sat over the spring, or fluttered from bough to bough of the soft white-pines over my head; or the red squirrel, coursing down the nearest bough, was particularly familiar and inquisitive. You only need sit still long enough in some attractive spot in the woods that all its inhabitants may exhibit themselves to you by turns.

I was witness to events of a less peaceful character. One day when I went out to my wood-pile, or rather my pile of stumps, I observed two large ants, the one red, the other much larger, nearly half an inch long, and black, fiercely contending with one another. Having once got hold they never let go, but struggled and wrestled and rolled on the chips incessantly. Looking farther, I was surprised to find that the chips were covered with such combatants, that it was not a *duellum*, but a *bellum*, a war between two races of ants, the red always pitted against the black, and frequently two red ones to one black. The legions of these Myrmidons covered all the hills and vales in my woodyard, and the ground was already strewn with the dead and dying, both red and black. It was the only battle which I have ever witnessed, the only battlefield I ever trod while the battle was raging; internecine war; the red republicans on the one hand, and the black imperialists on the other. On every side they were engaged in deadly combat, yet without any noise that I could hear, and human soldiers never fought so resolutely. I watched a couple that were fast locked in each other's embraces, in a little sunny valley amid the chips, now at noon-day prepared to fight till the sun went down, or life went out. The smaller red champion had fastened himself like a vice to his adversary's front, and through all the tumblings on that field never for an instant ceased to gnaw at one of his feelers near the root, having already caused the other to go by the board; while the stronger black one dashed him from side to side, and, as I saw on looking nearer, had already divested him of several of his members. They fought with more pertinacity than bulldogs. Neither manifested the least disposition to retreat. It was evident that their battle-cry was "Conquer or die." In the meanwhile there came along a single red ant on the hill-side of this valley, evidently full of excitement, who either had despatched his foe, or had not yet taken part in the battle; probably the latter, for he had lost none of his limbs; whose mother had charged him to return with his shield or upon it. Or perchance he was some Achilles, who had nourished his wrath apart, and had now come to avenge or rescue his Patroclus. He saw this unequal combat from afar,—for the blacks were nearly twice the size of the red,—he drew near with rapid pace till he stood on his guard within half an inch of the combatants; then, watching his opportunity, he sprang upon the black warrior, and commenced his operations near the root of his right fore-leg, leaving the foe to select among his own members; and so there were three united for life, as if a new kind of attraction had been invented which put all other locks and cements to shame. I should not have wondered by this time to find that they had their respective musical bands stationed on some eminent chip, and playing their national airs the while, to excite the slow and cheer the dying combatants. I was myself excited somewhat even as if they had been men. The more you think of it, the less the difference. And certainly there is not the fight recorded in Concord history, at least, if in the history of America, that will bear a moment's comparison with this, whether for the numbers engaged in it, or for the patriotism and heroism displayed. For numbers and for carnage it was an Austerlitz or Dresden. Concord Fight! Two killed on the patriots' side, and Luther Blanchard wounded! Why here every ant was a Buttrick,—"Fire! for God's sake fire!"—and thousands shared the fate of Davis and Hosmer. There was not one hireling there. I have no doubt that it was a principle they fought for, as much as our ancestors, and not to avoid a three-penny tax on their tea; and the results of this battle will be as important and memorable to those whom it concerns as those of the battle of Bunker Hill, at least.

I took up the chip on which the three I have particularly described were struggling, carried it into my house, and placed it under a tumbler on my window-sill, in order to see the issue. Holding a microscope to the first mentioned red ant, I saw that, though he was assiduously gnawing at the near fore-leg of his enemy, having severed his remaining feeler, his own breast was all torn away, exposing what vitals he had there to the jaws of the black warrior, whose breast-plate was apparently too thick for him to pierce; and the dark carbuncles of the sufferer's eyes shone with ferocity such as war only could excite. They struggled half an hour longer under the tumbler, and when I looked again the black soldier had severed the heads of his foes from their bodies, and the still living heads were hanging on either side of him like ghastly trophies at his saddle-bow, still apparently as firmly fastened as ever, and he was endeavoring with feeble struggles, being without feelers and with only the remnant of a leg, and I know not how many other wounds, to divest himself of them; which at length, after half an hour more, he accomplished. I raised the glass, and he went off over the window-sill in that crippled state. Whether he finally survived that combat, and spent the remainder of his days in some Hotel des Invalides, I do not know; but I thought that his industry would not be worth much thereafter. I never learned which party was victorious nor the cause of the war; but I felt for the rest of that day as if I had had my feelings excited and harrowed by witnessing the struggle, the ferocity and carnage, of a human battle before my door.

Kirby and Spence tell us that the battles of ants have long been celebrated and the date of them recorded, though they say that Huber is the only modern author who appears to have witnessed them. "Aeneas Sylvius," say they, "after giving a very circumstantial account of one contested with great obstinacy by a great and small species on the trunk of a pear tree," adds that " 'This action was fought in the pontificate of Eugenius the Fourth, in the presence of Nicholas Pistoriensis, an eminent lawyer, who related the whole history of the battle with the greatest fidelity.' A similar engagement between great and small ants is recorded by Olaus Magnus, in which the small ones, being victorious, are said to have buried the bodies of their own soldiers, but left those of their giant enemies a prey to the birds. This event happened previous to the expulsion of the tyrant Christiern the Second from Sweden." The battle which I witnessed took place in the Presidency of Polk, five years before the passage of Webster's Fugitive-Slave Bill.

Alan Devoe

Our Enemy, the Cat

1

We tie bright ribbons around their necks, and occasionally little tinkling bells, and we affect to think that they are as sweet and vapid as the coy name "kitty" by which we call them would imply. It is a curious illusion. For, purring beside our fireplaces and pattering along our back fences, we have got a wild beast as uncowed and uncorrupted as any under heaven.

It is five millenniums since we snared the wild horse and broke his

OUR ENEMY, THE CAT   From *The American Mercury*, December 1937. Reprinted by permission.

spirit to our whim, and for centuries beyond counting we have been able to persuade the once-free dog to fawn and cringe and lick our hands. But a man must be singularly blind with vanity to fancy that in the three—ten? —thousand years during which we have harbored cats beneath our roof-trees, we have succeeded in reducing them to any such insipid estate. It is not a "pet" (that most degraded of creatures) that we have got in our house, whatever we may like to think. It is a wild beast; and there adheres to its sleek fur no smallest hint of the odor of humanity.

It would be a salutary thing if those who write our simpering verses and tales about "tabby-sit-by-the-fire" could bring themselves to see her honestly, to look into her life with eyes unblurred by wishful sentiment. It would be a good thing—to start at the beginning—to follow her abroad into the moonlight on one of those raw spring evenings when the first skunk-cabbages are thrusting their veined tips through the melting snow and when the loins of catdom are hot with lust.

The love-play of domestic creatures is mostly a rather comic thing, and loud are the superior guffaws of rustic humans to see the clumsy, fumbling antics that take place in the kennels and the stockpen. But the man had better not laugh who sees cats in their rut. He is looking upon something very like aboriginal passion, untainted by any of the overlaid refinements, suppressions, and modifications that have been acquired by most of mankind's beasts. The mating of cats has neither the bathetic clumsiness of dogs' nor the lumbering ponderousness of cattle's, but—conducted in a lonely secret place, away from human view—is marked by a quick concentrated intensity of lust that lies not far from the borderline of agony. The female, in the tense moment of the prelude, tears with her teeth at her mate's throat, and, as the climax of the creatures' frenzy comes, the lean silky-furred flanks quiver vibrantly as a taut wire. Then quietly, in the spring night, the two beasts go their ways.

It will be usually May before the kittens come; and that episode, too, will take place secretly, in its ancient feline fashion, where no maudlin human eye may see. Great is the pique in many a house when "pussy," with dragging belly and distended dugs, disappears one night—scorning the cushioned maternity-bed that has been prepared for her—and creeps on silent feet to the dankest cranny of the cellar, there in decent aloneness to void her blood and babies. She does not care, any more than a lynx does, or a puma, to be pried upon while she licks the birth-hoods from her squirming progeny and cleans away the membrane with her rough pink tongue.

A kitten is not a pretty thing at birth. For many days it is a wriggling mite of lumpy flesh and sinew, blind and unaware, making soft sucking noises with its wet, toothless mouth, and smelling of milk. Daily, hourly, the rough tongue of the tabby ministers to it in its helplessness, glossing the baby-fur with viscid spittle, licking away the uncontrolled dung, cleaning away the crumbly pellet of dried blood from its pointed ears. By that tenth or fourteenth day when its eyes wholly unseal, blue and weak in their newness, the infant cat is clean to immaculateness, and an inalienable fastidiousness is deep-lodged in its spirit.

It is now—when the kitten makes its first rushes and sallies from its birthplace, and, with extraordinary gymnastics of its chubby body, encounters chair-legs and human feet and other curious phenomena—that it elicits from man those particular expressions of gurgling delight which we reserve for very tiny fluffy creatures who act very comically. But the infant cat has no coy intent to be amusing. If he is comic, it is only because of the incongruity of so demure a look and so wild a heart. For in that furry head of his, grim and ancient urges are already dictating.

Hardly larger than a powder-puff, he crouches on the rug and watches a fleck of lint. His little blue eyes are bright, and presently his haunches tense and tremble. The tiny body shivers in an ague of excitement. He pounces, a little clumsily perhaps, and pinions the fleeting lint-fleck with his paws. In the fractional second of that lunge, the ten small needles of his claws have shot from their sheaths of flesh and muscle. It is a good game; but it is not an idle one. It is the kitten's introduction into the ancient ritual of the kill. Those queer little stiff-legged rushes and prancings are the heritage of an old death-dance, and those jerkings of his hind legs, as he rolls on his back, are the preparation for that day when—in desperate conflict with a bigger beast than himself—he will win the fight by the time-old feline technique of disembowelment. Even now, in his early infancy, he is wholly and inalienably a cat.

While he is still young he has already formulated his attitude toward the human race into whose midst he has been born. It is an attitude not easily described, but compounded of a great pride, a great reserve, a towering integrity. It is even to be fancied that there is something in it of a sort of bleak contempt. Solemnly the cat watches these great hulking two-legged creatures into whose strange tribe he has unaccountably been born —and who are so clumsy, so noisy, so vexing to his quiet spirit—and in his feline heart is neither love nor gratitude. He learns to take the food which they give him, to relish the warmth and the comfort and the caresses which they can offer, but these profferments do not persuade his wild mistrustful heart to surrender itself. He will not sell himself, as a dog will, for a scrap of meat; he will not enter into an allegiance. He is unchangeably and incorruptibly a cat, and he will accommodate himself to the ways and spirit of mankind no more than the stern necessity of his unnatural environment requires.

2

Quietly he dozes by the fire or on a lap, and purrs in his happiness because he loves the heat. But let him choose to move, and if any human hand tries to restrain him for more than a moment he will struggle and unsheath his claws and lash out with a furious hate. Let a whip touch him and he will slink off in a sullen fury, uncowed and outraged and unrepenting. For the things which man gives to him are not so precious or essential that he will trade them for his birth-right, which is the right to be himself—a furred four-footed being of ancient lineage, loving silence and aloneness and the night, and esteeming the smell of rat's blood above any possible human excellence.

He may live for perhaps ten years; occasionally even for twenty. Year after year he drinks the daily milk that is put faithfully before him, dozes in laps whose contours please him, accepts with casual pleasure the rubbing of human fingers under his chin—and withdraws, in every significant hour of his life, as far away from human society as he is able. Far from the house, in a meadow or a woods if he can find one, he crouches immobile for hours, his lithe body flattened concealingly in the grass or ferns, and waits for prey.

With a single pounce he can break a rabbit's spine as though it were a brittle twig. When he has caught a tawny meadow-mouse or a mole, he has, too, the ancient cat-ecstasy of toying and playing with it, letting it die slowly, in a long agony, for his amusement. Sometimes, in a dim remembrance from the remote past of his race, he may bring home his kill; but mostly he returns to the house as neat and demure as when he left, with his chops licked clean of blood.

Immaculate, unobtrusive, deep withdrawn into himself, he passes through the long years of his enforced companionship with humanity. He takes from his masters (how absurd a word it is) however much they may care to give him; of himself he surrenders nothing. However often he be decked with ribbons and cuddled and petted and made much over, his cold pride never grows less, and his grave calm gaze—tinged perhaps with a gentle distaste—is never lighted by adoration. To the end he adores only his own gods, the gods of mating, of hunting, and of the lonely darkness.

One day, often with no forewarning whatever, he is gone from the house and never returns. He has felt the presaging shadow of death, and he goes to meet it in the old unchanging way of the wild—alone. A cat does not want to die with the smell of humanity in his nostrils and the noise of humanity in his delicate peaked ears. Unless death strikes very quickly and suddenly, he creeps away to where it is proper that a proud wild beast should die—not on one of man's rugs or cushions, but in a lonely quiet place, with his muzzle pressed against the cold earth.

James Agee

Knoxville: Summer 1915

We are talking now of summer evenings in Knoxville, Tennessee in the time that I lived there so successfully disguised to myself as a child. It was a little bit mixed sort of block, fairly solidly lower middle class, with one or two juts apiece on either side of that. The houses corresponded: middle-sized gracefully fretted wood houses built in the late nineties and early nineteen hundreds, with small front and side and more spacious back yards, and trees in the yards, and porches. These were softwooded trees, poplars, tulip trees, cottonwoods. There were fences around one or two of the houses, but mainly the yards ran into each other with only now and then a low hedge that wasn't doing very well. There were few good friends among the grown people, and they were not poor enough for the other sort of intimate acquaintance, but everyone nodded and spoke, and even might talk short times, trivially, and at the two extremes of the general or the particular, and ordinarily nextdoor neighbors talked quite a bit when they happened to run into each other, and never paid calls. The men were mostly small businessmen, one or two very modestly executives, one or two worked with their hands, most of them clerical, and most of them between thirty and forty-five.

But it is of these evenings, I speak.

Supper was at six and was over by half past. There was still daylight, shining softly and with a tarnish, like the lining of a shell; and the carbon lamps lifted at the corners were on in the light, and the locusts were started, and the fireflies were out, and a few frogs were flopping in the

KNOXVILLE: SUMMER 1915   From *A Death in the Family* by James Agee, Copyright © 1957 by James Agee Trust. First published in *The Partisan Review*. Reprinted by permission of the publisher, Grosset & Dunlap, Inc.

dewy grass, by the time the fathers and the children came out. The children ran out first hell bent and yelling those names by which they were known; then the fathers sank out leisurely in crossed suspenders, their collars removed and their necks looking tall and shy. The mothers stayed back in the kitchen washing and drying, putting things away, recrossing their traceless footsteps like the lifetime journeys of bees, measuring out the dry cocoa for breakfast. When they came out they had taken off their aprons and their skirts were dampened and they sat in rockers on their porches quietly.

It is not of the games children play in the evening that I want to speak now, it is of a contemporaneous atmosphere that has little to do with them: that of the fathers of families, each in his space of lawn, his shirt fishlike pale in the unnatural light and his face nearly anonymous, hosing their lawns. The hoses were attached at spiggots that stood out of the brick foundations of the houses. The nozzles were variously set but usually so there was a long sweet stream of spray, the nozzle wet in the hand, the water trickling the right forearm and the peeled-back cuff, and the water whishing out a long loose and low-curved cone, and so gentle a sound. First an insane noise of violence in the nozzle, then the still irregular sound of adjustment, then the smoothing into steadiness and a pitch as accurately tuned to the size and style of stream as any violin. So many qualities of sound out of one hose: so many choral differences out of those several hoses that were in earshot. Out of any one hose, the almost dead silence of the release, and the short still arch of the separate big drops, silent as a held breath, and the only noise the flattering noise on leaves and the slapped grass at the fall of each big drop. That, and the intense hiss with the intense stream; that, and that same intensity not growing less but growing more quiet and delicate with the turn of the nozzle, up to that extreme tender whisper when the water was just a wide bell of film. Chiefly, though, the hoses were set much alike, in a compromise between distance and tenderness of spray, (and quite surely a sense of art behind this compromise, and a quiet deep joy, too real to recognize itself), and the sounds therefore were pitched much alike; pointed by the snorting start of a new hose; decorated by some man playful with the nozzle; left empty, like God by the sparrow's fall, when any single one of them desists: and all, though near alike, of various pitch; and in this unison. These sweet pale streamings in the light lift out their pallors and their voices all together, mothers hushing their children, the hushing unnaturally prolonged, the men gentle and silent and each snail-like withdrawn into the quietude of what he singly is doing, the urination of huge children stood loosely military against an invisible wall, and gentle happy and peaceful, tasting the mean goodness of their living like the last of their suppers in their mouths; while the locusts carry on this noise of hoses on their much higher and sharper key. The noise of the locust is dry, and it seems not to be rasped or vibrated but urged from him as if through a small orifice by a breath than can never give out. Also there is never one locust but an illusion of at least a thousand. The noise of each locust is pitched in some classic locust range out of which none of them varies more than two full tones: and yet you seem to hear each locust discrete from all the rest, and there is a long, slow, pulse in their noise, like the scarcely defined arch of a long and high set bridge. They are all around in every tree, so that the noise seems to come from nowhere and everywhere at once, from the whole shell heaven, shivering in your flesh and teasing your eardrums, the boldest of all the sounds of night. And yet it is habitual to summer nights, and is of the great order of noises, like the noises of the sea and of the blood her precocious grandchild, which you realize you are hearing only when you catch yourself listening. Meantime from low in the dark, just outside the swaying horizons of the hoses, conveying always grass in the damp of dew and its strong green-black smear of smell, the regular yet spaced noises of the crickets, each a sweet cold silver noise threenoted, like the slipping each time of three matched links of a small chain.

But the men by now, one by one, have silenced their hoses and drained and coiled them. Now only two, and now only one, is left, and you see only ghostlike shirt with the sleeve garters, and sober mystery of his mild face like the lifted face of large cattle enquiring of your presence in a pitchdark pool of meadow; and now he too is gone; and it has become that time of evening when people sit on their porches, rocking gently and talking gently and watching the street and the standing up into their sphere of possession of the trees, of birds hung havens, hangars. People go by; things go by. A horse, drawing a buggy, breaking his hollow iron music on the asphalt; a loud auto; a quiet auto; people in pairs, not in a hurry, scuffling, switching their weight of aestival body, talking casually, the taste hovering over them of vanilla, strawberry, pasteboard and starched milk, the image upon them of lovers and horsemen, squared with clowns in hueless amber. A street car raising its iron moan; stopping, belling and starting; stertorous; rousing and raising again its iron increasing moan and swimming its gold windows and straw seats on past and past and past, the bleak spark crackling and cursing above it like a small malignant spirit set to dog its tracks; the iron whine rises on rising speed; still risen, faints; halts; the faint stinging bell; rises again, still fainter; fainting, lifting, lifts, faints forgone: forgotten. Now is the night one blue dew.

Now is the night one blue dew, my father has drained, he has coiled the
      hose.

Low on the length of lawns, a frailing of fire who breathes.
Content, silver, like peeps of light, each cricket makes his comment over
and over in the drowned grass.
A cold toad thumpily flounders.
Within the edges of damp shadows of side yards are hovering children
nearly sick with joy of fear, who watch the unguarding of a telephone
pole.
Around white carbon corner lamps bugs of all sizes are lifted elliptic, solar
systems. Big hardshells bruise themselves, assailant: he is fallen on his
back, legs squiggling.
Parents on porches: rock and rock: From damp strings morning glories:
hang their ancient faces.
The dry and exalted noise of the locusts from all the air at once enchants
my eardrums.

On the rough wet grass of the back yard my father and mother have
spread quilts. We all lie there, my mother, my father, my uncle, my aunt,
and I too am lying there. First we were sitting up, then one of us lay down,
and then we all lay down, on our stomachs, or on our sides, or on our
backs, and they have kept on talking. They are not talking much, and the
talk is quiet, of nothing in particular, of nothing at all in particular, of
nothing at all. The stars are wide and alive, they seem each like a smile of
great sweetness, and they seem very near. All my people are larger bodies
than mine, quiet, with voices gentle and meaningless like the voices of
sleeping birds. One is an artist, he is living at home. One is a musician, she
is living at home. One is my mother who is good to me. One is my father
who is good to me. By some chance, here they are, all on this earth; and
who shall ever tell the sorrow of being on this earth, lying, on quilts, on
the grass, in a summer evening, among the sounds of the night. May God
bless my people, my uncle, my aunt, my mother, my good father, oh, remember them kindly in their time of trouble; and in the hour of their
taking away.

After a little I am taken in and put to bed. Sleep, soft smiling, draws
me unto her: and those receive me, who quietly treat me, as one familiar
and well-beloved in that home: but will not, oh, will not, not now, not
ever; but will not ever tell me who I am.

Ken Kesey

One Flew Over the Cuckoo's Nest

They're out there. Black boys in white suits up before me to commit sex acts in the hall and get it mopped up before I can catch them.

They're mopping when I come out the dorm, all three of them sulky and hating everything, the time of day, the place they're at here, the people they got to work around. When they hate like this, better if they don't see me. I creep along the wall quiet as dust in my canvas shoes, but they got special sensitive equipment detects my fear and they all look up, all three at once, eyes glittering out of the black faces like the hard glitter of radio tubes out of the back of an old radio.

"Here's the Chief. The *soo*-pah Chief, fellas. Ol' Chief Broom. Here you go, Chief Broom. . . ."

Stick a mop in my hand and motion to the spot they aim for me to clean today, and I go. One swats the backs of my legs with a broom handle to hurry me past.

"Haw, you look at 'im shag it? Big enough to eat apples off my head an' he mine me like a baby."

They laugh and then I hear them mumbling behind me, heads close together. Hum of black machinery, humming hate and death and other hospital secrets. They don't bother not talking out loud about their hate secrets when I'm nearby because they think I'm deaf and dumb. Everybody thinks so. I'm cagey enough to fool them that much. If my being half Indian ever helped me in any way in this dirty life, it helped me being cagey, helped me all these years.

I'm mopping near the ward door when a key hits it from the other side and I know it's the Big Nurse by the way the lockworks cleave to the key, soft and swift and familiar she been around locks so long. She slides through the door with a gust of cold and locks the door behind her and I see her fingers trail across the polished steel—tip of each finger the same color as her lips. Funny orange. Like the tip of a soldering iron. Color so hot or so cold if she touches you with it you can't tell which.

She's carrying her woven wicker bag like the ones the Umpqua tribe sells out along the hot August highway, a bag shape of a tool box with a hemp handle. She's had it all the years I been here. It's a loose weave and I can see inside it; there's no compact or lipstick or woman stuff, she's got that bag full of a thousand parts she aims to use in her duties today—wheels and gears, cogs polished to a hard glitter, tiny pills that gleam like porcelain, needles, forceps, watchmakers' pliers, rolls of copper wire . . .

She dips a nod at me as she goes past. I let the mop push me back to the wall and smile and try to foul her equipment up as much as possible by not letting her see my eyes—they can't tell so much about you if you got your eyes closed.

In my dark I hear her rubber heels hit the tile and the stuff in her wicker bag clash with the jar of her walking as she passes me in the hall. She walks stiff. When I open my eyes she's down the hall about to turn into the glass Nurses' Station where she'll spend the day sitting at her desk and looking out of her window and making notes on what goes on out in front of her in the day room during the next eight hours. Her face looks pleased and peaceful with the thought.

Then . . . she sights those black boys. They're still down there together, mumbling to one another. They didn't hear her come on the ward. They sense she's glaring down at them now, but it's too late. They should of knew better'n to group up and mumble together when she was due on the ward. Their faces bob apart, confused. She goes into a crouch and advances on where they're trapped in a huddle at the end of the corridor. She knows what they been saying, and I can see she's furious clean out of control. She's going to tear the black bastards limb from limb, she's so furious. She's swelling up, swells till her back's splitting out the white uniform and she's let her arms section out long enough to wrap around the three of them five, six times. She looks around her with a swivel of her huge head. Nobody up to see, just old Broom Bromden the half-breed Indian back there hiding behind his mop and can't talk to call for help. So she really lets herself go and her painted smile twists, stretches to an open snarl, and she blows up bigger and bigger, big as a tractor, so big I can smell the machinery inside the way you smell a motor pulling too big a load. I hold my breath and figure, My God this time they're gonna do it! This time they let the hate build up too high and overloaded and they're gonna tear one another to pieces before they realize what they're doing!

But just as she starts crooking those sectioned arms around the black boys and they go to ripping at her underside with the mop handles, all the patients start coming out of the dorms to check on what's the hullabaloo, and she has to change back before she's caught in the shape of her hideous real self. By the time the patients get their eyes rubbed to where they can halfway see what the racket's about, all they see is the head nurse, smiling and calm and cold as usual, telling the black boys they'd best not stand in a group gossiping when it *is* Monday morning and there *is* such a lot to get done on the first morning of the week. . . .

". . . mean old Monday morning, you know, boys . . ."

"Yeah, Miz Ratched . . ."

". . . and we have quite a number of appointments this morning, so perhaps, if your standing here in a group talking isn't *too urgent* . . ."

"Yeah, Miz Ratched . . ."

She stops and nods at some of the patients come to stand around and stare out of eyes all red and puffy with sleep. She nods once to each. Precise, automatic gesture. Her face is smooth, calculated, and precision-made, like an expensive baby doll, skin like flesh-colored enamel, blend of white and cream and baby-blue eyes, small nose, pink little nostrils—everything working together except the color on her lips and fingernails, and the size of her bosom. A mistake was made somehow in manufacturing, putting those big, womanly breasts on what would of otherwise been a perfect work, and you can see how bitter she is about it.

The men are still standing and waiting to see what she was onto the black boys about, so she remembers seeing me and says, "And since it *is* Monday, boys, why don't we get a good head start on the week by shaving poor Mr. Bromden first this morning, before the after-breakfast rush on the shaving room, and see if we can't avoid some of the—ah—disturbance he tends to cause, don't you think?"

Before anybody can turn to look for me I duck back in the mop closet, jerk the door shut dark after me, hold my breath. Shaving before you get breakfast is the worst time. When you got something under your belt you're stronger and more wide awake, and the bastards who work for the Combine aren't so apt to slip one of their machines in on you in place of an electric shaver. But when you shave *before* breakfast like she has me do some mornings—six-thirty in the morning in a room all white walls and white basins, and long-tube-lights in the ceiling making sure there aren't any shadows, and faces all round you trapped screaming behind the mirrors—then what chance you got against one of their machines?

I hide in the mop closet and listen, my heart beating in the dark, and I try to keep from getting scared, try to get my thoughts off someplace else—try to think back and remember things about the village and the big Columbia River, think about ah one time Papa and me were hunting birds in a stand of cedar trees near The Dalles. . . . But like always when I try to place my thoughts in the past and hide there, the fear close at hand seeps in through the memory. I can feel that least black boy out there coming up the hall, smelling out for my fear. He opens out his nostrils like black funnels, his outsized head bobbing this way and that as he sniffs, and he sucks in fear from all over the ward. He's smelling me now, I can hear him snort. He don't know where I'm hid, but he's smelling and he's hunting around. I try to keep still. . . .

(Papa tells me to keep still, tells me that the dog senses a bird some-wheres right close. We borrowed a pointer dog from a man in The Dalles. All the village dogs are no-'count mongrels, Papa says, fish-gut eaters and no class a-tall; this here dog, he got *insteek!* I don't say anything, but I already see the bird up in a scrub cedar, hunched in a gray knot of feathers. Dog running in circles underneath, too much smell around for him to point for sure. The bird safe as long as he keeps still. He's holding out pretty good, but the dog keeps sniffing and circling, louder and closer. Then the bird breaks, feathers springing, jumps out of the cedar into the birdshot from Papa's gun.)

The least black boy and one of the bigger ones catch me before I get ten steps out of the mop closet, and drag me back to the shaving room. I don't fight or make any noise. If you yell it's just tougher on you. I hold back the yelling. I hold back till they get to my temples. I'm not sure it's one of those substitute machines and not a shaver till it gets to my temples; then I can't hold back. It's not a will-power thing any more when they get to my temples. It's a . . . *button*, pushed, says Air Raid Air Raid, turns me on so loud it's like no sound, everybody yelling at me, hands over their ears from behind a glass wall, faces working around in talk circles but no sound from the mouths. My sound soaks up all other sound. They start the fog machine again and it's snowing down cold and white all over me like skim milk, so thick I might even be able to hide in it if they didn't have a hold on me. I can't see six inches in front of me through the fog and the only thing I can hear over the wail I'm making is the Big Nurse whoop and charge up the hall while she crashes patients outta her way with that wicker bag. I hear her coming but I still can't hush my hollering. I holler till she gets there. They hold me down while she jams wicker bag and all into my mouth and shoves it down with a mop handle.

(A bluetick hound bays out there in the fog, running scared and lost because he can't see. No tracks on the ground but the ones he's making, and he sniffs in every direction with his cold red-rubber nose and picks up no scent but his own fear, fear burning down into him like steam.) It's gonna burn me just that way, finally telling about all this, about the hospital, and her, and the guys—and about McMurphy. I been silent so long now it's gonna roar out of me like floodwaters and you think the guy telling this is ranting and raving my *God*; you think this is too horrible to have really happened, this is too awful to be the truth! But, please. It's still hard for me to have a clear mind thinking on it. But it's the truth even if it didn't happen.

Tom Wolfe

Cosmo's Tasmanian Deviltry

If only there were the perfect place, which would be a place big enough for the multitudes and isolated enough to avoid the cops, with their curfews and eternal hassling. Shortly after that they found the perfect place, by acci—

By *ac*cident, Mahavira?

The third Acid Test was scheduled for Stinson Beach, 15 miles north of San Francisco. Stinson Beach was already a gathering place for local heads. You could live all winter in little beach cottages there for next to nothing. There was a nice solid brick recreation hall on the beach, all very nice—but at the last minute that whole deal fell through, and they shifted to Muir Beach, a few miles south. The handbills were already out, all over the head sections of San Francisco, CAN *YOU* PASS THE ACID TEST, advertising Cassady & Ann Murphy Vaudeville and celebrities who *might be* there, which included anybody who happened to be in town, or might make it to town, the Fugs, Ginsberg, Roland Kirk. There were always some nice chiffon subjunctives and the future conditionals in the Prankster handbill rhetoric, but who was to deny who *might* be drawn into the Movie . . .

COSMO'S TASMANIAN DEVILTRY   From *The Electric Kool-Aid Acid Test* by Tom Wolfe. Reprinted with permission of Farrar, Straus & Giroux, Inc.

Anyway, at the last minute they headed for Muir Beach instead. The fact that many people wouldn't know about the change and would go to Stinson Beach and merely freeze in the darkness and never find the right place—somehow that didn't even seem distressing. It was part of some strange analogical order of the universe. Norman Hartweg hooked down his LSD—it was in the acid gas capsules that night—and thought of Gurdjieff. Gurdjieff wouldn't announce a meeting until the last minute. We're gonna get together tonight. The people that got there, got there; and there was message in that alone. Which was, of course: *you're either on the bus or off the bus.*

Those who were on the bus, even if they weren't Pranksters, like Marshall Efron, the round Mercury of Hip California, or the Hell's Angels . . . all found it. The cops, however, never did. They were apparently thrown off by the Stinson Beach handbills.

Muir Beach had a big log-cabin-style lodge for dances, banquets, and the like. The lodge was stilted up out in a waste of frigid marsh grass. A big empty nighttime beach in winter. Some little log tourist cabins with blue doors on either side, all empty. The lodge had three big rooms and was about 100 feet long, all logs and rafters and exposed beams, a tight ship of dark wood and Roughing It. The Grateful Dead piled in with their equipment and the Pranksters with theirs, which now included a Hammond electric organ for Gretch and a great strobe light.

The strobe! The strobe, or stroboscope, was originally an instrument for studying motion, like the way a man's legs move when he is running. In a darkened chamber, for example, you aim a bright light, flashing on and off, at the runner's legs as he runs. The light flashes on and off very rapidly, maybe three times as fast as a normal heartbeat. Every time the light flashes on, you see a new stage in the movement of the runner's legs. The successive images tend to freeze in your mind, because the light flashes off before the usual optical blur of the motion can hit you. The strobe has certain magical properties in the world of the acid heads. At certain speeds stroboscopic lights are so synched in with the pattern of brain waves that they can throw epileptics into a seizure. Heads discovered that strobes could project them into many of the sensations of an LSD experience without taking LSD. *The strobe!*

To people standing under the mighty strobe everything seemed to fragment. Ecstatic dancers—their hands flew off their arms, frozen in the air—their glistening faces came apart—a gleaming ellipse of teeth here, a pair of buffered highlit cheekbones there—all flacking and fragmenting into images as in an old flicker movie—a man in slices!—all of history pinned up on a butterfly board; the *experience*, of course. The strobe, the projectors, the mikes, the tapes, the amplifiers, the variable lag Ampex—it was all set up in a coiling gleaming clump in the Lincoln Log lodge, the communal clump, Babbs working over the dials, talking into the microphones to test them. Heads beginning to pour in. Marshall Efron and Norman, Norman already fairly zonked . . . Then in comes Kesey, through the main door—

Everyone watches. His face is set, his head cocked slightly. He is going to *do* something; everyone watches, because this seems terribly important. Drawn in right away by the charismatic vacuum cleaner, they are. Kesey heads for the control center, saying nothing to anyone, reaches into the galaxy of dials, makes . . . a single minute adjustment . . . yes! one toggle switch, double-pole, single-throw, double-break, in the allegory of Control . . .

Babbs is there, bombed, but setting up the intricate glistening coils of the tapes and projectors and the rest of it. Each of the Pranksters, bombed, has some fairly exacting task to do. Norman is staring at the dials—and he can't even see the numbers, he is so bombed, the numbers are wriggling off like huge luminous parasites under a microscope—but—*function under acid*. Babbs says, "One reason we're doing this is to learn how to function on acid." Of course! Prepare for the Day—when multitudes, millions, civilizations are on acid, seeking satori, it is coming, the wave is spreading.

The heads are all sitting around on the floor, about 300 of them. Into the maelstrom! Yes. At Big Nig's in San Jose, a lot of the kids the Pranksters had corralled coming out of the Rolling Stones show did not take LSD that night, although there were enough heads at Big Nig's stoned on various things to create that sympathetic vibration known as the "contact high." But this is different. Practically everybody who has found the place, after the switch from Stinson Beach, is far enough into the thing to know what the "acid" in the Acid Test means. A high percentage took LSD about four hours ago, rode out the first rush and are ready . . . now to groove . . . The two projectors shine forth with The Movie. The bus and the Pranksters start rolling over the walls of the lodge, Babbs and Kesey rapping on about it, the Bus lumping huge and vibrating and bouncing in great swells of heads and color—Norman, zonked, sitting on the floor, is half frightened, half ecstatic, although something in the back of his mind recognizes this as his Acid Test pattern, to sit back and watch, holding on through the rush, until 3 or 4 A.M., in the magic hours, and then dance—but so much of a rush this time! The Movie and Roy Seburn's light machine pitching the intergalactic red science-fiction seas to all corners of the lodge, oil and water and food coloring pressed between plates of glass and projected in vast size so that the very ooze of cellular Creation seems to ectoplast into the ethers and then the Dead coming in with their immense submarine vibrato vibrating, *garanging*, from the Aleutian rocks to the baja griffin cliffs of the Gulf of California. The Dead's weird sound! agony-in-ecstasis! submarine somehow, turbid half the time, tremendously loud but like sitting under a waterfall, at the same time full of sort of ghoul-show vibrato sounds as if each string on their electric guitars is half a block long and twanging in a room full of natural gas, not to mention their great Hammond electric organ, which sounds like a movie house Wurlitzer, a diathermy machine, a Citizens' Band radio and an Auto-Grind garbage truck at 4 A.M., all coming over the same frequency . . . Then suddenly another movie

THE FROGMAN

Babbs and Gretch and Hagen made it down in Santa Cruz, the story of Babbs the Frogman, arising from the Pacific in black neopreme Frogman suit from flippers to insect goggles, the pranking monster, falling in love with the Princess, Gretch, with floods of frames from elsewhere—the Bus Movie?—brittering in stroboscopically Frogman woos her and wins her and loses her to the Pacific Chohans in submarinal projection

BABBS! GRETCH!

Norman has never seen a movie while under acid before and it deepens, deepens, deepens in perspective, this movie, the most 3-D movie ever made, until they are standing right before him, their very neopreme fairy tails and the Pacific is so far in the distance and black out beyond the marshes around the Muir Beach lodge until Babbs and Gretch are now in the room in the flesh in two separate spots, here before me on the beach and over here in this very room in this very lodge on the beach, Babbs at the microphone and Gretch nearby at the new Hammond organ—such *synch!* that they should narrate and orchestrate their own lives like this, in variable lag, layer upon layer of variable lags

HEEEEEEEEE

into the whirlpool who should appear but Owsley. Owsley, done up in his $600 head costume, has emerged from his subterrain of espionage and paranoia to come see the Prankster experiment for himself, and in the middle of the giddy contagion he takes LSD. They never saw him take it before. He takes LSD and

RRRRRRRRRRRRRRRRRRRRRRRRRROIL

the whirlpool picks him up and spins him down into the stroboscopic stereoptic prankster panopticon in full variable lag

SUCH CREATURES

Hell's Angels come reeling in, shrieking Day-Glo, then clumping together on the floor under the black light and then most gentle Buddha blissly passing around among themselves various glittering Angel esoterica, chains, Iron Crosses, knives, buttons, coins, keys, wrenches, spark plugs, grokking over these arcana winking in the Day-Glo. Orange & Silver devil gliding through the dancers grinning his Zea-lot grin in every face, and Kesey crouched amid the gleaming coils, at the

CONTROLS

Kesey looks out upon the stroboscopic whirlpool—the dancers! flung and flinging! *in ecstasis!* gyrating! levitating! men in slices! in ping-pong balls! in the creamy bare essence! and it reaches a

SYNCH

he never saw before. Heads from all over the acid world out here and all whirling into the pudding. Now let a man see what

CONTROL

is. Kesey mans the strobe and a twist of the mercury lever

UP

and they all speed up

NOW

the whole whirlpool, so far into it, they are. Faster they dance, hands thrown up off their arms like confetti in the strobe flashing, blissful faces falling apart and being exchanged, for I am you and you are me in Cosmo's Tasmanian deviltry. Turn it

DOWN

and they slow down—or We turn down—It—Cosmo—turns down, still in perfect synch, one brain, one energy, a single flow of intersubjectivity. It is *possible*, this alchemy so dreamed of by all the heads. It is happening before him

CONTROL

Questions

Diction and Structure

1. As a nineteenth-century prose writer, Thoreau used somewhat more formal diction than most of the other writers included in this book. Cite instances in his essay of words now archaic or seldom used. Notice also the use of inverted sentences, with the verb coming before the subject. How do these usages affect the general character of the essay?

2. Look up the roots of the following polysyllabic, Latinate words used by Thoreau: "contending," "bellum," "internecine,"

"adversary," "pertinacity," "divested," "assiduously," "carnage,"
"pontificate." If they were replaced by shorter, more common
words—e.g., fighting, war, bloody, enemy, and so on—how
would this change the essay?

3. "The Battle of the Ants" contains many references to Roman
and American history. Show instances of these and indicate how
they are all part of the same system of images that build up the
point of the essay.

4. What are the obvious characteristics of Alan Devoe's word
choices in "Our Enemy, the Cat" (that is, formality, harshness,
objectivity, euphemism, and so on)? Why does he use words of
this sort?

5. Is Devoe's choice of diction consistently on the same level or
not? Consider "the superior guffaws of rustic humans," "bathetic
clumsiness," "wriggling mite of lumpy flesh and sinew," "viscid
spittle," "chops licked clean of blood."

6. What is the organizing principle of Devoe's essay?

7. Is James Agee's diction in "Knoxville: Summer 1915" formal
or informal, by and large? Is this appropriate to the subject?

8. Agee's essay is not written with the language a child might
use. How does this fact meet the stated purpose of the essay to
describe the child's recollection?

9. Examine in detail the paragraph on page 120 beginning,
"Supper was at six and was over by half past." Are the words
and phrases in any way unusual? What effect is created by the
paragraph? How is it done?

10. Look up the term *onomatopoeia*. How important is it as a
device in Agee's essay? How is it related to the central portion of
the description?

11. Like Agee's description of Knoxville, Ken Kesey's description
of the mental hospital is based on fact but is fictional in many
details. Which of the two compositions most successfully creates
the feeling of verisimilitude ("reality") for you? What devices
of diction especially help to do this?

12. Many of the sentences in Kesey's description are grammatically and syntactically at fault. How do you explain such
poor grammar and sentence structure? Does it work against the
effect of the description, or does it assist in creating the effect?

13. The concluding paragraphs of Kesey's description suggest
that the mood of Chief Bromden's memories will be one of
horror and raving madness. Is the language of this section
particularly emotional or "horrible"? Do euphemisms such as
"sex act" belong in Kesey's description?

14. In *One Flew,* Kesey refers to men of the Negroid race as *Negroes.* At various times in the last twenty years all of the following words or terms have been used to describe members of this race: "colored," "Negro," "Afro-American," "Blacks," and "blacks." How can you explain this variety of terms? Is one word in itself more pejorative or accurate or euphemistic than the others? What determines acceptable usage? What determines whether a term has connotations of racial prejudice? (Note, for example, the terms used by Stevenson, Kesey, Baldwin, and Podhoretz.)

15. What is the meaning of Tom Wolfe's title, "Cosmo's Tasmanian Deviltry"? What is a Tasmanian Devil? Who is Cosmo in the essay?

16. How does Tom Wolfe organize his description of a mass meeting of the Merry Pranksters, a drug cult led by Ken Kesey, author of *One Flew Over the Cuckoo's Nest?* Wolfe follows a time sequence (chronological order) but how does he alter it to convey his descriptive intent?

17. What are the associations of these words in Wolfe's description: Mahavira, hassling, "heads," synch, zonked? Why are certain words italicized?

18. Why would slang, jargon, and cant be unlikely to be widely used in descriptive writing by authors of the caliber included here? Can descriptive diction truly be put into a single dominant category—such as formal, informal, technical, or nontechnical? Explain your answer.

Style and Rhetoric

1. What is the relationship of the opening paragraphs of Thoreau's essay to his description of the ant battle? What is the rhetorical effect of describing first the battle at large and then the combat of the three ants in close detail?

2. What is the purpose and the effect of such terms as "legions of Myrmidons," "Conquer or die," "return with his shield or on it," "Austerlitz or Dresden," "Concord Fight!"?

3. Is Thoreau's style too exalted for describing a struggle between insects? Why does he use such elaborate diction and sentence patterns?

4. "We tie bright ribbons . . ." begins Devoe's essay on the cat. What is his reason for using the first person plural in this way? Does he use the form consistently throughout his composition?

5. In describing cats, does Devoe write about particular breeds or not? Is he concerned with what might be called "catness" or "felinity"? Are his statements too generalized to be true?

6. Does Devoe's description correspond to your own observations of cats? How do your personal attitudes toward cats, favorable or unfavorable, affect your reading of Devoe's description? Is your reaction an indication of Devoe's objectivity or not?

7. Judging from his style, does Devoe himself "like" cats? Show how his diction and style reflect his views toward his subject.

8. James Agee uses the series or list more obviously than other writers of descriptions in this section. He also uses long sentences made up of successive phrases that qualify or add to each other. Show examples of these uses and suggest their purpose and effects.

9. Is Agee's style more heavily adjectival than Devoe's or Thoreau's? Is his use of adjectives different in any way from theirs? How?

10. What mood is Agee trying to describe in his essay? Is it a familiar one to you? If you have not experienced this mood yourself, does the description by Agee create it for you?

11. Make a list of some ten or fifteen single words used by Agee in a passage that you think is most successful at description. What are the connotations of these words? Are they richly allusive in themselves, or are they connotative only within the context of their phrases (or sentences)? Compare Agee with Devoe in this regard. Is descriptive style more a matter of selecting vivid words or making unusual combinations of words?

12. The speaker in Ken Kesey's chapter from *One Flew Over the Cuckoo's Nest* is an insane, poorly educated Indian. Is the style of the selection appropriate to such a speaker?

13. Notice how comparison and contrast are used in the descriptions of the head nurse as she enters and as she confronts the Negro workers. What is the purpose of these passages? How effective are they in accomplishing this purpose?

14. One of the major devices of the fiction writer is the use of dialogue. Compare Kesey's use of dialogue with that in the essay by Wolfe.

15. The symbol can be an effective device in description. Look up the word *symbol* in a comprehensive dictionary or handbook of literary terms, and review its use by Fromm in his essay on page 50. How important are symbols in the essays by Lynes, Thoreau, and Devoe respectively? Are symbols more significant in the fictional pieces by Agee and Kesey than in the essays by the other three?

16. Tom Wolfe is noted as a "new-style" journalist: a reporter who is especially vivid in his descriptions. Do you find his style particularly "vivid"? In what ways? Is it "accurate" reporting? Discuss.

17. From what (or whose) vantage point is Wolfe describing the "acid love-in": Kesey's, an unidentified observer's, all of the participants', none of these, or what? Why does he use this technique? Does it work?

18. Wolfe's description deals with a place and actions, on one level. What else is he trying to describe besides a setting and actions? Is this sort of description unusually difficult in any way? Does Wolfe attempt to imitate Kesey's own style and perceptions in *One Flew?*

Theme and Viewpoint

1. Modern behavioral scientists are quite interested in what animal behavior reveals about human emotions and human society; the writings of Dr. Konrad Lorenz are a good example of literature on the subject. Read one of Lorenz's essays on animal behavior and compare it with Thoreau's essay on the ants in method, attitude, and conclusions.

2. What is Thoreau's apparent attitude toward ants—amusement, pity, disgust, detachment, indignation, horror, indifference?

3. Devoe compares and contrasts dogs, cows, and cats. Does his description in any way suggest Kronenberger's classifications of people? Look up the meanings of *anthropomorphism*. Is Devoe's essay anthropomorphic in any way? Is Thoreau's?

4. Apply F. L. Lucas's criteria for good style to Agee's description of Knoxville and Kesey's description of the hospital. Are Lucas's criteria applicable to descriptive writing?

5. Both Agee and Kesey write descriptive passages dealing with recollections of the past, of a lost childhood. Compare and contrast their attitudes toward childhood and the past and their descriptive prose styles in those passages.

6. Compare the treatments of the parent-child relationship in Agee and Kesey with that in Ian Stevenson's essay. Are the descriptions of Agee and Kesey more revealing in their insights into filial relationships than the "scientific" one? How so or not?

7. Is Tom Wolfe's description of Ken Kesey in the throes of cosmic madness in any way a commentary on Kesey as a thinker and writer? What *is* Wolfe's attitude toward Kesey? Compare

and contrast the treatment of "madness" in "One Flew Over the Cuckoo's Nest" and "Cosmo's Tasmanian Deviltry."

8. Does Wolfe's account of an "electric Kool-Aid acid test" bear any relationship to the scientific definition of a "drug" advanced by Nowlis? Comment.

Characterizing

Characterization is a specialized kind of descriptive writing: the verbal portrait of a human being. In describing someone, the writer seeks to create the vitality of that person by presenting lifelike details that conjure up the presence and the character of a recognizable being. Whether the figure is real or imagined, historical or fictitious, the characterization must possess the semblance of reality, the *feel* of fact. Whether in the form of the short story, novel, biography, autobiography, interview, or sketch, the characterization in prose must aim for verisimilitude: the appearance of life.

Some kinds of writing border on characterization without truly conveying the vital or living qualities of their subjects. Consider, for instance, the kind of "biography" or "life-writing" to be found in *Who's Who*. There may be a long list of facts: place and date of birth, where educated, mother's maiden name, jobs held, books published, elective offices gained, and so on. The reader may amass plenty of information about the subject, but may still lack any real sense of what that person is like.

Another sort of writing that approximates characterization

without fully realizing it is caricature. This is the exaggeration of several surface qualities that suggest the total human being. Novelists in particular use this method to sketch minor figures: Charles Dickens was the past master of the technique, being able to combine two or three physical details—a shock of red hair, a perpetual snigger, a smirking phrase—into a "character" in *David Copperfield* or *Bleak House*. Often the caricature is a stereotype, a simplified figure who represents a category or class of people: the man in the gray flannel suit; the bleached-blonde, wise-cracking chorus girl; the bespectacled and befuddled absent-minded professor. The skillful writer may be able to convince us that one of these stereotypes is a unique, vital person; but usually, despite their seeming dimensions of character, both the stereotype and the caricature are "flat" characterizations rather than complexly rounded people.

Detailed description of physical appearance may aid in characterizing someone; but it alone is unlikely to create a full presence. The old saw "You can tell everything about people by the way they look" is not only a dubious psychological proposition; it is also fallacious if applied to prose characterization. In past times, it was thought that certain physical traits denoted traits of character as well. Thus Chaucer could clue his reader that the Wife of Bath was sensuous by nature because there was a gap between her two front teeth, or Shakespeare could indicate nobility and intelligence by describing a king's high forehead. Today, the "science" of physiognomy is discredited, although many people still retain their suspicions about such features as close-set eyes, cleft chins, and bucked teeth. The prose description of physical appearance may rely on these associations or try to create new ones. What it chiefly does is to suggest that some physical detail is the principle by which a character may be placed into a larger category with well-established traits. To describe Samuel Taylor Coleridge by saying that he once dyed his hair green and took a lobster walking on a leash appears to be a colorful characterization; but it really provides only enough information for the reader to place Coleridge into the category of eccentrics (or individualists) and it provides almost no insight into his motivation or character. Was he insane? Vain? Desirous of shocking people? Humorless? Or full of humor? Bored? Angry? Protesting something? External description alone does not give any clear answer to such questions.

To be sure, external details may assist the observer to understand the inner nature of a person, what is called *character* or *personality* or some other term connoting the inner being. Such externals as appearance, dress, speech, gestures, habits, possessions, surroundings come from and reflect the inner self. The characters of those we meet in real life are ascertainable to us largely through extrinsic evidence in speech, behavior, and style. Such nebulous qualities as intelligence, taste, judgment, imagination, and feeling must be gauged in another human being from words, acts, and surroundings. Thus the writer who wants to capture the essence of character must often choose visible, concrete details about the subject and present them in such a way as to suggest their relationship to invisible or intangible character traits.

The best kind of prose characterization convinces its readers that they are meeting someone both familiar and new. We are all human beings; and a prose characterization must reflect the common qualities of humanity as we know them. Science fiction writers either dehumanize their Martians and Venusians to make them unsympathetic and repellent, or else they endow their fictional creatures with human attributes to appeal to the reader's sympathy. We must be able to empathize, to "feel with" characters if we are truly to believe in them. But if like us in some ways, the prose character must also differ significantly in others to engage our interest. The ordinary and commonplace, in life and in literature, possess little appeal. The accomplished writer is able to take the ordinary and by slightly heightening or exaggerating it to make it new. This is what Anton Chekhov does to make postal clerks and housewives memorable; this is how Harold Pinter converts truck drivers and landlords into frightening or terrified characters. Many writers, however, choose distinctive or unusual figures deliberately. Perhaps they speak in an odd dialect, behave in a peculiar fashion, have undergone some strange experience, or have a special forcefulness or vitality. Whatever the unique quality, the prose character must be distinctively individual as well as humanly recognizable.

The writer's attitude toward his or her subject is especially important in characterization. It may be sentimental—or hostile, ironic, amused, outraged, possibly bathetic or awed— but in some way or another the writer must be involved with the person described. To convince the reader, an author must respond strongly to his or her characters, identify with them, understand how and why they feel as they do, and, most importantly, know what factors made them what they are. Ultimately, of course, the composition must stress the subject and not the writer (except in autobiography); the writer's understanding should result in the careful choosing of descriptive, revealing details and the establishing of an implicit attitude toward the character. Readers may share that attitude or not, but they will never gain the "feel" of the character unless the writer has first responded to the character and later identified the factors that caused this response.

Katherine Anne Porter

The Witness

Uncle Jimbilly was so old and had spent so many years bowed over things, putting them together and taking them apart, making them over and making them do, he was bent almost double. His hands were closed and stiff from gripping objects tightly, while he worked at them, and they could not open altogether even if a child took the thick black fingers and tried to turn them back. He hobbled on a stick; his purplish skull showed through patches in his wool, which had turned greenish gray and looked as if the moths had got at it.

He mended harness and put half soles on the other Negroes' shoes; he built fences and chicken coops and barn doors; he stretched wires and put in new window panes and fixed sagging hinges and patched up roofs; he repaired carriage tops and cranky plows. Also he had a gift for carving miniature tombstones out of blocks of wood; give him almost any kind of piece of wood and he could turn out a tombstone, shaped very like the real ones, with carving, and a name and date on it if they were needed. They were often needed, for some small beast or bird was always dying and having to be buried with proper ceremonies: the cart draped as a hearse, a shoe-box coffin with a pall over it, a profuse floral outlay, and, of course, a tombstone. As he worked, turning the long blade of his bowie knife deftly in circles to cut a flower, whittling and smoothing the back and sides, stopping now and then to hold it at arm's length and examine it with one eye closed, Uncle Jimbilly would talk in a low, broken, abstracted murmur, as if to himself; but he was really saying something he meant one to hear. Sometimes it would be an incomprehensible ghost story; listen ever so carefully, at the end it was impossible to decide whether Uncle Jimbilly himself had seen the ghost, whether it was a real ghost at all, or only another man dressed like one; and he dwelt much on the horrors of slave times.

"Dey used to take 'em out and tie 'em down and whup 'em," he muttered, "wid gret big leather strops inch thick long as yo' ahm, wid round holes bored in 'em so's evey time dey hit 'em de hide and de meat done come off dey bones in little round chunks. And when dey had whupped 'em wid de strop till dey backs was all raw and bloody, dey spread dry cawnshucks on dey backs and set 'em afire and pahched 'em, and den dey poured vinega all ovah 'em . . . Yassuh. And den, the ve'y nex day dey'd got to git back to work in the fiels or dey'd do the same thing right ovah agin. Yassah. Dat was it. If dey didn't git back to work dey got it all right ovah agin."

The children—three of them: a serious, prissy older girl of ten, a thoughtful sad looking boy of eight, and a quick flighty little girl of six— sat disposed around Uncle Jimbilly and listened with faint tinglings of embarrassment. They knew, of course, that once upon a time Negroes had been slaves; but they had all been freed long ago and were now only servants. It was hard to realize that Uncle Jimbilly had been born in slavery, as the Negroes were always saying. The children thought that Uncle Jimbilly had got over his slavery very well. Since they had known him, he had never done a single thing that anyone told him to do. He did his work just as he pleased and when he pleased. If you wanted a tombstone, you had to be very careful about the way you asked for it. Nothing could have been more impersonal and faraway than his tone and manner of talking about slavery, but they wriggled a little and felt guilty. Paul would have changed the subject, but Miranda, the little quick one, wanted to know the worst. "Did they act like that to you, Uncle Jimbilly?" she asked.

"No, *mam*," said Uncle Jimbilly. "Now whut name you want on dis one? Dey nevah did. Dey done 'em dat way in the rice swamps. I always worked right here close to the house or in town with Miss Sophia. Down in the swamps . . ."

"Didn't they ever die, Uncle Jimbilly?" asked Paul.

"Cose dey died," said Uncle Jimbilly, "cose dey died—dey died," he went on, pursing his mouth gloomily, "by de thousands and tens upon thousands."

"Can you carve 'Safe in Heaven' on that, Uncle Jimbilly?" asked Maria in her pleasant, mincing voice.

"To put over a tame jackrabbit, Missy?" asked Uncle Jimbilly indignantly. He was very religious. "A heathen like dat? No, *mam*. In de swamps dey used to stake 'em out all day and all night, and all day and all night and all day wid de hans and feet tied so dey couldn't scretch and let de muskeeters eat 'em alive. De muskeeters 'ud bite 'em tell dey was all swole up like a balloon all over, and you could heah em howlin and prayin all ovah the swamp. Yassuh. Dat was it. And nary a drop of watah noh a moufful of braid . . . Yassah, dat's it. Lawd, dey done it. Hosanna! Now take dis yere tombstone and don' bother me no more . . . or I'll . . ."

Uncle Jimbilly was apt to be suddenly annoyed and you never knew why. He was easily put out about things, but his threats were always so exorbitant that not even the most credulous child could be terrified by them. He was always going to do something quite horrible to somebody and then he was going to dispose of the remains in a revolting manner. He was going to skin somebody alive and nail the hide on the barn door, or he was just getting ready to cut off somebody's ears with a hatchet and pin them on Bongo, the crop-eared brindle dog. He was often all prepared in his mind to pull somebody's teeth and make a set of false teeth for Ole Man Ronk . . . Ole Man Ronk was a tramp who had been living all summer in the little cabin behind the smokehouse. He got his rations along with the Negroes and sat all day mumbling his naked gums. He had skimpy black whiskers which appeared to be set in wax, and angry red eyelids. He took morphine, it was said; but what morphine might be, or how he took it, or why, no one seemed to know . . . Nothing could have been more unpleasant than the notion that one's teeth might be given to Ole Man Ronk.

The reason why Uncle Jimbilly never did any of these things he threatened was, he said, because he never could get round to them. He always had so much other work on hand he never seemed to get caught up on it. But some day, somebody was going to get a mighty big surprise, and meanwhile everybody had better look out.

Katherine Anne Porter

The Last Leaf

Old Nannie sat hunched upon herself expecting her own death momentarily. The Grandmother had said to her at parting, with the easy prophecy of the aged, that this might be their last farewell on earth; they embraced and kissed each other on the cheeks, and once more promised to meet each other in heaven. Nannie was prepared to start her journey at once. The children gathered around her: "Aunt Nannie, never you mind! We love you!" She paid no attention; she did not care whether they loved her or not. Years afterward, Maria, the elder girl, thought with a pang, they had not really been so very nice to Aunt Nannie. They went on depending upon her as they always had, letting her assume more burdens and more, allowing her to work harder than she should have. The old woman grew silent, hunched over more deeply—she was thin and tall also, with a nobly modeled Negro face, worn to the bone and a thick fine sooty black, no mixed blood in Nannie—and her spine seemed suddenly to have given way. They could hear her groaning at night on her knees beside her bed, asking God to let her rest.

When a black family moved out of a little cabin across the narrow creek, the first cabin empty for years, Nannie went down to look at it. She came back and asked Mister Harry, "Whut you aim to do wid dat cabin?" Mister Harry said, "Nothing," he supposed; and Nannie asked for it. She wanted a house of her own, she said; in her whole life she never had a place of her very own. Mister Harry said, of course she could have it. But the whole family was surprised, a little wounded. "Lemme go there and pass my last days in peace, chil'ren" she said. They had the place scrubbed and whitewashed, shelves put in and the chimney cleaned, they fixed Nannie up with a good bed and a fairly good carpet and allowed her to take all sorts of odds and ends from the house. It was astonishing to discover that Nannie had always liked and hoped to own certain things, she had seemed so contented and wantless. She moved away, and as the children said afterwards to each other, it was almost funny and certainly very sweet to see how she tried not to be too happy the day she left, but they felt rather put upon, just the same.

Thereafter she sat in the serene idleness of making patchwork and braiding woolen rugs. Her grandchildren and her white family visited her, and all kinds of white persons who had never owned a soul related to Nannie, went to see her, to buy her rugs or leave little presents with her.

She had always worn black wool dresses, or black and white figured calico with starchy white aprons and a white ruffled mobcap, or a black taffety cap for Sundays. She had been finicking precise and neat in her ways, and she still was. But she was no more the faithful old servant Nannie, a freed slave: she was an aged Bantu woman of independent means, sitting on the steps, breathing the free air. She began wearing a blue bandanna wrapped around her head, and at the age of eighty-five she took to smoking a corncob pipe. The black iris of the deep, withdrawn old eyes turned a chocolate brown and seemed to spread over the whole surface of the eyeball. As her sight failed, the eyelids crinkled and drew in, so that her face was like an eyeless mask.

The children, brought up in an out-of-date sentimental way of thinking, had always complacently believed that Nannie was a real member of the family, perfectly happy with them, and this rebuke, so quietly and firmly administered, chastened them somewhat. The lesson sank in as the years went on and Nannie continued to sit on the doorstep of her cabin. They were growing up, times were changing, the old world was sliding from under their feet, they had not yet laid hold of the new one. They missed Nannie every day. As their fortunes went down, and they had very few servants, they needed her terribly. They realized how much the old woman had done for them, simply by seeing how, almost immediately after she went, everything slackened, lost tone, went off edge. Work did not accomplish itself as it once had. They had not learned how to work for themselves, they were all lazy and incapable of sustained effort or planning. They had not been taught and they had not yet educated themselves. Now and then Nannie would come back up the hill for a visit. She worked then almost as she had before, with a kind of satisfaction in proving to them that she had been almost indispensable. They would miss her more than ever when she went away. To show their gratitude, and their hope that she would come again, they would heap upon her baskets and bales of the precious rubbish she loved, and one of her great grandsons Skid or Hasty would push them away beside her on a wheelbarrow. She would again for a moment be the amiable, dependent, like-one-of-the-family old servant: "I know my chil'ren won't let me go away empty-handed."

Uncle Jimbilly still pottered around, mending harness, currying horses, patching fences, now and then setting out a few plants or loosening the earth around shrubs in the spring. He muttered perpetually to himself, his blue mouth always moving in an endless disjointed comment on things past and present, and even to come, no doubt, though there was nothing about him that suggested any connection with even the nearest future . . . Maria had not realized until after her grandmother's death that Uncle Jimbilly and Aunt Nannie were husband and wife . . . That marriage of convenience, in which they had been mated with truly royal policy, with an eye to the blood and family stability, had dissolved of itself between them when the reasons for its being had likewise dissolved . . . They took no notice whatever of each other's existence, they seemed to forget they had children together (each spoke of "my children"), they had stored up no common memories that either wished to keep. Aunt Nannie moved away into her own house without even a glance or thought for Uncle Jimbilly, and he did not seem to notice that she was gone . . . He slept in a little attic over the smoke-house, and ate in the kitchen at odd hours, and did as he pleased, lonely as a wandering spirit and almost as invisible . . . But one day he passed by the little house and saw Aunt Nannie sitting on her steps with her pipe. He sat down awhile, groaning a little as he bent himself into angles, and sunned himself like a weary old dog. He would have stayed on from that minute, but Nannie would not have him. "Whut you doin with all this big house to yoself?" he wanted to know. " 'Tain't no more than just enough fo' me," she told him pointedly; "I don' aim to pass my las' days waitin on no man," she added, "I've served my time, I've done my do, and dat's all." So Uncle Jimbilly crept back up the hill and into his smoke-house attic, and never went near her again . . .

✦

On summer evenings she sat by herself long after dark, smoking to keep away the mosquitoes, until she was ready to sleep. She said she wasn't afraid of anything: never had been, never expected to be. She had long ago got in the way of thinking that night was a blessing, it brought the time when she didn't have to work any more until tomorrow. Even after she stopped working for good and all, she still looked forward with longing to the night, as if all the accumulated fatigues of her life, lying now embedded in her bones, still begged for easement. But when night came, she remembered that she didn't have to get up in the morning until she was ready. So she would sit in the luxury of having at her disposal all of God's good time there was in this world.

When Mister Harry, in the old days, had stood out against her word in some petty dispute, she could always get the better of him by slapping her slatty old chest with the flat of her long hand and crying out: "Why, Mister Harry, you, ain't you ashamed to talk lak dat to me? I nuhsed you at dis bosom!"

Harry knew this was not literally true. She had nursed three of his elder brothers; but he always said at once, "All right, Mammy, all right, for God's sake!"—precisely as he had said it to his own mother, exploding in his natural irascibility as if he hoped to clear the air somewhat of the smothering matriarchal tyranny to which he had been delivered by the death of his father. Still he submitted, being of that latest generation of sons who acknowledged, however reluctantly, however bitterly, their mystical never to be forgiven debt to the womb that bore them, and the breast that suckled them.

Margaret Truman

Harry Truman and Bess Wallace

My childhood memories are rich in love and laughter. But this book is about my father, not about me, so I won't burden it with my reminiscences, such as the time he gave me a baby grand piano for Christmas, hoping to speed my recovery from a bout of pneumonia. I had been hoping for electric trains. I burst into tears and refused to touch the piano. Besides, now that I am an adult, I have developed a kind of second memory about Dad that historians may consider more valuable, and I find more interesting. This second memory is composed of answers I have received to innumerable questions I have asked my mother and my father, my grandmothers when they were living, my father's sister, Aunt Mary, and my Cousin Ethel Noland who was our family historian. From their memories and from not a few yellowed newspaper clippings that I had the Truman Library put on microfilm, lest they crumble away at my touch, I have extended my memories of my father back into the years before Mary Margaret Truman entered his life.

There is really nothing very surprising about this, if you stop to think about it. No one's memories are limited to his own life. When you grow up in a big family as I did, with grandmothers who lived into their nineties, the years before your birth are in some ways as vivid as your childhood years. In that sense my memories go all the way back to the Civil War. My father was even more interested in the family's past than I was, and he often talked to me or prompted my Grandmother Truman— Mamma Truman, as we called her—into talking about her memories of Missouri in those days, when Northern and Southern guerrillas roamed the state, shooting and stealing.

There was an enormously strong intellectual-emotional bond between Dad and his mother—the sort of bond which, I have discovered from my delvings into presidential lore, has existed between an astonishing number of presidents and their mothers. No less than twenty-one of the thirty-six American presidents to date have been their mothers' first boy and almost every one of them were the favorite sons of strong-minded women.

That brings us to the other side of Dad's relationship with his mother. Even in her seventies and eighties, when I knew her best, Mamma Truman was a woman with a glint in her eye. She had a mind of her own on almost every subject from politics to plowing. Although she spent most of her long life on a farm, she never milked a cow. "Papa told me that if I never learned, I'd never have to do it," she explained once to her daughter Mary Jane. Something else I learned from my mother only a year or two ago. Mamma Truman hated to cook, and only made one dish that was praiseworthy—fried chicken. In her early years she supervised a kitchen that fed as many as twenty field hands, but servants did the real cooking. In her later years, Aunt Mary handled the stove work. Neither she nor anyone else in the family let me in on this secret all during my girlhood years, when we spent almost every Sunday visiting Mamma Truman and dined on her delicious fried chicken. For a while I was convinced that I was a female dropout, because I loathed the idea of cooking from a very early age, and still do it under protest.

Any boy who spent a lot of time with a mother like Martha Ellen

Truman could only emerge from the experience the very opposite of a conventional mamma's boy. This is one among many reasons why my father always bridled when a writer or reporter tried to pin this image on him. The rest of the family, knowing Mamma Truman, simply guffawed at the notion.

But Martha Ellen Truman gave her son much else, besides moral fiber. She passed on to him her strong interest in books, music, and art. This may startle some readers. For too many people, particularly in the East, the word "farm" is synonymous with ignorance and poverty. It conjures up images from *Tobacco Road* or *The Grapes of Wrath*. Missourians are constantly astonished by this cultural parochialism. Martha Ellen Young Truman came from a family that was, if not aristocratic, certainly upper-middle class. Even in the early 1900s, when her father's farm was reduced from 2,000 to 600 acres, it regularly earned $15,000 a year—the equivalent of $50,000 to $60,000 today. She had an excellent education, having graduated from the Baptist Female College in Lexington, Missouri, where she majored—if that is not too strong a word—in music and art. I have already noted that she taught my father to read before he was five; she had him playing the piano not much later.

Mamma Truman was the moving spirit behind the family decision to set up housekeeping in Independence. They had been living on the Young farm for three or four years, but the country schools in nearby Grandview were decidedly inadequate, compared to those in Independence. At this point in time—1890—Independence was by no means the quaint little farming community that some of my father's biographers have imagined. It was a very genteel town, with plenty of what might be called "old money" in it, if we foreshorten the term a little. In its heyday, before the railroad spanned the West, Independence had been the jumping-off point for both the Santa Fe and Oregon trails. There were only about 6,000 people living in the town in 1890, but there was a remarkable number of houses built along spacious Victorian lines.

The Trumans moved into one of these, on Chrysler Street, formerly owned by a wealthy family named Blitz. Kansas City, only a few miles away at the western end of Jackson County, was a roaring boom town of 55,000. But neither the Trumans nor the Youngs would ever have dreamt of living there. That was the "Yankee town." Independence was the stronghold of the old original pioneers in Jackson County, most of whom, like the Trumans and the Youngs, came from Kentucky. The atmosphere in Independence was Southern in the best sense of that much abused word.

The pace was slow and dignified, the people friendly. The word "family" included numerous cousins, and the bond between "kin" was strong.

The past was very important. I am sure my father's interest in history was born in his numerous discussions of the Civil War with his mother. She always talked as if the Yankee guerrillas from Kansas Territory—"Jayhawkers" as they were called—had appeared at the Young farm only a few weeks ago to slaughter the pigs and cattle, kill the chickens, and steal the family silver and featherbeds. When she recalled these memories for me, she always seemed to reserve a special resentment for the loss of those featherbeds—something that long puzzled me. Only when I was an adult did I realize that it took months of plucking geese to create a featherbed, and they were extremely valuable.

This absorption in the Southern side of our historic quarrel led my father inevitably to an equally strong interest in politics—on the side of the Democratic party. Democrats were not made by campaign promises and rational debate, in Independence. They were born. As for Republicans, Mamma Truman always talked about them as if, at that very moment, somewhere in Kansas they were all collectively dining off her mother's silver.

Most of the time, my father's world revolved around his mother. A story my Cousin Ethel liked to tell illustrates this fact as well as Mamma Truman's strength of character. The boys along Chrysler Street had, it seemed, a habit of bombarding the local chickens with rocks. One woman neighbor repeatedly accused my father of being involved in this mischief and Mamma Truman steadfastly denied it. Finally, one day the neighbor appeared in a monumental rage.

"Your older boy was in it this time," she said. "Now don't say he wasn't because this time he was."

Calmly Mamma Truman replied, "Well, just wait and we'll see, we'll find out. If he was why we're not going to excuse him but we won't blame him unless he's guilty."

She promptly summoned all the boys within calling distance and asked each one of them if my father had done any rock throwing. Vivian and all the rest of them confessed their guilt, but they unanimously exonerated my father. "The neighbor went home a little crestfallen," Cousin Ethel recalled.

I am sure that it was Mamma Truman who sustained Dad's years of studying the piano, in spite of hoots and sneers from his less artistically minded contemporaries. The fact that he was a very talented pianist helped, of course. Dad's stringent modesty when describing his own achievements has confused a lot of people about his musical ability. At first he studied with Miss Florence Burrus, who lived next door. But he soon outgrew her scope, and Mamma Truman sent him to Mrs. E. C. White, a Kansas City teacher who had studied under Theodor Leschetitzky, a very famous European master of the time, the teacher of Paderewski. Twice a week Dad journeyed to Mrs. White's house for lessons, and practiced at least two hours a day. When Paderewski came through Kansas City on a tour in 1900, Mrs. White took Dad to meet him, and the great man showed Dad how to play the "turn" in his Minuet in G. By this time, Dad was playing Bach, Beethoven, Liszt, and he had acquired what was later called "a good foundation." Mrs. White thought he should aim at a musical career. But when he was seventeen, Dad quit because—he says—"I wasn't good enough." There was another reason, which we will see in a few pages.

My father's glasses did not entirely separate him from boys his own age. During his first years in Independence, the Truman home was one of the star attractions of the neighborhood, thanks to its extensive animal farm. John Anderson Truman built a little wagon and had harnesses especially made for a pair of goats that he hitched to it, and every boy in town was soon begging my father and his brother for a ride. When the boys grew older and turned to sports, my father would occasionally join them, at least during the baseball season as umpire.

But my father spent most of his time reading books that Mamma Truman carefully selected for him. His favorite was a red-backed four-volume set of biographies by Charles Francis Horne, *Great Men and Famous Women*. These were the books that made him fall in love with history. To this day he still insists that reading biographies is the best way to learn history. He is also a firm believer in what some cynical historians have called the great man theory. Dad sums it up more positively. "Men make history. History does not make the man."

My father's second preference, after Mr. Horne's biographies, was the Bible. By the time he was twelve, he had read it end to end twice and was frequently summoned to settle religious disputes between the various branches of the Truman and Young families, who were divided among Baptists, Presbyterians, and Methodists. He also discovered the Independence Public Library, and by the time he had graduated from high school, Dad had devoured all of the books on its shelves that might interest a boy. Included in this diet, of course, were great gobs of history. He remained totally fascinated by all aspects of the past. At one point, he and a group of his friends spent weeks constructing a model of a bridge Julius Caesar built across the Rhine. My Cousin Ethel remembered another season when Dad's big enthusiasm was fencing.

Studious though he was, my father was not the brightest boy in his class. This title went to Charlie Ross, a gangling, rather shy young man who read at least as many books as Dad, and had a talent for handling words that won him the admiration of the school's favorite teacher, Miss

Tillie Brown. Charlie was editor of the year book and the class valedic-
torian. On graduation day Miss Tillie gave him a big kiss. Dad was one of
several boys who protested this favoritism. But Miss Tillie refused to
apologize. "When the rest of you do something worthwhile, you'll get your
reward, too," she said. As we shall see, Dad never forgot those words.

Charlie was one of my father's closest friends. But more than friendship attracted him to another member of the class—a very pretty blonde
girl named Elizabeth Virginia Wallace, known to her friends as Bess.
They had already known each other for a long time. They had attended
Sunday school together at the First Presbyterian Church when they were
kindergarten age. My father often says it took him another five years to
get up the nerve to speak to her, but this can be partly explained by
geography. They went to different grammar schools until the Trumans
sold their house on Chrysler Street and moved to new quarters on Waldo
Street. When Dad transferred to fifth grade in the Columbian School, he
found Bess Wallace in his new class. Everyone in the family seems to
agree that he was in love with her, even then. "To tell the truth," my
Cousin Ethel said, "there never was but one girl in the world for Harry
Truman, from the first time he ever saw her at the Presbyterian kindergarten." This was the voice of authority speaking. Cousin Ethel went all
through school with Dad and Mother. In high school they used to meet
regularly at the Noland house to study Latin with the help of Cousin
Ethel's sister, Nellie, who was a whiz in the language. They apparently
spent most of their time fencing, however.

I am sure that Mother was the best female fencer in town, and she
was probably better than most of the boys. To this day I find it hard to
listen to stories of my mother's girlhood without turning an envious green,
or collapsing into despair. She was so many things that I am not. She was
a marvelous athlete—the best third baseman in Independence, a superb
tennis player, a tireless ice skater—and she was pretty besides. Sometimes I
think she must have reduced most of the boys in town to stuttering awe.
Mother also had just as many strong opinions at eighteen as she has now,
and no hesitation about stating them Missouri style—straight from the
shoulder. What man could cope with a girl like that—especially when she
could also knock down a hot grounder and throw him out at first or wallop
him six love at tennis? Sometimes, when someone looks skeptical about my
thesis that my father was always an extraordinary man, I'm tempted to
give them the best capsule proof I know—he married my mother. Only
someone who was very confident that he was no ordinary man would have
seen himself as Bess Wallace's husband.

Although they were frequently together in the big crowd of cousins
and friends who picnicked and partied during their high school years,

they drifted apart after they graduated. Again, geography was the villain. John Anderson Truman took a terrible beating, speculating on the Kansas City grain market in 1901, and in 1902 the Trumans had to sell their house on Waldo Street and move to Kansas City, Missouri. My father had hoped—in fact expected—to go to college. But that was out of the question now. He tried for West Point and Annapolis, but was turned down because of his bad eyes. So, like most young men his age (seventeen), he went to work. To the great distress of his teacher, Mrs. White, he also abandoned his piano lessons. The long years of preparation necessary for a classical pianist's career seemed out of the question now.

My father worked for a summer as a timekeeper with the Santa Fe Railroad. Then for several years he was a bank clerk. He made considerable progress at this job, going from $35 to $120 a month, and handling a million dollars a day in his cage. One of his fellow fledgling bankers was Arthur Eisenhower, whose younger brother Ike was still in high school in Abilene, Kansas. On Saturdays Dad ushered at the local theaters to make extra money—and enjoy free of charge all the vaudeville acts and traveling drama groups that came to Kansas City.

In 1906, John Anderson Truman asked my father to return to the Young farm and help him run this 600-acre establishment, as well as 300 acres nearby, which belonged to Dad's uncle, Harrison Young, after whom he was named. It was sometime during these years—no one seems to remember precisely the date—that Dad regained Bess Wallace's attention, this time permanently.

My Cousin Ethel Noland was the unchallengeable authority on the occasion, because it was from her home that my father returned the famous (in the Truman family, anyway) cake plate, which enabled him to renew the acquaintance. "Mrs. Wallace was very neighborly," Cousin Ethel explained, "and she loved to send things over to us—a nice dessert or something, just to share it." As a result, there were often Wallace cake plates sitting around the Noland house, waiting to be returned. One Saturday or Sunday my father was visiting, when Cousin Ethel remarked that it was about time someone got around to returning one of these plates. Dad volunteered with something approaching the speed of light, and the young lady who answered his knock at the Wallace door was the very person he wanted to see.

I believe there really are no explanations that completely explain why two people fall in love with each other. But if you live with them long enough, you can see glimpses of explanations, and I will advance one here that throws some light on my father's character at the same time. I think the secret of his success with my mother was his absolute refusal to argue with her—a policy he has followed to this day. From his very early years, my father was known as the peacemaker in the Truman-Young families. Even among his Noland cousins he is still remembered as an expert in resolving arguments. Right straight through his presidential years, he continued to play this role in our highly combative clan. Occasionally he complained mightily to me in his letters about the prevalence of "prima donnas," as he called the more difficult members of the family. But he continued to exercise this gift for peacemaking in private—and in public.

Contrary to her public image, my mother is a very combative person. There is nothing vindictive or mean about her. She just likes to argue. I am the same way. To this day we cannot get together for more than twenty minutes without locking verbal horns. (Whereupon Dad will groan, "Are you two at it again?") Who else but a young man smart enough *not* to argue with Bess Wallace could have persuaded a girl like that to marry him?

By 1914, when my grandfather, John Anderson Truman, died, it was more or less understood that Mother and Dad were paired. She went to my grandfather's funeral, and my father was a regular visitor at the Wallace house on North Delaware Street. Contrary to some of the biographical legends, he did not commute by horseback from the farm at Grandview. At first he came by train and streetcar and later in a magnificent 1910 Stafford with a brass-rimmed windshield and Prest-O-Lite lamps.

Some people have claimed that he bought the car to impress his future mother-in-law, Mrs. Wallace, who supposedly did not approve of the match. But no one in the family believes that story. Sometimes the tale is embellished, to make my mother the richest girl in Independence and my father some poor disheveled dirt farmer, desperately attempting to hide his poverty behind a high-powered engine. This is plain nonsense. By now I trust I have established as undeniable fact that the Trumans were not poor. They had suffered financial reverses, but they still had those 900 acres of prime Missouri topsoil on the Young farms to fall back on. As my Cousin Ethel often said, "There was always a feeling of security there."

What good times they had in that cousinly, neighborly crowd! Whether my father was commuting from his bank job in Kansas City, where he lived with his first cousins, the Colgans, or from the farm at Grandview, when he got to Independence, there always seemed to be a party in progress. My Cousin Ethel had a wonderful picture of the crowd enjoying a watermelon feast in the Colgan backyard. My mother and her brothers are there, all, as Cousin Ethel put it, "into watermelon up to our ears." *Life* magazine once begged her to let them publish it, but they received a frosty no because Cousin Ethel thought Mother looked undignified.

There were practical jokes galore that kept everyone laughing. No one loves a practical joke more than my father, so it doesn't surprise me that he was deep in most of them. Among the favorites was one Dad helped cook up on his cousin, Fred Colgan, and another friend, Edwin Green. They and the girls in the crowd went picnicking on the banks of the Missouri one day. Fred Colgan and Ed Green decided, just for the fun of it, to put a message in a bottle, toss it in the river, and see if they got an answer. My father and the other young jokers promptly concocted two imaginary girls in Mississippi who wrote deliciously teasing letters to Messrs. Colgan and Green. Pretty soon there was a veritable romance budding, with my father and his fellow jokers fiendishly mailing letters and even phony pictures to friends in Mississippi who remailed them to poor Fred Colgan and Ed Green, who were by now getting desperately lovesick. Finally, one of the older members in the family put a stop to it, lest they have a couple of romantic nervous breakdowns on their hands. Fred Colgan took the news especially hard, and, I have been told, did not speak to my father or the other jokers for months.

With Dad's ability to play the piano, and his love of a good joke, he was often the life of the party. Another story that everyone loves to tell concerns his antics en route to a wedding in 1913. The bridegroom was a highly successful young businessman, and he had a very formal wedding. Dad borrowed a tuxedo from one friend and an opera hat from my mother's brother, Frank Wallace. The hat was collapsible, and en route to the reception, riding in a horse-drawn cab, Dad tried to put his head out the window to tell the driver the address. His hat hit the top of the window and collapsed. Everyone went into hysterics at "the little fried egg thing sitting on the top of his head," to quote my Cousin Ethel. Dad let the hat perch there all the way over to the reception, while the cab rocked with laughter. When they finally arrived, they had to sit outside the bride's house for a good five minutes, recovering their senses. "We were carefree and a little irresponsible, I think," my Cousin Ethel said. Those words are a pretty good paraphrase of the fundamental, almost idyllic happiness that comes through to me in the recollections I have heard and overheard of my father's youth in pre-World War I Independence.

Happy memories are a priceless asset to a man when he becomes a public servant. They deepen and broaden his vision of his country's value and make him more generous, I think, more committed to widening the opportunities for happiness for the generations that follow him.

These years also helped to form in my father his deliberate, methodical approach to problems. From his early twenties to his early thirties, he was a farmer—not a gentleman farmer but a working one, toiling most of the time under John Anderson Truman's stern eye. Off the political platform, when he talked about learning how to plow a straight furrow, he often added, "It had to be straight. If it wasn't, I heard about it from my father for the next year." These were the years when Dad also developed that sturdy physique which prompted us to snort with indignation when someone called him "the little man in the White House." Riding a gang-plow across a field behind a team of four horses or four mules took muscle, and added some every time you did it.

When my father discussed his farming days he made you realize the sheer physical labor involved. "I used to milk cows by hand. I used to plow with a four-horse team, instead of a tractor," he said once during the White House years. "I have two nephews on the same farm that get much more out of that farm than I ever did. But they do it with machinery. They milk cows by machine, and they plow with a tractor and they plant with a tractor and they bale hay with a tractor. I don't think that those boys could follow me up a corn row to save their lives, because they ride and I walked."

But the most important thing about a farmer's life is the steady, methodical nature of his work. Dad could count the revolutions of a gang-plow's wheel, and figure out exactly how long it would take him to plow a field half a mile square. Things had to be done on a schedule, but nothing much could be done to hurry the growth of the corn or the wheat. The pace of the farm was reflected in the pace of the era. There was no sense of frantic urgency, no burning need to hurry. As Cousin Ethel said, "Harry was always a deliberate man."

J. Robert Oppenheimer

On Albert Einstein

Though I knew Einstein for two or three decades, it was only in the last decade of his life that we were close colleagues and something of friends. But I thought that it might be useful, because I am sure that it is not too

ON ALBERT EINSTEIN From *The New York Review of Books,* March 17, 1966. Originally delivered as a lecture in the UNESCO House, Paris, December 13, 1965. Reprinted by permission.

soon—and for our generation perhaps almost too late—to start to dispel the clouds of myth and to see the great mountain peak that these clouds hide. As always, the myth has its charms; but the truth is far more beautiful.

Late in his life, in connection with his despair over weapons and wars, Einstein said that if he had to live it over again he would be a plumber. This was a balance of seriousness and jest that no one should now attempt to disturb. Believe me, he had no idea of what it was to be a plumber; least of all in the United States, where we have a joke that the typical behavior of this specialist is that he never brings his tools to the scene of the crisis. Einstein brought his tools to his crises; Einstein was a physicist, a natural philosopher, the greatest of our time.

What we have heard, what you all know, what is the true part of the myth is his extraordinary originality. The discovery of quanta would surely have come one way or another, but he discovered them. Deep understanding of what it means that no signal could travel faster than light would surely have come; the formal equations were already known; but this simple, brilliant understanding of the physics could well have been slow in coming, and blurred, had he not done it for us. The general theory of relativity which, even today, is not well proved experimentally, no one but he would have done for a long, long time. It is in fact only in the last decade, the last years, that one has seen how a pedestrian and hard-working physicist, or many of them, might reach that theory and understand this singular union of geometry and gravitation; and we can do even that today only because some of the *a priori* open possibilities are limited by the confirmation of Einstein's discovery that light would be deflected by gravity.

Yet there is another side besides the originality. Einstein brought to the work of originality deep elements of tradition. It is only possible to discover in part how he came by it, by following his reading, his friendships, the meager record that we have. But of these deep-seated elements of tradition—I will not try to enumerate them all; I do not know them all—at least three were indispensable and stayed with him.

The first is from the rather beautiful but recondite part of physics that is the explanation of the laws of thermodynamics in terms of the mechanics of large numbers of particles, statistical mechanics. This was with Einstein all the time. It was what enabled him from Planck's discovery of the laws of black body radiation to conclude that light was not only waves but particles, particles with an energy proportional to their frequency and momentum determined by their wave-number, the famous relations that de Broglie was to extend to all matter, to electrons first and then clearly to all matter.

It was this statistical tradition that led Einstein to the laws governing the emission and absorption of light by atomic systems. It was this that enabled him to see the connection between de Broglie's waves and the statistics of light-quanta proposed by Bose. It was this that kept him an active proponent and discoverer of the new phenomena of quantum physics up to 1925.

The second and equally deep strand—and here I think we do know where it came from—was his total love of the idea of a field: the following of physical phenomena in minute and infinitely subdividable detail in space and in time. This gave him his first great drama of trying to see how Maxwell's equations could be true. They were the first field equations of physics; they are still true today with only very minor and well-understood modifications. It is this tradition which made him know that there had to be a field theory of gravitation, long before the clues to that theory were securely in his hand.

The third tradition was less one of physics than of philosophy. It is a form of the principle of sufficient reason. It was Einstein who asked what do we mean, what can we measure, what elements in physics are conventional? He insisted that those elements that were conventional could have no part in the real predictions of physics. This also had roots: for one the mathematical invention of Riemann, who saw how very limited the geometry of the Greeks had been, how unreasonably limited. But in a more important sense, it followed from the long tradition of European philosophy, you may say starting with Descartes—if you wish you can start it in the Thirteenth Century, because in fact it did start then—and leading through the British empiricists, and very clearly formulated, though probably without influence in Europe, by Charles Pierce: One had to ask how do we do it, what do we mean, is this just something that we can use to help ourselves in calculating, or is it something that we can actually study in nature by physical means? For the point here is that the laws of nature not only describe the results of observations, but the laws of nature delimit the scope of observations. That was the point of Einstein's understanding of the limiting character of the velocity of light; it also was the nature of the resolution in quantum theory, where the quantum of action, Planck's constant, was recognized as limiting the fineness of the transaction between the system studied and the machinery used to study it, limiting this fineness in a form of atomicity quite different from and quite more radical than any that the Greeks had imagined or than was familiar from the atomic theory of chemistry.

In the last years of Einstein's life, the last twenty-five years, his tradition in a certain sense failed him. They were the years he spent at Princeton and this, though a source of sorrow, should not be concealed. He had a right to that failure. He spent those years first in trying to prove that the quantum theory had inconsistencies in it. No one could have been more ingenious in thinking up unexpected and clever examples; but it turned out that the inconsistencies were not there; and often their resolution could be found in earlier work of Einstein himself. When that did not work, after repeated efforts, Einstein had simply to say that he did not like the theory. He did not like the elements of indeterminacy. He did not like the abandonment of continuity or of causality. These were things that he had grown up with, saved by him, and enormously enlarged; and to see them lost, even though he had put the dagger in the hand of their assassin by his own work, was very hard on him. He fought with Bohr in a noble and furious way, and he fought with the theory which he had fathered but which he hated. It was not the first time that this has happened in science.

He also worked with a very ambitious program, to combine the understanding of electricity and gravitation in such a way as to explain what he regarded as the semblance—the illusion—of discreteness, of particles in nature. I think that it was clear then, and believe it to be obviously clear today, that the things that this theory worked with were too meager, left out too much that was known to physicists but had not been known much in Einstein's student days. Thus it looked like a hopelessly limited and historically rather accidentally conditioned approach. Although Einstein commanded the affection, or, more rightly, the love of everyone for his determination to see through his program, he lost most contact with the profession of physics, because there were things that had been learned which came too late in life for him to concern himself with them.

Einstein was indeed one of the friendliest of men. I had the impression that he was also, in an important sense, alone. Many very great men are lonely; yet I had the impression that although he was a deep and loyal friend, the stronger human affections played a not very deep or very central part in his life taken as a whole. He had of course incredibly many disciples, in the sense of people who, reading his work or hearing it taught by him, learned from him and had a new view of physics, of the philosophy of physics, of the nature of the world that we live in. But he did not have, in the technical jargon, a school. He did not have very many students who were his concern as apprentices and disciples. And there was an element of the lone worker in him, in sharp contrast to the teams we see today, and in sharp contrast to the highly cooperative way in which some other parts of science have developed. In later years, he had people working with him. They were typically called assistants and they had a wonderful life. Just being with him was wonderful. His secretary had a wonderful life. The sense of grandeur never left him for a minute, nor his sense of humor. The assistants did one thing which he lacked in his young days. His early papers are paralyzingly beautiful, but there are many errata. Later there were none. I had the impression that, along with its miseries, his fame gave him some pleasure of meeting people but the extreme pleasure of music played not only with Elizabeth of Belgium but more with Adolf Busch, for he was not that good a violinist. He loved the sea and he loved sailing and was always grateful for a ship. I remember walking home with him on his seventy-first birthday. He said, "You know, when it's once been given to a man to do something sensible, afterward life is a little strange."

Einstein is also, and I think rightly, known as a man of very great good will and humanity. Indeed, if I had to think of a single word for his attitude towards human problems, I would pick the Sanscrit word *Ahinsa*, not to hurt, harmlessness. He had a deep distrust of power; he did not have that convenient and natural converse with statesmen and men of power that was quite appropriate to Rutherford and to Bohr, perhaps the two physicists of this century who most nearly rivaled him in eminence. In 1915, as he made the general theory of relativity, Europe was tearing itself to pieces and half losing its past. He was always a pacifist. Only as the Nazis came into power in Germany did he have some doubts, as his famous and rather deep exchange of letters with Freud showed, and began to understand with melancholy and without true acceptance that, in addition to understanding, man sometimes has a duty to act.

After what you have heard, I need not say how luminous was his intelligence. He was almost wholly without sophistication and wholly without worldliness. I think that in England people would have said that he did not have much "background," and in America that he lacked "education." This may throw some light on how these words are used. I think that this simplicity, this lack of clutter and this lack of cant, had a lot to do with his preservation throughout of a certain pure, rather Spinoza-like, philosophical monism, which of course is hard to maintain if you have been "educated" and have a "background." There was always with him a wonderful purity at once childlike and profoundly stubborn.

Einstein is often blamed or praised or credited with these miserable bombs. It is not in my opinion true. The special theory of relativity might not have been beautiful without Einstein; but it would have been a tool for physicists, and by 1932 the experimental evidence for the interconvertibility of matter and energy which he had predicted was overwhelming. The feasibility of doing anything with this in such a massive way was not clear until seven years later, and then almost by accident. This was not what Einstein really was after. His part was that of creating an intellectual revolution, and discovering more than any scientist of our time how profound were the errors made by men before then. He did write a letter to Roosevelt about atomic energy. I think this was in part his agony at the evil of the Nazis, in part not wanting to harm anyone in any way; but I ought to report that that letter had very little effect, and that Einstein himself is really not answerable for all that came later. I believe he so understood it himself.

His was a voice raised with very great weight against violence and cruelty wherever he saw them and, after the war, he spoke with deep emotion and I believe with great weight about the supreme violence of these atomic weapons. He said at once with great simplicity: Now we must make a world government. It was very forthright, it was very abrupt, it was no doubt "uneducated," no doubt without "background"; still all of us in some thoughtful measure must recognize that he was right.

Without power, without calculation, with none of the profoundly political humor that characterized Gandhi, he nevertheless did move the political world. In almost the last act of his life, he joined with Lord Russell in suggesting that men of science get together and see if they could not understand one another and avert the disaster which he foresaw from the arms race. The so-called Pugwash movement, which has a longer name now, was the direct result of this appeal. I know it to be true that it had an essential part to play in the Treaty of Moscow, the limited test-ban treaty, which is a tentative, but to me very precious, declaration that reason might still prevail.

In his last years, as I knew him, Einstein was a twentieth-century Ecclesiastes, saying with unrelenting and indomitable cheerfulness, "Vanity of vanities, all is vanity."

Jane Kramer

Allen Ginsberg and His Father

On a snowy Sunday morning in Paterson, New Jersey, Allen Ginsberg and his father, Louis, settled into a pair of plumped chintz armchairs in Mr. Ginsberg's living room to read the New York *Times* together and talk over the schedule for a father-and-son poetry reading that they were going to

ALLEN GINSBERG AND HIS FATHER   From *Allen Ginsberg in America*, by Jane Kramer. Copyright © 1968, 1969 by Jane Kramer. Reprinted by permission of Random House, Inc. Originally appeared in *The New Yorker*.

give at Paterson State College that night. Ginsberg's stepmother, Edith, was in the kitchen fixing a big breakfast of bagels, bialy, lox, cream cheese, and scrambled eggs, and Maretta, who had come home with Ginsberg for the weekend, was still asleep. It was Ginsberg's first visit to the house since early fall, when a warrant had been issued in Paterson for his arrest on a marijuana charge. The mayor of Paterson, who was on his way out of office, had ordered the arrest after Ginsberg informed the audience at another family reading, at the local Young Men's Hebrew Association, that he had "heightened the experience" of a poetic pilgrimage to the Passaic Falls that morning with his father. Paterson's policemen had thereupon combed the city for Ginsberg, who had last been seen carrying his purple bookbag and wearing his owlish horn-rimmed glasses, his tan hiking shoes, unmatching gray socks, rumpled khaki pants, a relatively threadbare brown tweed jacket, an old white button-down shirt, finger cymbals, and a Tibetan oracle's ring, and after a few days they had spotted a likely-looking beard near a bar downtown. By the time the gentleman with the beard was released as a sartorial follower of Ginsberg rather than the genuine poetic article, Ginsberg was safely across the state line in New York. He thought about returning to Paterson with a phalanx of reporters, to be arrested publicly as a first move in a marijuana-law test case, but he abandoned the scheme as "too embarrassing" to his father, and left for the West Coast, to teach at Berkeley, instead. While he was away, a friendlier mayor took office, and now the case against him had been dismissed, on the ground of insufficient evidence, by the Paterson Municipal Court.

Ginsberg remarked to his father that his five months as "the poet who was wanted in Paterson" reminded him of a letter he had written to William Carlos Williams from San Francisco back in 1956, just before shipping out as a yeoman storekeeper aboard a freighter bound for the Arctic: ". . . I have NOT absconded from Paterson. I do have a whitmanic mania & nostalgia for cities and detail & panorama and isolation in jungle and pole, like the images you pick up. When I've seen enough I'll be back to splash in the Passaic again only with a body so naked and happy City Hall will have to call out the Riot Squad. When I come back I'll make big political speeches in the mayoralty campaigns like I did when I was 16 only this time I'll have W. C. Fields on my left and Jehovah on my right. Why not? Paterson is only a big sad poppa who needs compassion. . . . In any case Beauty is where I hang my hat. And reality. And America. . . . I mean to say Paterson is not a task like Milton going down to hell, it's a flower to the mind too. . . ." Peering over the top of the "News of the Week in Review," Mr. Ginsberg said that he remembered the letter. At seventy-one, Louis Ginsberg was compact and jaunty, with quizzical, popping eyes, a scrubbed-to-gleaming forehead, and a favorite expression of slightly oppressed seniority. For forty years he had taught English in the Paterson public high schools, and for fifty he had been writing and steadily publishing lyric poems. At the moment, he was stagestruck, according to Mrs. Ginsberg, who dated this new passion of her husband's from the night of the first reading by the Ginsbergs, *père et fils*, in March of 1966.

"You did bring home some good clothes for the reading tonight, didn't you, Allen?" Mr. Ginsberg, who was already dressed for the event in a blue serge suit and a new polka-dot bow tie, asked.

Ginsberg looked up from Section 1, which he was scouring for hippie news, and laughed. "Yeah, I've got *my* suit, too," he said.

Mr. Ginsberg sighed. "We'll show them that the Ginsberg name means poetry," he said, and he added, philosophically, "You know, Allen, you're popular with the college crowd, but with a real audience you need me for balance. I'm like the stamp to your letter."

Ginsberg, smiling, shook his head.

"I told you that one," Mr. Ginsberg said. "The one where the stamp says to the letter, 'I may be square, but I send you.'"

Ginsberg groaned.

His father, who has long been known in the Passaic County press as "the Paterson pun-dit" or, alternatively, "the Paterson punny man," went on to say that he had just recatalogued his pun collection by subjects, such as "Flirtation," "Love," "Automobiles," and "Alcoholics," and now had a thick folder just on beatniks. He stood up to get it from his desk, in the sunroom, but Ginsberg waved him down.

"You know, Louis, I think you secretly dig my poetry," Ginsberg said.

Louis Ginsberg shrugged. "You're a new generation, Allen," he said. "I believe in poetic coexistence, but you young people—you don't like a nice, regular, flexible metre. You don't like discipline. You don't like rhyme. You say it's not natural. I ask you: What could be more natural than rhyme? Rhymes are so enchanting, so instinctive. Children make rhymes as soon as they can speak." Mr. Ginsberg sighed again, and went right on, "And you've got such new mores. For instance, you use four-letter words that I was brought up not to use in company. And the way you live. You don't have to live like that, Allen. You're a world-famous poet."

Ginsberg made a mudra—a potent Oriental gesture—to assure his father that he recognized and respected the soul of another sentient being in the living room. Then he said "*Om*," signifying the ultimate oneness of all views.

"And these odd religions," Mr. Ginsberg said. He seemed to be warming to the opportunity at hand, and Ginsberg chuckled. In December, he had taken his father to a birthday party for his friend Swami Satchidananda, a Hindu yoga and holy man who lived on West End Avenue.

Mr. Ginsberg had had indigestion after three spoonfuls of the Swami's party food, and had ever since displayed a certain impatience with the customs of the East.

"I bet it was that curry, Louis," Ginsberg said.

Mr. Ginsberg shook his head. He said it was really Maretta that was bothering him. She had arrived at the house the night before with a sack of equipment for her rather unnerving meditations—a tattered paperback copy of the "The Tibetan Book of the Dead," a pair of finger cymbals, Ginsberg's big metal dorja, her own faceted gazing crystal, and a packet of incense sticks—and had emptied it out on the living-room couch for the Ginsbergs to see. Then, just before going to bed, she had informed Mr. Ginsberg that her sadhana was hashish. "What's with this Maretta?" Mr. Ginsberg asked. "Why can't you bring home a nice Jewish girl?"

Ginsberg, laughing, threw up his hands. "Louis," he said, "here for years you've been saying, 'Please, just bring home a *girl* for a change,' and now that I do, you want a *Jewish* one?"

"You're such an *experimenter*, Allen," Mr. Ginsberg said. "Tibetan Buddhist girl friends. Swamis. Drugs. All this talk from you about pot. 'It's so elevating, Louis. So ecstatic. My soul is outside my body. I see ultimate reality.'" Mr. Ginsberg frowned. "You know what *I* say? I say, 'Allen, take it easy.'"

Ginsberg, who had removed his shoes and was sitting in the lotus position in the chintz chair, leaned forward and took his father's hand. "*You* should take it easy, Louis," he said. "You'll wear yourself out straightening me out."

"Look, Allen, it's been a long time since I've been able to get you to the old homestead," Mr. Ginsberg said. "Your father waits, counts the days."

"Well, the troubles are over now," Ginsberg said. "Was it bad for you here? With the trial?"

Mr. Ginsberg shook his head. "You know, some people talk," he said. "You hear all sorts of odd things." He shuffled through a pile of papers on an end table by his chair and handed a clipping to his son. It was a letter to the editor of the Paterson *Call*:

> In reference to Allen Ginsberg, whom your reporter, George James, described as a poet, living legend, and international traveler. So what! I was extremely disgusted with your paper's continuously shielding and glorifying this poet. One would think that you were trying to defend a moral saintly man instead of a person who openly admitted that he was smoking marijuana, which is unlawful. . . . I was a student attending Central High School and remember his

father, Louis Ginsberg, who taught there. Being a parent myself I do not condemn him because of his son, but I am shocked that he has joined his son as a team in the poetry readings. It seems that he must certainly enjoy all this publicity, despite what kind it may be. . . .

Ginsberg tossed the clipping back on the table.

"Some people are like that," Mr. Ginsberg said. "I've got no axiom to grind."

"I was just wondering what the gossip in the coffee shops was, that's all," Ginsberg said.

"Allen, I *told* you," Mr. Ginsberg said. "Everybody thought that it was pretty silly of the previous mayor to make a fuss. That the evidence was flimsy. Everybody's glad it turned out fine. Still . . ." Mr. Ginsberg looked up.

"Go ahead," Ginsberg said.

"Well, *my* feeling," Mr. Ginsberg said, "is really that you should obey the law, and then when the law is changed, you can go ahead and smoke all you want."

Maretta walked into the living room, yawning.

"I felt I didn't need the drugs," Mr. Ginsberg told her. "I felt that with my own imagination I could receive the majesty and grandeur of the Falls."

Maretta nodded, and began poking her long hair into a new fringed shawl, which she had wrapped around her head. She was dressed for breakfast in baggy black ski pants and purple sari cloth. The dorja and the crystal were both on strings around her neck. Mr. Ginsberg stared, speechless, as she arranged herself on a brown-slipcovered couch.

"Well, young lady, how do you like it here?" Mr. Ginsberg asked, finally, with a sweep of his hand.

Maretta contemplated the small, tidy living room. It was painted a rosy tan and had beige carpeting and silvery nylon window curtains. There were urns of bright-green plastic leaves in a fireplace at one end and, at the other, a gilt-trimmed white secretary and an enormous television set. Photographs of various Ginsberg grandchildren were displayed along the walls, and above the brown couch were two Montmartre flower-market scenes, which Mr. Ginsberg pointed out to Maretta, telling her proudly that he had picked them out himself.

Maretta, however, was busy scrutinizing a lampshade through her crystal bead.

Mr. Ginsberg tried again. "I imagine you're meditating. Do you meditate often?"

"I've sat in a few caves," Maretta said.

"And have you been gazing and ciphering ancient Buddhist texts?" Mr. Ginsberg went on. "Are you wiser now than before?"

"Yeah," Maretta said.

Mr. Ginsberg put down his paper. "With you young people," he said, "it's like the one about children—you can love them in the abstract, but it's hard in the concrete."

"Maretta speaks Tibetan," Ginsberg said.

"So what's wrong with English?" Mr. Ginsberg said.

Questions

Diction and Structure

1. Much of Katherine Anne Porter's characterization of Uncle Jimbilly depends on the use of dialect. (Check the meaning of the term in your dictionary.) Since dialect is spoken rather than written language, and informal rather than formal, what problems are connected with using it as extensively as Porter does? Compare the use of dialect here with that used in the depiction of Old Nannie.

2. The narrator in Porter's essays uses a level of diction and a tone that contrast with the speech of the characters themselves. Describe this tone and diction and indicate their role in characterizing Uncle Jimbilly and Old Nannie.

3. What significance have the titles "The Witness" and "The Last Leaf"? Do their associations impart anything to the character sketches?

4. How important are descriptive words (adjectives, adverbs) in Porter's stories? How does she get her effects?

5. What levels of diction does Margaret Truman use in her essay on her father and mother? Is there a significant difference between the language she uses as a writer and the spoken language she quotes? What is the effect?

6. Notice the use of colloquialisms in the Truman essay. What is their purpose?

7. "Harry Truman and Bess Wallace" is Chapter Two of a full-scale biography of the former president. Does this brief excerpt

succeed in showing *all* of Truman's character? What does it do? How is the chapter organized?

8. J. Robert Oppenheimer's depiction of Albert Einstein employs many terms from modern physics: Planck's discovery, light-quanta, discreteness, and so on. Does the author expect his reader to know these terms? Does he explain them? Is a knowledge necessary in order to understand the points Oppenheimer is making?

9. From how many different languages and fields of knowledge does Oppenheimer draw his terminology? Are these terms used consistently and combined to produce one effect or do they jar with each other?

10. What is the meaning of these words used in Jane Kramer's essay on Allen Ginsberg: bagels, bialy, lox, *père et fils*, mudra, om, dorja, sadhana? Are they necessary in describing Ginsberg? Explain their function, if any.

11. Kramer uses dialogue in her characterizations. Compare and contrast her usage with those of Porter and Truman. What problems might arise in setting dialogue down on paper?

12. Of the four pieces in this section, Porter's are fictional sketches; Oppenheimer's is a reminiscence; and Kramer's is based on a series of interviews. What differences in form do you see to correspond to these various kinds of characterization?

Style and Rhetoric

1. Katherine Anne Porter has been called one of the great prose stylists in America. Examine several of her paragraphs carefully; identify the types of sentences she uses (grammatically, rhetorically, and syntactically), the kinds of words she chooses (concrete or abstract, common or proper, single or collective), and the way she organizes her ideas. Can you make any generalizations about her preference for certain kinds of diction and sentences? Does her style satisfy F. L. Lucas's requirements? (See p. 20 above.)

2. Which does Porter use most extensively in creating the characters of Uncle Jimbilly and Old Nannie; their actions, words, thoughts, possessions? How important are their appearances?

3. Do you understand the minds of Uncle Jimbilly and Old Nannie after reading Porter's sketches? What sort of understanding about them do you have?

4. How does Porter use comparison and contrast to create her

characters? What other characters does she show besides the two major ones?

5. Is Oppenheimer more concerned with Einstein's mind, his character, or his personality? Defend your answer by reference to the essay.

6. Point out evidences of Oppenheimer's own character in his essay. Does it overshadow the portrait of Einstein, supplement it, or contrast with it?

7. The characterization of Einstein appears to break into two parts, the second half beginning, "In the last years of Einstein's life . . ." (p. 158). How are these related?

8. Caricature is to characterization as a cartoon is to a portrait: it is a deliberate exaggeration of certain features or qualities. Point out examples of caricature (if any) in the essays.

9. Although both her father and mother were still alive when Margaret Truman was writing about their youth and courtship, she never refers to their own recollections or quotes them talking about the past. Why? Is this a strength or weakness in her characterization?

10. How many people other than her father and mother are characterized by Margaret Truman? Compare and contrast the ways they are depicted.

11. Does Truman reveal any implicit biases or prejudices in her characterization? Does she characterize herself in any way(s)?

12. What methods of characterizing are most important in Kramer's essay? Which does she find more interesting: the older or younger Ginsberg? Explain your answer.

13. Does Kramer use dialect in her characterization? Notice the use of rhetorical questions by the Ginsbergs; what is their effect? Is their speech unusual in any other way?

14. How do the following act as symbols in the Kramer essay: The *New York Times*; Paterson, New Jersey; finger cymbals; the joint poetry reading; the discussion of poetic meter; Maretta's crystal; the plastic leaves?

15. Find instances of symbols in the other characterizing selections. How can symbols aid in characterization?

Theme and Viewpoint

1. Minority groups are sometimes represented in stereotyped characterizations. Compare and contrast the depiction of the Negro by Katherine Anne Porter and Ken Kesey. Is one writer

more dependent on stereotypes than the other? Justify your answer. Is either entirely free of stereotyped qualities in his or her description?

2. What is Porter's attitude toward Uncle Jimbilly and Old Nannie: patronizing, sentimental, detached, condescending, annoyed, loving, or none of these? Compare her attitude toward her subjects with Kesey's attitude toward his. Does either writer show evidence of "prejudice," as Ian Stevenson describes it?

3. Do the children in Porter's sketches display any "prejudices" toward Uncle Jimbilly and Old Nannie? Compare and contrast their attitudes with that of the author.

4. Porter uses a Southern background for her sketches; and Margaret Truman emphasizes the "Southern" background of the Trumans. Do the two writers define "Southern" in the same implicit way? Discuss.

5. Does Reik's theory of the ego-ideal serve to explain the love of Harry Truman and Bess Wallace or not? Does it suggest anything about Truman's relationship with his mother? (Notice Margaret Truman's comments about American presidents and their mothers. What do you make of her facts?)

6. Would Elizabeth Janeway consider "Mamma Truman" and Bess Wallace "liberated" or not? Does Margaret Truman appear to be a "liberated woman" in her essay? Is Margaret Truman's humor like or unlike that of Janeway?

7. Is the atmosphere of Independence, Missouri, in the Truman essay similar to that of Knoxville, Tennessee, in Agee's essay or not? How do you explain this? Who is more proficient at evoking the small town atmosphere: Truman or Agee? Is it a matter of style or something else?

8. Do J. Robert Oppenheimer and John Steele hold the same views about science and scientists or not? (Look back at Steele's essay.) Would Steele feel toward Einstein as Oppenheimer does? Explain.

9. Does Louis Ginsberg speak English, Ameridish, Yinglish, or all three? (Reread Rosten's essay before you answer.) How does his speech help to characterize Louis? What does the speech of the father (himself a poet) suggest about Allen Ginsberg's own interest in poetry?

10. Are Louis Ginsberg's views on poetry compatible with those of Graham Hough?

11. By Kronenberger's standards are the Ginsbergs individualists? Eccentrics? Cranks? Nonconformists? What?

12. According to Hans Selye, stress is a vital part of living. Do

any of the characterizations given here show their subjects in a state of stress? How do the people in these essays seem to deal with stress? Are they unusual "characters" partly because of the ways they deal with the stresses of life?

13. Which of the selections read earlier use characterization as a rhetorical technique?

Illustrating
and exemplifying

The words *description* and *illustration,* as they are used to differentiate kinds of prose techniques, may seem to be alike in their root meanings—"picturing something in words" —but they denote two separate rhetorical methods. The List of Illustrations often found at the beginning of a book is a list of drawings, woodcuts, photographs, and pictures in the literal sense. Illustrations of this sort help to make written prose clearer by providing a visual embodiment of certain points made in the text itself. But the verbal text uses illustration of another kind. One pictured illustration may be worth a thousand words in certain instances; but it is not always possible to picture abstractions (mercy, justice, education); procedures and processes (dying, writing a poem, growing up); or generalizations (the human family, the decline of American culture, the inevitability of human warfare). In cases like these, thousands of words may be necessary, and they take the form of verbal illustration or examples.

The rhetorical method of illustrating simply means making a more or less intangible concept clear and immediate by showing how it takes a specific form. Paranoia is a highly com-

171

plex psychological condition; to explain it in technical medical language will enlighten only those already specially trained. But suppose that the behavior of Adolph Hitler is used as a concrete instance of paranoid behavior: his morbid suspicion of other people, his fear of being plotted against, his desire to attack violently and destroy his supposed enemies, his ceaseless desire to be venerated by masses of followers, his belief that he was godlike. This illustration gives us a lucid idea of what paranoia is.

All students are familiar with the technique of illustration from the practice of their teachers. "Let me show you what I mean," the teacher may say, meaning "Let me illustrate how this principle, idea, or belief works in a particular instance." The writer who has a specialized knowledge of child psychology or who has reached certain beliefs about human beings' fear of death may explain these personal opinions by using a case history or by giving instances of behavior in burial ceremonies around the world. These examples stand as proof for the broader, more generalized, and more abstract views about mental illness or social behavior. The writer tries to embody in one or two vivid instances the truth about a larger category or to show how a general principle operates in a given example.

As they are commonly used to indicate rhetorical method, illustration and exemplification mean pretty much the same thing. Illustration is more often the term used to indicate the use of one extended instance to clarify a somewhat abstract phenomenon, as Bruno Bettelheim uses Joey to show autism in children or Stephen Spender uses his own experience in writing one poem to show how the poet works. Exemplification, or giving examples, may then be defined as the use of several particularized instances to validate a general condition, state, or practice, as Smith and Todes cite death customs in varying cultures to reveal human attitudes toward dying, or as Julian Huxley uses instances from history and animal behavior to back up his views of war as a biological phenomenon.

Although illustration and exemplification are among the most helpful ways of developing an essay, they are valueless or even harmful if they stem from lazy, uninformed, or prejudiced thinking. To illustrate the disenchantment of modern students with their society by singling out one mentally disturbed ringleader at Berkeley or Columbia as an "example" of what all student protesters are like is "illustration" of a shoddy and inept type. It is equally useless to illustrate the necessity for clerical celibacy by holding up Pope John XXIII as a typical example of its benefits, or to "prove" the decadence of American society by using as examples of depravity the audiences for "porno films" or "skin flicks." Good illustrations must not oversimplify ("All kids today are like Mick Jagger"); nor should they ignore aspects of the thing they discuss ("The Democratic Party is the War Party; Democrats start wars"); nor should they be based on some nonessential or tangential aspect of the phenomenon they purport to explain ("The essence of the Hippie Movement was long hair").

Because illustration and exemplification are very effective and frequently used techniques, the reader must be especially aware of their limitations when he or she meets them in a prose essay. On the one hand, they may be vivid and concise ways of coming to understand the nature of something; on the other, they may confuse and mislead. If they are used accurately as a way of explaining, they are commendable rhetorical devices. But if they are used to argue for the writer's point of view by ignoring or distorting or slanting the evidence, they must be tested by the principles of logical reasoning. These principles are discussed in the section Reasoning, below.

Huston Smith & Samuel Todes

The Point of Death

Franz Josef, the last real emperor of Austria-Hungary, was given one of the most magisterial funerals in history. The body lay in state in the Cathedral of St. Stephen in Vienna, whence the funeral cortege, led by the young Emperor Charles and Empress Zita, proceeded on foot for the burial to a Capuchin monastery, whose monks were known for their gentleness and kindly humanitarianism. A vast crowd stood in reverent silence along the route of the procession, but when the cortege reached the

THE POINT OF DEATH by Huston Smith and Samuel Todes is reprinted by permission of Charles Scribner's Sons from *The Patient, Death, and the Family* by Stanley B. Troup and William A. Greene. Copyright © 1974 Charles Scribner's Sons.

monastery gates they were closed. The grand major domo, white plumes on his hat, knocked loudly, but there was no response. The knocking turned into pounding. Finally a tiny window opened on an upper story, disclosing a wizened face in a brown hood.

"Who knocks?" it asked.

"Franz Josef, Emperor of Austria, Apostolic King of Hungary," came the reply.

"We know no such man," and the window closed.

More pounding. At length the face reappeared to put the same question.

"Franz Josef, Heir to the House of Anjou, Protector of the House of Hapsburg, King of Bohemia, Lord of Bosnia and Herzegovina . . ." The titles seemed endless.

"We know no such man."

A third time the drama was repeated, but this time to "Who knocks?" the answer came back, "A poor mortal." The gates swung open. Only the casket was admitted, carried by the brothers.

In surface respects, attitudes toward death and rituals relating to it differ markedly from culture to culture. In China, as recently as a generation ago, paid mourners could be hired, on the death of someone well-to-do, to wail the clock around for days. Bought grief has been known in the West, too, but it offends modern sensibilities. It seems inappropriate to the point of being perverse.

Balinese fishing tribes dispose of their dead by exposing them in a special site along the shore, which—for sanitary reasons—is secluded from the villages. In the Parsee Towers of Silence in Bombay, human corpses are exposed to vultures. But Balinese tribesmen are shocked when told of the Bombay custom. To allow a human body to be devoured by vultures, a lower form of life, strikes them as barbaric. A Westerner might not see any difference in principle between being eaten by maggots and being eaten by vultures, but to the Balinese the difference is important. Maggots and vermin derive from the corpse itself, they point out; in being consumed by them the corpse isn't preyed upon; it self-destructs.

Such variations respecting death and the dead could be multiplied indefinitely, but hand-in-hand with the multiplicity goes unity. Except for the contemporary, secularized West, every known culture has seen death as in some way a continuation of life rather than its abrogation. This .of course precludes equating man with his body. The distinction—between man in his entirety and his bodily component—has seemed to all traditional societies plausible. Dreams provide evidence for it: in dreams something in man can journey forth—go hunting, visit a friend—without his body's leaving the room. Hallucinations occasioned by psychedelic vegetables or fevered delirium provide complementary evidence; users of mescaline and other hallucinogenics have reported the experience of leaving the body and viewing it from the outside. Finally, corpses themselves are sometimes viewed as proof that bodies are not life's full equivalent. Something seems conspicuously absent from them. Something has "gone out," departed.

If we call this "something" soul, life has generally been taken across the whole face of humanity to be a meld of body and soul. On the way the two are related, however, peoples have differed markedly. In ancient Egypt it was believed that souls after death continued to depend on their original bodies; the two were separated spatially but the body had to remain intact if the soul was to survive. It was this view that catapulted embalming and architectural engineering to advanced sciences: Egyptian mummies are still around, and the pyramids that housed them, fortresses against enemies and elements alike, remain wonders of the world. In ancient China it was believed that if a corpse did not decompose, its soul had become immortal; some of the elixirs concocted by the Taoists were in actuality effective embalming agents.

The Zoroastrian-Judeo-Christian version of the soul's attachment to its original host took the form of believing that the original body would resurrect, though in its Christian version such "celestial" bodies will be spiritualized; they will be, in the words of St. Paul, glorified and incorruptible. In India souls are believed to shed their initial bodies to acquire successively subsequent ones on the same plane; this belief is called the doctrine of reincarnation. In the words of the Bhagavad Gita:

> Worn-out garments
> Are shed by the body;
> Worn-out bodies
> Are shed by the dweller
> Within the body.

Finally, in the Platonic, Manichaean, and Gnostic views, souls are released completely from their bodies; these are examples of the doctrine of the immortality of the soul unalloyed. Taxonomically, the three views of the soul have been that the soul is permanently identified with one body, that it passes through a number of bodies, and that it sheds its bodily components altogether.

Given the majority opinion that physical death is not an absolute end, it is not difficult to believe that it has been faced serenely. We do not know what Eskimo grandmothers felt when they voluntarily crawled off into the snow to die in times of famine, but it does not strain credulity to imagine a quiet repose.

In China coffins can be seen on display in living rooms as status symbols; their impending occupants show them off with the pleasure some Americans would reserve for a new Cadillac.

The English philosopher Gerald Heard tells of an elderly woman who gave a farewell party for herself. A good time was had by all, and only at the evening's close did the hostess disclose the party's object. Her duties in life, she announced in an after-dinner speech, had been fulfilled and she had gathered her friends to say goodbye. The following morning she was dead.

Although there is little sociological documentation, anecdotes about voluntary death abound in many cultures. In the early 1960s a case was reported on Melville Island, off the coast of Australia. A man of perhaps sixty, in seeming health, had remarked to a friend that his life was over, that there was nothing remaining for him to do. He did a routine day's work, then retired. The next morning he appeared to be normal but declined to get up. Within an hour he was dead, from no discernible cause; persons had been in the room throughout.

The account of the death of Yamamoto Roshi, Abbot of Ryutaku Zen temple, is better documented. Aged 96 and almost blind, he decided it was time to die and stopped eating.

When asked by his monks why he refused his food, he replied that he had outlived his usefulness and was only a bother to everybody. They told him, "If you die now [January] when it is so cold, everybody will be uncomfortable at your funeral and you will be an even greater nuisance, so please eat!" He thereupon resumed eating, but when it became warm again he stopped, and not long after quietly toppled over and died.

Shunryu Suzuki, the roshi of the San Francisco Zen Center, prepared his students for his passing by telling them: "When I die, if I suffer physical agony or spiritual agony, that is all right, that is not a problem. That is suffering Buddha. No confusion in it. We should be very grateful to have a limited body like mine, or like yours. If you had a limitless life it would be a real problem for you."

It is absorbing to consider what death has meant to other peoples. Even more absorbing—and more difficult—is the question: What can death mean to those who live in modernized, industrialized, "enlightened" America? The title of this essay is intentionally ambiguous. "The point of death" can denote either when death occurs or why it occurs—why in the sense not of cause but of significance.

When death occurs has proved to be more complicated than was once supposed. To date it at the stopping of heart and lungs turns out to be premature; if these organs are reactivated within five minutes, full organismic functioning can be resumed. If death denotes a point of no return it must be fixed later. How much later depends on definition. Psychic death occurs about five minutes after anoxia, when the cells of the cortex die and coma becomes irreversible. Vegetative death—the expiration of the slightly tougher cells of the vegetative brain (which control the body's autonomic functions)—occurs about eight minutes after anoxia.

On the "when" of death philosophers have nothing to say to physiologists—philosophers are concerned only with death's "why." But before the question of death's why, there is a prior "why": Why are people concerned about death's point or purpose? One reason, presumably, is to enable the living to be of greater help to those who are dying and to the bereaved. This purpose renders irrelevant all objective explanations of death. It could be pointed out, for example, that without death there could be no birth. There could not be sex or children: there would be no room for people or food—entries presuppose exits. There is a need for new blood and for the removal of dead wood and oppressive seniority. In Washington, where the dead weight of seniority on congressional committees is conspicuous, there is a saying. "Here today, here tomorrow." There is a story of an aging Texas businessman who was heir-designate to his father's thriving empire. Alas, the father himself was so healthy that the son found himself approaching normal retirement age without having come into his own. He is reported to have remarked ruefully, "If he can't take it with him, apparently he isn't going."

One of the services of death is to serve as a blessed disposal unit, to clear the ground for oncoming freshness. Concomitantly, a nightmare attending the computer is that it may foil this function. Giant retrieval systems with their seemingly bottomless memory banks can retain too much, saddle us with the past unduly, rule out fresh beginnings, the new leaf.

Objectively it is not difficult to see point and purpose in death, but death to the die-er is not objective. It is subjective—to a degree unparalleled by any other experience. Death is an experience wherein company is absolutely precluded. Even if people seem to be "dying together," each is facing death alone. The person who is dying is further along than those at his bedside. He has passed them by.

Objective theories as to the point of death are irrelevant, but when modern American doctors attempt to help those who are facing death as a subjective phenomenon, they find that their culture has ill-served them in at least two ways, one specific, the other general.

A specific way modern culture impedes the doctor's task of ministering to the dying is by bureaucratizing the practice of medicine—rules, regulations, queues, "take a number," "fill out this form," "don't forget your social security."

> It couldn't be called ungentle.
> But how thoroughly departmental*

Legalisms dehumanize by placing categories ahead of persons. No one likes them, but imposed on the ill they seem especially inappropriate, for they treat as objects those whose distress throws objectivity itself into question, both the capacity for objectivity and the need for it.

Another consequence of the bureaucratizing of medical practice is the removal of death from the home. People no longer die surrounded by loved ones but in enameled hospital beds where, far from being important centers of interest, they are anonymous objects of efficient systems. "What man shall live and not see death?" a psalmist inquires. It is an important fact of contemporary life that most Americans have not seen death, and that a large proportion of those who have, have seen it, not in the course of their life at home, but in combat far away.

While the bureaucratization of medical practice is the specific way in which modern society makes it difficult for the doctor to render to the needs of the dying, the general obstacle is the nature of modern life itself. Life in modern impersonal, bureaucratic, mobile society has become "abstract"—in contrast to former times when life was rooted in primary, face-to-face communities.

It is often remarked that death and sex have changed places since Victorian times. To the Victorian, death was a public obsession and sex was taboo. Table legs were alluded to as limbs (the word "leg" being considered provocative) and were frequently covered with ruffles against indecent exposure. Today sex is displayed and death concealed, or denied, or pretended out of existence in the manner of Forest Lawn Cemetery and *The Loved One.*

Even the next of kin may be unwillingly "shielded" from the sight of death. In a letter written to one of the authors of this essay, a widow described the way the doctors and nurses employed various ruses to get her out of her husband's room as he was dying. She went into a waiting room and a few minutes later was told that her husband was dead. She realized that he must have died while she was still in his room and resented the fact that she was not told when it happened. She felt that she had a right

* From "Departmental" from *The Poetry of Robert Frost* edited by Edward Connery Lathem. Copyright 1936 by Robert Frost. Copyright © 1964 by Lesley Frost Ballantine. Copyright © 1969 by Holt, Rinehart, and Winston. Reprinted by permission of Holt, Rinehart, and Winston, Publishers.

to know and that the "beating around the bush" was heartless and wrong, even if it was kindly meant.

This reversal in attitudes toward sex and death is related to the change from a rooted to an abstract form of life. In a rooted life, lived out in abiding primary groups, *who* acts is more important than what he does. By contrast, abstract life is role-dominated, role behavior being defined as behavior in which what counts is what is done, not who does it. Persons within roles are interchangeable, any number of persons being able to fill the role of bus driver or bank teller without affecting the character of the roles themselves; the more human life is lived in terms of roles, the more individuality idles—or never comes into being. Indeed, if people ever come to the point where they live only their roles, there will be no individuality at all. In rooted societies a man's action was personal because what he did was valued as *his* action; each town, for example, would have its doctor who was greeted as a person while being greeted as a professional, a situation which continues in small towns where the word "Doctor," or its abbreviation, "Doc," doubles as both common and proper noun. Mobility has made this a vanishing phenomenon. The average American now moves every five years and changes careers three times. This mobility reduces the personal component in his life in ratio to role behavior.

The impersonality of modern life has a great deal to do with modern attitudes toward death. The sense of awkwardness in seeing people die stems basically from the realization that they haven't lived. This age of surgical transplants and interchangeable organs is also an age of interchangeable lives. An interchangeable life is a life that has not been fully lived. As André Gide expressed it in *Fruits of the Earth*, "Death is dreadful to those who have not lived their lives." Or, in the words of Thoreau (in *A Plea for John Brown*), "In order to die you must first have lived."

Not only is the doctor hampered by society in his efforts to minister well to the dying; current medical training compounds his difficulties.

Life seeks to move from lacks to fulfillment, from minus to plus. In this technological age people tend to look to science to erase life's minus and to produce its plus. There are three movements:

1. From minus to zero. To effect this shift is the task of science and technology. They can increase comfort and prolong survival.

2. From zero to finite plus. This is the domain of love and work, of mastery, achievement, and realized potential.

3. From finite plus to infinity. This is the domain of religion or one's basic life stance, of meaning and significance wherein one seeks affirmation that the whole was worth while and acceptable.

Many people still seem to hold the view that science, potentially, can save us; that if it were to come into its own completely, all human needs would be fulfilled. Actually, if science were to do all it could, life would be completely comfortable but no more.

Technological achievement is achievement in one dimension only. A large part of us is mute, unanswered. To satisfy the neglected dimension of our being we need a deeper sense of reality, and this in turn calls for placing technology in perspective.

Medicine is biological technology, and to say that it too can serve man fully only when practiced in perspective is to acknowledge that coming to terms with death does not pertain exclusively to the patient and his family. A doctor's first inclination is to assume that the problem is basically the patient's and that it concerns death, but the problem is equally the doctor's and concerns life. For there can be no adequate understanding of death which is not rooted in an adequate understanding of life.

Medicine as an autonomous endeavor—that is, when not seen in perspective—is premised on the concept of life as survival. The body is a fortress, disease is attack, death is "the last great enemy," medicine is defense. One corollary of this view is that organic functioning should be prolonged whatever its psychic concomitant. Pumps and tubes and pacers —more and more the request is heard: "Don't let them make a vegetable out of me." Another corollary is that in order to insure health, risks should be minimized. Pleasures may have to be foregone and spontaneity curtailed, but in the interests of life-as-prolongation such restrictions are warranted.

When life is no longer viewed as survival but as need for fulfillment, stress falls on achievement and a life aimed at completion. Survival is not completable, but achievement is. To survive means to survive and continue to survive. The concept is to continue to take one more step—until finally one cannot. But if life can be completed there can be death with dignity. On this view death need not be defeat; it can be finale. Instead of cancellation, it can be consummation.

Life as survival is a straight line which can only be cut off. Life as fulfillment can achieve closure. It can become a circle.

The days of our years are forked at every moment, one fork pointing toward death as annihilation, the other toward death as fulfillment. A person whose life is moving toward completion is not only not a problem to others, he is a help to others. He is a source of life to others, not an embarrassment and a burden.

It is possible to die for something, not just from something or of something. Death can be from something that attacks life, that breaks in on life and is not reached by life itself, but this is not death's only form.

To the extent that doctors equate life with survival they are restricted in their capacity to minister to the dying, for on this view no meaningful view of death is possible. If death is simply life's opposite, to the extent that we affirm life we must oppose death. Its only meaning is obliteration, and despair is the only honest stance we can adopt toward it.

For some, death is annihilation, but this is not death's definition. If we feel uncomfortable in the presence of the dying generally, this indicates that deep down we assume that annihilation is what death comes to.

Nothing turns on conscious articulation in life's closing hours. Closure can pertain to lives cut down at midpoint, like those of the Kennedy brothers. Both lives were inscribing their circles; death continued their trajectories. If a life is moving in a curve, death closes the circle. Death says, this being where it was going, this is what it comes to. So seen, death is both poignant and noble. It completes. The Kennedy deaths turned what might have been into what would have been. Instead of depriving their lives of promise, death stressed the promise implicit in them by virtue of the direction in which they were moving. From what the Kennedys achieved in the time they had, the curvature of their lives can be extrapolated.

What a life consists of is not confined to its own experience. It is also accessible to others, conceivably in ways more lucid than to itself, just as past historical epochs are in some ways better understood than one's own period of history.

Linear lives are defensive lives; always they face the threat of their termination. Concomitantly, they are empty lives: a flat line holds no water. Jones has survived up to this point. So what?

The point of death is to sum up, to complete, to indicate what a life has achieved and yielded. If life has been fully lived, death puts its seal on this fact; it symbolizes completion. Linearly, death equals zero. In closing the circle of a "curved" life, it equals infinity.

Julian Huxley

War as a Biological Phenomenon

Whenever we tend to become completely absorbed in an enterprise or an idea, it is a good thing to stand off from it now and again and look at it from the most dispassionate point of view possible. War is no exception. Quite rightly, all our major efforts must to-day be devoted to the urgent business of making sure that we win the war* and win it as quickly as possible. We are for most purposes immersed in the war; however, it will not merely do no harm, but will actually be of service, if now and again we try to get outside it and to look at it as objectively as we can in long perspective.

The longest possible perspective is that of the biologist, to whom man is a single animal species among hundreds of thousands of others, merely one of the products (albeit the latest and the most successful) of millions of years of evolution.

How does war look when pinned out in the biologist's collection? In the first place, he is able to say with assurance that war is not a general law of life, but an exceedingly rare biological phenomenon. War is not the same thing as conflict or bloodshed. It means something quite definite: an organized physical conflict between groups of one and the same species. Individual disputes between members of the same species are not war, even if they involve bloodshed and death. Two stags fighting for a harem of hinds, or a man murdering another man, or a dozen dogs fighting over a bone, are not engaged in war. Competition between two different species, even if it involves physical conflict, is not war. When the brown rat was accidentally brought to Europe and proceeded to oust the black rat from most of its haunts, that was not war between the two species of

WAR AS A BIOLOGICAL PHENOMENON From *On Living in a Revolution* by Julian Huxley. Copyright 1942 by Julian S. Huxley. Reprinted by permission of Harper & Row, Publishers, Inc.
* I.e., World War II. [editor's note]

rat; nor is it war in any but a purely metaphorical sense when we speak of making war on the malaria mosquito or the boll-weevil. Still less is it war when one species preys upon another, even when the preying is done by an organized group. A pack of wolves attacking a flock of sheep or deer, or a peregrine killing a duck, is not war. Much of nature, as Tennyson correctly said, is "red in tooth and claw"; but this only means what it says, that there is a great deal of killing in the animal world, not that war is the rule of life.

In point of fact, there are only two kinds of animals that habitually make war—man and ants. Even among ants war is mainly practised by one group, comprising only a few species among the tens of thousands that are known to science. They are the harvester ants, inhabitants of arid regions where there is little to pick up during the dry months. Accordingly they collect the seeds of various grasses at the end of the growing season and store them in special underground granaries in their nests. It is these reserve supplies which are the object of ant warfare. The inhabitants of one nest set out deliberately to raid the supplies of another group. According to Forel and other students of ant life, they may employ quite elaborate military tactics, and the battles generally result in heavy casualties. If the attackers win, they remove the stores grain by grain to their own nest. Ant wars never last nearly so long as human wars. One campaign observed by the American myrmecologist McCook in Penn Square in the centre of Philadelphia, lasted almost 3 weeks. The longest on record is 6½ weeks.

Harvesters are the only kind of ants to go in for accumulating property, as well as the chief kind to practise war. This association of property with war is interesting, as various anthropologists believe that in the human species war, or at any rate habitual and organized war, did not arise in human evolution until man had reached the stage of settled civilization, when he began to accumulate stores of grain and other forms of wealth.

Less deliberate wars may also occur in some other species, between communities whose nests are so close that they compete for the same food-territory. When similarly provoked conflicts occur between closely related species, the term war may perhaps be extended to them. On the other hand, the raids of the slave-making ants are not true war, but a curious combination of predation and parasitism.

There is another group of ants called army-ants, which suggests military activity; but the phrase is really a mis-nomer, for these army-ants are in reality simply predatory species which happen to hunt in packs: they are the wolves of the insect world, not the war-mongers.

So much then for war as a biological phenomenon. The facts speak for themselves. War, far from being a universal law of nature, or even a common occurrence, is a very rare exception among living creatures; and where it occurs, it is either associated with another phenomenon, almost equally rare, the amassing of property, or with territorial rights.

Biology can help put war in its proper perspective in another way. War has often been justified on biological grounds. The program of life, say war's apologists, depends on the struggle for existence. This struggle is universal and results in what Darwin called "Natural Selection," and this in its turn results in the "Survival of the Fittest." Natural Selection, of course, works only in a mass way, so that those which survive in the struggle will merely have an average of fitness a little above those which perish or fail to reproduce themselves. But some of the qualities which make for success in the struggle, and so for a greater chance of survival, will certainly be inherited; and since the process continues generation after generation not merely for thousands but for millions of years, the average fitness and efficiency of the race will steadily and continuously be raised until it can be pushed no higher. In any case, say the believers in this doctrine, struggle is necessary to maintain fitness; if the pressure of competition and conflict is removed, biological efficiency will suffer, and degeneration will set in.

Darwin's principle of Natural Selection, based as it is on constant pressure of competition or struggle, has been invoked to justify various policies in human affairs. For instance, it was used, especially by politicians in late Victorian England, to justify the principles of *laisser-faire* and free competition in business and economic affairs. And it was used, especially by German writers and politicians from the late nineteenth century onwards, to justify militarism. War, so ran this particular version of the argument, is the form which is taken by Natural Selection and the Struggle for Existence in the affairs of the nations. Without war, the heroic virtues degenerate; without war, no nation can possibly become great or successful.

It turns out, however, that both the *laisser-faire* economists and the militarists were wrong in appealing to biology for justification of their policies. War is a rather special aspect of competition between members of the same species—what biologists call "intra-specific competition." It is a special case because it involves physical conflict and often the death of those who undertake it, and also because it is physical conflict not between individuals but between organized groups; yet it shares certain properties in common with all other forms of intra-specific struggle or competition. And recent studies of the way in which Natural Selection works and how the Struggle for Existence operates in different conditions have resulted in this rather surprising but very important conclusion—that intra-specific competition need not, and usually does not, produce results of any advantage to the species as a whole.

A couple of examples will show what I mean. In birds like the peacock or the argus pheasant, the males are polygamous—if they can secure a harem. They show off their gorgeous plumage before the hen birds in an elaborate and very striking display, at definite assembly grounds where males and females go for the purpose of finding mates. The old idea that the hen deliberately selects the male she thinks the most beautiful is putting the matter in human terms which certainly do not apply to a bird's mind; but it seems certain that the brilliant and exciting display does have an effect on the hen bird, stimulating her to greater readiness to mate. Individual male birds meet with different degrees of success in this polygamous love business: some secure quite a number of mates, others only one or a few, and some get none at all. This puts an enormous biological premium on success: the really successful male leaves many times more descendants than the unsuccessful. Here, then, is Natural Selection working at an exceedingly high pitch of intensity to make their display plumage and display actions more effective in their business of stimulating the hens. Accordingly, in polygamous birds of this kind, we often find the display plumage developed to a fantastic extent, even so far as to be a handicap to the species as a whole. Thus the display organ of the peacock, his train of enormously over-grown tail-covert feathers, is so long and cumbersome that it is a real handicap in flight. In the argus pheasant the chief display organs are the beautifully adorned wings which the male throws up and forward in display so that he looks like a gigantic bell-shaped flower. The business of display has been so important that it has overridden the business of flying, and now the male argus pheasant can fly only with difficulty, a few feet at a time.

Here are two good examples of how a purely intra-specific struggle, in this case between individual rival males, can produce results which are not merely useless, but harmful to the species as a whole in its struggle for existence against its enemies and the forces of nature. In general, selection for success in reproduction reaches greater intensities than selection for individual survival, for the simple reason that reproduction implies multiplication: the individual is a single unit, but, as we have just seen for polygamous birds, success in reproduction may give the individual's characteristics a multiple representation in later generations.

In flowering plants, the intra-specific struggle for reproduction between different individuals often produces results which, if not directly harmful to the species, are at least incredibly wasteful. We need only think of the fantastic profusion of bloom on flowering trees like dogwood or hawthorn or catalpa, or the still more fantastic profusion of pollen in trees which rely on fertilization by the wind, like pine and fir. The individual trees are competing for the privilege of surviving in their descendants; the species could certainly perpetuate itself with a much more modest expenditure of living material.

One final example. Naturalists have often noted the almost unbelievable perfection of the protective resemblance of certain insects to their surroundings. The most extraordinary cases are the resemblances of various butterflies, like the Kallima, to dead leaves. Not only do the folded wings perfectly resemble a dead leaf in shape and colour, not only do they have a projection to imitate the stalk, and dark lines which perfectly simulate the veins, but some even go so far as to be marked with imitation mould-spots and holes!

Now, in all butterflies the survival of the species depends to a preponderant degree on the capacity of the defenceless and juicy caterpillar and chrysalis to survive. Selection presses with much greater intensity on the larval and pupal stages than on the adult. Furthermore, there is some sort of balance between the number of adults which survive to reproduce themselves and the intensity of selection which presses on the next generation of caterpillars. If more adults reproduce, there will be many more caterpillars, and they will be more easily found by their enemies, especially the tiny parasitic wasps which lay eggs inside the caterpillars, the eggs growing into grubs which devour the unfortunate animals from within. Conversely, if fewer adults reproduce, there are many fewer caterpillars, but each of them has a better chance of surviving to the butterfly stage. Accordingly, the protection of the adults is, from the point of view of the species, a secondary matter. Of course they must be protected sufficiently well for a reasonable number to survive and reproduce, but after this it is quite unimportant—for the species—if a slightly higher or a slightly lower proportion survives.

It is unimportant for the species but it remains important for the individual. If one kind of adult is better protected than another, it will automatically leave a higher average number of offspring; and so the intraspecific struggle for reproduction among the individual adult butterflies will continue to push any protective devices they possess on toward ever greater efficiency, even though this may be quite immaterial to the survival of the species. The perfection of the Kallima's resemblance to a dead leaf is one of the marvels of nature; not the least marvelous part of it is that it is of no value to the species as a whole.

On the other hand, intra-specific competition and struggle need not always lead to results which are useless to the species. The competition between individuals may concern qualities which are also useful in the struggle of the species against its enemies, as in deer or zebra or antelope —the same extra turn of speed which gives one individual an advantage over another in escaping from wolf or lion or cheetah will also stand the whole species in good stead. Or it may concern qualities which help the species in surviving in a difficult environment; an extra capacity for resisting drought in an individual cactus or yucca will help the species in colonizing new and more arid regions. It will not be useless or harmful to the species unless the competition is directed solely or mainly against other individuals like itself.

Furthermore, the results will differ according to conditions. When there is competition for mates among male birds, it will become really intense only when polygamy prevails and the advantage of success is therefore multiplied. Monogamous birds also stimulate their mates with a display of bright plumage, but in this case the display plumage is never developed to a pitch at which it is actually harmful in the general struggle for existence; the balance is struck at a different level.

All these considerations apply to war. In the first place it is obvious that war is an example of intra-specific competition—it is a physical conflict between groups within the same species. As such, it might be not merely useless but harmful to the species as a whole—a drag on the evolutionary progress of humanity. But, further, it might turn out to be harmful in some conditions and not in others. This indeed seems to be the truth. Those who say that war is always and inevitably harmful to humanity are indulging in an unjustified generalization (though not nearly so unjustified as the opposite generalization of the militarists who say that war is both necessary and beneficial to humanity). Warfare between peoples living on the tribal level of early barbarism may quite possibly have been on balance a good thing for the species—by encouraging the manly virtues, by mixing the heritage of otherwise closed communities through the capture of women, by keeping down excessive population-pressure, and in other ways. War waged by small professional armies according to a professional code was at least not a serious handicap to general progress. But long-continued war in which the civilian population is starved, oppressed, and murdered and whole countries are laid waste, as in the Thirty Years War—that is harmful to the species; and so is total war in the modern German sense in which entire populations may be enslaved and brutalized, as with Poland or Greece to-day, whole cities smashed, like Rotterdam, the resources of large regions deliberately destroyed, as in the Ukraine. The more total war becomes, both intensively, as diverting more of the energies of the population from construction to destruction, and extensively, as involving more and more of the countries of the globe, the more of a threat does it become to the progress of the human species. As H. G. Wells and many others have urged, it might even turn back the clock of civilization and force the world into another Dark Age. War of this type is an intra-specific struggle from which nobody, neither humanity at large nor any of the groups engaged in the conflict, can really reap any balance of advantage, though of course we may snatch particular advantages out of the results of war.

But it is one thing to demonstrate that modern war is harmful to the species, another thing to do something about abolishing it. What has the biologist to say to those who assert that war is inevitable, since, they say, it is a natural outcome of human nature and human nature cannot possibly be changed?

To this the biologist can give a reassuring answer. War is not an inevitable phenomenon of human life; and when objectors of this type talk of human nature they really mean the expression of human nature, and this can be most thoroughly changed.

As a matter of observable fact, war occurs in certain conditions, not in others. There is no evidence of prehistoric man's having made war, for all his flint implements seem to have been designed for hunting, for digging, or for scraping hides; and we can be pretty sure that even if he did, any wars between groups in the hunting stage of human life would have been both rare and mild. Organized warfare is most unlikely to have begun before the stage of settled civilization. In man, as in ants, war in any serious sense is bound up with the existence of accumulations of property to fight about.

However, even after man had learned to live in cities and amass property, war does not seem to have been inevitable. The early Indus civilization, dating from about 3000 B.C., reveals no traces of war. There seem to have been periods in early Chinese history, as well as in the Inca civilization in Peru, in which war was quite or almost absent.

As for human nature, it contains no specific war instinct, as does the nature of harvester ants. There is in man's make-up a general aggressive tendency, but this, like all other human urges, is not a specific and unvarying instinct; it can be moulded into the most varied forms. It can be canalized into competitive sport, as in our own society, or as when certain Filipino tribes were induced to substitute football for head-hunting. It can be sublimated into non-competitive sport, like mountain-climbing, or into higher types of activity altogether, like exploration or research or social crusades.

There is no theoretical obstacle to the abolition of war. But do not let us delude ourselves with the idea that this will be easy. The first step needed is the right kind of international machinery. To invent that will not be particularly simple: sanctions against aggressors, the peaceful reconciliation of national interests in a co-operative international system, an international police force—we can see in principle that these and other necessary bits of anti-war machinery are possible, but it will take a great deal of hard thinking to design them so that they will really work.

The second step is a good deal more difficult. It is to find what William James called a "moral equivalent for war," while at the same time reducing the reservoir of potential aggressiveness which now exists in every powerful nation. This is a psychological problem. Thanks to Freud and modern psychology in general, we are now beginning to understand how the self-assertive impulses of the child may be frustrated and repressed in such a way as to drive them underground. There in the subconscious they may persist in the form of crude urges to aggression and cruelty, which are all the more dangerous for not being consciously recognized.

To prevent the accumulation of this store of psychological dynamite and to find ways in which our self-assertive impulses can issue along conscious and constructive channels is a big job. It means a better structure of social and family life, one which does not inflict such frustrations on the growing human personality; it means a new approach to education; it means providing outlets in the form of physical or mental adventure for the impulses which would otherwise be unused even if not repressed. It is a difficult task; but by no means an impossible one.

Thus in the perspective of biology war first dwindles to the status of a rare curiosity. Further probing, however, makes it loom larger again. For one thing, it is a form of intra-specific struggle, and as such may be useless or even harmful to the species as a whole. Then we find that one of the very few animal species which make war is man; and man is to-day not merely the highest product of evolution, but the only type still capable of real evolutionary progress. And, war, though it need not always be harmful to the human species and its progress, indubitably is so when conducted in the total fashion which is necessary in this technological age. Thus war is not merely a human problem; it is a biological problem of the broadest scope, for on its abolition may depend life's ability to continue the progress which it has slowly but steadily achieved through more than a thousand million years.

But the biologist can end on a note of tempered hope. War is not inevitable for man. His aggressive impulses *can* be canalized into other outlets; his political machinery *can* be designed to make war less likely. These things *can* be done: but to do them will require a great deal of hard thinking and hard work. While waging this particular war with all our might, we have a duty to keep a corner of our minds open, engaged on the job of thinking out ways and means of preventing war in general in the future.

Bruno Bettelheim

Joey: A "Mechanical Boy"

Joey, when we began our work with him, was a mechanical boy. He functioned as if by remote control, run by machines of his own powerfully creative fantasy. Not only did he himself believe that he was a machine but, more remarkably, he created this impression in others. Even while he performed actions that are intrinsically human, they never appeared to be other than machine-started and executed. On the other hand, when the machine was not working we had to concentrate on recollecting his presence, for he seemed not to exist. A human body that functions as if it were a machine and a machine that duplicates human functions are equally fascinating and frightening. Perhaps they are so uncanny because they remind us that the human body can operate without a human spirit, that body can exist without soul. And Joey was a child who had been robbed of his humanity.

Not every child who possesses a fantasy world is possessed by it. Normal children may retreat into realms of imaginary glory or magic powers, but they are easily recalled from these excursions. Disturbed children are not always able to make the return trip; they remain withdrawn, prisoners of the inner world of delusion and fantasy. In many ways Joey presented a classic example of this state of infantile autism. In any age, when the individual has escaped into a delusional world, he has usually fashioned it from bits and pieces of the world at hand. Joey, in his time and world, chose the machine and froze himself in its image. His story has a general relevance to the understanding of emotional development in a machine age.

Joey's delusion is not uncommon among schizophrenic children today. He wanted to be rid of his unbearable humanity, to become completely automatic. He so nearly succeeded in attaining this goal that he could al-most convince others, as well as himself, of his mechanical character. The descriptions of autistic children in the literature take for their point of departure and comparison the normal or abnormal human being. To do justice to Joey I would have to compare him simultaneously to a most inept infant and a highly complex piece of machinery. Often we had to force ourselves by a conscious act of will to realize that Joey was a child. Again and again his acting-out of his delusions froze our own ability to respond as human beings.

During Joey's first weeks with us we would watch absorbedly as this at once fragile-looking and imperious nine-year-old went about his me-chanical existence. Entering the dining room, for example, he would string an imaginary wire from his "energy source"—an imaginary electric outlet—to the table. There he "insulated" himself with paper napkins and finally plugged himself in. Only then could Joey eat, for he firmly believed that the "current" ran his ingestive apparatus. So skillful was the pantomime that one had to look twice to be sure there was neither wire nor outlet nor plug. Children and members of our staff spontaneously avoided stepping on the "wires" for fear of interrupting what seemed the source of his very life.

For long periods of time, when his "machinery" was idle, he would sit so quietly that he would disappear from the focus of the most conscien-tious observation. Yet in the next moment he might be "working" and the center of our captivated attention. Many times a day he would turn him-self on and shift noisily through a sequence of higher and higher gears until he "exploded," screaming "Crash, crash!" and hurling items from his ever present apparatus—radio tubes, light bulbs, even motors or, lack-ing these, any handy breakable object. (Joey had an astonishing knack for snatching bulbs and tubes unobserved.) As soon as the object thrown had shattered, he would cease his screaming and wild jumping and retire to mute, motionless nonexistence.

Our maids, inured to difficult children, were exceptionally attentive to Joey; they were apparently moved by his extreme infantile fragility, so strangely coupled with megalomaniacal superiority. Occasionally some of the apparatus he fixed to his bed to "live him" during his sleep would fall down in disarray. This machinery he contrived from masking tape, card-board, wire and other paraphernalia. Usually the maids would pick up such things and leave them on a table for the children to find, or disregard them entirely. But Joey's machine they carefully restored: "Joey must have the carburetor so he can breathe." Similarly they were on the alert to pick up and preserve the motors that ran him during the day and the exhaust pipes through which he exhaled.

How had Joey become a human machine? From intensive interviews with his parents we learned that the process had begun even before birth. Schizophrenia often results from parental rejection, sometimes combined ambivalently with love. Joey, on the other hand, had been completely ignored.

"I never knew I was pregnant," his mother said, meaning that she had already excluded Joey from her consciousness. His birth, she said, "did not make any difference." Joey's father, a rootless draftee in the wartime civilian army, was equally unready for parenthood. So, of course, are many young couples. Fortunately most such parents lose their indifference upon the baby's birth. But not Joey's parents. "I did not want to see or nurse him," his mother declared. "I had no feeling of actual dislike—I simply didn't want to take care of him." For the first three months of his life Joey "cried most of the time." A colicky baby, he was kept on a rigid four-hour feeding schedule, was not touched unless necessary and was never cuddled or played with. The mother, preoccupied with herself, usually left Joey alone in the crib or playpen during the day. The father discharged his frustrations by punishing Joey when the child cried at night.

Soon the father left for overseas duty, and the mother took Joey, now a year and a half old, to live with her at her parents' home. On his arrival the grandparents noticed that ominous changes had occurred in the child. Strong and healthy at birth, he had become frail and irritable; a responsive baby, he had become remote and inaccessible. When he began to master speech, he talked only to himself. At an early date he became preoccupied with machinery, including an old electric fan which he could take apart and put together again with surprising deftness.

Joey's mother impressed us with a fey quality that expressed her insecurity, her detachment from the world and her low physical vitality. We were struck especially by her total indifference as she talked about Joey. This seemed much more remarkable than the actual mistakes she made in handling him. Certainly he was left to cry for hours when hungry, because she fed him on a rigid schedule; he was toilet-trained with great rigidity so that he would give no trouble. These things happen to many children. But Joey's existence never registered with his mother. In her recollections he was fused at one moment with one event or person; at another, with something or somebody else. When she told us about his birth and infancy, it was as if she were talking about some vague acquaintance, and soon her thoughts would wander off to another person or to herself.

When Joey was not yet four, his nursery school suggested that he enter a special school for disturbed children. At the new school his autism was immediately recognized. During his three years there he experienced a slow improvement. Unfortunately a subsequent two years in a parochial school destroyed his progress. He began to develop compulsive defenses, which he called his "preventions." He could not drink, for example, except through elaborate piping systems built of straws. Liquids had to be "pumped" into him, in his fantasy, or he could not suck. Eventually his behavior became so upsetting that he could not be kept in the parochial school. At home things did not improve. Three months before entering the Orthogenic School he made a serious attempt at suicide.

To us Joey's pathological behavior seemed the external expression of an overwhelming effort to remain almost nonexistent as a person. For weeks Joey's only reply when addressed was "Bam." Unless he thus neutralized whatever we said, there would be an explosion, for Joey plainly wished to close off every form of contact not mediated by machinery. Even when he was bathed he rocked back and forth with mute, engine-like regularity, flooding the bathroom. If he stopped rocking, he did this like a machine too; suddenly he went completely rigid. Only once, after months of being lifted from his bath and carried to bed, did a small expression of puzzled pleasure appear on his face as he said very softly: "They even carry you to your bed here."

For a long time after he began to talk he would never refer to anyone by name, but only as "that person" or "the little person" or "the big person." He was unable to designate by its true name anything to which he attached feelings. Nor could he name his anxieties except through neologisms of word contaminations. For a long time he spoke about "master paintings" and "a master painting room" (i.e., masturbating and masturbating room). One of his machines, the "criticizer," prevented him from "saying words which have unpleasant feelings." Yet he gave personal names to the tubes and motors in his collection of machinery. Moreover, these dead things had feelings; the tubes bled when hurt and sometimes got sick. He consistently maintained this reversal between animate and inanimate objects.

In Joey's machine world everything, on pain of instant destruction, obeyed inhibitory laws much more stringent than those of physics. When we came to know him better, it was plain that in his moments of silent withdrawal, with his machine switched off, Joey was absorbed in pondering the compulsive laws of his private universe. His preoccupation with machinery made it difficult to establish even practical contacts with him. If he wanted to do something with a counselor, such as play with a toy that has caught his vague attention, he could not do so: "I'd like this very much, but first I have to turn off the machine." But by the time he had fulfilled all the requirements of his preventions, he had lost interest. When a toy was offered to him, he could not touch it because his motors and his tubes did not leave him a hand free. Even certain colors were dangerous and had to be strictly avoided in toys and clothing, because "some colors turn off the current, and I can't touch them because I can't live without the current."

Joey was convinced that machines were better than people. Once when he bumped into one of the pipes on our jungle gym he kicked it so violently that his teacher had to restrain him to keep him from injuring himself. When she explained that the pipe was much harder than his foot, Joey replied: "That proves it. Machines are better than the body. They don't break; they're much harder and stronger." If he lost or forgot something, it merely proved that his brain ought to be thrown away and replaced by machinery. If he spilled something his arm should be broken and twisted off because it did not work properly. When his head or arm failed to work as it should, he tried to punish it by hitting it. Even Joey's feelings were mechanical. Much later in his therapy, when he had formed a timid attachment to another child and had been rebuffed, Joey cried: "He broke my feelings."

Gradually we began to understand what had seemed to be contradictory in Joey's behavior—why he held on to the motors and tubes, then suddenly destroyed them in a fury, then set out immediately and urgently to equip himself with new and larger tubes. Joey had created these machines to run his body and mind because it was too painful to be human. But again and again he became dissatisfied with their failure to meet his need and rebellious at the way they frustrated his will. In a recurrent frenzy he "exploded" his light bulbs and tubes, and for a moment became a human being—for one crowning instant he came alive. But as soon as he had asserted his dominance through the self-created explosion, he felt his life ebbing away. To keep on existing he had immediately to restore his machines and replenish the electricity that supplied his life energy.

What deep-seated fears and needs underlay Joey's delusional system? We were long in finding out, for Joey's preventions effectively concealed the secret of his autistic behavior. In the meantime we dealt with his peripheral problems one by one.

During his first year with us Joey's most trying problem was toilet behavior. This surprised us, for Joey's personality was not "anal" in the Freudian sense; his original personality damage had antedated the period of his toilet-training. Rigid and early toilet-training, however, had certainly contributed to his anxieties. It was our effort to help Joey with this problem that led to his first recognition of us as human beings.

Going to the toilet, like everything else in Joey's life, was surrounded by elaborate preventions. We had to accompany him; he had to take off all his clothes; he could only squat, not sit, on the toilet seat; he had to touch the wall with one hand, in which he also clutched frantically the vacuum tubes that powered his elimination. He was terrified lest his whole body be sucked down.

To counteract this fear we gave him a metal wastebasket in lieu of a toilet. Eventually, when eliminating into the wastebasket, he no longer needed to take off all his clothes, nor to hold on to the wall. He still needed the tubes and motors which, he believed, moved his bowels for him. But here again the all-important machinery was itself a source of new terrors. In Joey's world the gadgets had to move their bowels, too. He was terribly concerned that they should, but since they were so much more powerful than men, he was also terrified that if his tubes moved their bowels, their feces would fill all of space and leave him no room to live. He was thus always caught in some fearful contradiction.

Our readiness to accept his toilet habits, which obviously entailed some hardship for his counselors, gave Joey the confidence to express his obsessions in drawings. Drawing these fantasies was a first step toward letting us in, however distantly, to what concerned him most deeply. It was the first step in a year-long process of externalizing his anal preoccupations. As a result he began seeing feces everywhere; the whole world became to him a mire of excrement. At the same time he began to eliminate freely wherever he happened to be. But with this release from his infantile imprisonment in compulsive rules, the toilet and the whole process of elimination became less dangerous. Thus far it had been beyond Joey's comprehension that anybody could possibly move his bowels without mechanical aid. Now Joey took a further step forward; defecation became the first physiological process he could perform without the help of vacuum tubes. It must not be thought that he was proud of this ability. Taking pride in an achievement presupposes that one accomplishes it of one's own free will. He still did not feel himself an autonomous person who could do things on his own. To Joey defecation still seemed enslaved to some incomprehensible but utterly binding cosmic law, perhaps the law his parents had imposed on him when he was being toilet-trained.

It was not simply that his parents had subjected him to rigid, early training. Many children are so trained. But in most cases the parents have a deep emotional investment in the child's performance. The child's response in turn makes training an occasion for interaction between them and for the building of genuine relationships. Joey's parents had no emotional investment in him. His obedience gave them no satisfaction and won him no affection or approval. As a toilet-trained child he saved his mother labor, just as household machines saved her labor. As a machine he was not loved for his performance, nor could he love himself.

So it had been with all other aspects of Joey's existence with his parents. Their reactions to his eating or noneating, sleeping or wakening, urinating or defecating, being dressed or undressed, washed or bathed did not flow from any unitary interest in him, deeply embedded in their personalities. By treating him mechanically his parents made him a machine. The various functions of life—even the parts of his body—bore no integrating relationship to one another or to any sense of self that was acknowledged and confirmed by others. Though he had acquired mastery over some functions, such as toilet-training and speech, he had acquired them separately and kept them isolated from each other. Toilet-training had thus not gained him a pleasant feeling of body mastery; speech had not led to communication of thought or feeling. On the contrary, each achievement only steered him away from self-mastery and integration. Toilet-training had enslaved him. Speech left him talking in neologisms that obstructed his and our ability to relate to each other. In Joey's development the normal process of growth had been made to run backward. Whatever he had learned put him not at the end of his infantile development toward integration but, on the contrary, farther behind than he was at its very beginning. Had we understood this sooner, his first years with us would have been less baffling.

It is unlikely that Joey's calamity could befall a child in any time and culture but our own. He suffered no physical deprivation; he starved for human contact. Just to be taken care of is not enough for relating. It is a necessary but not a sufficient condition. At the extreme where utter scarcity reigns, the forming of relationships is certainly hampered. But our society of mechanized plenty often makes for equal difficulties in a child's learning to relate. Where parents can provide the simple creature-comforts for their children only at the cost of significant effort, it is likely that they will feel pleasure in being able to provide for them; it is this, the parents' pleasure, that gives children a sense of personal worth and sets the process of relating in motion. But if comfort is so readily available that the parents feel no particular pleasure in winning it for their children, then the children cannot develop the feeling of being worthwhile around the satisfaction of their basic needs. Of course parents and children can and do develop relationships around other situations. But matters are then no longer so simple and direct. The child must be on the receiving end of care and concern given with pleasure and without the exaction of return if he is to feel loved and worthy of respect and consideration. This feeling gives him the ability to trust; he can entrust his well-being to persons to whom he is so important. Out of such trust the child learns to form close and stable relationships.

For Joey relationship with his parents was empty of pleasure in comfort-giving as in all other situations. His was an extreme instance of a plight that sends many schizophrenic children to our clinics and hospitals.

Many months passed before he could relate to us; his despair that anybody could like him made contact impossible.

When Joey could finally trust us enough to let himself become more infantile, he began to play at being a papoose. There was a corresponding change in his fantasies. He drew endless pictures of himself as an electrical papoose. Totally enclosed, suspended in empty space, he is run by unknown, unseen powers through wireless electricity.

As we eventually came to understand, the heart of Joey's delusional system was the artificial, mechanical womb he had created and into which he had locked himself. In his papoose fantasies lay the wish to be entirely reborn in a womb. His new experiences in the school suggested that life, after all, might be worth living. Now he was searching for a way to be reborn in a better way. Since machines were better than men, what was more natural than to try rebirth through them? This was the deeper meaning of his electrical papoose.

As Joey made progress, his pictures of himself became more dominant in his drawings. Though still machine-operated, he has grown in self-importance. Another great step forward is represented in a picture in which he has acquired hands that do something, and he has had the courage to make a picture of the machine that runs him. Later still the papoose became a person, rather than a robot encased in glass.

Eventually Joey began to create an imaginary family at the school: the "Carr" family. Why the Carr family? In the car he was enclosed as he had been in his papoose, but at least the car was not stationary; it could move. More important, in a car one was not only driven but also could drive. The Carr family was Joey's way of exploring the possibility of leaving the school, of living with a good family in a safe, protecting car.

Joey at last broke through his prison. In this brief account it has not been possible to trace the painfully slow process of his first true relations with other human beings. Suffice it to say that he ceased to be a mechanical boy and became a human child. This newborn child was, however, nearly 12 years old. To recover the lost time is a tremendous task. That work has occupied Joey and us ever since. Sometimes he sets to it with a will; at other times the difficulty of real life makes him regret that he ever came out of his shell. But he has never wanted to return to his mechanical life.

One last detail and this fragment of Joey's story has been told. When Joey was 12, he made a float for our Memorial Day parade. It carried the slogan: "Feelings are more important than anything under the sun." Feelings, Joey had learned, are what make for humanity; their absence, for a mechanical existence. With this knowledge Joey entered the human condition.

Stephen Spender

The Making of a Poem

Apology

It would be inexcusable to discuss my own way of writing poetry unless I were able to relate this to a wider view of the problems which poets attempt to solve when they sit down at a desk or table to write, or walk around composing their poems in their heads. There is a danger of my appearing to put across my own experiences as the general rule, when every poet's way of going about his work and his experience of being a poet are different, and when my own poetry may not be good enough to lend my example any authority.

Yet the writing of poetry is an activity which makes certain demands of attention on the poet and which requires that he should have certain qualifications of ear, vision, imagination, memory and so on. He should be able to think in images, he should have as great a mastery of language as a painter has over his palette, even if the range of his language be very limited. All this means that, in ordinary society, a poet has to adapt himself, more or less consciously, to the demands of his vocation, and hence the peculiarities of poets and the condition of inspiration which many people have said is near to madness. One poet's example is only his adaptation of his personality to the demands of poetry, but if it is clearly stated it may help us to understand other poets, and even something of poetry.

Today we lack very much a whole view of poetry, and have instead many one-sided views of certain aspects of poetry which have been advertised as the only aims which poets should attempt. Movements such as free verse, imagism, surrealism, expressionism, personalism and so on, tend to make people think that poetry is simply a matter of not writing in metre or rhyme, or of free association, or of thinking in images, or of a

THE MAKING OF A POEM   From *Partisan Review*, Summer 1946. Copyright 1946 by Stephen Spender. Reprinted by permission of Harold Matson Company, Inc.

kind of drawing room madness (surrealism) which corresponds to drawing room communism. Here is a string of ideas: Night, dark, stars, immensity, blue, voluptuous, clinging, columns, clouds, moon, sickle, harvest, vast camp fire, hell. Is this poetry? A lot of strings of words almost as simple as this are set down on the backs of envelopes and posted off to editors or to poets by the vast army of amateurs who think that to be illogical is to be poetic, with that fond question. Thus I hope that this discussion of how poets work will imply a wider and completer view of poets.

Concentration

The problem of creative writing is essentially one of concentration, and the supposed eccentricities of poets are usually due to mechanical habits or rituals developed in order to concentrate. Concentration, of course, for the purposes of writing poetry, is different from the kind of concentration required for working out a sum. It is a focussing of the attention in a special way, so that the poet is aware of all the implications and possible developments of his idea, just as one might say that a plant was not concentrating on developing mechanically in one direction, but in many directions, towards the warmth and light with its leaves, and towards the water with its roots, all at the same time.

Schiller liked to have a smell of rotten apples, concealed beneath the lid of his desk, under his nose when he was composing poetry. Walter de la Mare has told me that he must smoke when writing. Auden drinks endless cups of tea. Coffee is my own addiction, besides smoking a great deal, which I hardly ever do except when I am writing. I notice also that as I attain a greater concentration, this tends to make me forget the taste of the cigarette in my mouth, and then I have a desire to smoke two or even three cigarettes at a time, in order that the sensation from the outside may penetrate through the wall of concentration which I have built round myself.

For goodness' sake, though, do not think that rotten apples or cigarettes or tea have anything to do with the quality of the work of a Schiller, a de la Mare, or an Auden. They are a part of a concentration which has already been attained rather than the causes of concentration. Da la Mare once said to me that he thought the desire to smoke when writing poetry arose from a need, not of a stimulus, but to canalize a distracting leak of his attention away from his writing towards the distraction which is always present in one's environment. Concentration may be disturbed by someone whistling in the street or the ticking of a clock. There is always a slight tendency of the body to sabotage the attention of the mind by providing some distraction. If this need for distraction can be directed into one channel—such as the odor of rotten apples or the taste of tobacco or tea—then other distractions outside oneself are put out of competition.

Another possible explanation is that the concentrated effort of writing poetry is a spiritual activity which makes one completely forget, for the time being, that one has a body. It is a disturbance of the balance of body and mind and for this reason one needs a kind of anchor of sensation with the physical world. Hence the craving for a scent or taste or even, sometimes, for sexual activity. Poets speak of the necessity of writing poetry rather than of a liking for doing it. It is spiritual compulsion, a straining of the mind to attain heights surrounded by abysses and it cannot be entirely happy, for in the most important sense, the only reward worth having is absolutely denied: for, however confident a poet may be, he is never quite sure that all his energy is not misdirected nor that what he is writing is great poetry. At the moment when art attains its highest attainment it reaches beyond its medium of words or paints or music, and the artist finds himself realizing that these instruments are inadequate to the spirit of what he is trying to say.

Different poets concentrate in different ways. In my own mind I make a sharp distinction between two types of concentration: one is immediate and complete, the other is plodding and only completed by stages. Some poets write immediately works which, when they are written, scarcely need revision. Others write their poems by stages, feeling their way from rough draft to rough draft, until finally, after many revisions, they have produced a result which may seem to have very little connection with their early sketches.

These two opposite processes are vividly illustrated in two examples drawn from music: Mozart and Beethoven. Mozart thought out symphonies, quartets, even scenes from operas, entirely in his head—often on a journey or perhaps while dealing with pressing problems—and then he transcribed them, in their completeness, onto paper. Beethoven wrote fragments of themes in notebooks which he kept beside him, working on and developing them over years. Often his first ideas were of a clumsiness which makes scholars marvel how he could, at the end, have developed from them such miraculous results.

Thus genius works in different ways to achieve its ends. But although the Mozartian type of genius is the more brilliant and dazzling, genius, unlike virtuosity, is judged by greatness of results, not by brilliance of performance. The result must be the fullest development in a created aesthetic form of an original moment of insight, and it does not matter whether genius devotes a lifetime to producing a small result if that result be immortal. The difference between two types of genius is that one type (the Mozartian) is able to plunge the greatest depths of his own experience by the tremendous effort of a moment, the other (the Beethovenian) must dig deeper and deeper into his consciousness, layer by layer. What counts in either case is the vision which sees and pursues and attains the end; the logic of the artistic purpose.

A poet may be divinely gifted with a lucid and intense and purposive intellect; he may be clumsy and slow; that does not matter, what matters is integrity of purpose and the ability to maintain the purpose without losing oneself. Myself, I am scarcely capable of immediate concentration in poetry. My mind is not clear, my will is weak, I suffer from an excess of ideas and a weak sense of form. For every poem that I begin to write, I think of at least ten which I do not write down at all. For every poem which I do write down, there are seven or eight which I never complete.

The method which I adopt therefore is to write down as many ideas as possible, in however rough a form, in notebooks (I have at least twenty of these, on a shelf beside my desk, going back over fifteen years). I then make use of some of the sketches and discard others.

The best way of explaining how I develop the rough ideas which I use, is to take an example. Here is a Notebook begun in 1944. About a hundred pages of it are covered with writing, and from this have emerged about six poems. Each idea, when it first occurs, is given a number. Sometimes the ideas do not get beyond one line. For example No. 3 (never developed) is the one line:—

A language of flesh and roses.

I shall return to this line in a few pages, when I speak of inspiration. For the moment, I turn to No. 13, because here is an idea which has been developed to its conclusion. The first sketch begins thus:—

a) There are some days when the sea lies like a harp
Stretched flat beneath the cliffs. The waves
Like wires burn with the sun's copper glow
        [*all the murmuring blue every silent*]

Between whose spaces every image
Of sky [*field and*] hedge and field and boat
Dwells like the huge face of the afternoon.
[*Lies*]

When the heat grows tired, the afternoon
Out of the land may breathe a sigh
[*Across these wires like a hand. They vibrate With*]

> Which moves across those wires like a soft hand
> [*Then the vibration*]
> Between whose spaces the vibration holds
> Every bird-cry, dog's bark, man-shout
> And creak of rollock from the land and sky
> With all the music of the afternoon.

Obviously these lines are attempts to sketch out an idea which exists clearly enough on some level of the mind where it yet eludes the attempt to state it. At this stage, a poem is like a face which one seems to be able to visualize clearly in the eye of memory, but when one examines it mentally or tries to think it out, feature by feature, it seems to fade.

The idea of this poem is a vision of the sea. The faith of the poet is that if this vision is clearly stated it will be significant. The vision is of the sea stretched under a cliff. On top of the cliff there are fields, hedges, houses. Horses draw carts along lanes, dogs bark far inland, bells ring in the distance. The shore seems laden with hedges, roses, horses and men, all high above the sea, on a very fine summer day when the ocean seems to reflect and absorb the shore. Then the small strung-out glittering waves of the sea lying under the shore are like the strings of a harp which catch the sunlight. Between these strings lies the reflection of the shore. Butterflies are wafted out over the waves, which they mistake for the fields of the chalky landscape, searching them for flowers. On a day such as this, the land, reflected in the sea, appears to enter into the sea, as though it lies under it, like Atlantis. The wires of the harp are like a seen music fusing seascape and landscape.

Looking at this vision in another way, it obviously has symbolic value. The sea represents death and eternity, the land represents the brief life of the summer and of one human generation which passes into the sea of eternity. But let me here say at once that although the poet may be conscious of this aspect of his vision, it is exactly what he wants to avoid stating, or even being too concerned with. His job is to recreate his vision, and let it speak its moral for itself. The poet must distinguish clearly in his own mind between that which most definitely must be said and that which must not be said. The unsaid inner meaning is revealed in the music and the tonality of the poem, and the poet is conscious of it in his knowledge that a certain tone of voice, a certain rhythm, are necessary.

In the next twenty versions of the poem I felt my way towards the clarification of the seen picture, the music and the inner feeling. In the first version quoted above, there is the phrase in the second and third lines

> The waves
> Like wires burn with the sun's copper glow.

This phrase fuses the image of the sea with the idea of music, and it is therefore a key-phrase, because the theme of the poem is the fusion of the land with the sea. Here, then, are several versions of these one and a quarter lines, in the order in which they were written:—

    b)   The waves are wires
          Burning as with the secret song of fires

    c) The day burns in the trembling wires
          With a vast music golden in the eyes

    d) The day glows on its trembling wires
          Singing a golden music in the eyes

    e) The day glows on its burning wires
          Like waves of music golden to the eyes.

    f) Afternoon burns upon its wires
          Lines of music dazzling the eyes

    g) Afternoon gilds its tingling wires
          To a visual silent music of the eyes

In the final version, these two lines appear as in the following stanza:—

    h) There are some days the happy ocean lies
          Like an unfingered harp, below the land.
          Afternoon gilds all the silent wires
          Into a burning music of the eyes.
          On mirroring paths between those fine-strung fires
          The shore, laden with roses, horses, spires,
          Wanders in water, imaged above ribbed sand.

Inspiration

The hard work evinced in these examples, which are only a fraction of the work put into the whole poem, may cause the reader to wonder whether there is no such thing as inspiration, or whether it is merely Stephen Spender who is uninspired. The answer is that everything in poetry is work except inspiration, whether this work is achieved at one swift stroke, as Mozart wrote his music, or whether it is a slow process of evolution from stage to stage. Here again, I have to qualify the word 'work,' as I qualified the word 'concentration': the work on a line of poetry may take the form of putting a version aside for a few days, weeks or years, and then taking it up again, when it may be found that the line has, in the interval of time, almost rewritten itself.

Inspiration is the beginning of a poem and it is also its final goal. It is the first idea which drops into the poet's mind and it is the final idea which he at last achieves in words. In between this start and this winning post there is the hard race, the sweat and toil.

Paul Valéry speaks of the *"une ligne donnée"* of a poem. One line is given to the poet by God or by nature, the rest he has to discover for himself.

My own experience of inspiration is certainly that of a line or a phrase or a word or sometimes something still vague, a dim cloud of an idea which I feel must be condensed into a shower of words. The peculiarity of the key word or line is that it does not merely attract, as, say, the word "braggadocio" attracts. It occurs in what seems to be an active, male, germinal form as though it were the centre of a statement requiring a beginning and an end, and as though it had an impulse in a certain direction. Here are examples:—

A language of flesh and roses.

This phrase (not very satisfactory in itself) brings to my mind a whole series of experiences and the idea of a poem which I shall perhaps write some years hence. I was standing in the corridor of a train passing through the Black Country. I saw a landscape of pits and pitheads, artificial mountains, jagged yellow wounds in the earth, everything transformed as though by the toil of an enormous animal or giant tearing up the earth in search of prey or treasure. Oddly enough, a stranger next to me in the corridor echoed my inmost thought. He said: "Everything there is man-made." At this moment the line flashed into my head

A language of flesh and roses.

The sequence of my thought was as follows: the industrial landscape which seems by now a routine and act of God which enslaves both employers and workers who serve and profit by it, is actually the expression of man's will. Men willed it to be so, and pitheads, slag-heaps and the ghastly disregard of anything but the pursuit of wealth, are a symbol of modern man's mind. In other words, the world which we create—the world of slums and telegrams and newspapers—is a kind of language of our inner wishes and thoughts. Although this is so, it is obviously a language which has got outside our control. It is a confused language, an irresponsible senile gibberish. This thought greatly distressed me, and I started thinking that if the phenomena created by humanity are really like words in a language, what kind of language do we really aspire to? All this sequence of thought flashed into my mind with the answer which came before the question: A *language of flesh and roses*.

I hope this example will give the reader some idea of what I mean by inspiration. Now the line, which I shall not repeat again, is a way of thinking imaginatively. If the line embodies some of the ideas which I have related above, these ideas must be further made clear in other lines. That is the terrifying challenge of poetry. Can I think out the logic of images? How easy it is to explain here the poem that I would have liked to write! How difficult it would be to write it. For writing it would imply living my way through the imaged experience of all these ideas, which here are mere abstractions, and such an effort of imaginative experience requires a lifetime of patience and watching.

Here is an example of a cloudy form of thought germinated by the word *cross*, which is the key word of the poem which exists formlessly in my mind. Recently my wife had a son. On the first day that I visited her after the boy's birth, I went by bus to the hospital. Passing through the streets on the top of the bus, they all seemed very clean, and the thought occurred to me that everything was prepared for our child. Past generations have toiled so that any child born today inherits, with his generation, cities, streets, organization, the most elaborate machinery for living. Everything has been provided for him by people dead long before he was born. Then, naturally enough, sadder thoughts colored this picture for me, and I reflected how he also inherited vast maladjustments, vast human wrongs. Then I thought of the child as like a pin-point of present existence, the moment incarnate, in whom the whole of the past, and all possible futures *cross*. This word *cross* somehow suggested the whole situation to me of a child born into the world and also of the form of a poem about his situation. When the word *cross* appeared in the poem, the idea of the past should give place to the idea of the future and it should be apparent that the *cross* in which present and future meet is the secret of an individual human existence. And here again, the unspoken secret which lies beyond the poem, the moral significance of other meanings of the word "cross" begins to glow with its virtue that should never be said and yet should shine through every image in the poem.

This account of inspiration is probably weak beside the accounts that other poets might give. I am writing of my own experience, and my own inspiration seems to me like the faintest flash of insight into the nature of reality beside that of other poets whom I can think of. However, it is possible that I describe here a kind of experience which, however slight it may be, is far truer to the real poetic experience than Aldous Huxley's account of how a young poet writes poetry in his novel *Time Must Have a Stop*. It is hard to imagine anything more self-conscious and unpoetic than Mr. Huxley's account.

Memory

If the art of concentrating in a particular way is the discipline necessary for poetry to reveal itself, memory exercised in a particular way is the natural gift of poetic genius. The poet, above all else, is a person who never forgets certain sense-impressions which he has experienced and which he can re-live again and again as though with all their original freshness.

All poets have this highly developed sensitive apparatus of memory, and they are usually aware of experiences which happened to them at the earliest age and which retain their pristine significance throughout life. The meeting of Dante and Beatrice when the poet was only nine years of age is the experience which became a symbol in Dante's mind around which the *Divine Comedy* crystallized. The experience of nature which forms the subject of Wordsworth's poetry was an extension of a childhood vision of "natural presences" which surrounded the boy Wordsworth. And his decision in later life to live in the Lake District was a decision to return to the scene of these childhood memories which were the most important experiences in his poetry. There is evidence for the importance of this kind of memory in all the creative arts, and the argument certainly applies to prose which is creative. Sir Osbert Sitwell has told me that his book *Before the Bombardment,* which contains an extremely civilized and satiric account of the social life of Scarborough before and during the last war, was based on his observations of life in that resort before he had reached the age of twelve.

It therefore is not surprising that although I have no memory for telephone numbers, addresses, faces and where I have put this morning's correspondence, I have a perfect memory for the sensation of certain experiences which are crystallized for me around certain associations. I could demonstrate this from my own life by the overwhelming nature of associations which, suddenly aroused, have carried me back so completely into the past, particularly into my childhood, that I have lost all sense of the present time and place. But the best proofs of this power of memory are found in the odd lines of poems written in notebooks fifteen years ago. A few fragments of unfinished poems enable me to enter immediately into the experiences from which they were derived, the circumstances in which they were written, and the unwritten feelings in the poem that were projected but never put into words.

> . . . Knowledge of a full sun
> That runs up his big sky, above
> The hill, then in those trees and throws
> His smiling on the turf.

That is an incomplete idea of fifteen years ago, and I remember exactly a balcony of a house facing a road, and, on the other side of the road, pine trees, beyond which lay the sea. Every morning the sun sprang up, first of all above the horizon of the sea, then it climbed to the tops of the trees and shone on my window. And this memory connects with the sun that shines through my window in London now in spring and early summer. So that the memory is not exactly a memory. It is more like one prong upon which a whole calendar of similar experiences happening throughout years, collect. A memory once clearly stated ceases to be a memory, it becomes perpetually present, because every time we experience something which recalls it, the clear and lucid original experience imposes its formal beauty on the new experiences. It is thus no longer a memory but an experience lived through again and again.

Turning over these old notebooks, my eye catches some lines, in a projected long poem, which immediately re-shape themselves into the following short portrait of a woman's face:—

> Her eyes are gleaming fish
> Caught in her nervous face, as if in a net.
> Her hair is wild and fair, haloing her cheeks
> Like a fantastic flare of Southern sun.
> There is madness in her cherishing her children.
> Sometimes, perhaps a single time in years,
> Her wandering fingers stoop to arrange some flowers—
> Then in her hands her whole life stops and weeps.

It is perhaps true to say that memory is the faculty of poetry, because the imagination itself is an exercise of memory. There is nothing we imagine which we do not already know. And our ability to imagine is our ability to remember what we have already once experienced and to apply it to some different situation. Thus the greatest poets are those with memories so great that they extend beyond their strongest experiences to their minutest observations of people and things far outside their own self-centredness (the weakness of memory is its self-centredness: hence the narcissistic nature of most poetry).

Here I can detect my own greatest weakness. My memory is defective and self-centred. I lack the confidence in using it to create situations outside myself, although I believe that, in theory, there are very few situations in life which a poet should not be able to imagine, because it is a fact that most poets have experienced almost every situation in life. I do not mean by this that a poet who writes about a Polar Expedition has actually been to the North Pole. I mean, though, that he has been cold, hungry, etc., so that it is possible for him by remembering imaginatively his own felt experiences to know what it is like to explore the North Pole. That is where I fail. I cannot write about going to the North Pole.

Faith

It is evident that a faith in their vocation, mystical in intensity, sustains poets. There are many illustrations from the lives of poets to show this, and Shakespeare's sonnets are full of expressions of his faith in the immortality of his lines.

From my experience I can clarify the nature of this faith. When I was nine, we went to the Lake District, and there my parents read me some of the poems of Wordsworth. My sense of the sacredness of the task of poetry began then, and I have always felt that a poet's was a sacred vocation, like a saint's. Since I was nine, I have wanted to be various things, for example, Prime Minister (when I was twelve). Like some other poets I am attracted by the life of power and the life of action, but I am still more repelled by them. Power involves forcing oneself upon the attention of historians by doing things and occupying offices which are, in themselves, important, so that what is truly powerful is not the soul of a so-called powerful and prominent man but the position which he fills and the things which he does. Similarly, the life of "action" which seems so very positive is, in fact, a selective, even a negative kind of life. A man of action does one thing or several things because he does not do something else. Usually men who do very spectacular things fail completely to do the ordinary things which fill the lives of most normal people, and which would be far more heroic and spectacular perhaps, if they did not happen to be done by many people. Thus in practice the life of action has always seemed to me an act of cutting oneself off from life.

Although it is true that poets are vain and ambitious, their vanity and ambition are of the purest kind attainable in this world, for the saint renounces ambition. They are ambitious to be accepted for what they ultimately are as revealed by their inmost experiences, their finest perceptions, their deepest feelings, their uttermost sense of truth, in their poetry. They cannot cheat about these things, because the quality of their own being is revealed not in the noble sentiments which their poetry expresses, but in sensibility, control of language, rhythm and music, things which cannot be attained by a vote of confidence from an electorate, or by the office of

Poet Laureate. Of course, work is tremendously important, but, in poetry, even the greatest labor can only serve to reveal the intrinsic qualities of soul of the poet as he really is.

Since there can be no cheating, the poet, like the saint, stands in all his works before the bar of a perpetual day of judgment. His vanity of course is pleased by success, though even success may contribute to his understanding that popularity does not confer on him the favorable judgment of all the ages which he seeks. For what does it mean to be praised by one's own age, which is soaked in crimes and stupidity, except perhaps that future ages, wise where we are foolish, will see him as a typical expression of this age's crimes and stupidity? Nor is lack of success a guarantee of great poetry, though there are some who pretend that it is. Nor can the critics, at any rate beyond a certain limited point of technical judgment, be trusted.

The poet's faith is therefore, firstly, a mystique of vocation, secondly, a faith in his own truth, combined with his own devotion to a task. There can really be no greater faith than the confidence that one is doing one's utmost to fulfil one's high vocation, and it is this that has inspired all the greatest poets. At the same time this faith is coupled with a deep humility because one knows that, ultimately, judgment does not rest with oneself. All one can do is to achieve nakedness, to be what one is with all one's faculties and perceptions, strengthened by all the skill which one can acquire, and then to stand before the judgment of time.

In my Notebooks, I find the following Prose Poem, which expresses these thoughts:

> Bring me peace bring me power bring me assurance. Let me reach the bright day, the high chair, the plain desk, where my hand at last controls the words, where anxiety no longer undermines me. If I don't reach these I'm thrown to the wolves, I'm a restless animal wandering from place to place, from experience to experience.
>
> Give me the humility and the judgment to live alone with the deep and rich satisfaction of my own creating: not to be thrown into doubt by a word of spite or disapproval.
>
> In the last analysis don't mind whether your work is good or bad so long as it has completeness, the enormity of the whole world which you love.

Song

Inspiration and song are the irreducible final qualities of a poet which make his vocation different from all others. Inspiration is an experience in which a line or an idea is given to one, and perhaps also a state of mind in which one writes one's best poetry. Song is far more difficult to define. It is the music which a poem as yet unthought of will assume, the empty womb of poetry for ever in the poet's consciousness, waiting for the fertilizing seed.

Sometimes, when I lie in a state of half-waking half-sleeping, I am conscious of a stream of words which seem to pass through my mind, without their having a meaning, but they have a sound, a sound of passion, or a sound recalling poetry that I know. Again sometimes when I am writing, the music of the words I am trying to shape takes me far beyond the words, I am aware of a rhythm, a dance, a fury, which is as yet empty of words.

In these observations, I have said little about headaches, midnight oil, pints of beer or of claret, love affairs, and so on, which are supposed to be stations on the journeys of poets through life. There is no doubt that writing poetry, when a poem appears to succeed, results in an intense physical excitement, a sense of release and ecstasy. On the other hand, I dread writing poetry, for, I suppose, the following reasons: a poem is a terrible journey, a painful effort of concentrating the imagination; words are an extremely difficult medium to use, and sometimes when one has spent days trying to say a thing clearly one finds that one has only said it dully; above all, the writing of a poem brings one face to face with one's own personality with all its familiar and clumsy limitations. In every other phase of existence, one can exercise the orthodoxy of a conventional routine: one can be polite to one's friends, one can get through the day at the office, one can pose, one can draw attention to one's position in society, one is—in a word —dealing with men. In poetry, one is wrestling with a god.

Usually, when I have completed a poem, I think "this is my best poem," and I wish to publish it at once. This is partly because I only write when I have something new to say, which seems more worth while than what I have said before, partly because optimism about my present and future makes me despise my past. A few days after I have finished a poem, I relegate it to the past of all my other wasted efforts, all the books I do not wish to open.

Perhaps the greatest pleasure I have got from poems that I have written is when I have heard some lines quoted which I have not at once recognized. And I have thought "how good and how interesting," before I have realized that they are my own.

In common with other creative writers I pretend that I am not, and I am, exceedingly affected by unsympathetic criticism, whilst praise usually makes me suspect that the reviewer does not know what he is talking about. Why are writers so sensitive to criticism? Partly, because it is their business to be sensitive, and they are sensitive about this as about other things. Partly, because every serious creative writer is really in his heart concerned with reputation and not with success (the most successful writer I have known, Sir Hugh Walpole, was far and away the most unhappy about his reputation, because the "highbrows" did not like him). Again, I suspect that every writer is secretly writing for *someone*, probably for a parent or teacher who did not believe in him in childhood. The critic who refuses to "understand" immediately becomes identified with this person, and the understanding of many admirers only adds to the writer's secret bitterness if this one refusal persists.

Gradually one realizes that there is always this someone who will not like one's work. Then, perhaps, literature becomes a humble exercise of faith in being all that one can be in one's art, of being more than oneself, expecting little, but with a faith in the mystery of poetry which gradually expands into a faith in the mysterious service of truth.

Yet what failures there are! And how much mud sticks to one; mud not thrown by other people but acquired in the course of earning one's living, answering or not answering the letters which one receives, supporting or not supporting public causes. All one can hope is that this mud is composed of little grains of sand which will produce pearls.

Questions

Diction and Structure

1. Smith and Todes say their title, "The Point of Death," is intentionally ambiguous, that it is meant to suggest separate ways of thinking about death. Which meaning did you first take? Does that indicate something to you about your own attitudes toward death. What?

2. Death is a subject laden with emotion, as Smith and Todes admit. How does their diction control the inherent emotionalism of the topic?

3. Trace the development of the Smith and Todes essay. How are its separate sections related to each other? For what audience would you suppose this essay was written?

4. Julian Huxley's definition of *war* is crucial to his discussion of it as a biological manifestation. How does he define it? What

definitions does he reject? Is his final definition overly inclusive or exclusive?

5. Outline the stages of Huxley's essay. Does the section beginning "All of these considerations apply to war" (p. 187) alter the basic approach used in the earlier section? If so, how and why? What is the relationship of the concluding section (beginning on p. 189) to the first parts?

6. Look up these words: albeit, peregrine, myrmecologist, predation, parasitism, *laisser-faire*, polygamous, canalized. Could synonyms for any of these have been better used than the terms that Huxley does use? Explain.

7. Bruno Bettelheim is a psychiatrist, and his study of Joey is a case history. Is it intended for a professional audience? Justify your opinion.

8. Bettelheim uses the term "neologism" to describe Joey's speech. What does it mean? What examples of neologisms does Bettelheim give? What do they indicate, according to him?

9. Are the following terms used by Bettelheim medical ones or otherwise technical: megalomania, paraphernalia, ingestive apparatus, schizophrenic, autism (or autistic), pathological? Why does he use them?

10. Stephen Spender asserts that a poet is supremely sensitive to words and their connotations. Does his prose (not poetic specimens) strike you as unusual in any way; that is, in its imagery or phraseology or diction or sentence patterns? Would Spender himself assert that good poets must write good prose?

11. How do the various subsections ("Concentration," "Inspiration" . . . "Song") pertain to the central purpose of Spender's essay?

12. Point out instances where Spender deliberately uses repetition in order to emphasize, develop, or qualify his ideas.

13. Examine closely the changes Spender made in his poem (p. 201). Do you see how his mind was working as he went from version *a*) to version *h*)? Can you make any general observations about the kinds of changes his language was undergoing?

Style and Rhetoric

1. What central idea or assertion are the various references to the Balinese, Indians, Eskimos, and so forth used to develop in "The Point of Death"? Are these illustrations or examples?

2. Point out instances in which Smith and Todes rely on

comparison and contrast to give emphasis to their illustrative techniques.

3. Note the different definitions of "death" given in the essay. Which is the "true" or "real" definition? Can all of the definitions be "real"? Can they all be true though different? Why or why not?

4. Suggest the different ways that Huxley uses examples in his discussion of war as a biological phenomenon. Are his examples all of the same thesis, or of different but related theses?

5. Exactly what is Huxley explaining: animal behavior patterns, human behavior patterns, the correspondence between animal and human behavior, or none of these? Is he illustrating an established but intangible truth in this essay or is he trying to prove his own theory and thus establish it? Defend your answer.

6. Why does Huxley use the "we" or first person plural voice in his essay? Is it a device to interest and involve his reader, to establish some sense of a common cause between England and America, or does it have a deeper purpose?

7. Is Bettelheim's title "Joey: A 'Mechanical Boy'" a good indication of the contents of the essay to follow? Why is "Mechanical Boy" in quotation marks? Does the punctuation add to or detract from the interest of the title?

8. Consider some of the other titles of essays you have read in this collection. Which do you find particularly interesting and suggestive? What qualities do these share? What do you think makes an essay title a good one?

9. In the passages describing Joey's toilet habits, Bettelheim uses a number of euphemisms. (If you do not know what a euphemism is, find its meaning in the dictionary.) Are they necessary here? How does their use affect the essay as a whole?

10. Is Bettelheim concerned with explaining why Joey was autistic or does he simply want to illustrate the nature of autism? Support your answer by citing specific sections in the essay. Is illustration (or exemplification) used in the other essays in this section for the sake of telling *why* or only *how?*

11. What is the reason for Spender's "Apology" at the beginning of his "The Making of a Poem"? How does it illuminate the nature of illustration as a literary technique and point out its perils?

12. Is Spender illustrating a process, a state of mind, a system, the elements in a poem, or none of these? Is he illustrating one idea or a system of ideas? How are the various illustrations from his own experience related to each other?

13. Would Spender's essay qualify as an analysis as readily as an illustration? How does he use comparison and contrast? Does the Spender essay suggest anything to you about the differences or similarities between analysis and illustration?

Theme and Viewpoint

1. Compare Julian Huxley's ideas on intraspecific strife with Ian Stevenson's discussion of the nature of prejudice. Does Huxley confirm Stevenson's views? Would they agree about "canalizing" emotions?

2. Reread Thoreau's account of the battle of the ants. Does Thoreau provide further evidence to support Huxley's opinions about war as a biological phenomenon? Do Thoreau and Huxley share the same belief about the nature of human aggressiveness?

3. Does the behavior of cats, as their activities are described by Alan Devoe, confirm Huxley's views on intraspecific strife? Do cats wage war, by Huxley's definition of the term?

4. Compare Huxley's discussion of animal mating habits with Devoe's account of the cat's breeding (p. 117), Reik's discussion of love and lust (p. 102), and Porter's account of the mating of Negro slaves (p. 146). Do all of these authors think, like Huxley, that human behavior is analogous to animal behavior?

5. Compare and contrast the ways that Margaret Mead uses examples of diverse cultures to make her points in "New Year's —A Universal Birthday" and the ways Smith and Todes use the same device in "The Point of Death." Do you see any inherent reason for drawing on diverse cultures to deal with the subjects of "birth" and "death"?

6. Mead is an anthropologist; Smith and Todes are philosophers. Would you expect their interests to be different or not? Their literary techniques? Do Mead and Smith/Todes confirm or refute John Steele's assertions about the scientist and the humanist?

7. Is Bettelheim's interest in Joey purely "scientific"? Explain. What part does emotion play in the "science" of behavior?

8. How does Joey's verbal behavior, as Bettelheim describes it, illustrate Eric Fromm's theories of symbolic language? What does Joey's language symbolize?

9. Could Joey's autism be considered a way to meet stress on his part? What caused Joey's stress? If his mother refused even to fight with him, how could he have been under any stress?

10. Joey's mental condition is revealed in his thinking of himself as a machine, according to Bettelheim. In Kesey's story, the mental patient sees the head nurse as a mechanical being with machine-like parts. Do Bettelheim's explanations of a real mental case provide insight into the mind of the narrator of Kesey's sketch?

11. Several writers included in this collection have been concerned with the relationship between verbal ability, intelligence, and emotional adjustment. Compare the views on the relationship held by Lucas, Janeway, Reik, Kesey, Porter, and Bettelheim.

12. Does Spender agree with Graham Hough about the nature of poetry? Does he appear to agree with the views of Louis Ginsberg? Would Spender find Fromm's ideas on symbolic language useful in understanding how poetry functions?

13. If Spender is correct in his statements about poetry, what kinds of prose would most resemble poetry: definition, analysis, description, etc.? What kinds would least resemble it? Might poetry simply be certain kinds of prose put into meter?

14. By Spender's criteria, would Agee's description of Knoxville be a poem of sorts? Would Wolfe's "Cosmo's Tasmanian Deviltry"? Devoe's description of cats?

15. Spender uses Mozart and Beethoven to illustrate his idea of two kinds of genius. Is musical or poetic genius unlike logical or scientific genius? (Compare the views of Steele and Oppenheimer here.) Does Spender disagree with Steele about intuitive and logical genius as they are to be found in the poet and the scientist?

16. Would the views about individuality expressed by Smith and Todes be compatible with those of Kronenberger?

17. Several authors in this book deal with the death of animals and insects (Devoe, Thoreau) and others with human death (Porter, Williams, Roueché, Faulkner, Fletcher). Are the concluding opinions of Smith and Todes about attitudes toward death applicable to nonhuman death? Which of the depictions of human death indicate the author's agreement/disagreement with the view of death as a completion, the infinite fulfillment of a circle rounded off?

Demonstrating causality

Possibly the most commonly asked question is one of the briefest—"Why?" From the child's query, "Why is the sky blue?" to Albert Einstein's cosmic speculations about the velocity of light, the curiosity of Western people has taken the form of inquiring what causes the things we observe. The ancient Indo-European word from which *why* is derived meant the same thousands of years ago as the word *why* does today: for what reason, from what cause or motive. And the term that usually begins any answer to the question "Why?" again states the basic assumption that events or phenomena are related in a sequence or line of causality—"Because . . . " or "by cause or reason of." A major part of European and American thought rests upon the belief that everything has some causal explanation.

So dominant a concept has causality been that generations of philosophers formulated fundamental theories of the original or first causes of things: God, natural law, historical momentum, human nature. At one time, the First Cause of all the chains of effects in the universe was called the *Primum Mobile*, or First Mover; and it was supposed that everything could be traced back to it. In the present century, both philosophers and scientists place less stress on the idea of causation as universal and inevitable. Thinkers as diverse as David Hume and Marshall McLuhan have criticized the idea of a "logical" and "rational" pattern of causality as the explanation for all things; and many schools of thought, from skepticism to mysticism, have denied that events exist in a cause-and-effect relationship. Nevertheless, the human desire to form systematic explanations assures that causality will continue to be an important way of organizing ideas and presenting them in prose. Even those who wish to deny the "scientific" emphasis on causation often substitute a superstitious belief in its place: the horoscope that outlines the "influence" of the stars is as surely an instance of causal thinking as the domino theory of Communist warfare in Asia, the longstanding debate about whether the personality is determined by heredity or environment, or the Surgeon General's assertions about the link between cigarette smoking and lung cancer. All assume the validity of causality.

When writers deal with events or phenomena in terms of why they occur, they are demonstrating causality. They attempt to show the overt or covert relationship between some thing—an event, situation, condition, or some other phenomenon—and the factors that preceded it and presumably shaped it. At times the descriptive writer implicitly suggests why the subject is the way it is: for instance, a beautiful valley may be seen as the result of glacial erosion. Writing that characterizes may also suggest causation: Harry Truman's character was shaped by a strong-willed mother. In its most clearcut rhetorical form, however, causality is an explanation of why and how something came to be, to manifest itself in its specific way. The writer wishes to demonstrate an intrinsic relationship between phenomena in time, showing that one event or condition *follows* another necessarily through some operative law—of God, nature, human society, or psychological motivation. Thus Sir James Jeans explains the blue color of the sky as an instance of the laws governing physical and optical phenomena; Jeff Greenfield sees the songs of the Beatles as a popular expression of new cultural values; Jane Jacobs asserts that the physical plan of city streets results from certain wrong psychological assumptions that produce undesirable effects; and Victor Cline explains the outbreak of violence among the young in America as the result of overexposure to acts of criminal violence on television.

Obviously, identifying the causes for things we observe is not always possible. Some of the most ordinary phenomena can be described without our knowing precisely what causes them: hiccoughs, homosexuality, market surpluses, inflation, the aurora borealis—not even the "experts" can explain exactly what factors produce such effects. Causality is sometimes conjectural; the presumed cause for an observed situation is a *hypothesis*, and many cause-and-effect relationships are hypothetical. Indeed, it is extremely difficult to prove incontrovertibly that a given phenomenon will inevitably produce a given result. Our knowledge of variants is often too limited to enable us to assert positively that B will always follow A; David Hume insisted that the fact the sun has always risen on previous mornings does not prove it will rise tomorrow.

If causality is often hypothetical, nevertheless it proves accurate in enough instances to justify our confidence in it as an intellectual and rhetorical method. Only the most eccentric person would insist today that infantile paralysis is caused by evil spirits or a vengeful God or the child's disobeying the parents; nor would anyone reasonably deny that vaccines have the effect of preventing polio. There are hundreds of instances in which causal relationships are apparent. We need not go back to a theoretical *Primum Mobile* to find a causal explanation for air pollution, traffic-accident rates, gasoline taxes, and many other observable phenomena. Effects can be seen and their causes identified. In isolating the cause, we may be able to control the effect. In any case, causal explanation gives us a sense of meaning and order in events and thereby satisfies our innate desire to understand why things are the way we observe them to be.

Sir James Jeans

Why the Sky Looks Blue

Imagine that we stand on an ordinary seaside pier, and watch the waves rolling in and striking against the iron columns of the pier. Large waves pay very little attention to the columns—they divide right and left and re-unite after passing each column, much as a regiment of soldiers would if a tree stood in their road; it is almost as though the columns had not been there. But the short waves and ripples find the columns of the pier a much more formidable obstacle. When the short waves impinge on the columns, they are reflected back and spread as new ripples in all directions. To use the technical term, they are "scattered." The obstacle provided by the iron columns hardly affects the long waves at all, but scatters the short ripples.

We have been watching a sort of working model of the way in which sunlight struggles through the earth's atmosphere. Between us on earth and outer space the atmosphere interposes innumerable obstacles in the form of molecules of air, tiny droplets of water, and small particles of dust. These are represented by the columns of the pier.

The waves of the sea represent the sunlight. We know that sunlight is a blend of many colors—as we can prove for ourselves by passing it through a prism, or even through a jug of water, or as nature demonstrates to us when she passes it through the raindrops of a summer shower and produces a rainbow. We also know that light consists of waves, and that the different colors of light are produced by waves of different lengths, red light by long waves and blue light by short waves. The mixture of waves which constitutes sunlight has to struggle past the columns of the pier. And these obstacles treat the light waves much as the columns of the pier treat the sea-waves. The long waves which constitute red light are hardly affected but the short waves which constitute blue light are scattered in all directions.

WHY THE SKY LOOKS BLUE   From *The Stars in Their Courses* by Sir James Jeans. Reprinted by permission of Cambridge University Press, New York.

Thus the different constituents of sunlight are treated in different ways as they struggle through the earth's atmosphere. A wave of blue light may be scattered by a dust particle, and turned out of its course. After a time a second dust particle again turns it out of its course, and so on, until finally it enters our eyes by a path as zigzag as that of a flash of lightning. Consequently the blue waves of the sunlight enter our eyes from all directions. And that is why the sky looks blue.

Jeff Greenfield

The Beatles: They Changed Rock, Which Changed the Culture, Which Changed Us

They have not performed together on stage for more than eight years. They have not made a record together in five years. The formal dissolution of their partnership in a London courtroom last month was an echo of an ending that came long ago. Now each of them is seeking to overcome the shadow of a past in which they were bound together by wealth, fame and adulation of an intensity unequaled in our culture. George Harrison scorns talk of reunion, telling us to stop living in the past. John Lennon told us years ago that "the dream is over."

He was right: When the Beatles broke up in 1970 in a welter of lawsuits and recriminations, the sixties were ending as well—in spirit as well as by the calendar. Bloodshed and bombings on campus, the harsh realities beneath the facile hopes for a "Woodstock nation," the shabby refuse of counterculture communities, all helped kill the dream.

What remains remarkable now, almost 20 years after John Lennon started playing rock 'n' roll music, more than a decade after their first worldwide conquest, is how appealing this dream was; how its vision of the world gripped so much of a generation; how that dream reshaped our recent past and affects us still. What remains remarkable is how strongly this dream was triggered, nurtured and broadened by one rock 'n' roll band of four Englishmen whose entire history as a group occurred before any of them reached the age of 30.

Their very power guarantees that an excursion into analysis cannot fully succeed. Their songs, their films, their lives formed so great a part of what we listened to and watched and talked about that everyone affected by them still sees the Beatles and hears their songs through a personal prism. And the Beatles themselves never abandoned a sense of self-parody and put-on. They were, in Richard Goldstein's phrase, "the clown-gurus of the sixties." Lennon said more than once that the Beatles sometimes put elusive references into their songs just to confuse their more solemn interpreters. "I am the egg man," they sang, not "egghead."

Still, the impact of the Beatles cannot be waved away. If the Marx they emulated was Groucho, not Karl, if their world was a playground instead of a battleground, they still changed what we listened to and how we listened to it; they helped make rock music a battering ram for the youth culture's assault on the mainstream, and that assault in turn changed our culture permanently. And if the "dream" the Beatles helped create could not sustain itself in the real world, that speaks more to our false hopes than to their promises. They wrote and sang songs. We turned it into politics and philosophy and a road map to another way of life. The Beatles grew up as children of the first generation of rock 'n' roll, listening to and imitating the music of Little Richard, Larry Williams, Chuck Berry, Elvis Presley, and the later, more sophisticated sounds of the Shirelles and the Miracles. It was the special genius of their first mentor, Brian Epstein, to package four Liverpool working-class "rockers" as "mods," replacing their greasy hair, leather jackets, and on-stage vulgarity with jackets, ties, smiles and carefully groomed, distinctive haircuts. Just as white artists filtered and softened the raw energy of black artists in the nineteen-fifties, the Beatles at first were softer, safer versions of energetic rock 'n roll musicians. The words promised they only wanted to hold hands; the rhythm was more insistent.

By coming into prominence early in 1964, the Beatles probably saved rock 'n' roll from extinction. Rock in the early nineteen-sixties existed in name only; apart from the soul artists, it was a time of "shlock rock," with talentless media hypes like Fabian and Frankie Avalon riding the crest of the American Bandstand wave. By contrast, the Beatles provided a sense of musical energy that made successful a brilliant public-relations effort. Of course, the $50,000 used to promote the Beatles' first American appearance in February, 1964, fueled some of the early hysteria; so did the timing of their arrival.

Coming as it did less than a hundred days after the murder of John Kennedy, the advent of the Beatles caught America aching for any diversion to replace the images of a flag-draped casket and a riderless horse in the streets of Washington.

I remember a Sunday evening in early February, standing with hundreds of curious collegians in a University of Wisconsin dormitory, watching these four longhaired (!) Englishmen trying to be heard over the screams of Ed Sullivan's audience. Their music seemed to me then derivative, pleasant and bland, a mixture of hard rock and the sounds of the black groups then popular. I was convinced it would last six months, no more.

The Beatles, however, had more than hype; they had talent. Even their first hits, "I Want to Hold Your Hand," "She Loves You," "Please Please Me," "I Saw Her Standing There," had a hint of harmonies and melodies more inventive than standard rock tunes. More important, it became immediately clear that the Beatles were hipper, more complicated, than the bovine rock stars who could not seem to put four coherent words together.

In the spring of 1964, John Lennon published a book, "In His Own Write," which, instead of a ghost-written string of "groovy guides for keen teens," offered word plays, puns and black-humor satirical sketches. A few months later came the film "A Hard Day's Night," and in place of the classic let's-put-on-a-prom-and-invite-the-TeenChords plot of rock movies, the Beatles and director Richard Lester created a funny movie parodying the Beatles's own image.

I vividly recall going to that film in the midst of a National Student Association congress; at that time, rock 'n' roll was regarded as high-school nonsense by this solemn band of student-body presidents and future C.I.A. operatives. But after the film, I sensed a feeling of goodwill and camaraderie among that handful of rock fans who had watched this movie: The Beatles were media heroes without illusion, young men glorying in their sense of play and fun, laughing at the conventions of the world. They were worth listening to and admiring.

The real surprise came at the end of 1965, with the release of the "Rubber Soul" album. Starting with that album, and continuing through "Revolver" and "Sgt. Pepper's Lonely Hearts Club Band," the Beatles began to throw away the rigid conventions of rock 'n' roll music and lyrics. The banal abstract, second-hand emotions were replaced with sharp, sometimes mordant portraits of first-hand people and experiences, linked to music that was more complicated and more compelling than rock had ever dared attempt. The Beatles were drawing on their memories and feelings, not those cut from Tin Pan Alley cloth.

"Norwegian Wood" was about an unhappy, inconclusive affair ("I once had a girl/or should I say/she once had me"). "Michelle" and "Yesterday" were haunting, sentimental ballads, and Paul McCartney dared sing part of "Michelle" in French—most rock singers regarded English as a foreign language. "Penny Lane" used cornets to evoke the suggestion of a faintly heard band concert on a long-ago summer day. Staccato strings lent urgency to the story of "Eleanor Rigby."

These songs were different from the rock music that our elders had scorned with impunity. Traditionally, rock 'n' roll was rigidly structured: 4/4 tempo, 32 bars, with a limited range of instruments. Before the Beatles, rock producer Phil Spector had revolutionized records by adding strings to the drums, bass, sax and guitar, but the chord structure was usually limited to a basic blues or ballad pattern. Now the Beatles, with the kind of visibility that made them impossible to ignore, were expanding the range of rock, musically and lyrically. A sitar—a harpsichord effect—a ragtime piano—everything was possible.

With the release of "Sgt. Pepper" in the spring of 1967, the era of rock as a strictly adolescent phenomenon was gone. One song, "A Day in the Life," with its recital of an ordinary day combined with a dreamlike sense of dread and anxiety, made it impossible to ignore the skills of Lennon and McCartney. A decade earlier, Steve Allen mocked the inanity of rock by reading "Hound Dog" or "Tutti-Frutti" as if they were serious attempts at poetry. Once "Sgt. Pepper" was recorded, Partisan Review was lauding the Beatles, Ned Rorem proclaimed that "She's Leaving Home" was "equal to any song Schubert ever wrote," and a Newsweek critic meant it when he wrote: " 'Strawberry Fields Forever' [is] a superb Beatleizing of hope and despair in which the four minstrels regretfully recommend a Keatsian lotus-land of withdrawal from the centrifugal stresses of the age."

"We're so well established," McCartney had said in 1966, "that we can bring fans along with us and stretch the limits of pop." By using their fame to help break through the boundaries of rock, the Beatles proved that they were not the puppets of backstage manipulation or payola or hysterical 14-year-olds. Instead, they helped make rock music *the* music of an entire international generation. Perhaps for the first time in history, it was possible to say that tens of millions of people, defined simply by age, were all doing the same thing: they were listening to rock 'n' roll. That fact changed the popular culture of the world.

Rock 'n' roll's popularity had never been accompanied by respectability, even among the young. For those of us with intellectual pretenses, rock 'n' roll was like masturbation: exciting, but shameful. The culturally alienated went in for cool jazz, and folk music was the vehicle for the politically active minority. (The growth of political interest at the start of the sixties sparked something of a folk revival.)

Along with the leap of Bob Dylan into rock music, the Beatles destroyed this division. Rock 'n' roll was now broad enough, free enough, to encompass every kind of feeling. Its strength had always been rooted in the sexual energy of its rhythms; in that sense, the outraged parents who had seen rock as a threat to their children's virtue were right. Rock 'n' roll made you want to move and shake and get physically excited. The Beatles proved that this energy could be fused with a sensibility more subtle than the "let's-go-down-to-the-gym-and-beat-up-the-Coke-machine" quality of rock music.

In 1965, Barry McGuire recorded the first "rock protest" song (excluding the teen complaints of the Coasters and Chuck Berry). In his "Eve of Destruction," we heard references to Red China, Selma, Alabama, nuclear war and middle-class hypocrisy pounded out to heavy rock rhythms. That same year came a flood of "good time" rock music, with sweet, haunting melodies by groups like the Lovin' Spoonful and the Mamas and the Papas. There *were* no limits to what could be done; and the market was continually expanding.

The teen-agers of the nineteen-fifties had become the young adults of the nineteen-sixties, entering the professions, bringing with them a cultural frame of reference shaped in good measure by rock 'n' roll. The "youth" market was enormous—the flood of babies born during and just after World War II made the under-25 population group abnormally large; their tastes were more influential than ever before. And because the music had won acceptability, rock 'n' roll was not judged indulgently as a "boys will be boys" fad. Rock music was expressing a sensibility about the tangible world—about sensuality, about colors and sensations, about the need to change consciousness. And this sensibility soon spilled over into other arenas.

Looking back on the last half of the last decade, it is hard to think of a cultural innovation that did not carry with it the influence of rock music, and of the Beatles in particular: the miniskirt, discothèques, the graphics of Peter Max, the birth of publications like Rolling Stone, the "mind-bending" effects of TV commercials, the success of "Laugh-In" on television and "Easy Rider" in the movies—all of these cultural milestones owe something to the emergence of rock music as the most compelling and pervasive force in our culture.

This is especially true of the incredible spread of drugs—marijuana and the hallucinogens most particularly—among the youth culture. From

"Rubber Soul" through "Sgt. Pepper," Beatle music was suffused with a sense of mystery and mysticism: odd choral progressions, mysterious instruments, dreamlike effects, and images that did not seem to yield to "straight" interpretation. Whether specific songs ("Lucy in the Sky with Diamonds," "A Little Help From My Friends") were deliberately referring to drugs is beside the point. The Beatles were publicly recounting their LSD experiences, and their music was replete with antirational sensibility. Indeed, it was a commonplace among my contemporaries that Beatle albums could not be understood fully without the use of drugs. For "Rubber Soul," marijuana; for "Sgt. Pepper," acid. When the Beatles told us to turn off our minds and float downstream, uncounted youngsters assumed that the key to this kind of mind-expansion could be found in a plant or a pill. Together with "head" groups like Jefferson Airplane and the Grateful Dead, the Beatles were, consciously or not, a major influence behind the spread of drugs.

In this sense, the Beatles are part of a chain: (1) the Beatles opened up rock; (2) rock changed the culture; (3) the culture changed us. Even limited to their impact as musicians, however, the Beatles were as powerful an influence as any group or individual; only Bob Dylan stands as their equal. They never stayed with a successful formula; they were always moving. By virtue of their fame, the Beatles were a giant amplifier, spreading "the word" on virtually every trend and mood of the last decade.

They were never pure forerunners. The Yardbirds used the sitar before the Beatles; the Beach Boys were experimenting with studio enhancement first; the Four Seasons were using elaborate harmonies before the Beatles. They were never as contemptuously antimiddle-class or decadent as the Kinks or the Rolling Stones; never as lyrically compelling as Dylan; never as musically brilliant as the Band; never as hallucinogenic as the San Francisco groups. John Gabree, one of the most perceptive of the early rock writers, said that "their job, and they have done it well, has been to travel a few miles behind the avant-garde, consolidating gains and popularizing new ideas."

Yet this very willingness meant that new ideas did not struggle and die in obscurity; instead, they touched a hundred million minds. Their songs reflected the widest range of mood of any group of their time. Their openness created a kind of salon for a whole generation of people, an idea exchange into which the youth of the world was wired. It was almost inevitable that, even against their will, their listeners shaped a dream of politics and lifestyle from the substance of popular music. It is testament both to the power of rock music, and to the illusions which can be spun out of impulses.

The Beatles were not political animals. Whatever they have done since going their separate ways, their behavior as a group reflected cheerful anarchy more than political rebellion. Indeed, as editorialists, they were closer to The Wall Street Journal than to Ramparts. "Taxman" assaults the heavy progressive income tax ("one for you, 19 for me"), and "Revolution" warned that "if you go carrying pictures of Chairman Mao/you ain't gonna make it with anyone anyhow."

The real political impact of the Beatles was not in any four-point program or in an attack on injustice or the war in Vietnam. It was instead in the counterculture they had helped to create. Somewhere in the nineteen-sixties, millions of people began to regard themselves as a class separate from mainstream society *by virtue of their youth and the sensibility that youth produced.*

The nineteen-fifties had produced the faintest hint of such an attitude in the defensive love of rock 'n' roll; if our parents hated it, it had to be good. The sixties had expanded this vague idea into a battle cry. "Don't trust anyone over 30!"—shouted from a police car in the first massive student protest of the decade at Berkeley—suggested an outlook in which the mere aging process was an act of betrayal, in which youth itself was a moral value. Time magazine made the "under-25 generation" its Man of the Year in 1967, and politicians saw in the steadily escalating rebellion among the middle-class young a constituency and a scapegoat.

The core value of this "class" was not peace or social justice; it was instead a more elusive value, reflected by much of the music and by the Beatles' own portrait of themselves. It is expressed best by a scene from their movie "Help!" in which John, Paul, George and Ringo enter four adjoining row houses. The doors open—and suddenly the scene shifts inside, and we see that these "houses" are in fact one huge house; the four Beatles instantly reunite.

It is this sense of communality that was at the heart of the youth culture. It is what we wished to believe about the Beatles, and about the possibilities in our own lives. If there is one sweeping statement that makes sense about the children of the last decade, it is that the generation born of World War II was saying "no" to the atomized lives their parents had so feverishly sought. The most cherished value of the counterculture—preached if not always practiced—was its insistence on sharing, communality, a rejection of the retreat into private satisfaction. Rock 'n' roll was the magnet, the driving force, of a shared celebration, from Alan Freed's first mammoth dance parties in Cleveland in 1951, to the Avalon Ballroom in San Francisco, to the be-ins in our big cities, to Woodstock itself. Spontaneous gathering was the ethic: Don't plan it, don't think about it, *do* it—you'll get by with a little help from your friends.

In their music, their films, their sense of play, the Beatles reflected this dream of a ceaseless celebration. If there *was* any real "message" in their songs, it was the message of Charles Reich: that the world would be changed by changing the consciousness of the new generation. "All you need is love," they sang. "Say the word [love] and you'll be free." "Let it be." "Everything's gonna be all right."

As a state of mind, it was a pleasant fantasy. As a way of life, it was doomed to disaster. The thousands of young people who flocked to California or to New York's Lower East Side to join the love generation found the world filled with people who did not share the ethic of mutual trust. The politicization of youth as a class helped to divide natural political allies and make politics more vulnerable to demagogues. As the Beatles found in their own personal and professional lives, the practical outside world has a merciless habit of intruding into fantasies; somebody has to pay the bills and somebody has to do the dishes in the commune and somebody has to protect us from the worst instincts of other human beings. John Lennon was expressing some very painful lessons when he told Rolling Stone shortly after the group's breakup that "nothing happened except we all dressed up . . . the same bastards are in control, the same people are runnin' everything."

He was also being unfair. If the counterculture was too shallow to understand how the world does get changed, the forces that were set loose in the nineteen-sixties have had a permanent effect. The sensuality that rock 'n' roll tapped will never again be bottled up. The vestiges of the communal dream have changed the nature of friendships and life-styles and marriages, in large measure for the better. And with the coming of harder economic times, the idea of abandoning private retreat for shared pleasures and burdens has a direct contemporary practicality.

For me, the final irony is that the Beatles themselves have unconsciously proven the value of communality. As a group, they seemed to hold each other back from excess: McCartney was lyrical, but not saccharine; Lennon was rebellious but not offensive; Harrison's mysticism was disciplined (Ringo was always Ringo, drummer and friend). Now, the sense of control seems to have loosened. Paul and Linda McCartney seem tempted by the chance to become the Steve and Eydie of rock; Lennon is still struggling to free himself from a Fad of the Month mentality; George Harrison's Gospel According to Krishna succeeded in boring much of his audience on his recent concert tour. Perhaps the idea they did so much to spread several years ago is not as dead as all that; perhaps we all need a little help from our friends. The enduring power of that idea is as permanent as any impact their music had on us, even if they no longer believe it.

Jane Jacobs

What Makes City Streets Unsafe?

This is something everyone already knows: A well-used city street is apt to be a safe street. A deserted city street is apt to be unsafe. But how does this work, really? And what makes a city street well used or shunned? Why is the sidewalk mall in Washington Houses,* which is supposed to be an attraction, shunned? Why are the sidewalks of the old city just to its west not shunned? What about streets that are busy part of the time and then empty abruptly?

A city street equipped to handle strangers, and to make a safety asset, in itself, out of the presence of strangers, as the streets of successful city neighborhoods always do, must have three main qualities:

First, there must be a clear demarcation between what is public space and what is private space. Public and private spaces cannot ooze into each other as they do typically in suburban settings or in projects.

Second, there must be eyes upon the street, eyes belonging to those we might call the natural proprietors of the street. The buildings on a street equipped to handle strangers and to insure the safety of both residents and strangers, must be oriented to the street. They cannot turn their backs or blank sides on it and leave it blind.

And third, the sidewalk must have users on it fairly continuously, both to add to the number of effective eyes on the street and to induce the people in buildings along the street to watch the sidewalks in sufficient numbers. Nobody enjoys sitting on a stoop or looking out a window at an empty street. Almost nobody does such a thing. Large numbers of people entertain themselves, off and on, by watching street activity.

In settlements that are smaller and simpler than big cities, controls on

WHAT MAKES CITY STREETS UNSAFE? From *The Death and Life of Great American Cities,* by Jane Jacobs. Copyright © 1961 by Jane Jacobs. Reprinted by permission of Random House, Inc.
* A public housing project in New York. [editor's note]

acceptable public behavior, if not on crime, seem to operate with greater or lesser success through a web of reputation, gossip, approval, disapproval and sanctions, all of which are powerful if people know each other and word travels. But a city's streets, which must control not only the behavior of the people of the city but also of visitors from suburbs and towns who want to have a big time away from the gossip and sanctions at home, have to operate by more direct, straightforward methods. It is a wonder cities have solved such an inherently difficult problem at all. And yet in many streets they do it magnificently.

It is futile to try to evade the issue of unsafe city streets by attempting to make some other features of a locality, say interior courtyards, or sheltered play spaces, safe instead. By definition again, the streets of a city must do most of the job of handling strangers for this is where strangers come and go. The streets must not only defend the city against predatory strangers; they must protect the many, many peaceable and well-meaning strangers who use them, insuring their safety too as they pass through. Moreover, no normal person can spend his life in some artificial haven, and this includes children. Everyone must use the streets.

On the surface, we seem to have here some simple aims: To try to secure streets where the public space is unequivocally public, physically unmixed with private or with nothing-at-all space, so that the area needing surveillance has clear and practicable limits; and to see that these public street spaces have eyes on them as continuously as possible.

But it is not so simple to achieve these objects, especially the latter. You can't make people use streets they have no reason to use. You can't make people watch streets they do not want to watch. Safety on the streets by surveillance and mutual policing of one another sounds grim, but in real life it is not grim. The safety of the street works best, most casually, and with least frequent taint of hostility or suspicion precisely where people are using and most enjoying the city streets voluntarily and are least conscious, normally, that they are policing.

The basic requisite for such surveillance is a substantial quantity of stores and other public places sprinkled along the sidewalks of a district; enterprises and public places that are used by evening and night must be among them especially. Stores, bars and restaurants, as the chief examples, work in several different and complex ways to abet sidewalk safety.

First, they give people—both residents and strangers—concrete reasons for using the sidewalks on which these enterprises face.

Second, they draw people along the sidewalks past places which have no attractions to public use in themselves but which become traveled and peopled as routes to somewhere else; this influence does not carry very far geographically, so enterprises must be frequent in a city district if they are to populate with walkers those other stretches of street that lack public places along the sidewalk. Moreover, there should be many different kinds of enterprises, to give people reasons for crisscrossing paths.

Third, storekeepers and other small businessmen are typically strong proponents of peace and order themselves; they hate broken windows and holdups; they hate having customers made nervous about safety. They are great street watchers and sidewalk guardians if present in sufficient numbers.

Fourth, the activity generated by people on errands, or people aiming for food or drink, is itself an attraction to still other people.

This last point, that the sight of people attracts still other people, is something that city planners and city architectural designers seem to find incomprehensible. They operate on the premise that city people seek the sight of emptiness, obvious order and quiet. Nothing could be less true. People's love of watching activity and other people is constantly evident in cities everywhere. This trait reaches an almost ludicrous extreme on upper Broadway in New York, where the street is divided by a narrow central mall, right in the middle of traffic. At the cross-street intersections of this long north-south mall, benches have been placed behind big concrete buffers and on any day when the weather is even barely tolerable these benches are filled with people at block after block after block, watching the pedestrians who cross the mall in front of them, watching the traffic, watching the people on the busy sidewalks, watching each other. Eventually Broadway reaches Columbia University and Barnard College, one to the right, the other to the left. Here all is obvious order and quiet. No more stores, no more activity generated by the stores, almost no more pedestrians crossing—and no more watchers. The benches are there but they go empty in even the finest weather. I have tried them and can see why. No place could be more boring. Even the students of these institutions shun the solitude. They are doing their outdoor loitering, outdoor homework and general street watching on the steps overlooking the busiest campus crossing.

It is just so on city streets elsewhere. A lively street always has both its users and pure watchers. Last year I was on such a street in the Lower East Side of Manhattan, waiting for a bus. I had not been there longer than a minute, barely long enough to begin taking in the street's activity of errand goers, children playing, and loiterers on the stoops, when my attention was attracted by a woman who opened a window on the third floor of a tenement across the street and vigorously yoo-hooed at me. When I caught on that she wanted my attention and responded, she shouted down, "The bus doesn't run here on Saturdays!" Then by a combination of shouts and pantomime she directed me around the corner. This woman was one of thousands upon thousands of people in New York who casually take care of the streets. They notice strangers. They observe everything going on. If they need to take action, whether to direct a stranger waiting in the wrong place or to call the police, they do so. Action usually requires, to be sure, a certain self-assurance about the actor's proprietorship of the street and the support he will get if necessary. But even more fundamental than the action and necessary to the action, is the watching itself.

Not everyone in cities helps to take care of the streets, and many a city resident or city worker is unaware of why his neighborhood is safe. The other day an incident occurred on the street where I live, and it interested me because of this point.

My block of the street, I must explain, is a small one, but it contains a remarkable range of buildings, varying from several vintages of tenements to three- and four-story houses that have been converted into low-rent flats with stores on the ground floor, or returned to single-family use like ours. Across the street there used to be mostly four-story brick tenements with stores below. But twelve years ago several buildings, from the corner to the middle of the block, were converted into one building with elevator apartments of small size and high rents.

The incident that attracted my attention was a suppressed struggle going on between a man and a little girl of eight or nine years old. The man seemed to be trying to get the girl to go with him. By turns he was directing a cajoling attention to her, and then assuming an air of nonchalance. The girl was making herself rigid, as children do when they resist, against the wall of one of the tenements across the street.

As I watched from our second-floor window, making up my mind how to intervene if it seemed advisable, I saw it was not going to be necessary. From the butcher shop beneath the tenement had emerged the woman who, with her husband, runs the shop; she was standing within earshot of the man, her arms folded and a look of determination on her face. Joe Cornacchia, who with his sons-in-law keeps the delicatessen, emerged about the same moment and stood solidly to the other side. Several heads poked out of the tenement windows above, one was withdrawn quickly and its owner reappeared a moment later in the doorway behind the man. Two men from the bar next to the butcher shop came to the doorway and waited. On my side of the street, I saw that the locksmith, the fruit man and the laundry proprietor had all come out of their shops and that the scene was also being surveyed from a number of windows besides ours. That man did not know it, but he was surrounded. Nobody was going to allow a little girl to be dragged off, even if nobody knew who she was.

I am sorry—sorry purely for dramatic purposes—to have to report that the little girl turned out to be the man's daughter.

Throughout the duration of the little drama, perhaps five minutes in all, no eyes appeared in the windows of the high-rent, small-apartment building. It was the only building of which this was true. When we first moved to our block, I used to anticipate happily that perhaps soon all the buildings would be rehabilitated like that one. I know better now, and can only anticipate with gloom and foreboding the recent news that exactly this transformation is scheduled for the rest of the block frontage adjoining the high-rent building. The high-rent tenants, most of whom are so transient we cannot even keep track of their faces,[1] have not the remotest idea of who takes care of their street, or how. A city neighborhood can absorb and protect a substantial number of these birds of passage, as our neighborhood does. But if and when the neighborhood finally *becomes* them, they will gradually find the streets less secure, they will be vaguely mystified about it, and if things get bad enough they will drift away to another neighborhood which is mysteriously safer.

In some rich city neighborhoods, where there is little do-it-yourself surveillance, such as residential Park Avenue or upper Fifth Avenue in New York, street watchers are hired. The monotonous sidewalks of residential Park Avenue, for example, are surprisingly little used; their putative users are populating, instead, the interesting store-, bar- and restaurant-filled sidewalks of Lexington Avenue and Madison Avenue to east and west, and the cross streets leading to these. A network of doormen and superintendents, of delivery boys and nursemaids, a form of hired neighborhood, keeps residential Park Avenue supplied with eyes. At night, with the security of the doormen as a bulwark, dog walkers safely venture forth and supplement the doormen. But this street is so blank of built-in eyes, so devoid of concrete reasons for using or watching it instead of turning the first corner off of it, that if its rents were to slip below the point where they could support a plentiful hired neighborhood of doormen and elevator men, it would undoubtedly become a woefully dangerous street.

Once a street is well equipped to handle strangers, once it has both a good, effective demarcation between private and public spaces and has a basic supply of activity and eyes, the more strangers the merrier.

Strangers become an enormous asset on the street on which I live, and the spurs off it, particularly at night when safety assets are most needed. We are fortunate enough, on the street, to be gifted not only with a locally supported bar and another around the corner, but also with a famous bar that draws continuous troops of strangers from adjoining neighborhoods and even from out of town. It is famous because the poet

---

[1] Some, according to the storekeepers, live on beans and bread and spend their sojourn looking for a place to live where all their money will not go for rent.

Dylan Thomas used to go there, and mentioned it in his writing. This bar, indeed, works two distinct shifts. In the morning and early afternoon it is a social gathering place for the old community of Irish longshoremen and other craftsmen in the area, as it always was. But beginning in midafternoon it takes on a different life, more like a college bull session with beer, combined with a literary cocktail party, and this continues until the early hours of the morning. On a cold winter's night, as you pass the White Horse, and the doors open, a solid wave of conversation and animation surges out and hits you; very warming. The comings and goings from this bar do much to keep our street reasonably populated until three in the morning, and it is a street always safe to come home to. The only instance I know of a beating in our street occurred in the dead hours between the closing of the bar and dawn. The beating was halted by one of our neighbors who saw it from his window and, unconsciously certain that even at night he was part of a web of strong street law and order, intervened.

A friend of mine lives on a street uptown where a church youth and community center, with many night dances and other activities, performs the same service for his street that the White Horse bar does for ours. Orthodox planning is much imbued with puritanical and Utopian conceptions of how people should spend their free time, and in planning, these moralisms on people's private lives are deeply confused with concepts about the workings of cities. In maintaining city street civilization, the White Horse bar and the church-sponsored youth center, different as they undoubtedly are, perform much the same public street civilizing service. There is not only room in cities for such differences and many more in taste, purpose and interest of occupation; cities also have a need for people with all these differences in taste and proclivity. The preferences of Utopians, and of other compulsive managers of other people's leisure, for one kind of legal enterprise over others is worse than irrelevant for cities. It is harmful. The greater and more plentiful the range of all legitimate interests (in the strictly legal sense) that city streets and their enterprises can satisfy, the better for the streets and for the safety and civilization of the city.

Victor B. Cline

How TV Violence Damages Your Children

ITEM: Shortly after a Boston TV station showed a movie depicting a group of youths dousing a derelict with gasoline and setting him afire for "kicks," a woman was burned to death in that city—turned into a human torch under almost identical circumstances.

ITEM: Several months ago, NBC-TV presented in early-evening, prime viewing time a made-for-TV film, *Born Innocent*, which showed in explicit fashion the sexual violation of a young girl with a broom handle wielded by female inmates in a juvenile detention home. Later a California mother sued NBC and San Francisco TV station KRON for $11,000,000, charging that this show had inspired three girls, ages 10 to 15, to commit a similar attack on her 9-year-old daughter and an 8-year-old friend three days after the film was aired.

ITEM: A 14-year-old boy, after watching rock star Alice Cooper engage in a mock hanging on TV, attempted to reproduce the stunt and killed himself in the process.

ITEM: Another boy laced the family dinner with ground glass after seeing it done on a television crime show.

ITEM: A British youngster died while imitating his TV hero, Batman. The boy was hanged while leaping from a cabinet in a garden shed. His neck became caught in a nylon loop hanging from the roof. His father blamed the TV show for his death—and for encouraging children to attempt the impossible.

These are just a sampling of many well-documented instances of how TV violence can cause antisocial behavior—instances that are proving that TV violence is hazardous to your child's health.

TV broadcasters can no longer plead that they are unaware of the potential adverse effects of such programs as *Born Innocent*. During the last decade, two national violence commissions and an overwhelming number of scientific studies have continually come to one conclusion: televised and filmed violence can powerfully teach, suggest—even legitimatize—extreme antisocial behavior, and can in some viewers trigger specific aggressive or violent behavior. The research of many behavioral scientists has shown that a definite cause-effect relationship exists between violence on TV and violent behavior in real life.

When U.S. Surgeon General Jesse Steinfeld appeared before the U.S. Senate subcommittee reviewing two years of scientific research on the issue, he bluntly concluded, "The overwhelming consensus and the unanimous Scientific Advisory Committee's report indicate that televised violence, indeed, does have an adverse effect on certain members of our society. . . . It is clear to me that the causal relationship between televised violence and antisocial behavior is sufficient to warrant appropriate and immediate remedial action. . . . There comes a time when the data are sufficient to justify action. That time has come."

The Federal Communications Commission was ordered by Congress to come up with a report by Dec. 31, 1974, on how children can be protected from televised violence (and sex). Hopefully, some concrete proposals will develop.

The television moguls have repeatedly paraded before various Congressional subcommittees over the last ten years, solemnly promising to reduce the overall amount of violence programmed, especially in time slots that had large numbers of child viewers. However, if we look at the data compiled throughout the 1960's and early 1970's, we find very little change in the average number of violent episodes per program broadcast by all three networks. In one study, the staff of U.S. Congressman John M. Murphy of New York found NBC leading the pack with violent sequences in 71 percent of its prime-time shows, followed by ABC with 67 percent and CBS with 57 percent.

With more and more mega-violent films coming to TV from the commercial theater market, as well as the increasing violence injected into made-for-TV movies, we find that the promise of television has been shamelessly ignored. In too many TV films, we see a glorification of violence that makes heroes of killers. The primary motivation for all of this is money and the fierce scramble for ratings. Thus the television industry's "repentance" for past wrongs, occurring after major national tragedies such as the assassination of the Kennedy brothers and Martin Luther King, Jr., with the transient public outrage and demand for change, has been all ritual with little substance.

We are a great free society with the power to shape our destiny and create almost any social-cultural environment we wish, but as the late

President John F. Kennedy put it, "We have the power to make this the best generation in the history of mankind, or the last." If one looks at crime statistics, we find that we are by far the most violent of all the great Western nations. Our homicide rate is about ten times greater than, say, the Scandinavian countries', or four times greater than Scotland's or Australia's. There are more murders per year on the island of Manhattan or in the city of Philadelphia than in the entire United Kingdom, with its nearly 60,000,000 people. Violent crime has been increasing at six to 10 times the rate of population growth in this country. And interestingly, if one analyzes the content of TV programs in England, we find that their rate of televised violence is half that of ours; in the Scandinavian countries it is much less even than that.

Thus one of the major social-cultural differences between the United States with its high homicide and violence rates and those countries with low violence rates is the amount of violence screened on public television.

"Monkey see, monkey do"

Much of the research that has led to the conclusion that TV and movie violence could cause aggressive behavior in some children has stemmed from work in the area of imitative learning or modeling which, reduced to its simplest expression might be termed, "monkey see, monkey do." Research by Stanford psychologist Albert Bandura has shown that even brief exposure to novel aggressive behavior *on a one-time basis* can be repeated in free play by as high as 88 percent of the young children seeing it on TV. Dr. Bandura also demonstrated that even a single viewing of a novel aggressive act could be recalled and produced by children six months later, without any intervening exposure. Earlier studies have estimated that the average child between the ages of five and 15 will witness, during this 10-year period, the violent destruction of more than 13,400 fellow humans. This means that through several hours of TV-watching, a child may see more violence than the average adult experiences in a lifetime. Killing is as common as taking a walk, a gun more natural than an umbrella. Children are thus taught to take pride in force and violence and to feel ashamed of ordinary sympathy.

According to the Nielsen Television Index, preschoolers watch television an average of 54 hours a week. During one year, children of school age spend more time in front of a TV set than they do in front of a teacher; in fact, they spend more time watching TV than any other type of waking activity in their lives.

So we might legitimately ask, What are the major lessons, values and attitudes that television teaches our children? Content analyses of large numbers of programs broadcast during children's viewing hours suggest that the major message taught in TV entertainment is that violence is the way to get what you want.

Who are the "good guys"?

Another major theme that many TV studies have shown to occur repeatedly is that violence is acceptable if the victim "deserved" it. This, of course, is a very dangerous and insidious philosophy. It suggests that aggression, while reprehensible in criminals, is acceptable for the "good guys" who have right on their side. But, of course, nearly every person feels that he or she is "right." And often the "good guys" are criminals whom the film happens to depict sympathetically, as in *The Godfather*. Who is "good" and who is "bad" merely depends on whose side you're on.

Studies by McLeod and Associates of boys and girls in junior and senior high school found that the more the youngster watched violent television fare, the more aggressive he or she was likely to be. Other studies revealed that the amount of television violence watched by children (especially boys) at age 9 influenced the degree to which they were aggressive 10 years later, at age 19.

The problem becomes increasingly serious because, even if your child is not exposed to a lot of media violence, the youngster still could become the *victim or target* of aggression by a child who is stimulated by the violence that he or she sees on TV.

And criminals are too frequently shown on TV as daring heroes. In the eyes of many young viewers, these criminals possess all that's worth having in life—fast cars, beautiful, admiring women, super-potent guns, modish clothes, etc. In the end they die like heroes—almost as martyrs—but then only to appease the "old folks" who insist on "crime-does-not-pay" endings.

The argument that you can't get high ratings for your show unless it is hyped up with violence is, of course, not true—as 20 years of *I Love Lucy* and, more recently, *All in the Family, Sanford & Sons, The Waltons* and scores of other shows have demonstrated. Action shows featuring themes of human conflict frequently have appeal, yet even they needn't pander to the antisocial side of man's nature or legitimatize evil.

The hard scientific evidence clearly demonstrates that watching television violence, sometimes for only a few hours, and in some studies even for a few minutes, can and often does instigate aggressive behavior that would not otherwise occur. If only 1 percent of the possibly 40,000,000 people who saw *The Godfather* on TV were stimulated to commit an aggressive act, this would involve 400,000 people. Or if it were only one in 10,000, it would involve 4,000 people—plus their victims.

Some parents believe that if their children are suitably loved, properly brought up and emotionally well-balanced, they will not be affected by TV violence. However, psychiatrist Fredric Wertham responds to this by noting that all children are impressionable and therefore susceptible. We flatter ourselves if we think that our social conditions, our family life, our education and our entertainment are so far above reproach that only emotionally sick children can get into trouble. As Dr. Wertham points out, if we believe that harm can come only to the predisposed child, this leads to a contradictory and irresponsible attitude on the part of adults. Constructive TV programs are praised for giving children constructive ideas, but we deny that destructive scenes give children destructive ideas.

It should also be noted that the "catharsis theory" in vogue a few years ago, which suggested that seeing violence is good for children because it allows them vicariously to discharge their hostile feelings, has been convincingly discarded. Just the opposite has been found to be true. Seeing violence stimulates children aggressively; it also shows them how to commit aggressive acts.

The author of this article has conducted research studying the "desensitization" of children to TV violence and its potential effects.

In our University of Utah laboratories, we set up two six-channel physiographs which had the capacity to measure emotional responsiveness in children while they watched violent TV shows. When most of our subjects saw violent films, those instruments measuring heart action, respiration, perspiration, etc., all hooked up to the autonomic nervous system, did indeed record strong emotional arousal. We studied 120 boys between the ages of 5 and 14. Half had seen little or no TV in the previous two years (hence had seen little media violence), and the other half had seen an average of 42 hours of TV a week for the past two years (hence a lot of violence). As our violent film, we chose an eight-minute sequence from the Kirk Douglas prizefighting film, *The Champion*, which had been shown many times on TV reruns but which none of the boys tested had ever seen. We considered other, more violent films, but they were too brutal, we felt, to be shown to children—even for experimental purposes. The boxing match seemed like a good compromise. Nobody was killed or seriously injured. Nothing illegal occurred. Yet the fight did depict very graphically human aggression that was emotionally arousing.

These two groups of boys watched our film while we recorded their emotional responses on the physiograph. The results showed that the boys with a history of heavy violence watching were significantly less aroused emotionally by what they saw—they had become habituated or "desensitized" to violence. To put it another way, our findings suggested that the heavy TV watchers appeared to be somewhat desensitized or "turned off" to violence, suggesting the possibility of an emotional blunting or less "conscience and concern" in the presence of witnessed violence. This means that they had developed a tolerance for it, and possibly an indifference toward human life and suffering. They were no longer shocked or horrified by it. It suggested to us the many instances of "bystander apathy," in which citizens in large urban areas have witnessed others being assaulted, yet did not come to their rescue or try to secure aid or help. Or incidents such as the My Lai massacre, in which American soldiers killed Vietnamese civilians. This suggests an unfeeling, indifferent, noncaring, dehumanized response to suffering or distress.

In any event, our research has presented the first empirical evidence that children who are exposed to a lot of TV violence do to some extent become blunted emotionally or desensitized to it.

Since our children are an important national resource, these findings suggest that we should teach them wisely. The kinds of fantasies to which we expose them may make a great deal of difference as to what kind of adults they become, and whether we will survive as a society.

The author, who is a psychotherapist and who treats many damaged children and families, was then faced with the problem of what to do about his own TV set and his own children, who regularly watched TV and had their favorite programs. The evidence had been stacking up in my laboratory—so what should I do about it at home? The thing that finally turned me from being the permissive, tolerant, "good-guy" dad to the concerned parent was the realization that whenever my children looked at TV for any lengthy period, especially violent action shows, they became frequently touchy, cross and irritable. Instead of playing outside, even on beautiful days, discharging tensions in healthy interaction with others, they sat passive for hours, too often hypnotized by whatever appeared on the tube. Frequently, homework didn't get done, chores were neglected, etc. One Saturday morning I was shocked to find my bright, 15-year-old son watching cartoons for four straight hours, having let all chores and other responsibilities go. It was then that we finally decided to turn off the TV set on a relatively permanent basis.

"No TV" is a turn-on

When we announced this decision, we found ourselves faced with a family revolt. There was much wailing and gnashing of teeth. It was as if the alcoholic had been deprived of his bottle, or as if we had suddenly announced that no more food would be served at our table.

However, the "storm" lasted only one week. Interestingly, during that week, the children went outside and played with each other and the neighbors much more, a lot more good books got read, homework was done on time, chores got finished, and the children got along with each other better. And very interestingly, the complaints about "no TV" suddenly stopped at the end of that week. Now, several years later, we do occasionally look at TV—some sports specials, a good movie, something required for school, even a mystery. But it's almost never on school nights —and it is no longer an issue in our home. Nobody feels deprived. It's now just not a major part of our lifestyle.

It should be stated, in all fairness, that television has the potential for great good—to teach children pro-social values and behavior, such as sharing with others, controlling one's impulses, solving problems through reason and discussion, being kind and thoughtful. Such programs as *The Waltons* suggest to me that such content can have wide popular appeal and be commercially marketable—if done with talent, care and commitment. In other words, television could be used for far more constructive programming than we have seen in the past. For the time being, parents should, in my judgment, be very cautious about what they expose their children to on television (as well as in movies). If something particularly objectionable is broadcast during children's prime-time hours, there are three things that can be done: 1) turn the television set off; 2) phone your local station expressing your concern; 3) write to the program's sponsor, indicating your objections (the firm's address will be found on the label of his merchandise).

The evidence is clear: a child's mind can be polluted and corrupted just as easily as his body can be poisoned by contaminants in the environment. Children are essentially powerless to deal with such problems. This means that the responsibility for effecting change rests with every adult citizen. Meaning you. Meaning me. Meaning us.

Questions

Diction and Structure

1. Look up the meaning of *analogy*. How is it related to illustration? How do they differ? Why is the use of analogy necessary in Jeans's "Why the Sky Looks Blue"?

2. Does Jeans ever define "blue"? Does he need to give a specific definition, granting the defined limits of his topic? Explain.

3. Why does Jeans use the first person plural point of view in his essay? Who is the "we" referred to by the author?

4. Jeff Greenfield uses some italicized statements in his essay on the Beatles. What is their purpose? Does it succeed?

5. Someone writing about rock music might be expected to use "rock language": the jargon or slang or "in" phrases of the rock community. Does Greenfield do this? Why or why not?

6. Make an outline of the chief points in Greenfield's essay. Does each point lead logically and inevitably to the next? Are the points presented in a logical sequence or merely a chronological sequence? How does this affect the essay?

7. Why does Jane Jacobs begin her discussion with a series of rhetorical questions? Are her questions about a specific area in New York City really questions about broader problems and conditions? Does she answer her own queries in the rest of the essay?

8. Jacobs's essay opens with an assumption in the first sentence. Is the assumption ever substantiated by further evidence or does it stand as self-evident: "This is something everyone already knows . . ."?

9. How does Jacobs organize her essay? Is it naturally divided into related sections or is the entire piece concerned with one central topic despite the many opening questions? How does the numbering of individual points (on pp. 229–30) affect the development of the essay?

10. Cline's essay on T.V. violence begins with a series of "facts" identified as "items." For what reason? How does the list of facts indicate the direction of the rest of the article?

11. How does the section of Cline's essay describing the conduct of his own children relate to the other sections? It is a digression? A repetition? A comparison and contrast with the other sections? Is it necessary?

12. Notice Cline's use of statistics and figures. How are these connected to the "items" and the personal anecdotes?

Style and Rhetoric

1. Jeans's explanation of why the sky looks blue is very brief as it stands; could it be made even more brief, say only a few sentences? What is lost in the condensation?

2. How does Jeans use the rhetorical technique of illustration to

develop his causal explanation? Do the other essayists rely on illustration or examples in demonstrating causality?

3. Is Jeans showing one cause and one effect? Several causes and several effects? A series of causes and effects? Explain.

4. What kind of cause does Jeans show in operation: physical or mental or both? Is his basic purpose to explain how our senses perceive something by showing a process of matter in motion?

5. Jeff Greenfield lists (and numbers) the steps in the causal sequence he believes led to the Beatles's changing contemporary culture. Which parts of the essay substantiate each of the three points? Does Greenfield "prove" each point?

6. Greenfield says the Beatles themselves were "influenced" by Brian Epstein and the music of other groups. Why did Greenfield choose the Beatles as the "first" cause and not Epstein or some other influence on the Beatles? What determines an essayist's choice of a "first" cause when demonstrating causality?

7. According to Greenfield, the Beatles changed marriage styles, manners, dress, motion pictures, and the entire national consciousness. Does he give evidence to support these assertions? Upon what body of personal experience do most of Greenfield's "effects" depend? Are they adequate or not?

8. Is there any real way of testing the validity of Greenfield's claims? Is he really expounding an hypothesis? Is the hypothesis a credible one?

9. Jane Jacobs provides two sets of causation: the factors that result in "safe" streets and those that cause "unsafe" streets. How are these related?

10. Jacobs's list of "musts" for safety (p. 228) are given as causes. How are the examples given later in the essay (of the episode involving the man and little girl, the bus stop, the White Horse bar) connected with this list?

11. How does Victor Cline define "violence"? Is the definition important or not? How significant is precise definition in demonstrating causality? (Note the word "changed" in Greenfield's essay. Is it a key word? Is its meaning clear?)

12. Do Cline's opening "items" plainly show that the crimes were the result of watching T.V.? Could they have been caused by other factors than T.V.? Such as what? Are the probable or possible "causes" you suggested really more likely than Cline's thesis about T.V.?

13. Judging from the essays included here, can any cause and effect sequence be considered anything more than a "probable" hypothesis? Discuss.

Theme and Viewpoint

1. Sir James Jeans, like Einstein, was one of the best known physicists in the early half of the twentieth century; however, unlike Einstein, Jeans attempted to "popularize" physics by writing explanations of the kind given above. Would John Steele ("The Fiction of Science," p. 64) approve of Jeans's efforts to close the gap between the scientist and the nonscientist by writing in this manner? Would Oppenheimer approve of efforts to "popularize" highly complex physical theories? Explain your answers.

2. Compare Jeans's purpose and technique in popularizing physics with Julian Huxley's purpose and technique in his essay on biological factors in warfare. Does one seek more than the other to argue and persuade? Which appears more interested in explaining? Can science be used to "prove" arguments about moral questions?

3. Selye, Oppenheimer, Huxley, Bettelheim, and Jeans are all "scientists" of varying persuasions. Do their essays indicate any common approach or assumptions or techniques of investigation that may be classed as "scientific"? How important is causation in each of their essays?

4. The nature and cause of violence has been dealt with directly or indirectly in at least seven of the earlier selections in this book. Does Victor Cline agree with the other writers about what violence is? Would any of them agree in his belief that juvenile violence can be controlled by curtailing T.V. watching?

5. Cline and Sedulus are much concerned with the effects of T.V. on American culture; and Greenfield mentions the impact of the Beatles when they first appeared on the Ed Sullivan Show. Do the essays agree on the degree of influence that television wields on culture? Do they agree about its injurious effects?

6. Greenfield suggests that the music of the Beatles provided a necessary sense of "community" to young Americans at a troubled time in history. Look at the essays by Mead and Janeway. What do they say about the sense of "community"? Is "community" an important factor to Jacobs?

7. Tom Wolfe's description of the Electric Kool-Aid Acid Test held by Ken Kesey shows one of the kinds of "together" sessions that Greenfield says the Beatles encouraged. Does Wolfe show the sort of "dream" that Greenfield describes? Does Wolfe's essay share Greenfield's attitude toward "community" gettogethers and their effects? Do the Wolfe and Greenfield articles imply

the same attitudes toward the youth cults of the '60s and their ultimate fates?

8. Would Sedulus approve of the Beatle phenomenon? Would he like the scene described in "Cosmo's Tasmanian Deviltry"? Justify your answer.

9. Does Cline think that T.V. could produce a race of "Joeys"? Does Sedulus think so?

10. In what ways does Jane Kramer's description of Allen Ginsberg and his father confirm Greenfield's points about the opposition of the older and younger generations? Does Kramer refute Greenfield in any way?

Reasoning

The essays in previous sections have demonstrated basic rhetorical methods: defining, comparing and contrasting, describing, illustrating, and so forth. You are now certainly aware that developing ideas in writing involves a great deal more than stringing words like so many colored crystals or even than in tying several ideological strands together, like Indian beadwork. Rhetoric embodies ways of thinking; and verbal formulations finally are no stronger, more intricate, or more useful than the thinking they represent. The most beautiful and complex specimen of Navajo beadwork will disintegrate if its sustaining wires are weak or poorly linked; likewise, the most elaborate and appealing prose composition will fall apart if its basic assumptions are weak or its ideas faultily joined together.

Though many philosophers and some psychologists have tried, it is nearly impossible to isolate the various ways in which each of us thinks or conceptualizes. Our ideas are of different types, and we entertain several simultaneously. We "think" in images or pictures, in words, in feelings or sensations, in emotions, perhaps even in extrasensory ways; some of our thoughts follow linear patterns and others do not. If you consider what goes on in your mind as you read a textbook or listen to a lecture, you will realize that it is possible to follow a sequence of historical events or a chemical experiment, be aware of the odor of spring flowers, dream about your current love, feel your left leg cramping, write down some cryptic symbols in your notebook, and think of a half-dozen other things at the same time. Some of these simultaneous ways of conceiving and shaping experience are incidental or temporary, soon to be forgotten. Others are recurrent. Some are the product of accidental associations, and some are a part of your permanent mental equipment. Some are intuitive or imaginative; others are logical and empirical.

Since one prose composition cannot cover every aspect of a given subject, the writer must select materials with a purpose or intention in view. The choice of materials includes or implies some viable and effective way of presenting them. Rhetorical techniques in several of the literary methods illustrated in earlier sections plainly stress intuitive or imaginative ways of thinking through verbal devices that are suggestive or connotative: description and characterization are instances. Other literary methods illustrated depend upon ways of thinking that are essentially empirical and logical: classification, definition, and analysis are examples. Still other methods—comparison, contrast, illustration, exemplification, demonstrating causality —basically depend on logical ways of thinking but they also contain intuitive elements.

The critical reader must apply as the tests of success of a work of prose not only the writer's explicit or implicit standards of judgment but the standards that the essay requires by its techniques and methods. Types of writing that employ logical, empirical methods of thinking must be subjected to testing by the principles of logic, even if the piece as a whole is imaginative or intuitive. A characterization that suggests a dubious or false premise ("All Negroes are shiftless and lazy," "All Jews are materialistic," "All white, Anglo-Saxon Protestants are bigots") must be adjudged by the validity of its assumption as well as the effectiveness of its style.

Testing assumptions may not always prove easy. To a degree, everything we presumably know is an assumption: either a "fact" against which no contradictory evidence is known or an unprovable "belief." The supposedly "hard facts" of the scientist frequently are hypotheses that all known evidence supports but which new evidence might overturn. The proof of the mathematician rests upon an assumption, a hypothesis or a theorem. Even the basic definitions of words are assumptions, Herbert Muller reminds us (p. 9). Yet, some assumptions are stronger than others, being supported by more evidence or explaining something more completely than other assumptions do. Some assumptions are derived *inductively;* others are established *deductively;* still others rest upon untestable belief or trust in authority. Robert Gorham Davis goes into fuller detail about how assumptions are tested in his essay "Logical Fallacies," which follows.

In essays that combine several rhetorical methods to present a configuration of related ideas, the reader must be ready to identify and evaluate combinations of truth and error in subtle degrees. If an essay combines definition with illustration and contrast or commingles description and analysis for the sake of proving an opinion, the reader must be alert to a wide variety of ideological and rhetorical combinations. The essayist may purport to be giving objective information about drug-taking on college campuses and insist that 98 percent of all students take drugs. If the essayist is tacitly defining aspirin as a "drug," the assertions may be correct but highly misleading. Similarly, the writer who, trying to prove that fluoridation of water will poison the population, compares fluoride to the poisonous phosgene on the grounds that they are both gases, must be criticized by logical as well as rhetorical standards. Any essay that presumes to give accurate information (Exposition), establish operable patterns in time (Narration), disclose working relationships (Explanation), or prove an opinion valid (Argumentation), must rely on logical methods in whole or in part and thus be subject to logical criteria.

Because of the complex nature of human thought, even honest and knowledgeable writers may inadvertently combine contradictory or inaccurate ideas into prose that is superficially convincing or even logical. "Logic" means "patterns," "plans," or "orderly schemes," and these plans may be established by arbitrary methods. Thus one can logically "prove" some of the most absurd or outrageous assumptions. Jonathan Swift "logically" argues in *A Modest Proposal* that, if the Irish are starving and need meat, they can end their problem by raising children to butcher; children are, after all, meat. Swift's fiercely ironic parody shows that "logical" solutions may be far from reasonable. There is a current argument that air and water pollution cannot be stopped because to do so would cost too much money. The assumption underlying such unreasonable logic is that money is worth more than human life. Clearly, reasoning involves logic but it involves other ways of thinking as well.

Reasoning relies on tested and workable logical methods; but it also includes seeing the real relationship between the specific and the general, applying broad principles to particular instances only when they are apt, discerning true differences and vital similarities, and holding in doubt any propositions, data, or conclusions which claim a greater validity and applicability than they demonstrate. In his essay, Robert Gorham Davis discusses the kinds of logical errors in thinking and writing that occur most often. In successive essays, Claire Boothe Luce, James Baldwin, David Truman, and R. M. Hutchins use various ways of reasoning to explain why they hold certain opinions. After studying these examples of deductive, inductive, and analogous thinking, you should be ready to confront and treat critically the complicated ideas embodied in the complex rhetoric of the essays in Part Two.

Robert Gorham Davis

Logical Fallacies

Undefined Terms

The first requirement for logical discourse is knowing what the words you use actually mean. Words are not like paper money or counters in a game. Except for technical terms in some of the sciences, they do not have a fixed face value. Their meanings are fluid and changing, influenced by many considerations of context and reference, circumstance and association. This is just as true of common words such as *fast* as it is of literary terms such as *romantic*. Moreover, if there is to be communication, words must have approximately the same meaning for the reader that they have for the

LOGICAL FALLACIES From *Form and Thought in Prose*, Third Edition, edited by W. Stone and R. Hoopes. Published by Ronald Press Company. Reprinted by permission of Robert Gorham Davis and the President and Fellows of Harvard University.

writer. A speech in an unknown language means nothing to the hearer. When an adult speaks to a small child or an expert to a layman, communication may be seriously limited by lack of a mature vocabulary or ignorance of technical terms. Many arguments are meaningless because the speakers are using important words in quite different senses.

Because we learn most words—or guess at them—from the contexts in which we first encounter them, our sense of them is often incomplete or wrong. Discussing the meaning of "cohort," James Thurber said that when his teacher read aloud Byron's famous lines:

> The Assyrian came down like the wolf on the fold
> And his cohorts were gleaming in purple and gold

he visualized one huge man coming down a hill dressed in some kind of fancy armor. Though now often used to mean "henchman," a cohort was originally a legion or large band of warriors. "A rift in the lute" suggests vaguely a cracked mandolin. Failure to ascertain the literal meaning of figurative language is a frequent reason for mixed metaphors. We are surprised to find that the "devil" in "the devil to pay" and "the devil and the deep blue sea" is not Old Nick, but part of a ship. Unless terms mean the same thing to both writer and reader, proper understanding is impossible.

Abstractions

The most serious logical difficulties occur with abstract terms. An abstraction is a word which stands for a quality found in a number of different objects or events from which it has been "abstracted" or taken away. We may, for instance, talk of the "whiteness" of paper or cotton or snow without considering qualities of inflammability or usefulness or cold which these materials happen also to possess. Usually, however, our minds carry over other qualities by association, as when whiteness suggests purity or illness. See the fascinating chapter called "The Whiteness of the Whale" in *Moby Dick*.

In much theoretic discussion the process of abstraction is carried so far that although vague associations and connotations persist, the original objects or events from which the qualities have been abstracted are lost sight of completely. Instead of thinking of words like *sincerity* and *Americanism* as symbols standing for qualities that have to be abstracted with great care from examples and test cases, we come to think of them as real things in themselves. We assume that Americanism is Americanism just as a bicycle is a bicycle, and that everyone knows what it means. We forget that before the question, "Was Hitler sincere?" can mean anything, we have to agree on the criteria of sincerity.

When we try to define such words and find examples, we discover that almost no one agrees on their meaning. The word *church* may refer to anything from a building on the corner of Spring Street to the whole tradition of institutionalized Christianity. *Germany* may mean a geographical section of Europe, a people, a governing group, a cultural tradition, or a military power. Abstractions such as *freedom, courage, race, beauty, truth, justice, nature, honor, humanism, democracy*, should never be used in a theme unless their meaning is defined or indicated clearly by the context. Freedom for whom? To do what? Under what circumstances? Abstract terms have merely emotional value unless they are strictly defined by asking questions of this kind. The study of a word such as *nature* in a good unabridged dictionary will show that even the dictionary, indispensable though it is, cannot determine for us the sense in which a word is being used in any given instance. Once the student understands the importance of definition, he will—hopefully—no longer be betrayed into fruitless arguments over such questions as whether free verse is "poetry" or whether you can change "human nature."

Name-Calling

It is a common unfairness in controversy to place in a generally odious category what the writer dislikes or opposes. The realist dismisses what he dislikes by calling it *romantic*; the liberal, by calling it *fascist*; the conservative, by calling it *communistic*. These terms tell the reader nothing. What is *piety* to some will be *bigotry* to others. *Non-Catholic Christians* would rather be called *Protestants* than *heretics*. What is *right-thinking* except a designation for those who agree with the speaker? Civil rights proponents become *outside agitators*; industrial organizations, *forces of reaction*; investigation into Communism, *witch hunts*; prison reform, *coddling*; progressive education, *fads and frills*. The "cool" disdain everything that is "square." Such terms are intended to block thought by an appeal to prejudice and associative habits. Three steps are necessary before such epithets have real meaning. First, they must be defined; second, it must be shown that the object to which they are applied actually possesses these qualities; third, it must be shown that the possession of such qualities in this particular situation is necessarily undesirable. Unless a person is alert and critical both in choosing and in interpreting words, he may be alienated from ideas with which he would be in sympathy if he had not been frightened by a mere name.

Generalization

Similar to the abuse of abstract terms and epithets is the habit of presenting personal opinions in the guise of universal laws. The student often
seems to feel that the broader the terms in which he states an opinion, the
more effective he will be. Ordinarily the reverse is true. An enthusiasm for
Thomas Wolfe should lead to a specific critical analysis of Wolfe's novels
that will enable the writer to explain his enthusiasm to others; it should
not be turned into the argument that Wolfe is "the greatest American
novelist," particularly if the writer's knowledge of American novelists is
somewhat limited. The same questions of *who* and *when* and *why* and
under what *circumstances* which are used to check abstract terms should
be applied to generalizations. Consider how contradictory proverbial wisdom is when detached from particular circumstances. "Look before you
leap," but "he who hesitates is lost."

Superlatives and the words *right* and *wrong*, *true* and *untrue*, *never*
and *always* must be used with caution in matters of opinion. When a student says flatly that X is true, he often is really saying that he or his family
or the author of a book he has just been reading, persons of certain tastes
and background and experience, *think* that X is true. If his statement is
based not on logic and examination of evidence, but merely reproduces
other people's opinions, it can have little value or relevance unless these
people are identified and their reasons for thinking so explained. Because
many freshmen are taking survey courses in which they read a single work
by an author or see an historical event through the eyes of a single historian whose bias they may not be able to measure, they must guard
against this error.

Sampling

Assertions of a general nature are frequently open to question because
they are based on insufficient evidence. Some persons are quite ready, after
meeting one Armenian or reading one medieval romance, to generalize
about Armenians and medieval romances. One ought, of course, to examine objectively as many examples as possible before making a generalization, but the number is far less important than the representativeness of
the examples chosen. The Literary Digest Presidential Poll, sent to hundreds of thousands of people selected from telephone directories, was far
less accurate than the Gallup Poll which questioned far fewer voters, but
selected them carefully and proportionately from all different social groups.

But then the Gallup Poll failed because its sampling methods were not sufficiently responsive to social change. The "typical" college student, as portrayed by moving pictures and cartoons, is very different from the "average" college student as determined statistically. We cannot let uncontrolled experience do our sampling for us; instances and examples which impress themselves upon our minds do so usually because they are exceptional. In propaganda and arguments extreme cases are customarily treated as if they were characteristic.

If one is permitted arbitrarily to select some examples and ignore others, it is possible to find convincing evidence for almost any theory, no matter how fantastic. The fact that the mind tends naturally to remember those instances which confirm its opinions imposes a duty upon the writer, unless he wishes to encourage prejudice and superstition, to look carefully for exceptions to all generalizations which he is tempted to make. We forget the premonitions which are not followed by disaster and the times which our hunches failed to select the winner in a race. Patent medicine advertisements print the letters of those who survived their cure, and not of those who died during it. All Americans did not gamble on the stock exchange in the twenties or become Marxists in the thirties, and all Vermonters are not thin-lipped and shrewd. Of course the search for negative examples can be carried too far. Outside of mathematics or the laboratory, few generalizations can be made airtight, and most are not intended to be. But quibbling is so easy that resort to it is very common, and the knowledge that people can and will quibble over generalizations is another reason for making assertions as limited and explicitly conditional as possible.

False Analogy

Illustration, comparison, analogy are most valuable in making an essay clear and interesting. It must not be supposed, however, that they prove anything or have much argumentative weight. The rule that what is true of one thing in one set of circumstances is not necessarily true of another thing in another set of circumstances seems almost too obvious to need stating. Yet constantly nations and businesses are discussed as if they were human beings with human habits and feelings; human bodies are discussed as if they were machines; the universe, as if it were a clock. It is assumed that what held true for seventeenth century New England or the thirteen Atlantic colonies also holds true for an industrial nation of 180,000,000 people. Carlyle dismissed the arguments for representative democracy by saying that if a captain had to take a vote among his crew every time he wanted to do something, he would never get around Cape Horn. This analogy calmly ignores the distinction between the lawmaking and the executive branches of constitutional democracies. Moreover, voters may be considered much more like the stockholders of a merchant line than its hired sailors. Such arguments introduce assumptions in a metaphorical guise in which they are not readily detected or easily criticized. In place of analysis they attempt to identify their position with some familiar symbol which will evoke a predictable, emotional response in the reader. The revival during the 1932 presidential campaign of Lincoln's remark, "Don't swap horses in the middle of the stream," was not merely a picturesque way of saying "Keep Hoover in the White House." It was concealed argument based on a very dubious analogy between fording a river and ending a depression. This propagandist technique can be seen most clearly in political cartoons.

Degree

Often differences in degree are more important than differences in kind. By legal and social standards there is more difference between an habitual drunkard and a man who drinks temperately, than between a temperate drinker and a total abstainer. In fact differences of degree produce what are regarded as differences of kind. At known temperatures ice turns to water and water boils. At an indeterminate point attraction becomes love or a man who needs a shave becomes a man with a beard. The fact that no men or systems are perfect makes rejoinders and counter-accusations very easy if differences in degree are ignored. Nazi newspapers in the '30's, answering American accusations of brutality and suppression, referred to lynchings and gangsterism here. Before a disinterested judge could evaluate such mutual accusations, he would have to settle the question of the degree to which violent suppression and lynching are respectively prevalent in the countries under consideration. On the other hand, differences in degree may be merely apparent. Lincoln Steffens pointed out that newspapers can create a "crime wave" any time they wish, simply by emphasizing all the minor assaults and thefts commonly ignored or given an inch or two on a back page. The great reported increases in insanity may be due to the fact that in a more urban and institutionalized society cases of insanity more frequently come to the attention of authorities and hence are recorded in statistics.

Causation

The most common way of deciding that one thing causes another thing is the simple principle: *post hoc, ergo propter hoc*, "After this, therefore because of this." Rome fell after the introduction of Christianity; therefore Christianity was responsible for the fall of Rome. Such reasoning illustrates another kind of faulty generalization. But even if one could find ten cases in which a nation "fell" after the introduction of Christianity, it still would not be at all certain that Christianity caused the fall. Day, it has frequently been pointed out, follows night in every observable instance, and yet night cannot be called the cause of day. Usually a combination of causes produces a result. Sitting in a draught may cause a cold, but only given a certain physical condition in the person sitting there. In such instances one may distinguish between necessary and sufficient conditions. Air is a necessary condition for the maintenance of plant life, but air alone is not sufficient to produce plant life. And often different causes at different times may produce the same result. This relation is known as plurality of causes. If, after sitting in a stuffy theatre on Monday, and then again after eating in a stuffy restaurant on Thursday, a man suffered from headaches, he might say, generalizing, that bad air gave him headaches. But actually the headache on Monday may have been caused by eye-strain and on Thursday by indigestion. To isolate the causative factor it is necessary that all other conditions be precisely the same. Except in very simple instances, such isolation is possible only in the laboratory, or with strict scientific controls. If a picture falls from the wall every time a truck passes, we can say with some certainty that the truck's passing is the immediate cause. Still, it is easier to use a larger picture hook than try to ban the trucks. But with anything as complex and conditional as a nation's economy or human character, the determination of cause is not easy or certain. A psychiatrist often sees a patient for an hour daily for a year or more before he feels that he understands his basic problem.

Ordinarily when we speak of cause we mean the proximate or immediate cause. The plants were killed by frost; we had indigestion from eating lobster salad. But any single cause is one in an unbroken series. When a man is murdered, is his death caused by the loss of blood from the wound, or by the firing of the pistol, or by the malice aforethought of the murderer? Was the World War "caused" by the assassination at Sarajevo? Were the Navigation Acts or the ideas of John Locke more important in "causing" the American Revolution? A complete statement of cause would comprise the sum total of the conditions which preceded an event, conditions stretching back indefinitely into the past. Historical events are so interrelated that the isolation of a causative sequence is dependent chiefly on the particular preoccupations of the historian. An economic determinist can "explain" history entirely in terms of economic developments; an idealist, entirely in terms of the development of ideas.

Syllogistic Reasoning

The formal syllogism of the type,

> All men are mortal
> John is a man
> Therefore John is mortal,

is not so highly regarded today as in some earlier periods. It merely fixes an individual as a member of a class, and then assumes that the individual has the given characteristics of the class. Once we have decided who John is, and what "man" and "mortal" mean, and have canvassed all men, including John, to make sure that they are mortal, the conclusion naturally follows. It can be seen that the chief difficulties arise in trying to establish acceptable premises. Faults in the premises are known as "material" fallacies, and are usually more serious than the "formal" fallacies, which are logical defects in drawing a conclusion from the premises. But although directly syllogistic reasoning is not much practiced, buried syllogism can be found in all argument, and it is often a useful clarification to outline your own or another writer's essay in syllogistic form. The two most frequent defects in the syllogism itself are the undistributed middle and the ambiguous middle. The middle term is the one that appears in each of the premises and not in the conclusion. In the syllogism,

> All good citizens vote
> John votes
> Therefore John is a good citizen,

the middle term is not "good citizens," but "votes." Even though it were true that all good citizens vote, nothing prevents bad citizens from voting also, and John may be one of the bad citizens. Distributing the middle term means putting an "all" in front of it, but only if the evidence justifies this. Forcing oneself to say "some" when tempted to say "all" is essential to fairness in argument. To distribute the middle term "votes" one might say (but only if that is what one meant),

> All voters are good citizens
> John is a voter
> Therefore John is a good citizen.

The ambiguous middle term is even more common. It represents a problem in definition, while the undistributed middle is a problem in generalization. All acts which benefit others are virtuous, losing money at poker benefits others, therefore losing at poker is a virtuous act. Here the middle term "act which benefits others" is obviously used very loosely and ambiguously.

Non-Sequitur

This phrase, meaning "it does not follow," is used to characterize the kind of humor found in pictures in which the Marx Brothers used to perform. It is an amusing illogicality because it usually expresses, beneath its apparent incongruity, an imaginative, associative, or personal truth. "My ancestors came over on the Mayflower; therefore I am naturally opposed to labor unions." It is not logically necessary that those whose ancestors came over on the Mayflower should be opposed to unions; but it may happen to be true as a personal fact in a given case. It is usually a strong personal conviction which keeps people from realizing that their arguments are non-sequiturs, that they do not follow the given premises with logical necessity. Contemporary psychologists have effectively shown us that there is often such a wide difference between the true and the purported reasons for an attitude that, in rationalizing our behavior, we are often quite unconscious of the motives that actually influence us. A fanatical antivivisectionist, for instance, may have temperamental impulses toward cruelty which he is suppressing and compensating for by a reasoned opposition to any kind of permitted suffering. We may expect, then, to come upon many conclusions which are psychologically interesting in themselves, but have nothing to do with the given premises.

Ignoratio Elenchi

This means, in idiomatic English, "arguing off the point," or ignoring the question at issue. A man trying to show that monarchy is the best form of government for Great Britain may devote most of his attention to the personalities of the royal family and the people's interest in them. Public debates over marijuana or violence on TV are usually hopelessly confused as to what the issues really are or what constitutes proof. In ordinary conversational argument it is almost impossible for disputants to keep to the point. Constantly turning up are tempting side-issues through which one can discomfit an opponent or force him to irrelevant admissions that seem to weaken his case.

Begging the Question; Arguing in a Circle

The first of these terms means to assume in the premises what you are pretending to prove in the course of your argument. The function of logic is to demonstrate that because one thing or group of things is true, another must be true as a consequence. But in begging the question you simply say in varying language that what is assumed to be true is assumed to be true. An argument which asserts that we shall enjoy immortality because we have souls which are immaterial and indestructible establishes nothing, because the idea of immortality is already contained in the assumption about the soul. It is the premise which needs to be demonstrated, not the conclusion. Arguing in a circle is another form of this fallacy. It proves the premise by the conclusion and the conclusion by the premise. The conscience forbids an act because it is wrong; the act is wrong because the conscience forbids it.

Arguments ad Hominem and ad Populum

It is very difficult for men to be persuaded by reason when their interest or prestige is at stake. If one wishes to preach the significance of physiognomy, it is well to choose a hearer with a high forehead and a determined jaw. The arguments in favor of repealing the protective tariff on corn or wheat in England were more readily entertained by manufacturers than by landowners. The cotton manufacturers in New England who were doing a profitable trade with the South were the last to be moved by descriptions of the evils of slavery. Because interest and desire are so deeply seated in human nature, arguments are frequently mingled with attempts to appeal to emotion, arouse fear, play upon pride, attack the characters of proponents of an opposite view, show that their practice is inconsistent with their principles; all matters which have, strictly speaking, nothing to do with the truth or falsity, the general desirability or undesirability, of some particular measure. If men are desperate enough they will listen to arguments suitable only to a mental hospital but which seem to promise them relief.

After reading these suggestions, which are largely negative, the student may feel that any original assertion he can make will probably contain one or several logical faults. This assumption is not true. Even if it were, we know from reading newspapers and magazines that worldly fame is not dimmed by the constant and, one suspects, conscious practice of illogicality. But generalizations are not made only by charlatans and sophists. Intelligent and scrupulous writers also have a great many fresh and provocative observations and conclusions to express and are expressing them influentially. What is intelligence but the ability to see the connection between things, to discern causes, to relate the particular to the general, to define and discriminate and compare? Any man who thinks and feels and observes closely will not lack ideas to express.

And in expressing them, he will find that a due regard for logic does not limit but rather increases the force of his argument. When statements are not trite, they are usually controversial. Men arrive at truth dialectically; error is weeded out in the course of discussion, argument, attack, and counterattack. Not only can a writer who understands logic show the weaknesses of arguments he disagrees with, but also, by anticipating the kind of attack likely to be made on his own ideas, he can so arrange them, properly modified with qualifications and exceptions, that the anticipated attack is made much less effective. Thus, fortunately, we do not have to depend on the spirit of fairness and love of truth to lead men to logic; it has the strong support of argumentative necessity and of the universal desire to make ideas prevail.

Claire Boothe Luce

Eating Our Way to Bad Behavior?

Liberalism, the dominant political creed of America since the 1930s, has a basic article of faith that poverty is the root of all evil, especially that greatest of all evils, violence and crime.

When poverty is stamped out, the orthodox liberal believes, the Great and Good Society will automatically come to pass.

In the past 40 years, Americans have spent billions of dollars waging

EATING OUR WAY TO BAD BEHAVIOR?   From the *Democrat and Chronicle*, October 20, 1974. Reprinted by permission of the *Democrat and Chronicle*, Rochester, New York.

the "war on poverty." Much to the chagrin of liberals, however, violence and crime have not diminished. On the contrary, they have increased so fast that in 1969 the cry for law and order forced the government to launch a multi-billion-dollar "war on crime."

Atty. Gen. William Saxbe recently reported that the five-year-old attack on crime is a dismal failure. Since it began, the crime rate has doubled and is still zooming upward. If Draconian measures are not taken soon, he warns, in a few years America will be "swamped" by crime.

The most disturbing news from the crime front is that our fastest-growing criminal group is the 14 to 20-year-olds; the second fastest, the 10 to 14-year-olds. Our young Bonnies are coming along so fast that soon every Clyde can have one. While ghettos and "underprivileged" homes remain the most prolific incubators of crime, crime in white suburbia and among the "privileged" is catching up.

Saxbe attributes some of the phenomenal increase of crime among youth of all classes to the general collapse of traditional moral and spiritual values.

Now, as the liberal credo also holds that the destruction of traditional values automatically leads to a more liberal, and consequently better, society, these are fighting words. No true liberal can concede that our bumper crop of child criminals might have anything to do with "moral and spiritual values." The very idea smacks of—well, er, you know, obsolete values like religion.

So let's see how a liberal approaches the Saxbe report. Here we have Nicholas von Hoffman, a widely-syndicated columnist of the Faith, in search of some amoral, non-spiritual explanation of youthful crime.

Liberals, writes von Hoffman, have difficulty analyzing the problem. Poor housing, he admits, doesn't explain criminality among well-housed youngsters. On the other hand, he writes: "Mr. Saxbe's causes—the three P's: parents, permissiveness and pornography" are "psychological" and "conservative" (!) explanations. Psychological explanations of all and every kind aren't persuasive (i.e., spiritual and moral values are out). They do not provide "a convincing chain of causality. We must look elsewhere for other causes of the epidemic of violent anti-social behavior."

Von Hoffman's use of the word "epidemic" is the clue to where he looks.

If crime is not caused by poverty, it must be caused by disease. And von Hoffman thinks he has not only found the disease—he has found its cause! Our criminal youngsters, he suggests, are innocent victims of hyperkinesis, a "newly-defined disorder" whose symptoms are "compulsive aggression, short attention span, easy frustration, and quick anger, poor coordination, and difficulty in sleeping." (Lots of nightmares.)

Hyperkinesis is what's causing so many young people to raise hell at home and school. It is why so many tend to behave less like their parents and teachers and more like the teen-age muggers, thieves, addicts, and sadists whom they spend hours every day, every year, watching on TV and in film. According to von Hoffman, nobody knew until recently what caused hyperkinesis and made our children, well, crime-prone—although a treatment was found some time ago.

"Because of the difficulty of diagnoses," von Hoffman reports, "absolutely reliable figures are not available, but it appears that literally hundreds of thousands of children are now being treated for this disorder." (Here readers will please take deep breaths.) "The standard treatment is large doses of amphetamines and tranquilizers, which the young patients must be kept on for years." (Distraught parents and school personnel, it seems, have for years been administering these drugs to their "hyperkinetic" charges.)

Von Hoffman himself has been in some doubt whether "this massive use of behavior-controlling drugs" is a desirable solution to the problem. But now he brings good news. We may not need to continue drugging our unfortunate "hyperkinetic" youngsters much longer. The probable cause of "hyperkinesis" has now been discovered: anti-social behavior is an allergy.

The discoverer of hyperkinesis' cause, von Hoffman tells us, is Dr. Ben Feingold, a researcher in food allergies. Not long ago Dr. Feingold "asked himself whether or not 'hyperkinetic' children might not be under the influence of a drug." His suspicions "came to focus on the 2,000 or so artificial substances used to give color and flavor" to commercially packaged foods, especially the cake, candy, cola and such-like goodies which children enjoy.

So Dr. Feingold prescribed for some "hyperkinetic" children a diet free of artificial additives. Within a week, he said, their anti-social behavior symptoms disappeared. Unhappily it apparently doesn't take much to revive them. Von Hoffman reports that "Feingold cites the case of a 7-year-old boy, whose disruptive, regressive behavior returned three hours after he'd eaten a commercially baked doughnut."

That one doughnut was enough to convince a liberal believer that "a convincing chain of causality" for crime in the young had been established. As adults also eat food chockfull of additives, von Hoffman wonders if food additives may also explain part of adult crime. His column closes optimistically: "The unexplained rising crime Saxbe is so rightly concerned about may be traceable to the involuntary ingestion of (artificial flavors and colors) in our food supply."

So there it is, folks: Additives add up to additional crime. Of course, now we must explain those millions of additive eaters who don't batter or burgle. But all we need now to knock down the crime rate is a billion-dollar government program to eliminate artificial flavors and colors from the daily diets of 220 million people.

So relax, all you permissive parents. It's okay if Junior spends more time watching TV crime and horror shows than he spends at school, and if your teen-agers spend their nights at the skin flicks, soaking up sadistic porn. Every liberal knows that what goes into their young minds has absolutely no effect on their behavior. Only what goes into their stomachs counts.

James Baldwin

Down at the Cross

White Americans find it as difficult as white people elsewhere do to divest themselves of the notion that they are in possession of some intrinsic value that black people need, or want. And this assumption—which, for example, makes the solution to the Negro problem depend on the speed with which Negroes accept and adopt white standards—is revealed in all kinds of striking ways, from Bobby Kennedy's assurance that a Negro can become President in forty years to the unfortunate tone of warm congratulation with which so many liberals address their Negro equals. It is the Negro, of course, who is presumed to have become equal—an achievement that not only proves the comforting fact that perseverance has no color but also overwhelmingly corroborates the white man's sense of his own value. Alas, this value can scarcely be corroborated in any other way; there is certainly little enough in the white man's public or private life that one should desire to imitate. White men, at the bottom of their hearts, know this. Therefore, a vast amount of the energy that goes into what we call the

DOWN AT THE CROSS Excerpted from *The Fire Next Time* by James Baldwin. Copyright © 1962, 1963 by James Baldwin. Reprinted with the permission of The Dial Press, Inc.

Negro problem is produced by the white man's profound desire not to be judged by those who are not white, not to be seen as he is, and at the same time a vast amount of the white anguish is rooted in the white man's equally profound need to be seen as he is, to be released from the tyranny of his mirror. All of us know, whether or not we are able to admit it, that mirrors can only lie, that death by drowning is all that awaits one there. It is for this reason that love is so desperately sought and so cunningly avoided. Love takes off the masks that we fear we cannot live without and know we cannot live within. I use the word "love" here not merely in the personal sense but as a state of being, or a state of grace—not in the infantile American sense of being made happy but in the tough and universal sense of quest and daring and growth. And I submit, then, that the racial tensions that menace Americans today have little to do with real antipathy—on the contrary, indeed—and are involved only symbolically with color. These tensions are rooted in the very same depths as those from which love springs, or murder. The white man's unadmitted—and apparently, to him, unspeakable—private fears and longings are projected onto the Negro. The only way he can be released from the Negro's tyrannical power over him is to consent, in effect, to become black himself, to become a part of that suffering and dancing country that he now watches wistfully from the heights of his lonely power and, armed with spiritual traveller's checks, visits surreptitiously after dark. How can one respect, let alone adopt, the values of a people who do not, on any level whatever, live the way they say they do, or the way they say they should? I cannot accept the proposition that the four-hundred-year travail of the American Negro should result merely in his attainment of the present level of the American civilization. I am far from convinced that being released from the African witch doctor was worthwhile if I am now—in order to support the moral contradictions and the spiritual aridity of my life—expected to become dependent on the American psychiatrist. It is a bargain I refuse. The only thing white people have that black people need, or should want, is power—and no one holds power forever. White people cannot, in the generality, be taken as models of how to live. Rather, the white man is himself in sore need of new standards, which will release him from his confusion and place him once again in fruitful communion with the depths of his own being. And I repeat: The price of the liberation of the white people is the liberation of the blacks—the total liberation, in the cities, in the towns, before the law, and in the mind. Why, for example—especially knowing the family as I do—I should *want* to marry your sister is a great mystery to me. But your sister and I have every right to marry if we wish to, and no one has the right to stop us. If she cannot raise me to her level, perhaps I can raise her to mine.

In short, we, the black and the white, deeply need each other here if we are really to become a nation—if we are really, that is, to achieve our identity, our maturity, as men and women. To create one nation has proved to be a hideously difficult task; there is certainly no need now to create two, one black and one white. But white men with far more political power than that possessed by the Nation of Islam movement have been advocating exactly this, in effect, for generations. If this sentiment is honored when it falls from the lips of Senator Byrd, then there is no reason it should not be honored when it falls from the lips of Malcolm X. And any Congressional committee wishing to investigate the latter must also be willing to investigate the former. They are expressing exactly the same sentiments and represent exactly the same danger. There is absolutely no reason to suppose that white people are better equipped to frame the laws by which I am to be governed than I am. It is entirely unacceptable that I should have no voice in the political affairs of my own country, for I am not a ward of America; I am one of the first Americans to arrive on these shores.

This past, the Negro's past, of rope, fire, torture, castration, infanticide, rape; death and humiliation; fear by day and night, fear as deep as the marrow of the bone; doubt that he was worthy of life, since everyone around him denied it; sorrow for his women, for his kinfolk, for his children, who needed his protection, and whom he could not protect; rage, hatred, and murder, hatred for white men so deep that it often turned against him and his own, and made all love, all trust, all joy impossible—this past, this endless struggle to achieve and reveal and confirm a human identity, human authority, yet contains, for all its horror, something very beautiful. I do not mean to be sentimental about suffering—enough is certainly as good as a feast—but people who cannot suffer can never grow up, can never discover who they are. That man who is forced each day to snatch his manhood, his identity, out of the fire of human cruelty that rages to destroy it knows, if he survives his effort, and even if he does not survive it, something about himself and human life that no school on earth—and, indeed, no church—can teach. He achieves his own authority, and that is unshakable. This is because, in order to save his life, he is forced to look beneath appearances, to take nothing for granted, to hear the meaning behind the words. If one is continually surviving the worst that life can bring, one eventually ceases to be controlled by a fear of what life can bring; whatever it brings must be borne. And at this level of experience one's bitterness begins to be palatable, and hatred becomes too heavy a sack to carry. The apprehension of life here so briefly and inadequately sketched has been the experience of generations of Negroes, and it helps to explain how they have endured and how they have been able to produce children of kindergarten age who can walk through mobs to get to school. It demands great force and great cunning continually to assault the mighty and indifferent fortress of white supremacy, as Negroes in this country have done so long. It demands great spiritual resilience not to hate the hater whose foot is on your neck, and an even greater miracle of perception and charity not to teach your child to hate. The Negro boys and girls who are facing mobs today come out of a long line of improbable aristocrats—the only genuine aristocrats this country has produced. I say "this country" because their frame of reference was totally American. They were hewing out of the mountain of white supremacy the stone of their individuality. I have great respect for that unsung army of black men and women who trudged down back lanes and entered back doors, saying "Yes, sir" and "No, Ma'am" in order to acquire a new roof for the schoolhouse, new books, a new chemistry lab, more beds for the dormitories, more dormitories. They did not like saying "Yes, sir" and "No, Ma'am," but the country was in no hurry to educate Negroes, these black men and women knew that the job had to be done, and they put their pride in their pockets in order to do it. It is very hard to believe that they were in any way inferior to the white men and women who opened those back doors. It is very hard to believe that those men and women, raising their children, eating their greens, crying their curses, weeping their tears, singing their songs, making their love, as the sun rose, as the sun set, were in any way inferior to the white men and women who crept over to share these splendors after the sun went down. But we must avoid the European error; we must not suppose that, because the situation, the ways, the perceptions of black people so radically differed from those of whites, they were racially superior. I am proud of these people not because of their color but because of their intelligence and their spiritual force and their beauty. The country should be proud of them, too, but, alas, not many people in this country even know of their existence. And the reason for this ignorance is that a knowledge of the role these people played—and play—in American life would reveal more about America to Americans than Americans wish to know.

David Truman

The Necessity of High Literacy

To say that "liberal education" in this country is in disarray, or even to observe that it is at present on the defensive, is not to be very original.

The rush in recent years to throw out requirements, whatever its justification (and there is some); the abandonment of a common learning, even as an ideal, and its replacement by little more than "doing one's own thing" at a smorgasbord of courses and activities; the confusion over what kinds of learning reasonably should be recognized among the qualifications for a degree in the liberal arts: all these speak to the disarray.

The demand for immediate practicality, always an awkward matter for the liberal arts, though one that in some degree is warranted, especially for young women; the current fad of "career education," explainable and in some respects and circumstances defensible; even the assumptions implicit in proposals for a three-year degree, which are not wholly foolish: these surely sketch the defensive posture.

Liberal education is in a critical state, and that is a serious matter not merely for the institutions that profess their dedication to the liberal arts but for the future of the society. For, although the weaknesses and deficiencies of liberal education in the colleges are less conspicuous than those in the secondary schools—the real chamber of horrors in American education—they are more ominous. The society must look to and rely upon people with liberally educated minds for leadership in the future even more than in the past. The strains and reassessments that lie ahead nationally and globally will call urgently for such minds, for the balance, breadth, and compassion that lie close to the ideal of liberal education.

If that increased reliance is indeed to be expected, then it is critically urgent that colleges nominally dedicated to meeting it look earnestly at themselves and at what they are up to. Above all, what is essential to the

THE NECESSITY OF HIGH LITERACY   Reprinted with permission from *The Chronicle of Higher Education*. Copyright © 1974 by Editorial Projects for Education, Inc.

learning and practice of the liberal arts, today and for tomorrow? No particular content, surely, no special subject matter—although we can acknowledge that some materials and some subjects lend themselves more readily than others to the pursuit of competence in the liberal arts.

The seven liberal arts of the medieval curriculum, the *trivium* and *quadrivium*—inherited from the Romans and bequeathed to later ages—have been expanded so enormously in content over the centuries that their forms are not recognizable today. A central intent, however, is still pertinent: precision of thought and especially of language to the end of intellectual management of the evidence of experience. Music was included in the *quadrivium* not for aesthetic reasons and not primarily for the utilitarian purposes of the cathedrals and monasteries but because, in the cosmology of the time, it was thought to contribute, along with geometry and astronomy, to an explanation of the patterns of the universe.

Precise control of the evidence of experience through thought and language: where does this direct our energies?

The essential, the indispensable means to liberal education can be stated in one word: literacy. Not the low functional literacy of the first two "R's," but a high literacy characterized by precision and range in the use of language, and above all the written language—including, of course, mathematics.

A mutual relation exists between language and thought. It is a relation that is often recognized but more often ignored. The English language ". . . becomes ugly and inaccurate because our thoughts are foolish, but the slovenliness of our language makes it easier for us to have foolish thoughts." That sentence appears in George Orwell's essay, "Politics and the English Language," in which he was ". . . not . . . considering the literary use of language, but merely language as an instrument for expressing and not for concealing or preventing thought." It was written in 1946, before the invasion by television, which has given urgent reality to his forebodings.

It does not require a McLuhan to suggest that we are living in a period in which the image on the face of the tube threatens to displace the written word. Humans have made use of the image in communication since before written language, and our emotional and aesthetic lives would be unthinkably poorer without the image. The critical point lies in the differential limitations and strengths of the image and the written language and in the consequences in human affairs when their relative prominence changes.

The functions of communication can be classified as arousal, expression, and statement. The visual image is unequaled as a means of arousal.

Its expressive potential is less reliable. Its capacity for statement, unaided by language or by a clear contextual code, is low—immeasurably lower than words, especially written words. The means of communication of humans and those of other animals share the functions of arousal and expression. It is the ability of words to make statements that is distinctively human—as are both knowledge and ignorance. I might exaggerate slightly if I were to say that if you can't write it, you do not know it, but I am painfully accurate in saying that the weakening of written language and its displacement by the image is a fundamental threat to life that is distinctively human.

In any society the ways in which people relate to one another have their roots in modes of communication. A change in those modes will change the society. The invention of printing made a long-term monopoly of literacy impossible and contributed to profound social readjustments, including the democratizing of the societies most exposed to its effects. The weakening or displacement of written language by the electronic image would have effects of comparable scale. When, in addition, the images are mass-produced, it is doubtful that the long-term results would be democratic.

The contemporary threat to language thus is a threat to the extension and development of the human capacity for precise statement, for the replacement of ignorance in all its forms with knowledge and intellectual control; it is also a threat to the ideal of human worth and dignity that is basic to the democratic dream. Hence the importance of literate precision if the goals of liberal education are to be served.

What about range, which I earlier coupled with precision of language and thought as essential characteristics of genuine literacy? Why range?

Precision of language is a common mark of the specialist. Although precision is not, or need not be, his alone, the tendency in a complex, interdependent society is to encourage and reward the specialist. When we live in a society in which ". . . we are wired together so tightly that a short circuit can fry us all," as Dean George Gerbner of the Annenberg School of Communications at Pennsylvania recently observed, we cannot do without the specialist. The potential difficulty lies not in the specialist's precision but in the lack of range that our dependence upon him can readily foster. It is true, of course, that specialists tend to talk primarily to each other. No harm, up to that subtle point where the specialists do not wish to or cannot talk to anyone else. The trouble comes from the tendency in all such enclaves to measure and assess goals, values, and strategies solely in terms of the perspective of specialists.

The dangerous feature, certainly during the 1950's and 1960's, of the semi-independence of the Central Intelligence Agency, particularly its clandestine division, lay in such narrowness. The anti-Communist, anti-Soviet perspective in "the agency," although not wholly mistaken, became dominant, preclusive, so that all options were seen in these terms and any otherwise foolish effort could be supported if it appeared to serve this purpose.

The danger of such narrowness is, of course, conspicuously present among the specialists in violence, whether the military or the police, and it is the reason for their necessary subordination to a civil authority that can be expected to correct the myopia of specialists from a perspective that is wider and less specialized. But these are not the only cases, perhaps not even the most dangerous ones, of threat from the specialist's limitation of range. And we all are acquainted with the specialist whose tolerance, whose acknowledgment of fallibility, does not extend beyond the conventions of his own field.

Mount Holyoke's statement of principles speaks of the college as ". . . a fellowship whose members are gentle of spirit and tolerant of human failing"; it uses words like "compassion"; and it sets high among our goals the development of individuals ". . . liberated from narrow definitions of themselves, of others, and of human problems in general." It is warning, in part, against the sinful, destructive tendency of the specialists toward a narrowness of perspective that induces a narrowness of definition.

This is a sinful tendency because it leads away from tolerance, which is not merely a winsome attribute of human tenderness or a slovenly, sentimental inability to see valid distinctions. Genuine tolerance is much more fundamental than that. It is at base an acknowledgment of the fallibility of one's own perspectives and consequently an indication of willingness and ability to see those perspectives refuted by evidence and reason. The tendency toward narrowness is in turn destructive of rationality, which may not exist apart from an awareness that one may be in error. In sum, to quote the cogent statement in Alasdair MacIntyre's critique of Marcuse, ". . . to foreclose on tolerance . . . is gravely to endanger one's own rationality by not admitting one's own fallibility."

Given the necessity for specialization, range is perhaps our best insurance against its risks. Both range and precision of language and thought are thus essential to the genuine literacy without which a liberal education cannot be achieved.

How wide the range? I have suggested that some subjects lend themselves more readily than others to the purpose of liberal education. Even though we cannot define the liberal arts in terms of particular subject matters, we can perhaps identify those that are most likely to foster the two attributes that I have emphasized. But no sharp boundary can be drawn, nor need one be drawn. Almost any subject can be so taught and studied as to assist acquisition of the liberal arts—and, I must add, any subject can be so taught and studied that it makes no such contribution. The test of substance and of pedagogy is relative effectiveness in developing genuine literacy, characterized by precision and range in language and thought.

This emphasis will raise objections. Some may argue that I exclude all but the cognitive, rational components of human existence. I do not and I would not. The aesthetic and emotional components of human life are real. It would be foolish, moreover, to assume that aesthetic-emotional experience bears no useful functional relation to the cognitive-rational. Therefore I would assert only that, for the objectives of liberal education and for the achievement of genuine literacy, the rational, cognitive component is primary.

Others may object to my concern for the threat to language from the pervasive intrusion of the visual image on the ground that it is an "elitist" view, that only a few can expect to achieve the skill in language and thought that I have put at the focus of liberal education. So it may be, but I know of no necessary, inescapable reason why it must be. If, for a time in the clash of values represented by dependence on the visual image and insistence on literacy, the partisans of language are indeed few, that is regrettable. The alternative, however, is not some egalitarian utopia, but rather subordination to an elite of less worthy human qualities. The corruption of language has accompanied the degrading of human dignity from the demise of Plato's democratic state to 1984.

Much more is riding on genuine liberal education than taste and sensitivity. Much more is at stake than the identification and development of individual talent. We are not concerned with an ornamental luxury but with a quality of being that is essential to any future on this planet that is acceptably human: a genuine literacy, precise and wide-ranging, that can lead to competence or even mastery in "the arts of thought, perception, and judgment."

Robert M. Hutchins

Doing What Comes Scientifically

We have some idea of what the chemists and physicists can do: they showed us in the last two world wars. Now the biologists are moving into the field. This is the prospect opened before us by Robert Sinsheimer, professor of biophysics at the California Institute of Technology: "How will you choose to intervene in the ancient designs of nature for man? Would you like to control the sex of your offspring? It will be as you wish. Would you like your son to be six feet tall? Seven feet? Eight feet? What troubles you? Allergy? Obesity? Arthritic pain? These will be easily handled. For cancer, diabetes, there will be genetic therapy. The appropriate DNA will be provided in the appropriate dose. Viral and microbial disease will be easily met. Even the timeless patterns of growth and maturity and aging will be subject to our design. We know of no intrinsic limits to the life-span. How long would you like to live? . . . The foundation of ethics is foresight. But how can we possibly predict the ultimate consequence of the alteration of ourselves? . . . In all of science we have been in a sense children, spewing change into society with scant thought for the consequence."

Professor Sinsheimer ends by expressing the hope for responsibility, wisdom, and nobility of spirit to match that freedom from earlier troubles which biology gives us. But this appears to be nothing but a hope. To the idea of the conquest of nature is now added that of the conquest of human nature. The record that has resulted from our efforts to conquer the physical world does not encourage us to be optimistic about the outcome of efforts to conquer human nature. Such efforts raise in the gravest form the question of who is to conquer whom.

DOING WHAT COMES SCIENTIFICALLY   Reprinted from the January 1969 issue of *The Center Magazine*, a publication of The Center for the Study of Democratic Institutions in Santa Barbara, California. Reprinted by permission.

Science began as part of the search for understanding. Now it is part of the search for power. President Johnson and his predecessor recommended large expenditures on scientific objects in the name of the power and prosperity of their country. In doing so they did not invent a new idea; they followed what has become a global fashion. What the fashion means is that science has become engineering. It is studied not because it is worth knowing in itself but because of its applications. John Wilkinson has pointed out that the time between a "scientific" discovery and its application is steadily diminishing; he estimates that by 1990 the interval will have shrunk to 5/1000 of a second. This means that the application is in the mind of the scientist from the beginning of his work; it also means that the scientist has become an engineer. He becomes the servant of a society that has almost exclusively technological preoccupations. Assisting in this process is what is called the "moral neutrality" of science. The scientist is not a check on the modern preoccupation with power but simply an adjunct to it.

Preoccupation with power, technology, and innovation has led to something new in the world—Big Science. The enormous costs associated with this phenomenon are met by persuading corporations and governments of the commercial and political value of science. Big Science is therefore a propaganda machine for more Big Science. In the United States Big Science is carried on principally in the universities. They thus become the instruments of corporations and the government: they seek to achieve the objects that those who put up the money have in view. Big Science changes the role of the professor. Instead of being a teacher and a man interested in understanding some aspect of nature, he becomes an executive, a money-raiser, a businessman, organizing and "selling" the work of others.

These tendencies have been intensified by the Cold War. Almost every technological outrage of recent years has been perpetrated under the protection of the slogan, "We have to do it because the Russians will." When I asked Arthur Compton, the Nobel Laureate who had directed the research at Chicago leading to the atomic bomb, what terrible thing he proposed next, he said, "Well, we *could* probably do something with hydrogen, but we really don't need to, because we can do so much damage with what we've got already." But the United States manufactured the hydrogen bomb because "We had to."

No wonder it is sometimes suggested that technology is autonomous. We do things not because we need to or want to, but because we can. Even if it were possible for one country to do what none has yet been able to accomplish, to guide and control the development of technology within its own borders, such control could be at best only temporary and illusory as long as the country remained convinced that it could not fall behind its present or potential enemies, that is, behind any other country in the world. The seabed struggle is one illustration. The unseemly space race that is now going on has in the United States an aim that is obviously idiotic, to put a man on the moon this year. In this frenzy the lives of three brave men have already been sacrificed and many millions of dollars and much scientific and engineering skill have been wasted; but the frenzy appears to be an inevitable accompaniment of international competition for power and prestige.

When prosperity, power, and prestige come through science, it is natural that everybody should want to be "scientific." To this there could be no objection if science were still regarded as the pursuit of truth or the attempt to understand the natural world. The universal desire to be scientific has swept over us, however, while we are oppressed with crude misunderstandings of the scope and method of science. In some way or other the report has gone round the world, and is widely believed, that only science is careful, accurate, honest, and objective. Anything that cannot be called science must therefore be careless, inaccurate, dishonest, and biased. The philosopher, for example, must either regard his subject as superstition or he must make it look as "scientific" as possible.

Since scientists do not judge the laws of nature, a social scientist cannot judge the laws of his society. I once asked a great expert on the American system whether the decision of the United States Supreme Court desegregating the schools was good or bad. He replied, "As a social scientist I do not make value judgments." He indicated that he had personal, unscientific views about the question I had asked but he exhibited no confidence in them, appearing to think that they were the accidental, and indefensible, product of his early environment.

Since physics, the most popular of all sciences, rests on mathematics, we are easily led to the conclusion that nothing without a mathematical base can be worth knowing, and that everything that might have a mathematical base achieves intellectual dignity by virtue of this possibility alone. Hence the tremendous effort to count that goes on in American social science, the greatest triumph of which is the public-opinion poll. The slogan is, If you can't count it, it doesn't count. It is not surprising that attempts have been made to understand love by measuring the increases in temperature and pulse rate that are said to occur under its influence.

In some circles in America the notion has gained ground that only science can give us the truth and that the only true science is laboratory science. It follows that nothing is true unless it can be experimentally verified in the laboratory. Thus a dean of the division of biological sciences of the University of Chicago once informed me that the truths of theology and metaphysics, if any, could be accepted only provisionally as substitutes for real truths. Natural science would discover these as soon as it had developed experimental techniques adequate to the purpose. Such an attitude must leave the laborers in disciplines other than experimental science with the uneasy feeling that at any moment they may have their foundations shot out from under them. It also leaves the people of the world with the impression that the questions that bother them most are questions that cannot be answered. For there is no possibility that laboratory techniques capable of coping with these questions can be worked out.

The questions that have afflicted mankind since time immemorial are those which were raised by Socrates, who, according to Plato's *Apology*, expressly abstained from the study of natural science in order to seek the answers to them. How should we act? How should we live? What are the aims of organized society? Why should men be treated differently from other animals? These and questions like them are fundamental, and they do not seem susceptible to any mathematical or experimental treatment.

Sir Richard Livingstone used to say that the Greeks could not broadcast the Aeschylean Trilogy but they could write it. We can broadcast it, if we can find a sponsor, but could we write it? If not, it may be because our misconception of science has led us to misconceive or ignore the great perennial problems of humanity.

This necessarily brief and hence inaccurate account of the present situation leads of course to asking what can be done about it. Divine Providence is too mysterious to be relied upon. The unseen hand that won the devotion of Adam Smith seems to be responsible for our present plight. Yet we cannot accept without a struggle the proposition that technology is autonomous, not subject to human guidance or control. Although nobody could or would propose to put a stop to scientific discovery or technical invention, it does seem time to ask how these great achievements can be directed toward the enhancement of human life. I suggest five possibilities that might brighten the prospects of this scientific and technological age.

The first is the redefinition and restoration of liberal education. The second is the redefinition of the university. The third is the redefinition and restoration of the idea of a profession. The fourth is the revival of philosophy. The fifth is the restoration of and resort to politics.

Liberal education aims to help people become human by helping them learn to use their minds. It prepares them to be free men in a free society. Its backbone is language and mathematics, which are implicated in all human activities, and which are indispensable to further study after formal liberal education is complete. Through liberal education young people develop standards of thought and action; they learn to communicate and to be communicated with. Hence they can become members of the community. Because the mobility of populations and the rate of technological changes make vocational training in the educational system a waste of time, since technical competence will more and more have to be acquired on the job, the justification of any system of universal, compulsory schooling lies in the unique capacity of the school to contribute to liberal education.

We see this clearly enough in the case of the university. The German university of imperial times could be a community of sorts, even though specialization flourished in it, because of the common culture provided by the humanistic Gymnasium. It is ironical that the German university was introduced into the United States just as the high school was beginning its long, slow intellectual decline. As a result, what we had here in America was a German university floating in midair. It had to disintegrate, because no common understanding sustained it.

A university that is not an intellectual community is not worthy of the name. The name is now coming under a cloud in America. It is being superseded by the name multiversity. The multiversity does not pretend to be either intellectual or a community. It has no organizing principle. It will do whatever its constituency asks, provided its constituency will put up the money. It is a miscellany of heterogeneous activities united only by the fact that they are conducted under the same name, administered by the same officers, with the legal responsibility resting in the same board. If the multiversity is the ideal toward which we should strive, we can have little expectation that the university-become-multiversity can help us guide and control science and technology. The principal reason why the multiversity has come into existence is the demand for technical proficiency, technical services, and technical "progress." The multiversity is not equipped to guide or control anything because it has no organizing principle that would permit it to endorse or reject any project or program.

Since the object of the university, as distinguished from the multiversity, is understanding, its organizing principle is that everything must be seen in the light of everything else. The university must be a community because every member of, and every discipline in, the academic body must criticize and be criticized by every other member and every other discipline. Interdisciplinary studies are the essence of the enterprise. Science and technology should be included among the objects of the university's attention not in order to produce more scientists and engineers, not in order to get ahead of the Russians, but because science and technology must understand and be understood by the other disciplines with which the university is concerned.

The university, as distinguished from the multiversity, is an institution existing for the purpose of putting everything in its place, including science and technology. If the university is to play any role in the guidance of science and technology, it will have to be a small, self-governing intellectual community rather than the principal factory of the nationalized knowledge industry. Even its technical and professional schools must be "pure" rather than "applied." Their object must be understanding. Otherwise there is no reason why they should be in the university. It is perfectly possible to train reasonably competent technicians of every kind without exposing them to the influence, which may be subversive, of the university. I can testify from personal experience that one can succeed in the study of the law without bothering to comprehend it—one can even be a successful teacher of the subject on the same terms. All you have to do is teach your students how to manipulate the rules. They will like you all the better for not filling their minds with any nonsense about jurisprudence.

The largely technical character of professional schools in the United States is both a cause and a result of the disappearance of the professional idea. The technical society demands trained hands and nothing can stand in the way of the production of trained hands who can go into any occupation and start contributing to the success of the undertaking on the first day of their employment.

In the United States the name "profession" is applied to any occupation. A professional organization, therefore, is simply another pressure group. Many occupations now have some claim to be called "learned" professions, because they insist on certain educational requirements. These requirements do not suggest that the occupations have any intellectual content in their own right. They merely reflect the desire of the occupational group to limit competition and gain social prestige. The university is asked to establish a school for the occupation. A law is then passed providing that only those who have graduated from such a school may enter the occupation. Competition is limited, social prestige is acquired, but there is nothing to learn and nothing to teach, and the result for the university is more confusion.

A profession is a group organized to perform a public service. There is usually a confidential relation to the recipient of the service, one of advice, guidance, and expert assistance, which makes the rule of *caveat emptor* particularly inappropriate. And there is an *esprit de corps* resting, among other things, on a common education and centering on the maintenance of standards. In theory, at least, the group seeks to perform the service and to maintain the standards even though more money, power, influence, and prestige could be gained in ways that would endanger the confidential relation and the quality of the work. A learned profession is one based on an intellectual discipline. It has intellectual content and has it in its own right. A learned profession has something of its own that it can bring to the task of drawing the circle of knowledge, putting everything in its place, and facing the problems of modern man.

Scott Buchanan went so far as to say, "If the scientist's concern is truth, it is his responsibility to be sure that science is not misused so that something false comes out of it." And again he said, "The heaviest responsibility of the scientist may be to refuse to make himself useful."

This is a statement of the professional ideal. It is one that has been adopted by many individual scientists who have declined to lend themselves to commercial or political plans of which they disapproved. If the condemnation of the scientific community could be visited upon such plans and upon those who make themselves useful to them, an element of guidance and control would be introduced into the present technological chaos. This would have to mean that the "moral neutrality" of science and technology was at an end. Neither science nor social science could be "value-free." The true would have to be seen under the aspect of the good.

This is indeed the implication of liberal education, of the university ideal, and of the professional idea. They all cause or result from the attempt to generate standards of judgment. They can only be realized in a philosophical spirit. Philosophy is systematic reflection upon the common experience of mankind. But this is what liberal education, the university ideal, and the professional idea all come to. Every human act is a moral act. A moral judgment, if it is to have any authority, must rest on something more than prejudice or social pressure.

I have referred previously in *The Center Magazine* to the articles on Political Science and on Political Philosophy in the current edition of the Encyclopedia Britannica. The first is written by a political scientist and the second by a political philosopher. The political scientist says that his subject is descriptive and as quantitative as possible, whereas political philosophy is "strongly normative." The political philosopher instantly repudiates this offensive remark. He says the normative elements of political philosophy have been driven back into ethics, and "ethical principles in their turn have been removed from the field of rational discussion." All that remains of political philosophy, the author says, is linguistic analysis. The result is that neither political science nor political philosophy contains any normative elements. In this case neither one can show us how to guide and control science and technology. They are both "value-free."

Science and technology cannot judge themselves. The scientist can judge an experiment as an experiment; the engineer can judge a weapon as a weapon. But, when they decide to conduct the experiment or manufacture the weapon, they are, whether they know it or not, entering the realm of moral and political philosophy. They have abandoned their moral neutrality.

The decay of political philosophy means that politics is nothing but the exercise of power. Harold Lasswell's *Politics: Who Gets What, How, and Why* is the title of one of the most popular American works in this field. Politics so conceived cannot help us find the means of guiding and controlling science and technology. On the contrary, the conception of politics as power has produced and will continue to reproduce the situation we have today, in which science and technology are being exploited for the purposes of power in such a way as to threaten the existence of the race.

Politics is and ought to be the architectonic science. It is the science of the common good. Good is a moral term. The common good is a good that accrues to every member of the community because he belongs to it; it is a good he would not have if he did not belong to it. The task of politics is to define the common good and to organize the community to achieve it. The task is to find the means, as Harvey Wheeler has said, of constitutionalizing the intellectual enterprise and in particular, since science is now an untamed power, of constitutionalizing science. We have to find out how to direct science to the service of the common good.

And the community we are bound to consider is not simply that of the nation-state. We have seen that science and technology have become a threat to the survival of the race largely because no nation-state can contemplate the possibility that any other can surpass it in acquiring the power science gives. The *furor technologicus* cannot be allayed unless science and technology can be constitutionalized on a world basis and made to serve the common good of the whole human community.

This is the great political task of the future. The right to think, speak, and write must be inalienable. So must the right to inquire and investigate. But the common good now requires that the application of scientific knowledge be regulated in the common interest.

Some of the more absurd consequences of international competition could be obviated without further international organization. For example, Linus Pauling has proposed that space investigation be a joint venture of those nations which want to engage in it. There is no reason why there should be a race, with all the dangerous and irrelevant pressures that the notion of such a contest brings with it. The object must be to bring science and technology under the rule of law. Law is an ordinance of reason directed to the common good.

The redefinition and restoration of liberal education, the redefinition of the university, the redefinition and restoration of the professional idea, the revival of philosophy, and the restoration of and resort to politics may have to be the work of countries that have not yet felt the full force of the technological fever, or that have not yet succumbed to it. Such countries are, of course, eager to get going. They can easily deceive themselves into thinking that vocational training and the multiversity, in a society dedicated to power and unrestrained by professional and philosophical standards, will give them the affluence and influence they desire. History suggests, however, that the unrestrained pursuit of power is suicidal, and not merely murderous. We may hope that this is a lesson our country will not have to learn from experience.

My theme is that science must once more be regarded as a branch of knowledge and that its uses must be regulated in the public interest. On these principles, nothing that science can give us would be lost except those applications of it which are destructive of both science and society.

Questions

Diction and Structure

1. Robert Gorham Davis begins his discussion of logic in "Logical Fallacies" with a section on undefined terms. How carefully does he define his own terms throughout his essay? What peculiar problems of definition does he face, and what methods of definition does he use?

2. What is the meaning of such terms as "syllogism," "non-sequitur," "ignoratio elenchi," "ad hominem," and "ad populum"? From what origins do they come? Does the development of logical reasoning as an academic exercise for medieval thinkers mean that logic is unsuited to the needs of modern, practical application?

3. Do the sections of Davis's essay follow any logical pattern? Are the sections examples of classification?

4. Claire Boothe Luce's essay heavily stresses the term "liberal"; does she define it anywhere? What meaning does it (or liberalism) have for her?

5. Look up "hyperkinetic" in the dictionary. Does it have a precise meaning? Is precision of meaning important to Luce?

6. What are the major points in the Luce argument? How many sections or parts are there to the essay? What does each do? Is the diction consistent throughout?

7. James Baldwin's essay is a portion of the chapter titled "Down at the Cross" from his book *The Fire Next Time*. Is this section a self-contained unit of thought or not? How does it relate to the chapter title? To the title of the book?

8. What type of diction does Baldwin use in his essay? Would the essay be more effective or more persuasive if he had used some other kind of diction?

9. Is Baldwin's diction largely concrete or abstract, tangible or intangible, general or specific? Do these qualities cause his writing to increase or decrease in emotional intensity? Is the topic inherently controversial or not?

10. Notice Baldwin's definition of "love" and its importance to his interpretation of white Americans and their motivation. Does Baldwin's definition of "love" agree with Reik's (p. 102)? Does the definition add to or detract from Baldwin's generalizations in any way?

11. Notice Baldwin's reference to the "infantile" qualities in white Americans (p. 262). Does he anywhere suggest a contrast between white and black people in terms of "love" and the "infantile"?

12. David Truman urges the need for a "liberal education" to-day through higher "literacy." Do the root meanings of "liberal" and "literacy" have any relationship? Are "liberalism" and "literacy" aspects of the same thing?

13. Compare Truman's use of "liberal" with Luce's. Do they give the word the same meaning? Is one "right" and the other "incorrect" in usage?

14. Point to examples of Truman's abstract language in his essay. Could he have made the same points in more specific, concrete language? Why or why not?

15. Outline the development of reasoning in Hutchins's "Doing What Comes Scientifically." How is the list on page 273 related to what comes before and after?

16. Several words are used by Hutchins in his essay as obviously emphatic and connotative terms: "science," "technology," "moral," "liberal." Does he define them anywhere? What do they mean?

17. In several places, Hutchins gives apparently impromptu or stipulative definitions: a "university" is "an intellectual community"; "a profession is a group organized to perform a public

service"; "politics" is "the science of the common good." Evaluate the techniques and methods used in these definitions, and point out other examples. Is Hutchins's essay in any sense an extended definition?

Style and Rhetoric

1. Notice the use of rhetorical questions in Davis's essay. What purpose(s) do they serve?

2. Which of Davis's fallacies relate to the mental processes he says comprise "intelligence" (p. 258)? Which are errors in seeing connections between things? Which are errors in discerning causes?

3. Read the two final paragraphs of Davis's "Logical Fallacies" carefully. Does Davis himself commit any logical errors—e.g., begging the question, arguing *ad hominem*, and so on? Explain your answer.

4. Exactly what is Luce doing in her essay "Eating Our Way to Bad Behavior"? Is she proving the fallacy of liberal ideology as a whole? Attacking von Hoffman's logic? Refuting a scientific hypothesis? Or what?

5. What are the main points in von Hoffman's logic about food additives causing hyperkinesis, as Luce summarizes them? Is her summary fair or not? What is the effect of her parenthetical exclamation points and occasional rhetorical questions or her informal diction?

6. Does Luce suggest what she herself believes to cause juvenile violence? Where and how does she do this? Is her hypothesis more substantially based than von Hoffman's or not? Does she prove it?

7. What logical errors defined by Davis does Luce imply that von Hoffman is guilty of? Does she commit any logical fallacies herself? Support your opinion with textual examples.

8. Baldwin's discussion of white Americans depends to a large extent on generalizations. How does he establish these? Are any of the generalizations fallacious by Davis's standards? Are Baldwin's statements about the Negro generally assumed or do they represent his private assumptions? Does he make a distinction clear here?

9. On page 262, Baldwin says that the only thing possessed by the white American that the black American wants or needs is "power." What is the meaning of "power" here? How does the meaning affect the argument of the essay?

10. What are the implications of such terms as "spiritual traveller's checks," "African witch doctor . . . American psychiatrist," "knowing the family as I do," "enough is certainly as good as a feast"? How do they work to establish a tone for the essay?

11. Precisely what is David Truman asserting in his essay? Does he beg the question in his opening remarks about the plight of liberal education today? Explain.

12. Make a step-by-step outline of the logical points that Truman presents to support his view that "liberal" education is vital and high "literacy" is the essential element in liberal education.

13. Does Truman commit any errors in reasoning? Are many of his statements generalizations? Are there any flaws of sampling or false generalizing in his reasoning?

14. How are "tolerance" and "compassion" related to "liberal" thinking? Does Truman prove their importance or merely assume it?

15. Is R. M. Hutchins's essay ostensibly cool and disinterested in its attitude toward science and education? What evidence, direct and indirect, can you find to support the personal bias and inclinations of the writer? Does Hutchins think of himself as disinterested?

16. Look closely at Hutchins's argument. Does he commit any errors of false generalization? sampling? *ad hominem? post-hoc?* Support your answer with specific statements by Hutchins.

17. Does Hutchins himself point out logical fallacies in the thought of other people? Point out examples of his discussion of other points of view, and assess Hutchins's effectiveness in dealing with them logically.

Theme and Viewpoint

1. Using what you have learned about logical fallacies from Robert Davis's essay, go back and reread essays in several different rhetorical categories and test one or more for the logical principles that apply: e.g., the definition essays for errors of defining; the classification essays for errors of sample; the comparison and contrast essays for errors of degree and false analogy; and so on.

2. Does Davis suppose that any one essay can be totally free of logical flaws and errors? Discuss the implications of his treatment of logical fallacies, especially in the light of his two concluding paragraphs.

3. Does James Baldwin show Negroes themselves as having prejudices or solely as being the object of prejudice? Does Baldwin's treatment of prejudice—in his depiction of both whites and blacks—conform to Ian Stevenson's views of how prejudice is formed?

4. Do the Negroes and children (or white adults) in Katherine Anne Porter's sketches of Uncle Jimbilly and Old Nannie illustrate or contradict Baldwin's generalizations? Would Baldwin accuse Porter herself of sharing the white American's prejudices? Support your opinion with specific statements from the Baldwin and Porter essays.

5. In what ways does Theodor Reik's theory of the ego-ideal support Baldwin's contentions about the white American's attitude toward the Negro?

6. Compare David Truman's opinion of T.V. with that of Claire Luce. Do they agree or not? Other writers who have dealt with T.V. include Sedulus and Cline. Do the educator, T.V. critic, psychologist, and political spokeswoman hold similar attitudes toward T.V. and its influence? If they all agree, is their agreement "proof" of the "truth" of their view or not? How can a concensus of opinion "prove" or "disprove" the logical validity of an opinion?

7. Luce scorns the idea that diet additives can affect behavior in the way von Hoffmann asserts. Would Helen Nowlis accept Luce's view? Would Michael Jacobson? Reread "Our Diets Have Changed . . ." (p. 92); would Jacobson be more likely to back up the views of Luce or those she criticizes?

8. Does Luce's exercise in logic succeed in refuting the interpretation of data (or the data itself) in the Jacobson essay? Is Jacobson a "liberal" as Luce defines the term? Does one's political (philosophical) outlook really affect the way one interprets statistical data? Discuss.

9. Does David Truman mean the same thing by "high literacy" that F. L. Lucas does by "style"? If not, what is the relationship, if any, between literacy and style?

10. Do Luce and Baldwin agree on the causes for violence as it manifests itself racially? Is Baldwin a "liberal" in Luce's terms? What term might Baldwin apply to Luce?

11. One leading feminist has suggested that "women are the blacks of the human race." Do James Baldwin and Elizabeth Janeway seem to think that both women and blacks are victimized or exploited minorities? Compare their views. If women and blacks are victims, who are the victimizers? Do Janeway and Baldwin see the same victimizer-exploiter for the two groups?

What is the relationship of "White Americans" to "Male Chauvinist Pigs"?

12. Do you see any similarity between Baldwin's reading of the white–black relationship in the human race and Thoreau's reading of the battle between ants of two different colors? Does Julian Huxley's essay support or refute Baldwin's ideas about human confrontation?

13. Is there a relationship between "stress" and "violence"? Between drugs and stress, according to Hans Selye? May we conclude syllogistically that there is a connection between drugs (food additives) and violence? Test the logic of the implied syllogism.

14. Compare Robert Hutchins's and John Steele's views of science and "moral neutrality." Are their attitudes the same? Does Hutchins make out a better case for the political involvement of the scientist than Steele does? Is Steele interested in political involvement?

15. Compare the essays of Hutchins and Oppenheimer. Do they hold like or unlike viewpoints toward science, politics, and morality? Is one more obviously "liberal" than the other by Hutchins's definition? By Luce's definition? Is one more passionate and interested in the import of science than the other? If so, which? Would you expect this?

part two

Modes
of discourse

Exposition:
arranging information

Arranging information shares several characteristics with the kind of public exhibition or fair that shares its name—exposition. From the famous St. Louis Exposition of 1904 to the Montreal Expo 67, these public displays of products have demonstrated the literal meaning of the Latin *ex ponere*—"to set out" or expose to view. If you attended Expo 67, or one of its variations in Seattle or New York, you saw a vast conglomeration of things, all collected and arranged to display some aspect of cultural values, abilities, or activities. Plotted out, sorted and placed, ranged on counters, set before symbolic backgrounds, these chosen materials were arranged to illustrate some central idea or purpose: the variety of Canadian products, American technological ingenuity, British tradition, or Roman Catholic artistry. Even in regional fairs, there are "exhibition halls," full of Macintosh apples, pumpkins, hand-sewn quilts, home-baked custard pies, all displayed to reveal the rich variety of Yoknapatawpha county and its farms. There are also "demonstrations": of 4-H handcrafting or atomic milking machines. In "demonstrating" or "setting forth" diverse data, expository prose similarly displays the evidence that purports to convey most cogently and fully the true nature of its subject.

Just as a collection of related physical objects (coins, stamps, matchbook covers) that serves little purpose if it is all thrown together in a heap, must reveal its selective principle through arrangement, so an expository essay should include only material that is relevant and arrange it to suit some central aim or intention. Only related materials should be included; and they should follow some pattern of orderly logic that reveals the total character of the subject they comprise. Consider, for a moment, how many ways a coin collection might be set forth to demonstrate the significant aspects of coinage. French coins might be placed beside Russian ones; English farthings ranged from their sixteenth-century versions to their final shapes in 1956; groupings made by shape or size or design; a single coin shown in cross sections to reveal its composition. These physical methods correspond to the comparative, definitive, classifying, and analytical methods of exposition.

The underlying purpose of all exposition is to give full and accurate information about some subject or field of knowledge: to increase the reader's store of facts and understanding of what something is, how it came to be that way, and what it signifies. Expository writers amass details—sometimes through systematic experimentation and observation, sometimes through wide reading and research—and then arrange these details through some combination of rhetorical methods. Encyclopedia articles are prime examples of expository writing; but so are book reviews, lab reports, Ph.D. theses, and papers read to medical conventions.

In its purest versions, the expository mode does not seek to justify or defend anything; it describes its subject as completely as possible to meet certain demands and needs for information. Of course, much exposition cannot be wholly divorced from the personal qualities of the writer, who selects and emphasizes data according to his or her own criteria of relevance and accuracy. If the topic is an inflammatory one—drugs or juvenile delinquency, for instance—it is difficult for a writer to be totally objective and disinterested, just as it is impossible for the reader to be a machine recording the data it receives. But if the most objective expository essay still contains elements of the writer's bias, it may well remain useful for its informational qualities.

As you read the following essays on the Shakers, Ann Landers, violence, and drugs, keep in mind that good exposition must be measured by the extent to which it chooses its

materials in order to inform; arranges these data in a logical
and appropriate manner; and consistently enlightens and in-
structs the reader.

Encyclopaedia Britannica (1965)

The Shakers

Shakers, an American celibate and communistic sect, known as the
"United Society of Believers in Christ's Second Appearing" and as the
"Millennial Church." Some of the leaders prefer the name "Alethians,"
for they consider themselves children of the truth. The society had its beginning in a Quaker revival in England (1747) which resulted in the
organization of a sect of which Jane and James Wardley were the leaders.
They were succeeded by Ann Lee. The distinctive merit of celibacy became an original tenet of the Shakers in England. They did not prohibit
marriage but refused to accept it as a Christian institution and considered
it less perfect than the celibate state.

Under stress of persecution and in response to a revelation, "Mother"
Ann led a band of six men and two women to America. They arrived in
New York city on Aug. 6, 1774, and after two years' stay there, settled in
the woods of Watervliet, not far from Albany, N.Y. In 1780 there was a
religious revival in New Lebanon, N.Y., and some of the converts became
disciples of Ann Lee. At this place, in 1787, the first Shaker society in the
United States was organized; the society at Watervliet was organized
immediately afterward. Ann Lee went from place to place preaching her
new doctrine and became known as a faith healer. At the time of her
death (1784) she had disciples in New York, Massachusetts and Connecticut. A group of Shakers came out of the Kentucky revival of 1800–02.
The community at Mount Lebanon, N.Y., sent three of their number to
Kentucky to bear witness to the people.

Though at first bitterly opposed, these Shaker preachers made a sufficient number of converts to found five societies, "two in Ohio, two in

THE SHAKERS Reprinted by permission, © *Encyclopaedia Britannica,* 14th edition
(1965).

Kentucky and one in Indiana." In 1894 the Mount Lebanon society founded a colony at Narcoosee, Fla., called the Union Village society. In 1910 it went into the hands of a receiver.

The Shakers held that God was both male and female, that Adam, having been created in the image of God, had in him the nature of both sexes, that even angels and spirits are both male and female. Christ, they believed, was one of the superior spirits and appeared in Jesus, the son of a Jewish carpenter, representing the male principle. In Mother Ann, daughter of an English blacksmith, the female principle in Christ was manifested, and in her the promise of the Second Coming was fulfilled. Christ's kingdom on earth began with the establishment of the Shaker Church.

The practical ideals of the community were the common possession of property, a life of celibacy, confession of sin, without which no one could become a member of the community, power over physical disease and separation from the world. Disease they regarded as a sin against God. Their separateness from the world was indicated by their manner of living in families of 30 to 50 individuals. Each family had its own house, the stories being divided between the men and women. They made no room for adornments in the way of pictures or other works of art. In their prescribed mode of dress for men and women, they also protested against the fashions of a vain world. For a time they made their own clothing and wove their own cloth. They made leather in New York for several years; but were more successful in selling herbs and garden seeds, and in making apple sauce, weaving linen and knitting underwear. Many of them, however, considered it a mistake to have left agriculture and entered into manufacturing.

In 1874 there were 58 Shaker communities with 2,415 members, owning 100,000 ac. of land; in 1905 the membership was reduced to about 1,000. By mid-20th century there were fewer than 100 members in five surviving communities.

BIBLIOGRAPHY—John P. MacLean, *A Bibliography of Shaker Literature With an Introductory Study of the Writings and Publications Pertaining to Ohio Believers* (Columbus, O., 1905), *Sketch of the Life and the Labors of Richard McNemar* (Franklin, O., 1905); C. E. Robinson, *A Concise History of the United States of Believers, called Shakers* (1893); Anna White and Leila S. Taylor, *Shakerism, Its Meaning and Message* (1905); F. W. Evans, *Shakers: Compendium of the Origin, History, Principles, Rules and Regulations, Governments and Doctrines of the United Society of Believers in Christ's Second Appearing* (1858), often elsewhere under other titles; C. E. Sears (comp.) *Gleanings From Old Shaker Journals* (1916); F. H. Noyes, *History of American Socialisms* (1870); C. Nordhoff, *The Communistic Societies of the United States* (1875).
(G. W. Ri.; X.)

Encyclopaedia Britannica (1974)

The Shakers

Shakers, common name for the UNITED SOCIETY OF BELIEVERS IN CHRIST'S SECOND APPEARING, celibate millenarian sect that established socialist communities in the U.S. Dedicated to productive labour as well as to a life of perfection, Shaker communities flourished economically and contributed a distinctive style of architecture, furniture, and handicraft to U.S. culture.

Shakers derived originally from a small branch of radical English Quakers who had adopted the French Camisards' ritual practices of shaking, shouting, dancing, whirling, and singing in tongues. The Shaker doctrine, as it came to be known in the U.S., was formulated by Ann Lee, an illiterate textile worker of Manchester, who was converted to the "Shaking Quakers" in 1758. After experiencing persecution and imprisonment for participation in noisy worship services, "Mother Ann" had a series of revelations, after which she regarded herself—and was so regarded by her followers—as the female aspect of God's dual nature and the second incarnation of Christ. She established celibacy as the cardinal principle of the sect.

In 1774 Ann Lee came to America with eight disciples, having been charged by a new revelation to establish the millennial church in the New World. Settling in 1776 at Niskeyuna (now Watervliet), N.Y., the small group of believers benefitted from an independent revival movement that was sweeping the district and, within five years, was enlarged by several thousand converts.

After Mother Ann's death (1784), the Shaker church came under the leadership of Elder Joseph Meacham and Eldress Lucy Wright, who together worked out the communal pattern that was to be the distinctive Shaker social organization. The first Shaker community, established at New Lebanon, N.Y., in 1787, remained the head of influence as the movement spread through New England and westward into Kentucky, Ohio, and Indiana. By 1826, 18 Shaker villages had been set up in eight states.

Although often persecuted for pacifism, or for bizarre beliefs falsely attributed to them, the Shakers won the admiration of "the world's people" for their model farms and orderly, prosperous communities. Their industry and ingenuity produced numerous (usually unpatented) inventions, of which the screw propeller, Babbitt metal, a rotary harrow, an automatic spring, a turbine waterwheel, a threshing machine, the circular saw, and the common clothespin are a few. They were the first to package and market seeds and were once the largest producers of medicinal herbs. In exchanges with the world they were noted for their fair dealing.

Shaker dances and songs are a genuine folk art, and the simple beauty, functionalism, and honest craftsmanship of their meeting houses, barns, and artifacts have had a lasting influence on American design.

The Shaker impulse reached its height during the 1840s, when about 6,000 members were enrolled in the church. It declined with the ebbing of spiritualism. By 1874 the society was advertising for members, emphasizing physical comfort above spiritual values. By 1905 there were only 1,000 members, and by the late 1960s only a few elderly survivors remained.

Judith Wax

"Dear Ann Landers, Is Incest Hereditary?"

The trouble was, he just wouldn't take her advice. "Oh, I always found him fairly easy to talk to," says the doll-sized woman in the leopard-print robe that reveals a lot of cleavage. "He was really quite a reasonable man."

"Whenever I had an opportunity to see him—say at a small social function—I would try to get him off to one side." (One pictures her advancing relentlessly in the black sequins-with-marabou she likes to wear for Occasions.) "I'd say, 'Now look! We've got to get rid of this war!' And then he'd say, 'I know, but how do you do it?'" She checks out her apartment's 15th-story view of Lake Michigan and Chicago's Gold Coast and sighs, "I never could do a thing with Lyndon Johnson."

As for Richard Nixon, he'd have resigned five months earlier had he taken the advice she directed his way in a speech at Notre Dame last April. But if the gang at the White House doesn't always listen to the lady with the syndicated dimples, 56-year-old Eppie (Esther Pauline) Lederer—who is Ann Landers to an audience she round-numbers at 60 million—has been affecting life, thought and social custom with a continuing impact such temporary kings might envy. Her "Ask Ann Landers" column appears in 810 newspapers from Medicine Hat, Canada, to Dothan, Ala., from Shamokin, Pa., to the Fiji Islands. ("They ask the same things in Fiji as they do in Toledo.") She survives a daily saturation bombing of mail soliciting her opinion on everything from whether "you do a woman a favor when you tell her she has lipstick on her teeth," (yes) to "Is incest hereditary?" (no)—from heartbreak questions of loss, despair, dysfunction and disability to speculations concerning the proclivity of raccoons to breed through the nose and gestate in the sinus cavity. Fortunately, some readers merely need to know—preferably by return mail—what life is.

Surveys that measure such things show that in paper after paper she is first-read and favorite; "Dear Ann Landers" is frequently digested with morning toast before the headlines. Hers is said to be the most widely followed column in the world, a claim also made on behalf of her twin sister, who writes similarly pungent counsel under the name of Abigail Van Buren.

Humorist George Ade would have called her a Sassy Savant. In her natural lunchbox style—pithy, punchy, earthy and often snappily amusing—she has addressed herself to a regular stock company of American characters: the "funny" uncle, the meddling mother-in-law, the boss who collects pornography, the miniskirted ("Nobody would ever dream I'm 36") mama who chicken-frugs away the night with teen-age daughter's boyfriend.

She brooks no nonsense. "Bubs," "Busters" and "Kiddos" by the columnload had better shape up and "quitcherkidden." Miss Icarus, who writes she wants to marry her fiancé's father, is advised to "Drop Daedalus," and the actress whose true love beats her to improve her art by acquainting her with the range of human emotions is cautioned, "If he doesn't know how Sarah Bernhardt lost a leg, don't tell him; he might get ideas."

Certain griefs earn compassion and special endearments: "honey," "dear" or even "buttercup." "Terrible things can happen to some very nice people," she says, and to these she doles out cheer, comfort, support (frequently with the names of appropriate community-service agencies) or a typical, "And don't forget about me, toots, anytime you want to unload. That's what I'm here for."

She is not always thanked. "This is to let you know that I took your advice and it wrecked my whole life," writes Heartbroken Edna, who went along with the suggestion that she tell her now-departed fiancé of the illegitimate child in her past. "Get your head out of mothballs!" yowl three 12-year-old "refined ladies from nice families." But she is publicly kissed by admiring strangers wherever she goes ("You helped me raise my children"), given standing ovations at schools ("I asked you things I didn't dare discuss at home"), has been named Woman of the Year by six organizations and is a regular on "Most Admired" and "Most Influential" lists.

A staff of eight secretaries ("They're almost all college graduates; I'm not!") sorts out the daily deluge of 1,000 or more letters. She calls this daily Krakatoa of correspondence "a sacred trust between me and my readers," and when a newspaper employe in the East recently violated that trust by penciling a comment on a forwarded "Dear Ann" letter, he got a crackling reminder of her eyes-only policy. Eyes only, too: a letter from pal Hubert Humphrey which she says concedes "I should have listened, Eppie; you were right about Vietnam." ("He couldn't do much with Lyndon, either," she notes, "which was one of his problems.") Nearly three-quarters of the letters are requests for advice or general reader comment. Of this number, half are anonymous, and these go to Landers herself. From them she selects the "gut letters" that will ultimately appear—three a day, seven days a week, in her column. Though she spends three hours a day in her Chicago Sun-Times office, actual column preparation and writing is done at home. She swears by her favorite possession, a paper-clipencrusted bust of John Kennedy, that every word under her byline is her own—columns, books and pamphlets. She is frequently accused of inventing reader letters. "A person would have to be psychotic to make this stuff up," she says.

One-quarter of the daily mail contains requests for Landers-written pamphlets: "Teen-Age Sex and Ten Ways to Cool it," "Alcoholism—Hope and Help," "The Key to Popularity" and nine other 25c-to-$1.00 miniguides to social behavior and contemporary crisis. Most of the mail that is signed and return-addressed receives prompt staff-written answers, based on Landers guidelines and custom-tailored to the inquiry. Difficult or unusual signed letters are flagged to Landers or community-service organizations and a vast referral file is maintained of health and counseling services throughout the country. A "philosophy session" held every few weeks with visiting medical and psychiatric consultants is meant to keep the secretarial staff *au courant* with latest opinions and Landers-approved viewpoints.

About a quarter of the mail is from teenagers and the bulk of the rest from 30- to 45-year-olds—nearly half of them male, she says. But she hears from prepubescents with sibling grief and a 103-year-old faithful follower in Cleveland who reads the column without glasses. A National Education Association survey once indicated that Landers had a larger following among teachers than any other columnist; in fact, it would be hard to find a social, economic or work category that doesn't "Dear Ann" her.

What are the biggest concerns? "Loneliness and people who don't know what to do with their lives . . . 'Should I leave him?' 'Should I kick him out?' 'What can I do about his—or her—drinking?' 'What are we to do about these kids?'

"With teenagers, it's a toss-up between sex and trouble with parents; the drug questions are tapering off. I'm very sympathetic with the kids *and* with the parents. There have been so many changes in the last 10 years and more in the last 25 than in the previous 250. A lot of kids hate their parents; probably kids always have, but they're expressing it now. Many are in therapy and *it* has screwed up a lot of them into thinking their parents wrecked them. I've said in my column, 'All right, if you don't like what you are, make some changes, Bub.' A good therapist will get a kid past hating and blaming his parents and on to understanding and building a life."

(Misery, however, is not her sole concern. A sort of Landers lechery poll has recently evolved from her mail. At a reader's request, she compiled a survey among women to determine which males—by occupation—most frequently try to seduce them. At final count, it was doctors by a stethoscope; clergy collared second, with dentists catching up, lawyers gaining and professors—"It's that or flunk"—closing in fast.)

"I view my column as an opportunity to educate. I want to let people in trouble know that others have problems, too. I want to be the shoulder to cry on," she says earnestly. "Maybe I can't solve the problem, but at least I can turn on the light so they can see it. People are lonely, anguished . . . if I can give some support, what a blessing! What more could anyone want out of life?"

"Eppie just loves telling the world how to behave," says a friend.

Is it frightening being mentor to millions? "Never! I answer one person and forget the 59,999,999 others." (That cool extends to private life. Trapped in her nightgown by a self-locking door in a St. Regis corridor, she commanded by house-phone, "Send up your oldest bellboy!")

Wedding etiquette and woe swell the mail sacks. A "Bride's Guide" booklet can be ordered from the Landers office for 35c, but it provides scant help for such letter writers as the pregnant bride whose father threatened to have groom-to-be arrested for the "rape" she denied ("Shut up," she reported papa yelled. "If I say you were raped, you were raped!").

It does, however, give such modern guidelines as proper roles for the wedding principal's illegitimate progeny (ring-bearing and flower-strewing are frowned upon) and garb for those pregnant and altar-bound: "Better not plan on a white bridal gown; the best bet is an ensemble with loose-fitting coat."

Drug-related queries have abated from the poisonous flowering in the late nineteen-sixties. "My answer to your questions," she characteristically writes, "would cut no mustard. You might as well ask your mother. The opinions of the country's most distinguished psychiatrists, however, might make a dent." She tries to achieve balance, though most reflect prevailing cautionary medical views. She opposes the legalization of marijuana but deplores criminalization of youthful offenders. Her booklet, "Straight Dope on Drugs," is a direct, unemotional and readable compilation of properties, effects and legal ramifications, marijuana to heroin.

It's a far cry from the fifties, when Landers-column headlines reflected the travail of the day: "IS TEACHER'S TIGHT DRESS CORRUPTING PUPILS?" or, "TWO FLASHY GIRLS LURE BOYS TO APARTMENT." ("My buddy and I were in a high-class lounge and before you could say, 'rum and Coca-Cola,' they were sitting at our table.") "Stay away from dogs if you don't want fleas" answers then came a lot easier than those addressed more recently to "Speed Freak" and "Nothing to Live For."

Mind-jarring trivia and slipped-gear logic provide respite from the daily litanies of anguish. One man solicited the legal requirements for having himself embalmed and buried at the wheel of his beloved 1939 Dodge. Landers's underground adviser (her funeral-director son-in-law) recommended either three adjoining plots to lodge the Dodge or cremation and storage in the car's ashtray. A not-quite widow devoted five pages of inquiry to contemplated funerary chic: "Could a veil like Jackie Kennedy's be worn with glasses, or should I get contact lenses? Are white gloves too dressy?"

Despite such letters, she is never contemptuous of her readers' need for her. "I have been very lucky," she says. "I have good health, amazing vitality, good head, good body, a wonderful husband and daughter. Anybody who has it as good as I have has a responsibility to do something for those who haven't. And most haven't.

"I never insult or make fun of the person with the problem. And I never sacrifice sound advice for a laugh."

Almost before her column is set in type, its reverberations can be felt from suburban breakfast nook to Senate Dining Room. A million Landers-inspired letters to legislators in support of the National Cancer Act, for instance, spurred a $100-million appropriation. Such power to mobilize support inundates her office with requests for backing—worthy cause and crank's fancy alike.

An inaccurate or controversial column reply, a provocative question or the most innocuous assertion can set off mushroom clouds of reader response and endless fallout concerning such things as acceptable hair lengths, the ability of a woman who has not been pregnant to breast-feed or the efficacy of doing housework in the nude.

Seven thousand lawyers wrote to protest gratuitous and incorrect advice from a letter signed Legal Secretary. (Ann is quick with a *mea culpa:* "Twenty swats for me with a rolled up writ of replevin" or "I'll take 10 lashes with an old prayer shawl.")

A newspaper error, the omission of an ingredient in a reader-requested Landers recipe favorite (meatloaf), unleashed 3,000 outraged "stick to advice, the dog wouldn't eat it" letters. Correction only loosed another torrent—helpful suggestions such as "try whipping cream for water."

"I wrote, 'Look, the recipe is a darn good one from my sister in Omaha, Mrs. David Brodkey. If you don't like it, eat lamb chops!' " Meatloaf purists rushed to dial the Nebraska sister and alerted the police when they couldn't get through to the by-now Bell-shocked Mrs. Brodkey. "A little bacon on top adds flavor," brought 17 rabbinical outcries; several thousand new requests poured in from those who "lost the first one."

Last in an estimated 20,000 meatloaf missives was an appeal for a Chinese translation of the recipe for the reader's Oriental cook. "Because your name is on the list of the most-admired women in the world, Miss Landers, means that you go out of your way for people." Landers, by then a dazed cookery drop-out, advised, "Try Mme. Chiang Kai-Shek; she was on the Most-Admired list too."

Critics accuse mail oracles of playing God-cum-Freud, and cite the danger and possible damage to the vulnerable. Readers' letters, they point out, may omit significant detail and bend situation reality to their own biased or neurotic view. Others try on advice that doesn't fit them. Worse, it's charged, newspaper nostrums may deter or delay disturbed people from getting live professional counsel; advice may be oversimplified and based on insufficient data or geared to the entertaining answer. Landers, they note—like most of her past and present colleagues—has had no experience in psychiatric or social work.

Ann herself is convinced of the solidity of her product and an army of medical and psychiatric advisers and auditors give her a glowing, sometimes panegyrical bill of health on all counts.

"I can't salvage a life that's been rotten for 20 years in a little bit of newspaper space. But in 810 cities, we know exactly where to send people for every imaginable problem. The dean of Harvard Medical School, Dr. Robert Ebert, says we run the most effective social-service agency in the world.

"I know that I'm giving the very best possible advice, and I work like a dog to get it." The phone calls to her network of experts cost more than $24,000 annually.

Dr. Robert Moser, editor of The Journal of the American Medical Association, says, "Her mind is somewhere between a buzz saw and a filing cabinet, and because of her incredible contacts she has at her fingertips a cadre of the best medical brains in the country. Everyone is willing to help her because she has enormous power. People ask her questions they'd never ask their doctor." She has taken doctors to task for just that in a recent magazine article, charging that many tune out the cries for help —particularly in sexual matters—that eventually end up in her mailbag.

She sits on the Board of Overseers of Harvard Medical School, is a trustee of the Menninger Foundation and Mayo Foundation Sponsors' Committee and the Chicago Rehabilitation Institute and is the only woman member of the National Dermatology (despair is often skin deep) Foundation. She is an active participant in all. "I mean business when I accept one of these positions; I won't allow my name to be used just to decorate stationery." Though irate readers have accused her of being a shill for the A.M.A. and the American Psychiatric Association, she can dish out strong medicine to an occasional errant Welby. Psychiatrists are especially subject to criticism. "Your chances of getting a good one are about 50-50," she says. (Her latest column-blast at chiropractors set off a predictable furious postal deluge, along with—anonymously—a photograph of a bulletin board whose sole message was, "DID YOU READ WHAT THE JEWISH BITCH SAID ABOUT CHIROPRACTORS NOW?")

To help with religious problems, she has rallied an ecumenical council of her own, and clear favorite on the side of the angels is the Rev. Theodore Hesburgh, president of the University of Notre Dame, to whom she often turns for theological and moral counsel. His photograph hangs in her hall, its signature, "Love, but no kisses." She signs her letters to him the same way, but sometimes adds a jaunty, "Darn it!"

Among the custom-made rugs, paneling imported from a British castle, mother-of-pearl inlaid chairs, huge 15th-century kneeling angels she calls "the girls," Picasso, Dali, Renoir and Ming treasures in the Landers/ Lederer apartment, an unexpected sculpture of a horse-drawn cart loaded with assorted poultry cages draws the eye. It may be a reminder of not-so-fine-feathered beginnings when her father peddled chickens in Sioux City, Iowa. Abraham Friedman fled Russia with his wife Rebecca to avoid conscription in the Czar's army and quickly parlayed the chicken-vending wagon into a movie and vaudeville chain that spanned three states.

"I am typically upper-middle class, Midwestern Jewish," and this—says Landers—has shaped her thinking, her humor, the column and its style. "I grew up," she once wrote, "in an atmosphere electric with Yiddish adages. My father was sort of a Jewish Lin Yutang and my mother had a talent for fitting an appropriate expression to any set of circumstances."

Identical twins Esther Pauline (Eppie/Ann Landers) and Pauline Esther (Popo/Abigail Van Buren) followed two older Friedman girls in 1918. Born center-stagers, both studied the violin and neither has ever been content to play second fiddle. They were a vibrant, dress-alike matched pair, in the classroom, on dates and finally at the altar in a double ceremony that continued their 21-year-old habit of astounding Sioux Cityites.

Ann Landers's unchanging warning of the perils of interfaith marriage apparently was absorbed at home with parental chopped liver. When fiancé Jules Lederer was introduced for family inspection, papa Friedman questioned—despite assurances—the blond young man's credentials in the faith. "Say something in Yiddish," demanded the patriarch.

Jules thought it over. "I vanna go for a valk," he ventured, which evidently was good enough. (Daughter Margo recalls that as a Brandeis student she once requested permission from home to date the Aga Khan's Harvard-based son. "You say the boy's name is Kahn?" said Eppie. "Go ahead, doll.")

"Most married people, if they are honest," she has written, "will admit that marriage isn't all they hoped it would be." In her own case, she admits, the gypsy violins of courtship were muted when she "settled down to the hardships of everyday living. We had a child and moved around a great deal—to wherever Jules could make another five dollars." Good marriages, she allows, may be made in heaven, but "the maintenance work must be done down here."

"Ann Landers can tell a woman to scrub floors and sweat over the kitchen stove because she doesn't have to! I'll bet that dame has hired help all over the place," an Ohio husband reported his wife as saying in reaction to a 1968 column chiding "sloppy housekeepers."

"Your wife is right. I don't do housework, but I did plenty of it the first 10 years of my marriage. And I didn't hate it or feel it was beneath my dignity. My house looked fairly presentable and so did my husband's shirts, which I ironed. And nobody ever died from my cooking."

She once comforted a struggling housewife, "Pity the poor millionaire;

he'll never know the thrill of paying the final installment." It is a thrill she has had to forgo. Husband Jules, former owner of Budget Rent-A-Car ("Pretty good," she says, "for a guy who took on the world with a ninth-grade education and a hole in his sock") now has international business interests that keep him away from their 14-room apartment at least one-third of the year. His constant travels, she says, "have taught me how to be alone without feeling sorry for myself. He really does enjoy my success, but he's always insisted on supporting me."

Though she warns that earth-bound unions lose heavenly transport, she is nonetheless inspired by her own to rhapsodic variations Liszt wouldn't have dared. In column and conversation, he is "my doll, my beautiful guy; he is my best friend and I am his." She inscribes the books she writes and the linings of a herd of fur coats, "Jules' Wife."

A new acquaintance recently said of daughter Margo Furth, "I just met the campiest lady; she has a big framed picture of Ann Landers in her bedroom!" Now 34 and mother of three, Margo once had her own syndicated column and—along with the familial urge to write—has the maternal luminous skin ("I envy people with a few wrinkles"), high cheekbones, and congenital outspokenness. "I think I've always scandalized my mother, but she's behaved very well and never asked me not to do something because it wouldn't be compatible with the image of her column. She tries very hard not to give advice, though she sometimes sneaks a little in."

Landers has had frequent admonitions for grandchildren-spoilers ("Don't tell me wait till I have some of my own; I do, and I'm a pretty tough old cookie") and meddlers ("Margo is perfectly capable of raising her own children").

"She's pretty businesslike with my kids," says Margo. "She wants to teach, instill values. They go to her house for a coloring contest—she's not an impartial judge; whoever needs the lift most, wins—and for dinner."

Basic Landers laws for inlaws are: live separately, be friendly, husbands and wives owe first allegiance to each other. Readers don't always get the message. One husband drove his mother to her bridge game when his wife's labor pains began. A lament signed "Miami" stated, "Whenever you print a letter knocking a mother-in-law, I receive two copies the next day. One I'm sure is from my daughter-in-law and the other from her miserable mother. I can't tell you how it hurts a mother's heart to raise a boy and then hand him over to a lazy good-for-nothing who uses plastic tablecloths and buys ready-made potato salad. You should live to be a hundred, Ann Landers, and never know from such things."

Her own mother-in-law, to whom she once awarded a "World's Best M.I.L." medal, called her "Eppeleh with the Keppeleh." "As God is my judge, we never exchanged one unpleasant word in 34 years," said the column tribute at her mother-in-law's death.

Two sons-in-law, past and present, give high marks to her ability to take her own advice and "M.Y.O.B.,"—a vintage Landersism meaning mind your own business.

In 1955, after a series of moves around the country, 37-year-old Eppie beat out 27 competitors for the just-vacated Ann Landers slot on The Chicago Sun-Times. The "Ann Landers" name was a 1952 inspiration of editor Pete Akers, who thought it had a nice ring. The first and only other "Landers," a nurse named Ruth Crowley, wrote the column till her death three years later. Sister Popo needed only six more months to create an identical role for herself on The San Francisco Chronicle. Before moving to Chicago, Eppie had begun to make her presence felt in Wisconsin politics when, in a 1954 effort to get her licks in at then-Senator Joseph McCarthy, she won a hotly-contested Democratic county chairmanship. But neither sister had ever held a job or published a word. Both had married before completing Methodist Morningside College in Sioux City. Their readers weren't worried about credentials, though, and the lively, irreverent columns were an immediate hit. Syndication in newspapers was not far behind, thus launching a race for space and a furious feud that finally exhausted itself in rapprochement years later. Since then, frequent phone calls, letters and joint anniversary celebrations attest to the détente.

Dr. George Engel, professor of psychiatry and medicine at the University of Rochester and himself a twin, says, "Most identical twins—torn between the need for preserving the unique and attention-getting relationship and finding singular identity—struggle vigorously to keep their competitive feelings under control. If a break occurs, it is likely to be serious and painful."

Deprived of "the other" during their rift, Popo and Eppie had compensatory, perhaps more perfect pairings—one with "Abby" and one with "Ann." ("Eppie never really reveals herself," says an intimate. "Sometimes I think *she's* gotten lost in the identity of Ann Landers.") It's intriguing to wonder if the biological caprice that is twinning, with its psychic effects on the Sioux City sibyls, has had secondary impact on all those Distraughts, Left Behinds and Troubled in Topekas out there in universal readerland.

In 1958, Widow, 34, solicited Landers's blessing for a proposed motor trip to Mount Rushmore. Son Ronnie, 8, would share a room with Widow's fiancé; separate quarters—of course—for her. "I hope you will see the educational value in this trip, Miss Landers," she ventured, "and say it's all right, since my son wants to report on Mount Rushmore to his class."

Hard lines for Widow, 34. She was briskly informed that trip to altar precedes trip to Great Stone Faces. "It is not proper for unmarried people to travel together, even with an 8-year-old chaperon."

"Eppie has always been a puritan," says an old friend. Through the years, the columns have been studded with laudatory references to "white-flower girls" (virgins), and cautionary tales of the seduced-and-abandoned.

Though her views on virginity have mellowed through the years, her pamphlet "Love and Sex—and How to Tell the Difference" still concludes, "I hope all of you someday will know this most exquisite of all experiences, the moment when you give your most precious gift—yourself—to your beloved in marriage. You will be glad you waited and ever thankful that you refused to settle for a shoddy substitute." ("If men admire virgins so ardently," counters a letter signed Knob Hill, "why don't they leave a few around?")

Teen-age attraction is "one set of glands calling to another;" her "Necking and Petting" rules specify "all hands on deck" (a neat trick for petters) "and four feet on the floor." However, she has been in the vanguard for sex education at home and in the classroom and was one of the first popular columnists to discuss V.D.

She was an early advocate, too, of experimentation and freedom of sexual expression between married people. Nothing is indecent or unnatural, she has counseled, that is pleasing to both and degrading to neither—not revolutionary doctrine, but liberating revelation in many American homes.

"Many are cold, but few are frozen," she has instructed U.S. husbands. "Communicate!" she exhorts wives. "Tell your husband what you like and what you don't." (A young bride's tearful complaint of unappreciated husbandly ear-blowing prompted telegraphed instructions from the column queen herself: "TELL HIM TO STOP IT!") Joyful spankers and spankees, swingers and swappers, husbands and wives with his-and-hers girdles and bras are sick, all sick, says Landers, but—she tells them—"If it's O.K. with you, it's O.K. with me."

"My two biggest changes over the years have been in the areas of divorce and virginity. There was a time when I thought that no unmarried girl, no matter how old, should have any physical relations with a man. Well, I see now that is not the brightest approach. Some girls can handle sex outside of marriage if they're sufficiently mature . . . an awfully smart 19 or a darn steady, stable 20. But I firmly believe high school girls should stay intact." And Landers standards preclude joint unwed domesticity, even as a test for marriage.

Perhaps the biggest shift in Landers's attitude has been toward divorce, once rigidly opposed. "How come your dateline isn't Vatican

City?" demanded Jaundiced Eye in 1962. A decade later, spiraling divorce rates and, friends say, her own daughter's divorce and remarriage, have moved her to countenance what man sometimes puts asunder. "Apparently," she concedes, "some people must live through one unsuccessful marriage to know how to make a second marriage work."

It is rumored that when sister "Dear Abby" decided to investigate a new sociological trend firsthand, she put on an "Ann Landers wig" and went to see a porno movie. Ann herself met the devil-in-the-flesh in a TV confrontation last year with actress-contortionist Linda Lovelace. For the edification of viewers who might have spent the previous six months in Nebuchadnezzar's hanging gardens, Landers unabashedly explained the Lovelace feat by saying that she "accommodates male genitalia deeply."

Years of bizarre mail had not prepared Landers for Linda and her magic tricks; two cultures have rarely run so counter. There was considerable discussion about commitment (or its absence) in coupling animals. At program's end, Ann, grim with professional concern, leaned toward the younger woman. "If you're ever in trouble, dear," she said, "don't hesitate to write me." Lovelace peered out from an explosion of curls to murmur, with identical solicitude, "And if *you're* ever in trouble, don't hesitate to contact me."

The pill and an alleged sexual revolution may have wrested Ann's grip from the chastity chalice, but on several controversial issues—such as support for strong gun-control legislation—she has a circulation-be-damned attitude. John G. Trezevant, executive vice-president of The Chicago Sun-Times and The Chicago Daily News, continues to edit her column daily, as he has done since he was a Sun-Times editor in 1966. ("I do it for friendship and fun, and it takes damn little work.") "Her policies and replies are all her own," he says, "though I urge her to stay out of such political things as specific endorsements of candidates or pending legislation. But Eppie's been able to break most of the accepted rules and do things the way she wants by sheer force of personality. If she decided to be a brain surgeon, she'd be cutting heads open in a couple of months . . . and finding new ways to do it."

Liquor advertisers have urged some client papers to stop teetotaling Landers from hitting the bottle so hard in her column, a pressure management has not passed on to her, she says. "I'll continue talking up A.A. and hammering away at so-called social drinkers who are really alcoholics. I don't drink or smoke, and it's paid off in enormous energy."

Her strong advocacy of abortion on demand and columns on birth control and vasectomy have loosed landslides of protesting mail. "If I get one more copy of 'The Diary of an Unborn Child,'" she says, "I'll kill myself." Her pro-abortion utterances cost her an honorary degree and the speech she was scheduled to give at one Catholic college, but clerical columnists such as the Rev. Paul Cuddy have nevertheless likened our lady of letters to St. Teresa of Avila.

Enraged by her refusal to endorse the American Psychiatric Association's removal of the word "sick" to describe them, a coalition of gay organizations recently picketed what they mistakenly believed to be her residence chanting, "Ann Landers, we won't take your slanders!" She counters that she has been urging self, family and community acceptance— and an end to discrimination—since 1966, when her first column on the subject prompted a Michigan publisher to announce, page one: "There will be no Ann Landers column today; the one she presented was not fit for a family newspaper."

There have been occasional protests from feminists, too, but she is relaxing her rigid posture that women belong in the home except in cases of financial need. Now she will say, "The average American woman whose kids don't drive her batty should stay at home at least till they go to nursery school." She points out that she began her own career when she was 37 and her daughter 15. "I probably could have run for Congress before that," she says, "but I wouldn't leave my family to go to Washington." It is clear that stable, hearth-hugging Mom is still Landers's ideal, but some of the zest is gone, one senses, from the good old "pick up his socks and iron the sheets if that's what your guy likes," pronouncements. (An enraged wife once wrote, "My husband threw his shirt on the floor and said, 'Ann Landers said you're supposed to pick it up.' ")

She has recently issued a statement of support for the Equal Rights Amendment, although "in the beginning, the women's movement turned me off—they were pushy, aggressive and antimale. But the more I began to think about it the more I realized, yeah—they really have something. Women are not paid what they're worth." (What she's worth—and gets, it is said—is comfortably six-figured, proof of the marketability of counsel.) She makes nearly 100 speeches throughout the country each year, some without charge for a cause she supports, sometimes for fees that range from $300 for a high-school address to $3,000 for business conventions. She has been paid as much as $5,000 for a single lecture. What she says is often news fodder. "And, if the publisher in some city doesn't like me to speak my mind, which I have to do for my self-respect, he can lump it." Since her column may attract more readership than page one in their papers, objecting publishers are likely to opt for the lumps.

"Look, there've got to be 8,000 letters here," she says, pointing to a pile that nearly buckles her home desk. "They're anonymous . . . who would know if I put a match to them? But I'll read every one. Now *that* some people would consider sick." With the same energy, she hits the floor for daily exercise, wears out relay teams of secretaries, makes innumerable public appearances, strides the mile to and from work and does her mandatory Olympics dash ("Good for the heart!") up the escalator to her office while lobby saunterers break for cover.

Her sense of mission sometimes approaches religiosity. "It's so late, dear," she tells an interviewer. "Why do you work so hard?" When reminded of her own dizzying day, she protests, "But this is a service!"

Later, she'll recline in perfumed bubbles, a buxom Venus in reading glasses, in the kind of mirrored, marbled bathroom they use to pose Miss Februarys for Playboy (not to be confused with her bathroom that has the sea-shell-shaped toilet and sink, or the other one with the hand-laid mosaics featuring water nymphs, fish, vines and Neptune). The famed pouf-wing hairdo ("I haven't changed in 20 years") survives the steamy mists while she selects column material from the agony, ineptitude, loneliness and dementia piled at tubside.

There is one on pale blue paper that begins, "Dear Miss Landers: The main reason I am writing is regarding Nixon, freedom of speech, the right to vote and my ex-husband."

(It is not known whether Widow, 34—she'd be pushing 50 by now— ever got to see Mount Rushmore.)

Arthur Miller

The Bored and the Violent

If my own small experience is any guide, the main difficulty in approaching the problem of juvenile delinquency is that there is very little evidence about it and very many opinions as to how to deal with it. By evidence I do not mean the news stories telling of gang fights and teen-age murders—there are plenty of those. But it is unknown, for instance, what the actual effects are on the delinquent of prison sentences, psychotherapy, slum-clearance projects, settlement-house programs, tougher or more lenient police attitudes, the general employment situation, and so on. Statistics are few and not generally reliable. The narcotics problem alone is an almost closed mystery.

Not that statistical information in itself can solve anything, but it might at least outline the extent of the disease. I have it, for instance, from an old and deservedly respected official—it is his opinion anyway— that there is really no great increase in delinquent acts but a very great intensification of our awareness of them. He feels we are more nervous now about infractions of the social mores than our ancestors, and he likes to point out Shakespeare, Boccaccio, and other writers never brought on stage a man of wealth or station without his bravos, who were simply his private police force, necessary to him when he ventured out of his house, especially at night. He would have us read *Great Expectations, Oliver Twist, Huckleberry Finn,* and other classics, not in a romantic mood but in the way we read about our own abandoned kids and their depredations. The difference lies mainly in the way we look at the same behavior.

The experts have only a little more to go on than we have. Like the surgeon whose hands are bloody a good part of the day, the social worker is likely to come to accept the permanent existence of the delinquency disease without the shock of the amateur who first encounters it.

A new book on the subject, *All the Way Down,*[1] reports the experience of a social worker—of sorts—who never got used to the experience, and does not accept its inevitability. It is an easy book to attack on superficial grounds because it has no evident sociological method, it rambles and jumps and shouts and curses. But it has a virtue, a very great and rare one, I think, in that it does convey the endless, leaden, mind-destroying boredom of the delinquent life. Its sex is without romance or sexuality, its violence is without release or gratification—exactly like the streets— movies and plays about delinquency notwithstanding.

Unlike most problems which sociology takes up, delinquency seems to be immune to the usual sociological analyses or cures. For instance, it appears in all technological societies, whether Latin or Anglo-Saxon or Russian or Japanese. It has a very slippery correlation with unemployment and the presence or absence of housing projects. It exists among the rich in Westchester and the poor in Brooklyn and Chicago. It has spread quickly into the rural areas and the small towns. Now, according to Harrison Salisbury, it is the big problem in the Soviet Union. So that any

[1] By Vincent Riccio and Bill Slocum, Simon & Schuster.

single key to its causation is nowhere visible. If one wants to believe it to be essentially a symptom of unequal opportunity—and certainly this factor operates—one must wonder about the Russian problem, for the Soviet youngster can, in fact, go right up through the whole school system on his ability alone, as many of ours cannot. Yet the gangs are roaming the Russian streets, just as they do in our relatively permissive society.

So no one knows what "causes" delinquency. Having spent some months in the streets with boys of an American gang, I came away with certain impressions, all of which stemmed from a single, overwhelming conviction—that the problem underneath is boredom. And it is not strange, after all, that this should be so. It is the theme of so many of our novels, our plays, and especially our movies in the past twenty years, and it is the hallmark of society as a whole. The outcry of Britain's so-called Angry Young Men was against precisely this seemingly universal sense of life's pointlessness, the absence of any apparent aim to it all. So many American books and articles attest to the same awareness here. The stereotype of the man coming home from work and staring dumbly at a television set is an expression of it, and the "New Wave" of movies in France and Italy propound the same fundamental theme. People no longer seem to know why they are alive; existence is simply a string of near-experiences marked off by periods of stupefying spiritual and psychological stasis, and the good life is basically an amused one.

Among the delinquents the same kind of mindlessness prevails, but without the style—or stylishness—which art in our time has attempted to give it. The boredom of the delinquent is remarkable mainly because it is so little compensated for, as it may be among the middle classes and the rich who can fly down to the Caribbean or to Europe, or refurnish the house, or have an affair, or at least go shopping. The delinquent is stuck with his boredom, stuck inside it, stuck to it, until for two or three minutes he "lives"; he goes on a raid around the corner and feels the thrill of risking his skin or his life as he smashes a bottle filled with gasoline on some other kid's head. In a sense, it is his trip to Miami. It makes his day. It is his shopping tour. It gives him something to talk about for a week. It is *life*. Standing around with nothing coming up is as close to dying as you can get. Unless one grasps the power of boredom, the threat of it to one's existence, it is impossible to "place" the delinquent as a member of the human race.

With boredom in the forefront, one may find some perspective in the mélange of views which are repeated endlessly about the delinquent. He is a rebel without a cause, or a victim of poverty, or a victim of undue privilege, or an unloved child, or an overloved child, or a child looking for a father, or a child trying to avenge himself on an uncaring society, or what-not. But face to face with one of them, one finds these criteria useless, if only because no two delinquents are any more alike than other people are. They do share one mood, however. They are drowning in boredom. School bores them, preaching bores them, even television bores them. The word rebel is inexact for them because it must inevitably imply a purpose, an end.

Other people, of course, have known boredom. To get out of it, they go to the movies, or to a bar, or read a book, or go to sleep, or turn on TV or a girl, or make a resolution, or quit a job. Younger persons who are not delinquents may go to their room and weep, or write a poem, or call up a friend until they get tired talking. But note that each of these escapes can only work if the victim is sure somewhere in his mind, or reasonably hopeful, that by so doing he will overthrow his boredom and with luck may come out on the other side where something hopeful or interesting waits. But the delinquent has no such sense of an imminent improvement. Most of the kids in the Riccio and Slocum book have never known a single good day. How can they be expected to project one and restrain themselves in order to experience such joy once more?

The word rebel is wrong, too, in that it implies some sort of social criticism in the delinquent. But that would confuse him with the bourgeois Beatnik. The delinquent has only respect, even reverence, for certain allegedly bourgeois values. He implicitly believes that there are good girls and bad girls, for instance. Sex and marriage are two entirely separate things. He is, in my experience anyway, deeply patriotic. Which is simply to say that he respects those values he never experienced, like money and good girls and the Army and Navy. What he has experienced has left him with absolute contempt, or more accurately, an active indifference. Once he does experience decency—as he does sometimes in a wife—he reacts decently to it. For to this date the only known cure for delinquency is marriage.

The delinquent, far from being the rebel, is the conformist par excellence. He is actually incapable of doing anything alone, and a story may indicate how incapable he is. I went along with Riccio and the gang in his book to a YMCA camp outside New York City for an overnight outing. In the afternoon we started a baseball game, and everything proceeded normally until somebody hit a ball to the outfield. I turned to watch the play and saw ten or twelve kids running for the catch. It turned out that not one of them was willing to play the outfield by himself, insisting that the entire group hang around out there together. The reason was that a boy alone might drop a catch and would not be able to bear the humiliation. So they ran around out there in a drove all afternoon, creating a stampede every time a ball was hit.

They are frightened kids, and that is why they are so dangerous. But again, it will not do to say—it is simply not true—that they are therefore unrelated to the rest of the population's frame of mind. Like most of us, the delinquent is simply doing as he was taught. This is often said but rarely understood. Only recently a boy was about to be executed for murder in New York State. Only after he had been in jail for more than a year after sentencing did a campaign develop to persuade the Governor to commute his sentence to life imprisonment, for only then was it discovered that he had been deserted by his father in Puerto Rico, left behind when his mother went to New York, wandered about homeless throughout his childhood, and so on. The sentencing judge only learned his background a week or two before he was to be officially murdered. And then what shock, what pity! I have to ask why the simple facts of his deprivation were not brought out in court, if not before. I am afraid I know the answer. Like most people, it was probably beyond the judge's imagination that small children sometimes can be treated much worse than kittens or puppies in our cities.

Gangs in Suburbia

It is only in theory that the solution seems purely physical—better housing, enlightened institutions for deserted kids, psychotherapy, and the rest. The visible surfaces of the problem are easy to survey—although we have hardly begun even to do that.

More difficult is the subterranean moral question which every kind of delinquency poses. Not long ago a gang was arrested in a middle-class section of Brooklyn, whose tack was to rob homes and sell the stuff to professional fences. Many of these boys were top students, and all of them were from good, middle-class backgrounds. Their parents were floored by the news of their secret depredations, and their common cry was that they had always given their sons plenty of money, that the boys were secure at home, that there was no conceivable reason for this kind of aberration. The boys were remorseful and evidently as bewildered as their parents.

Greenwich, Connecticut, is said to be the wealthiest community in the United States. A friend of mine who lives there let his sons throw a party for their friends. In the middle of the festivities a gang of boys arrived—their own acquaintances who attend the same high school. They tore the house apart, destroyed the furniture, pulled parts off the automobile and left them on the lawn, and split the skulls of two of the guests with beer cans.

Now if it is true that the slum delinquent does as he is taught, it must be true that the Greenwich delinquent does the same. But obviously the lines of force from example to imitation are subtler and less easily traced here. It is doubtful that the parents of this marauding gang rip up the furniture in the homes to which they have been invited. So that once again it is necessary to withhold one's cherished theories. Rich delinquency is delinquency but it is not the same as slum delinquency. But there is one clear common denominator, I think. They do not know how to live when alone. Most boys in Greenwich do not roam in gangs but a significant fraction in both places find that counterfeit sense of existence which the gang life provides.

Again, I think it necessary to raise and reject the idea of rebellion, if one means by that word a thrust of any sort. For perspective's sake it may be wise to remember another kind of youthful reaction to a failed society in a different order. We have been brought up to believe that if you worked hard, saved your money, studied, kept your nose clean, you would end up made. We found ourselves in the Depression, when you could not get a job, when all the studying you might do would get you a chance, at best, to sell ties in Macy's. Our delinquency consisted in joining demonstrations of the unemployed, pouring onto campuses to scream against some injustice by college administrations, and adopting to one degree or another a Socialist ideology. This, in fact, was a more dangerous kind of delinquency than the gangs imply, for it was directed against the social structure of capitalism itself. But, curiously, it was at the same time immeasurably more constructive, for the radical youth of the 'thirties, contemptuous as he was of the social values he had rejected, was still bent upon instituting human values in their place. He was therefore a conserver, he believed in *some* society.

Gide wrote a story about a man who wanted to get on a train and shoot a passenger. Any train, any passenger. It would be a totally gratuitous act, an act devoid of any purpose whatever, an act of "freedom" from purpose. To kill an unknown man without even anger, without unrequited love, without love at all, with nothing in his heart but the sheerly physical contemplation of the gun barrel and the target. In doing this one would partake of Death's irreproachable identity and commit an act in revolt against meaning itself, just as Death is, in the last analysis, beyond analysis.

To think of contemporary delinquency in the vein of the 'thirties, as a rebellion toward something, is to add a value to it which it does not have. To give it even the dignity of cynicism run rampant is also over-elaborate. For the essence is not the individual at all; it is the gang, the herd, and we should be able to understand its attractions ourselves. It is not the thrust toward individual expression but a flight from self in any defined form. Therefore, to see it simply as a protest against conformism is to stand it on its head; it is profoundly conformist but without the mottoes, the entablature of recognizable, "safe" conformism and its liturgy of religious, patriotic, socially conservative credos.

The Greenwich gang, therefore, is also doing as it was taught, just as the slum gang does, but more subtly. The Greenwich gang is conforming to the hidden inhumanity of conformism, to the herd quality in conformism; it is acting out the terror-fury that lies hidden under father's acceptable conformism. It is simply conformity sincere, conformity revealing its true content, which is hatred of others, a stunted wish for omnipotence, and the conformist's secret belief that nothing outside his skin is real or true. For which reason he must redouble his obeisance to institutions lest, if the act of obeisance be withheld, the whole external world will vanish, leaving him alone. And to be left alone when you do not sense any existence in yourself is the ultimate terror. But this loneliness is not the poet's, not the thinker's, not the loneliness that is filled with incommunicable feeling, insufficiently formed thought. It is nonexistence and must not be romanticized as it has been in movies and some of the wishful Beat literature. It is a withdrawal not from the world but from oneself. It is boredom, the subsidence of inner impulse, and it threatens true death unless it is overthrown.

All of which is said in order to indicate that delinquency is not the kind of "social problem" it is generally thought to be. That is, it transcends even as it includes the need for better housing, medical care, and the rest. It is our most notable and violent manifestation of social nihilism. In saying this, however, it is necessary to short-circuit any notion that it is an attempt by the youth to live "sincerely." The air of "sincerity" which so many writers have given the delinquent is not to be mistaken as his "purpose." This is romanticism and solves nothing except to sentimentalize brutality. The gang kid can be sincere; he can extend himself for a buddy and risk himself for others; but he is just as liable, if not more so than others, to desert his buddies in need and to treat his friends disloyally. Gang boys rarely go to visit a buddy in jail excepting in the movies. They forget about him. The cult of sincerity, of true human relations uncontaminated by money and the social rat race, is not the hallmark of the gang. The only moment of truth comes when the war starts. Then the brave show themselves, but few of these boys know how to fight alone, and hardly any without a knife or a gun. They are not to be equated with matadors or boxers or Hemingway heroes. They are dangerous pack hounds who will not even expose themselves singly in the outfield.

If, then, one begins to put together all the elements, this "social problem" takes on not merely its superficial welfare aspects but its philosophical depths, which I think are the controlling ones. It is not a problem of big cities alone but of rural areas too; not of capitalism alone but of socialism as well; not restricted to the physically deprived but shared by the affluent; not a racial problem alone or a problem of recent immigrants, or a purely American problem. I believe it is in its present form the product of technology destroying the very concept of man as a value in himself.

I hesitate to say what I think the cure might be, if only because I cannot prove it. But I have heard most of the solutions men have offered, and they are spiritless, they do not assume that the wrong is deep and terrible and general among us all. There is, in a word, a spirit gone. Perhaps two world wars, brutality immeasurable, have blown it off the earth; perhaps the very processes of technology have sucked it out of man's soul; but it is gone. Many men rarely relate to one another excepting as customer to seller, worker to boss, the affluent to the deprived and vice versa—in short, as factors to be somehow manipulated and not as intrinsically valuable persons.

Power was always in the world, to be sure, and its evils, but with us now it is strangely, surrealistically masked and distorted. Time was, for example, when the wealthy and the politically powerful flaunted themselves, used power openly as power, and were often cruel. But this openness had the advantage for man of clarity; it created a certain reality in the world, an environment that was defined, with hard but touchable barriers. Today power would have us believe—everywhere—that it is purely beneficent. The bank is not a place which makes more money with your deposits than it returns to you in the form of interest; it is not a sheer economic necessity, it is not a business at all. It is "Your Friendly Bank," a kind of welfare institution whose one prayer, day and night, is to serve your whims or needs. A school is no longer a place of mental discipline but a kind of day-care center, a social gathering where you go through a ritual of games and entertainments which insinuate knowledge and the crafts of the outside world. Business is not the practice of buying low and selling high, it is a species of public service. The good life itself is not the life of struggle for meaning, not the quest for union with the past, with God, with man that it traditionally was. The good life is the life of ceaseless entertainment, effortless joys, the air-conditioned, dust-free languor beyond the Mussulman's most supine dream. Freedom is, after all, comfort; sexuality is a photograph. The enemy of it all is the real. The enemy is conflict. The enemy, in a word, is life.

My own view is that delinquency is related to this dreamworld from two opposite sides. There are the deprived who cannot take part in the dreams; poverty bars them. There are the oversated who are caught in its indefiniteness, its unreality, its boring hum, and strike for the real now and then—they rob, they hurt, they kill. In flight from the nothingness of this comfort they have inherited, they butt against its rubber walls in order to feel a real pain, a genuine consequence. For the world in which comfort rules is a delusion, whether one is within it or deprived of it.

There are a few social theorists who look beyond poverty and wealth, beyond the time when men will orient themselves to the world as bread-winners, as accruers of money-power. They look to the triumph of technology, when at least in some countries the physical struggle to survive will no longer be the spine of existence. Then, they say, men will define themselves through varying "styles of life." With struggles solved, nature tamed and abundant, all that will be left to do will be the adornment of existence, a novel-shaped swimming pool, I take it, or an outburst of artistic work.

It is not impossible, I suppose. Certainly a lot of people are already living that way—when they are not at their psychiatrists'. But there is still a distance to go before life's style matters very much to most of humanity in comparison to next month's rent. I do not know how we ought to reach for the spirit again but it seems to me we must flounder without it. It is the spirit which does not accept injustice complacently and yet does not betray the poor with sentimentality. It is the spirit which seeks not to flee the tragedy which life must always be, but seeks to enter into it, thereby to be strengthened by the fullest awareness of its pain, its ultimate non sequitur. It is the spirit which does not mask but unmasks the true function of a thing, be it business, unionism, architecture, or love.

Riccio's and Slocum's book, with all its ugliness, its crudeness, its lack of polish and design, is good because it delivers up the real. It is only as hopeless as the situation is. Its implied solutions are good ones: reform an idiotic narcotics laws, a real attempt to put trained people at the service of bewildered, desperate families, job-training programs, medical care, reading clinics—all of it is necessary and none of it would so much as strain this economy. But none of it will matter, none of it will reach further than the spirit in which it is done. Not the spirit of fear with which so many face delinquency, nor the spirit of sentimentality which sees in it some virtue of rebellion against a false and lying society. The spirit has to be that of those people who know that delinquents are a living expression of our universal ignorance of what life ought to be, even of what it is, and of what it truly means to live. Bad pupils they surely are. But who from his own life, from his personal thought has come up with the good teaching, the way of life that is joy? This book shows how difficult it is to reach these boys; what the country has to decide is what it is going to say if these kids should decide to listen.

John Cashman

Assassins, Toads, and God's Flesh

Hallucinogenic substances are almost as old as time. From the soma of the ancient Aryan invaders of India to the new laboratory synthetics history has recorded hundreds of natural and man-made mind-expanding drugs. No part of the world that supports a varied vegetation is without one or more natural hallucinogens. In North and South America alone there are more than forty known naturally occurring hallucinogens.

Why, then, is there such a fuss over LSD, merely the most recent in a long list of hallucinogens? Primarily because LSD, which is more potent and quicker-acting and which possesses fewer side-effects than its sister drugs, is easy to produce in bulk and is more generally available. It has also caught the fancy of certain way-out groups. LSD has, therefore, become the subject of public controversy, while the other more esoteric hallucinogens remain, by and large, medical curiosities. In short, and for a variety of reasons, the other hallucinogens present little threat to established order.

Nevertheless, the current bitter debate over the spreading illicit use of LSD has its roots in the use of another hallucinogen, the peyote cactus of the Southwest United States and Mexico. Both the late Aldous Huxley, the spiritual leader of the current extra-legal LSD explosion, and Dr. Timothy Leary, the movement's St. Paul, first discovered the mixed joys of mind expansion through peyote. Both later switched to LSD as the more manageable and effective of the two drugs.

It was Huxley, too, who reached into history to reclaim soma, a hallucinogen of unknown plant origin, as one of the controlling substances in his 1932 novel *Brave New World*. In his terrifying view of the future Huxley portrayed a world of sheep held in subjugation by the inner glories of soma and a futuristic mode of television entertainment called the feelies, color productions a viewer could see, hear and *feel*.

Twenty-six years later in *Brave New World Revisited,* Huxley wrote:

> The original soma, from which I took the name of this hypothetical drug, was an unknown plant (possibly *Asclepias acida*) used by the ancient Aryan invaders of India in one of the most solemn of their religious rites. The intoxicating juice expressed from the stems of this plant was drunk by the priests and nobles in the course of an elaborate ceremony. In the Vedic hymns we are told that the drinkers of soma were blessed in many ways. Their bodies were strengthened, their hearts were filled with courage, joy and enthusiasm, their minds were enlightened and in an immediate experience of eternal life they received the assurance of their immortality.

Soma, also known as *haoma* and *suma,* probably came from Central Asia into India and Iran some 3,000 years ago. It was considered the drink of the gods. As related in *Book IX* of the *Rig-Veda,* soma was drunk by the god Indra, and inspired him to create the universe. Little else is known of the drug, except that it was fermented, mixed with milk or water and strained through wool before it was drunk. The use of soma was eventually restricted, then gradually replaced by meditation in the form of yoga.

Like soma, most of the other hallucinogens discovered through history became the focal points of religious ceremonies among various primitive and not-so-primitive societies. Many of the drugs, cloaked in mystery and magic trappings, were used for thousands of years before they were objectively examined as drugs. Most were not reduced to their chemical components until late in the 19th century.

The most notable of the hallucinogens that emerged from the darkness of magic ritual in the chemical enlightenment of the nineteenth century were cannabis (hemp, bhang, marijuana, etc.), peyote and its alkaloid mescaline, and the "magic" Mexican mushroom and its alkaloid psilocybin. There are equally potent hallucinogens, not as well publicized, that have been recognized and cataloged by intrepid botanists who have traveled deep into jungles and other backwashes to find them. This group includes bufotenine, cohoba, yaje, caapi, and fly agaric, among others. In addition, such readily available garden variety items as morning glory seeds and jimson weed were found to be hallucinogenic if taken in sufficient amounts.

And in recent years, following the laboratory development of LSD, chemists have synthesized several compounds that have hallucinogenic properties. Among them are mysterious-sounding substances such as JB-329, JB-318, DMT, MLD-41 and TMA, all laboratory shorthand for a number of interlinked chemical substances with long names.

So far as medical science can determine, none of the hallucinogens is addictive and only a few, such as fly agaric, are poisonous if taken in sufficient amounts. Far from being addictive, most of the hallucinogens quickly cause a buildup of tolerance that limits their use, for proper effect, to twice or three times a week, at most.

The most widely known and widely used of the natural hallucinogens is Indian hemp, or *cannabis sativa,* which was introduced into Europe in about 1500 B.C. from Asia. Today it is known throughout the world as hemp, cannabis, bhang, hashish, ganja, charas, marijuana and various other local names. It is one of the milder and most controllable of the hallucinogens, but in any of its various forms it is capable of inducing effects as odd as those of the stronger members of the family, including hallucinations and bursts of mental insight.

Cannabis, or hemp, was known to the ancient Chinese, Indians and Persians and is mentioned in Greek and Assyrian religious literature dating to 1000 B.C. In the Hindu religion cannabis, regarded as a holy plant brought from the ocean by the God Shiva, was used as an adjunct to religious meditation. In later Mohammedan circles it was considered by some sects as an embodiment of the spirit of a prophet, and still later became a virtual God among some Central African tribes.

Hemp became firmly entrenched in India, the Near and Middle East and in North Africa through the Middle Ages. In the 11th century cannabis became the controlling influence of a Shi'a Ismailite sect in northern Persia, a politically motivated group that was distinguished by the relish with which its members devoted themselves to brutal murders. The most powerful leader of the group was a man named Hasan Sabah, who introduced cannabis to his band of murderers as a reward for jobs well done. The cannabis, along with consenting women, was supplied both before and after assignments. This led to a certain fanatical disregard for their own and others' safety among members of Hasan's faithful following. The speed and glee with which they dispatched political enemies (and anybody else who got in the way, including quite a few Crusaders) made the sect the most feared band of cutthroats in Persia and Syria. Since Hasan was handing out the cannabis, it became known as hashish, or gift of Hasan. And since Hasan's men were usually high on hashish, they became known as "the men under the influence of hashish," or, in the Arabic, singular, hashshashin. The word survives today in various forms in several languages, including the English "assassin," with all its ugly connotations.

Hashish was introduced into Europe around 1800 and from there spread to almost every corner of the globe, including the United States, by way of Mexico, in the early 1920's. Cannabis is a hardy plant and grows wild in almost any country with a temperate climate for at least part of the year. A survey by the United Nations a few years ago estimated the worldwide use of cannabis to be in excess of 200 million persons. In this country about ten million persons are believed to have tried marijuana at least once.

About the various strengths of the cannabis preparations, Rand Corporation drug expert Dr. William H. McGlothlin had this to say in an informative article in the *Psychedelic Review*:

> There are three grades (of cannabis) prepared in India. Bhang is cheap, low in potency and usually ingested as a drink; ganja is two to three times as strong; the most potent is charas, the unadulterated resin obtained from the plant or dried flower. Smoking is the most common mode of consumption for ganja and charas. Cannabis preparations have many other names in various parts of the world—in Morocco it is called kif, in South Africa dagga, and in the United States and Latin America marijuana. These correspond roughly in potency to the bhang of India, though they are mostly smoked rather than ingested. The term hashish, when used correctly, is a powdered and sifted form of charas, or a preparation made from it; however, hashish is widely used in the literature to refer to any form of cannabis drug. The marijuana available in the United States is estimated to be one-fifth to one-eighth as potent as the charas resin of India.

Cannabis sativa, so named by the botanist Linnaeus in 1753, is a tall, weedy herb that has separate male and female plants. Stems of the male plant are used to make hemp rope. The resins from the tops of the female plant and from its flowers yield the hallucinogen. Even though cannabis is a true hallucinogen, it has never been considered one of the important members of the drug family. That distinction, although somewhat arbitrary, accrues to LSD, peyote and the so-called "magic" mushroom of Mexico.

Peyote, a cactus found in Mexico and the Southwest United States, was used for centuries prior to the Spanish conquest of Mexico by Aztecs and other Mexican Indians as well as several American Indian tribes, among them the Apache, Kiowa and Comanche. As with other natural hallucinogens, peyote was an integral part of the religious and spiritual life of the various cultures and tribes.

The peyote cactus (*Lopophora Williamsii*) grows in the arid region that runs from north of the Rio Grande down into Central Mexico. Mexican and American Indians sliced off the buttonlike heads of the low-growing plant, which they then dried and ate, usually as part of communal religious rites and special tribal ceremonial observances. The Spanish Conquistadores called peyote "the devil's money" and did their best to stamp out the widespread use of the hallucinogen among the Aztecs and other Mexican Indians. The Christian missionaries that followed fought even harder to drive peyote from religious observances, but didn't do much better than the Spanish soldiers.

Today, the 250,000-member Native American Church, which is predominantly an Indian church, still uses peyote as an important part of its rites, even though the church is definitely Christian. The church, by law, is allowed to use peyote and its alkaloid mescaline. A test case in California in 1964 reaffirmed this right. On the other hand, the sale and distribution of peyote and mescaline are outlawed in the United States, as are the sale and distribution of other hallucinogens, under the country's narcotics laws.

Peyote and its use in Indian rituals spread through the plains of the United States and up into Canada in the nineteenth century, carried by the Mescalero Apaches, who had dipped into Mexico during the great Indian wars of the southwest. The peyotism of the Mescaleros, from which the name mescaline comes, was picked up by the Comanches and Kiowas, among other American tribes. As peyotism became intertwined with Christianity the religious beliefs among the Indians were modified to allow that God had put some of his powers into the peyote plant and that Jesus Christ had given the plant to the Indians in a time of need. Members of the Native American Church, which was formed in 1918 to fight anti-peyote legislation, usually eat twelve to fifteen dried mescal buttons in a communal circle formed in a traditional tepee early on a Saturday night. The rest of the night and into Sunday morning is spent in prayer, ritual singing and introspective contemplation. The church preaches brotherly love, care of the family, self-reliance and abstinence from alcohol. Since it holds the belief that peyote is the mediator between the church members and God, the church has no use for ministers or priests.

Botanists discovered peyote in 1892 after samples of the plant were brought back to laboratories by explorers who had witnessed the peyote rituals of the Mexican Indians. The hallucinogenic alkaloid of the plant, mescaline, was isolated in 1896. Sigmund Freud, William James, Havelock Ellis and others became interested in the hallucinogenic aspects of mescaline, and in the early decades of this century there was much thought, discussion and experimentation with the new drug. The most important aspect of the peyote experimentation was the possible link between mental diseases and the chemistry of the body. Unfortunately, laboratory techniques at the time were not equal to the task. Serious experimentation was stymied. Such side-effects as nausea, dizziness, headaches, chest pains and poor coordination caused by mescaline did not help much either.

(The hopes of finding a chemical "key" to schizophrenia were rekindled fifty years later with the discovery of LSD, only to be dashed again in the cold light of the laboratory. Advanced techniques and a broader knowledge of mental disorders, however, would keep LSD in the laboratory.)

The hallucinogenic power of peyote, although of marginal importance in laboratories, was given another life outside the laboratory. In the hands of poets and philosophers peyote was touted as the great shortcut to mystical experience. The aforementioned Aldous Huxley tried mescaline in the early 1950's and put down his thoughts on the subject in a small book called *The Doors of Perception*, in 1954. Of mescaline, Huxley said:

> Most takers of mescalin experience only the heavenly part of schizophrenia. The drug brings hell and purgatory only to those who have had a recent case of jaundice, or who suffer from periodical depressions or a chronic anxiety. If, like the other drugs of remotely comparable power, mescalin were notoriously toxic, the taking of it would be enough, of itself, to cause anxiety. But the reasonably healthy person knows in advance that, so far as he is concerned, mescalin is completely innocuous, that its effects will pass off after eight or ten hours, leaving no hangover and consequently no craving for a renewal of the dose.

Later Huxley tells of an experience under mescaline:

> Confronted by a chair which looked like the Last Judgement —or, to be more accurate, by a Last Judgement which, after a long time and with considerable difficulty, I recognized as a chair—I found myself all at once on the brink of panic. This, I suddenly felt, was going too far. Too far, even though the going was into intenser beauty, deeper significance. The fear, as I analyse it in retrospect, was of being overwhelmed, of disintegrating under a pressure of reality greater than a mind accustomed to living most of the time in a cosy world of symbols could possibly bear. . . .

Huxley further recorded that his experience under mescaline was "the ultimate reality" and "at once beautiful and appalling, but always other than human, always totally incomprehensible." And he concluded as the drug wore off: "I had returned to that reassuring but profoundly unsatisfactory state known as 'being in one's right mind.'"

Mescaline was also taken by Beat poet Allen Ginsberg who wrote in 1960 in *Birth* of many flights of sight, sound and reality, and of the initial tastes and reactions to the drug:

> We're flowers to rocks. That was last nite's note. Took peyote at 8:30 A.M.—very unpleasant bitter metallic taste, I gagged at

second chunk—the yellow insides. Worst part of peyote the metallic
imaginary aftertaste & feeling of stomach sickness and heaviness of
body, nearly nausea. . . . After awhile, when sickness passed—
first thing I noticed: eyes closed toward light leaves in eye a golden
glow hue—which darkens when you pass hand over lidded eye. It
made me feel like a very transparent sort of organism. . . . The
world is full of strange noises, I turn on music which is the most
strange—I'm walking around house at a mad pitch, doing things
and writing—must go back to that rock—am at kitchen table now
. . . I have been going around grinning idiotically at people . . .
Peyote is not God—but is a powerful force—can see, if everybody
on, how they would organize their lives once every year, communicating with each other—what spiritual violence that day—what
secrets revealed . . .

There were other similar reports of the powers of peyote, but they remained, for the most part, limited to a small circle of intellectuals. Then,
in 1960, Dr. Timothy Leary of Harvard University traveled to Mexico and
tried the dried mescal buttons. They sent him into another world that he
has been advertising in this world ever since. Of that initial contact he has
written, "I was whirled through an experience which could be described in
many extravagant metaphors but which was above all and without question the deepest religious experience of my life."

Another of the pre-Columbian hallucinogens is the sacred mushroom
(*Psilocybe mexicana*) of Mexico, which is believed to have been used by
the wild revelers during Montezuma's coronation as high priest of the
Aztecs in 1502. As with peyote, the dried or powdered mushrooms were
used as a sacrament in religious ceremonies. But unlike other hallucinogens, the sacred mushroom was thought to have divination and prophesy-
ing powers, and was also administered as a panacea for any number of
diseases.

To the Aztecs the sacred mushrooms were *teonanacatl*, God's flesh,
and there were stiff penalties, even death, for those who would partake of
the wonders of *teonanacatl* without good religious or ritual reasons. With
the collapse of the Aztec empire, however, the sacred mushrooms became
widely used for a variety of purposes, including private trips into the mind.
One intrepid seventeenth-century Spanish friar, who along with his brothers of the cloth was unalterably opposed to the use of the mushroom and
sickened by its Indian name, wrote of Indians who "see visions, feel a
faintness of heart and are provoked to lust" while under the influence of
teonanacatl. And, taking a page from current reports on LSD, he also observed that there were Indians who "see themselves dying in a vision
[while] others see themselves being eaten by wild beasts."

In his excellent book *Drugs and the Mind* Robert S. DeRopp wrote of the sacred mushroom:

> Teonanacatl belongs to the group of fungi which favor cow pats as their place of growth. During the rainy season from June to September it sprouts out of the pat, its dome-shaped cap borne on a long slender stalk. It is eagerly gathered by the . . . Indians and dried for future use. . . . Usually about fifteen of the mushrooms are consumed, overdoses of fifty or sixty resulting in poisoning, and continued use of large quantities producing insanity. A general feeling of exhilaration and well-being is experienced soon after the mushrooms have been eaten. This state of exhilaration is followed by hilarity, incoherent talking, and fantastic visions in brilliant colors similar to those produced by *peyotl*. It appears that the . . . divinators pay rather a high price for their [continued] indulgence in this mildly poisonous mushroom. They are said to age rapidly and even at the age of thirty-five have the appearance of old men.

The various properties of *teonanacatl* were rediscovered by an amateur botanist named Gordon Wasson in 1953 on a trip into Mexico in search of new varieties of mushroom. Wasson tried the sacred mushrooms and publicized the mushroom's hallucinogenic powers in a series of articles, one in *Life*. After eating twelve of the mushrooms, which he described as having an acrid, rancid flavor, Wasson sat in darkness and saw his own personal visions:

> They were vivid in color, always harmonious. They began with art motifs, such as might decorate carpets or textiles . . . then I saw a mythological beast drawing a regal chariot. Later it was as though the walls of our house had dissolved, and my spirit had flown forth, and I was suspended in mid-air viewing landscapes of mountains, with camel caravans advancing slowly across the slopes . . . The visions were not blurred or uncertain. They were sharply focused, the lines and colors being so sharp that they seemed more real to me than anything I had seen with my own eyes. I felt that I was now seeing clearly, whereas ordinary vision gives us an imperfect view; I was seeing the archetypes, the Platonic ideas, that underlie the imperfect images of everyday life. The thought crossed my mind: could the divine mushrooms be the secret that lay behind the ancient Mysteries? . . . These reflections passed through my mind at the very time that I was seeing the visions, for the effect of the mushrooms is to bring about a fission of the split, a split in the person, a kind of schizophrenia, with the rational side continuing to reason and to observe the sensations that the other side is enjoying.

In the middle 1950's one of the active alkaloids of the sacred mushroom was isolated. It was called psilocybin. Although psilocybin is not as free from side-effects as is LSD, nor as powerful (LSD has 200 times the strength of psilocybin), it has been used extensively in research, sometimes interchangeably with LSD. It has been found to be as effective an hallucinogen as LSD, though much larger doses are required. It was the drug of choice in the early psychedelic experiments of Dr. Leary and is used in clinical investigation today, without, it might be added, the furor that has grown around the use of LSD.

One other mushroom deserves mention. This is a poisonous toadstool called *Amanita muscaria,* or fly agaric. It is a close cousin to the *Amanita phalloides,* or destroying angel, which is nearly 100 percent fatal. And fly agaric is almost as dangerous. Three toadstools can cause convulsions and death. But in small amounts the fly agaric is a hallucinogen. For obvious reasons, it has little use, in the laboratory or elsewhere. The active alkaloid in fly agaric is muscarine, which was isolated as long ago as 1869. Muscarine is so complicated a substance and so poisonous that there has been little further information available to researchers.

Fly agaric has been used as a hallucinogen for hundreds of years and is still used by some primitive peoples in central and northeast Siberia. The ferocious Tartars were known to use it, in addition to some tribes among the Norsemen. Since muscarine is not affected by the kidneys, anyone drinking the urine of a fly agaric eater will get the full effect of the drug. The English writer Oliver Goldsmith wrote in 1762 of such an occurrence he observed while traveling in Asia:

> The poorer sort, who love mushroom broth to distraction as well as the rich, but cannot afford it at first hand, post themselves on these occasions around the huts of the rich and watch the opportunity of the ladies and gentlemen as they come down to pass their liquor, and holding a wooden bowl catch the delicious fluid, very little altered by filtration, being still strongly tinctured with the intoxicating quality. Of this they drink with the utmost satisfaction and thus they get as drunk and as jovial as their betters.

So much for toadstools—but not for another of the classic ingredients of a witches' brew, the toad itself.

Bufotenine, another of the little-known hallucinogens, is extracted from the skins of certain toads. It is also found in cohoba, which is made from the leguminous plant *Piptadenia peregrina.* Since bufotenine loses its hallucinogenic powers when swallowed, the pre-Columbian natives of the West Indies and the northern parts of South America used it in a powder form as snuff, or in a liquid solution as an enema.

It seems only fitting to pause at this juncture to pay homage to the nameless men who first discovered the natural plants that were to supply so much other-worldliness to those who came after them, those intrepid experimenters who ate of the forbidden fruit and either died in the attempt or became great medicine men. Hunger probably had something to do with it, to say nothing of a few loose marbles. But it boggles the mind to try and re-create the scenes lost to history where the discoveries of fly agaric and bufotenine were made.

In any case bufotenine and its hallucinogenic properties were discovered. In experiments today snuff and enemas have given way to injections. After an injection of 16 milligrams of bufotenine, a volunteer reported: "When I start on a thought another one comes along and clashes with it, and I can't express myself clearly . . . I feel dopey but not sleepy. I feel physically tense and mentally clouded. I am here and not here." Bufotenine does have its drawbacks, though. The volunteer's face turned purple and he retched and vomited before his mind started to expand.

Mexico, which seems to have a complete garden of natural hallucinogens, was also the starting point for ololiuqui, a vision-producing drug that is found in the seeds of the morning glory. Chemically, it closely resembles LSD, although twenty times weaker. The hallucinogenic properties of morning glory seeds have been known since the seventeenth century, but received little notice in this country until the advent of the LSD controversy. A few years ago there was a run on the morning glory seed market, which followed laboratory reports that ololiuqui contained an LSD-like substance capable of producing an "experience." Only two wild morning glory varieties, *Rivea corymbosa* and *Impomoea violacea*, contain the substance. The hard black seeds are first soaked in water to soften them for chewing. As little as fifteen seeds have been known to cause mental transportation. Some people get no reaction whatsoever. Others get deathly sick, but no visions. Dr. Sidney Cohen in his perspective book on the hallucinogens, *The Beyond Within*, reports the case of one young man who tried ololiuqui:

> One young man after sedulously chewing 300 of the black seeds had an intense and glorious experience for eight hours. The next sixteen hours were spent in considerable doubt about his ability to "get back," but he did. Three weeks later the morning glory state unexpectedly recurred. He was upset and panicky about the possibility of going crazy. The odd feelings of strangeness, "looseness" and unreality came and went for a week. One morning he awoke, agitated about being "out of balance" again. He dressed, drove his car down a nearby hill at a speed estimated at 100 miles an hour and crashed into a house.

The wild-growing jimson weed also has hallucinogenic properties. The pods of these plants, if enough of them are eaten, can be fatal, and coma is not rare. In 1965 there were reports of widespread use of the jimson weed in California, which prompted State Senator Robert J. Lagomarsino to call on Governor Pat Brown to have anti-jimson weed legislation passed.

Two of the more interesting and newer of the natural hallucinogens, in point of discovery, are yage and caapi, two plant concoctions from South America's Amazon region. Both are extracted from jungle vines (yage from the *Haemadictyon amazenicum* and caapi from the *Banisteria caapi*) by boiling the plant's stalks. The two hallucinogens, considered as potent if not more so than LSD, were rediscovered in 1956. As yet, little in the way of experiment has been done, but early reports indicate that yage and caapi are both capable not only of expanding minds, but of reducing man to his basic, prehistoric self. Visions of beasts and large serpents abound. One subject clearly saw his mother and father in the sexual act. Another was swallowed by a large snake. Another was attacked by panthers. Still another grew wings and flew.

But powerful or weak, strange or common, ageless or new, all the hallucinogens have taken a back seat to LSD, which began its life in a quiet Swiss laboratory during the summer of 1938.

Questions

Diction and Structure

1. Into how many distinct sections is the 1965 *Encyclopaedia Britannica* article on the Shakers divided? What is the purpose of each section? How are they all related? How does this compare with the 1974 article?

2. What is the organizing principle of the third paragraph in the 1965 Shaker article? What relationship to this purpose has the final sentence? What is the organizing principle in the 1974 article?

3. Why does the 1965 *Encyclopaedia* essay not define the term "Shaker"? Is its meaning apparent? Notice the origin of the term is given in the 1974 edition. Does the information add anything factual to your knowledge of the sect?

4. What is the ostensible relationship between the contents of

the 1965 Shaker article and the bibliography of longer works given at its conclusion? Why is the bibliography omitted in the 1974 edition? Can we assume that the later version is more factually complete and accurate than the earlier version? Is the 1965 article itself a mere précis of the encyclopaedist's reading and research? How do you know?

5. The prose used in Judith Wax's essay, "Dear Ann Landers . . .", has a marked resemblance to recorded conversation. Point out instances of informal or conversational uses, both in quotes and out. Is the same level of diction used throughout the essay? If so, why?

6. Wax mentions the impact a Jewish family background and the Yiddish language had on Ann Landers. Using Leo Rosten's essay on page 69 as reference, point to instances of Yiddish usage in the Wax article. Show also the uses of what Rosten calls "Yinglish." If you are a Landers reader, have you ever been aware before of the presence of "Yinglish" in her column?

7. Is the Landers prose an example of what F. L. Lucas terms "style"? Justify your answer.

8. What it the effect of Arthur Miller's opening paragraphs on the subsequent organization of "The Bored and the Violent"? How are the two parts of the essay related to each other? Are they logical divisions of the subject or not? Explain.

9. What in general is the dictional level of Miller's prose? Consider these phrases: "stultifying spiritual and psychological stasis," "risking his skin or his life as he smashes a bottle filled with gasoline on some other kid's head," "Their parents were floored by the news of their secret depredations." How is this kind of diction related to Miller's topic?

10. What is the significance of John Cashman's title, "Assassins, Toads, and God's Flesh"? How is it connected to his subject? How does it illustrate definition by root meaning?

11. How many different kinds of technical or specialized language appear in Cashman's essay? Does he define all the unusual and specialized terms? Is he writing for the same approximate audience as Helen Nowlis (p. 12) or not?

12. Make a paragraph outline of Cashman's essay. Do you consider the essay well planned and structured or not? Why?

Style and Rhetoric

1. Encyclopaedia articles are noted for their impersonal style. Are there any clues as to the personality of the author in either

of the essays on the Shakers? Is there an appreciable difference in style or tone in the two essays? Is this a merit or demerit for either article?

2. To what extent does the 1965 Shaker article use the rhetorical methods of definition, analysis, comparison and contrast, description, and showing causality? Which method is most important in the 1974 version? How does the shift in usage of rhetorical techniques indicate a changing focus of interest and emphasis from the earlier to the later version?

3. What rhetorical techniques are conspicuously absent from the 1965 Shaker essay? From the 1974 essay? Point out examples of places where you wish the author had supplemented the information with excursions into these methods of development.

4. The Wax essay on Esther Lederer (Ann Landers) obviously depends on some of the techniques of characterizing. Where do these appear most importantly? How are the concluding paragraphs of the essay related to characterization?

5. Point out places in the Wax essay where each of these techniques of rhetoric is predominant: comparison and contrast, analyzing, illustrating, classifying.

6. Who or what besides Ann Landers is characterized by Wax?

7. How is Arthur Miller's opening statement in "The Bored and the Violent" an indication of his awareness of the fallacies of sampling and generalization? Show the way he compensates for his limited data in the remainder of the essay. Do his qualifications make his statements more or less valid?

8. Examine Miller's discussion of the "causes" of juvenile delinquency and his conclusion (p. 311). Is this essay itself an exercise in showing causation? In suggesting causes, does Miller contradict himself or not?

9. How important are comparison and contrast, analysis, illustration, and classification to Miller? What other rhetorical devices, if any, does he use?

10. What basic rhetorical method(s) does Cashman use? Compare his approach to drugs with that of Nowlis. How do their uses of definition differ? Does Cashman accept the Nowlis definition, reject it, or alter it somewhat?

11. The danger of writing expository prose as full of data as Cashman's is that the reader will be lost in a flood of details. What principles of organization and style does Cashman use? Do you as a reader find his essay clear in direction, unified, and helpful in its emphases?

12. The Cashman selection probably contains more extensive quotations from other authors than any other selection in this anthology. Is this necessary for his purpose? Why is the use of citations from other sources more necessary in certain kinds of expository writing than in others? Compare Cashman's use of quotations with Miller's. Are the uses essentially similar in purpose?

13. Compare and contrast the use of quotations in expository writing with their use in definition, analysis, and characterization.

Theme and Viewpoint

1. According to Judith Wax, Ann Landers is directly opposed to many of the values and beliefs typified by the Beatles. What are some of these opposite views? What are their cultural implications? Both Wax and Greenfield claim that our culture has been greatly influenced by Ann Landers and the Beatles; can both claims be true? What evidence can you draw from the articles to establish the greater influence of one or the others?

2. Would Ann Landers approve of the culture and principles of the Shakers? Explain your answer.

3. Ann Landers wrote an approving comment for the book jacket of the work by Bach and Wyden from which the essay on page 43 was taken. In what ways do her views and theirs coincide?

4. The Wax article represents Ann Landers and her husband as having a very stable and peaceful marriage; but only a few weeks after the article was printed, the marriage broke up. Do you find any evidence in the Wax article that the Lederer marriage was in trouble? Do the views of Bach and Wyden or Eric Fromm throw any light on the situation?

5. In a recent essay published in the *Smithsonian* magazine, Richard Williams represents the remaining Shakers as living a life free from stress, violence, and the other threats that many essayists in this collection have been concerned with. How would their principles, as stated on page 290, account for this? Are the Shaker principles viable for modern society as a whole?

6. If Theodor Reik is correct in his theories about all of us searching for an ego-ideal through love, how does the celibate life of the Shakers affect his theory?

7. The bored, violent culture described by Miller contrasts dramatically with the peaceful life of the Shakers. Would the

Shakers' beliefs satisfy Miller's criteria for "life" as he establishes them in the closing section of his essay?

8. Compare the picture of life in Independence, Missouri, given by Margaret Truman, with the description of life in Westchester and New York by Miller. How do you account for the change in American culture from one to the other in a period of sixty years? How would Miller account for it? Would Miller find Harry Truman's life a working model for others?

9. Look back at Bruno Bettelheim's account on page 190 of Joey's alternately "mechanical" and violently emotional behavior. Does Miller's discussion of young Americans suggest a race of "Joeys"? Do Bettelheim's investigations support Miller's position or not?

10. Does the behavior of the hospital inmates in Kesey's *One Flew Over the Cuckoo's Nest* bear any resemblance to the behavior described by Miller? Do Kesey and Miller appear to hold the same beliefs about the causes of apathy and violence?

11. Does Miller's evidence about juvenile violence in the suburbs and the city support the contentions of Jane Jacobs? If Jacobs's proposals about city planning were carried out, would youthful violence decrease?

12. Do Julian Huxley's theories of violence and biology throw any additional light on Miller's views?

13. In what ways is Cashman's interest in drugs similar to that of Helen Nowlis? In what ways does it differ? Does Cashman think marijuana, peyote, LSD, and so forth are harmless or dangerous? Cite evidence in his essay to support your opinion.

14. Cashman quotes a section of Allen Ginsberg's record of his experience with mescaline in the poem *Birth* (p. 319). Compare Ginsberg's "creative" experience with that of Stephen Spender. Are they completely unalike?

Narration:
recounting events in time

In his critical analysis, *Aspects of the Novel,* E. M. Forster has identified the most essential elements of narrative prose: our sense of life in time and our desire to know what comes next. We all make sense of what happens to us by thinking of it as a sequence, a movement, or a succession of events while the clock ticks on, marking steps or stages in time. And we want to understand the larger pattern of these events in terms of their relationship to each other; thus we anticipate a second event when we hear of a first one—"And then?" Antecedents and consequents in time are the materials of which a narrative, a story or narrated series of events, is composed.

"Tell us a story," children beg. "What happened?" the adult demands. Narrative prose takes many forms, ranging from the simplest anecdote ("A funny thing happened to me on my way to the studio") to the most complex of novels. Tales, legends, myths, stories factual and fictional, epics, novels, biographies, autobiographies, and histories are all versions of the narrative mode. All rely upon some structure of events in time that reveal patterns of change, development, and alteration, and thus have significance. The narrative creates suspense and tension in us as readers by relying on our natural curiosity to know what happens next and how it will all end. "And so they lived happily ever after."

Not all narratives depend on obvious time structures; but the vital characteristic of the narrative mode is that it is tied to some inherent chronological plan. The narrative may begin in the middle of things, what Aristotle terms *in medias res,* then through exposition reveal what came before, finally proceeding to the logical and temporal conclusion of the series of events under examination. Or it may begin at the beginning, or some arbitrarily defined point in time, and proceed chronologically through an account of events or episodes to some arbitrary closing point. Textbooks that "survey" literary developments from 1550 to 1640 or treat the unification of Italy from 1870 to 1927 are such arbitrary versions of narrative. Some narratives use the "flashback" technique to emphasize the irony, comedy, or pathos of events. Other narratives coordinate widely diverse events that occurred simultaneously in time. Still others suggest succession in time but not duration or relationship among events. There are many ways of viewing time and many kinds of literary chronology; but the narrative mode always uses some kind of chronology.

Events in time may or may not be related in a causal sequence. Some narratives thus recount a sequence without suggesting that x directly led to y, which then caused z. Morton W. Bloomfield's chronological account of the development of the English language correlates linguistic changes with historical events but does not attempt to establish definite patterns of causality. On the other hand, Berton Roueché narrates the search of a public health officer for the cause of a man's strange death from trichinosis, thereby combining a sequence of actions with the motivation of locating an original cause. If the narrative employs causation, it must of course be judged by its adherence to certain logical rules; it must not commit *non sequitur* or *post hoc* errors.

Point of view in narration is also important. A narrative is *told* by somebody. Who is he or she? What authority has he for the events he tells about? Did she witness them personally? Was he physically involved? If so, could he see everything that went on? And was he intellectually and emotionally equipped to *understand* what he saw and heard? Did she depend on the reports of others? If so, how did she decide what was accurate and what was not? Robert Benchley plainly did not witness all that he reports in "A Good Old-Fashioned Christmas." From what vantage point—physical, intellectual, emotional, historical

—is he viewing his subject? William Faulkner's story "Dry September" explores the complexities of point of view and the difficulty of establishing the truth about events from second-hand reports or even firsthand experience.

Since a large part of all verbal communication takes a narrative form—from news items to world histories—narration is not only one of the most flexible prose modes but also one of the most useful. It both satisfies our sense of the continuity of life and supplies the patterns for comprehending it. Its protean nature, however, makes it a difficult type of prose to write. Furthermore, reading it demands much more attention and analytical effort than the primitive response of "Then what happened?"

Morton W. Bloomfield

A Brief History of the English Language

Language, like other important patterns of human behavior, slowly but constantly evolves from older forms into newer ones. When different groups of people speaking one language become separated by geographical, political, or social barriers, each group gradually develops its own variety of the language, which we call a dialect. So long as the differences between two varieties do not make mutual comprehension impossible (though they may make it difficult), and so long as the speakers of each do not consider themselves to be speaking a different language, we may say that these varieties are dialects of the same language.

However, the tendency of language throughout the early centuries of human civilization, as tribal groups broke up into subdivisions and mi-

A BRIEF HISTORY OF THE ENGLISH LANGUAGE   Morton W. Bloomfield, "A Brief History of the English Language," from *The American Heritage Dictionary of the English Language.* © Copyright 1969, 1970 by American Heritage Publishing Co., Inc. Reprinted by permission.

grated, was to split again and again into dialects that in time became mutually incomprehensible. At that point they are recognized as separate languages. Most of the languages spoken today in western Asia and Europe can be traced back to a remote "ancestor" language which we call Indo-European. It was an unwritten language and therefore, of course, no records of it survive. Yet . . . it can be reconstructed. The character of its words and phrases and of its grammatical structure can be inferred by comparative study of the many languages which are its descendants.

As a matter of fact, the early history of any given descendant has to be reconstructed too, by essentially the same method, for written records are a relatively recent development. In the case of English, which is our subject here, we have no written records surviving from earlier than the eighth century A.D., and they do not become common before the tenth and eleventh centuries. But by studying the written records of other languages that clearly show a common ancestry with English—Dutch and German, for example—and by assuming that evolutionary changes before the existence of writing were generally similar in kind to observable changes since, we can make a reasonable guess as to the vocabulary and structure of the earlier forms of the three sister languages, as well as of their common parent. Thus, for instance, the Modern English *blue eyes* and the modern German *blaue Augen* are both traced back to a presumed parent language which we designate as West Germanic; this in turn is considered to be a major dialect of Primitive or Common Germanic, in which language the phrase is reconstructed as *blaewō augona*. All the steps from *blaewō augona* to *blue eyes* can be traced or reasonably assumed.

Various kinds of historical evidence indicate that about 1,500 years ago three closely related tribes, the Angles, the Saxons, and the Jutes, dwelt beside each other on the North Sea shore in what is today northern Germany and southern Denmark. Their language was a variety of West Germanic; and when it began to show significant differences from the other West Germanic dialects spoken around them, we may say that the English language was born. The speakers of this language were probably not aware for some time that it was different, but ultimately political and geographical circumstances created such an awareness. For many decades, however, Old English (as we call it) must have been very similar to other West Germanic dialects, and especially to the other North Sea dialects of Old Saxon and Old Frisian. A modern variant of Old Frisian is still spoken in the northern Netherlands and the extreme northeast of Germany. Old Frisian and Old English uniquely share certain sound developments. But gradually Old English became a distinctively different language, even though it continued to bear, as its modern form still bears, marks of its Germanic ancestry.

The chief political events that tended toward the development of Old English as a separate language were no doubt the effects of the invasion of England by the Angles and the Saxons, which began around the middle of the fifth century. We do not know exactly what pressures caused the Germanic invaders to cross the channel, but it seems clear that the ease with which they overcame the native Britons encouraged further invasion and settlement. Britain, of course, had already been subdued by Caesar's Roman legions in the first century, and only the gradual collapse of the Roman Empire, including Roman withdrawal from Britain, made the success of the Germanic tribes possible.

During the next two or three centuries these tribes conquered most of England and parts of Scotland. They drove back the British inhabitants into Wales and Cumberland, killing many and enslaving others. They developed kingdoms and a settled form of life. So complete was their domination of their new land that almost no words have come down to us from the older forms of Celtic, the language of the ancient Britons. Welsh, the language of Wales, is a modern descendant of Celtic, and in more recent centuries there have been borrowings from Welsh. Meanwhile, even as Old English continued to evolve away from its West Germanic sister languages on the continent, it began to develop regional dialects of its own. The evidence indicates that the four main dialects, identified as West Saxon, Kentish, Mercian, and Northumbrian, differed mostly in pronunciation, their syntax and vocabularies remaining more or less similar.

The West Saxon dialect occupies an especially important role in Old English. It is the dialect of most of the documents that have come down to us, and was the basis of a kind of standard language which by the tenth century was widely used as the cultural linguistic norm of England. The political dominance of Wessex among the various Anglo-Saxon kingdoms assured the victory of its dialect. A standard language meant that there was a prestigious, relatively fixed form of Old English which was widely understood, and that the scribes who wrote down literary, political, and legal documents were learned in the use of it. Anglo-Saxon England is remarkable in Europe, after the fall of Rome, in having developed a standard literary and official language centuries before all the other European countries. However, as we shall see, this standardization was to be violently upset by political events.

As a Germanic language, Old English had inflectional endings resembling those of modern German. New words were largely formed by compounding and derivation; borrowing from other languages was not frequent, although some Latin and Greek words and a few from other tongues did enter Old English. The language had a much freer word order than

Modern English because the inflectional endings indicated grammatical relations which are shown by function words and word order in the language as we speak it today. However, Old English is by no means as free in its word order as Latin, various constraints of linguistic custom operating to restrict its freedom. There is a kind of compression in its style that gives Old English prose a special kind of dignity. Old English poetry had a very rich vocabulary, probably partly archaic at the time of its use. The verse was composed in great measure by formulas, using phrases of fixed metrical pattern which could be repeated in endless and fascinating variation. As we have noted, grammatical forms were much like those of modern German, with a number of noun declensions (although in later Old English these tend to fall together), strong and weak adjectives (two sets of declensions for all adjectives, depending on degree of particularity wished for), and strong and weak verbs rather like the same categories in Modern English. Nouns were of the masculine, feminine, or neuter gender, which determined the form of accompanying adjectives and the gender (and form) of referential pronouns. One cannot understand Old English without special study, yet even the most untutored reader of Modern English can grasp the meaning of some words or phrases. Here is Mark 12:1 in Old English:

> Sum monn him plantode wingeard and betynde hine ond dealf anne seath and getimbrode anne stiepel and gesette hine mid eorthtilium and ferde on eltheodignesse.

Here is a fairly literal translation of it:

> A certain man planted a vineyard for himself and enclosed it (him) and dug a pit and built a tower (steeple) and peopled (set) it (him) with farmers (earth-tillers) and went into a foreign country.

Old English is preserved in a rich literature, the oldest of any produced by the Germanic peoples, and in legal documents, inscriptions, and glosses. Much of this must be credited to the conversion of the Anglo-Saxon people to Christianity in the seventh and eighth centuries. The clerical scribes learned Latin, the language of their church, and then began to represent the vernacular language, Old English, with adaptations of the Roman alphabet. A few early inscriptions are preserved in the runic alphabet, which is an older form of the Roman alphabet borrowed by the Germanic peoples from the Romans much earlier. It is largely because we know rather precisely what sounds the Latin letters stand for that we can reconstruct the pronunciation of Old English with considerable certainty.

Some Old English literature is in the form of translations from religious classics; some of it consists of paraphrases and reworkings of religious stories. There are also original meditations, saints' lives, epics, practical work like collections of charms, and entertaining moralistic works like gnomes and riddles. It is an impressive body of work, and owes much to King Alfred (849–899), who actively encouraged the widespread literary use of Old English. He was himself a writer and translator, and he employed many other scholars at his court.

During much of King Alfred's reign, and again early in the 11th century, England was under invasion by Danes and Norwegians—or, as they are often called, the Vikings. The linguistic result of extended Viking occupation of parts of the country was a good deal of exchange and assimilation between the languages of the rival peoples. Since, however, the two were still quite closely related Germanic tongues at this point in their development, this interchange produced no striking shift in the history of English, despite the introduction of some Scandinavian (Old Norse) words and, to a lesser extent, grammatical forms.

A much more drastic change was brought about by the invasion and conquest of England by the Normans from northwestern France in 1066. Originally of Viking ancestry, the Normans had, by the middle of the 11th century, become Frenchified in language and culture; their language is designated as Norman French—a dialect of Old French. The effects of the Norman Conquest were profound in the field of language no less than in other fields. So immense were the changes this event brought about that we give a special name to the period of English after they begin to show themselves, from about 1100: we call the language, from then to about 1500, Middle English.

The replacement of the Anglo-Saxon upper classes by a French-speaking group led to the disappearance of the standard Old English language. As it lost its cultural linguistic center, English fell back completely onto its various dialects and became a language of peasants and laborers—and therefore, largely, unwritten. The early Middle English manuscripts that we have inherited simply represent late Old English, spelled in whatever way seemed to the local scribe (who was likely to be a Norman) to duplicate the sounds of the language as he heard it. This at least has the advantage of giving us clues to the changes that had been taking place in spoken Old English for many decades—changes that to some extent were concealed as long as the scribes used the standardized and relatively fixed literary language.

William the Conqueror and his successors ruled not only England but

Normandy, across the English Channel, until 1204. Then France won back the Duchy of Normandy, and the Anglo-Normans, politically detached from the continent, began to regard England as their permanent homeland. One result was the gradual adoption of English as their ordinary form of speech, rather than Norman French. But they brought to English, of course, the influence of Norman French, with its Latin background. Not only did French words come into the English vocabulary in large numbers, but English speech and literary style began to be receptive to borrowings from other languages, particularly Latin.

Middle English, then, comprises the various dialects of late Old English, modified both by evolutionary changes that were already in process and that continued for centuries, and by influences from Norman French. It is clear that English had been steadily losing or reducing its inflections, and consequently was becoming less free in word order; it was also losing its grammatical gender. By the later Middle English period, regardless of the many changes in sound and syntax yet to come, the essentials of Modern English had been created through these evolutionary changes and through the mingling of French and English, with an injection of Scandinavian.

The resurrection of English, in the 13th and 14th centuries, as the universal language of England once again made a standard dialect inevitable. Because London became the capital, its dialect won out over the other dialects of Middle English. Normally we recognize five of these: Northern (descended in the main from Northumbrian), spoken north of the Humber; Midland (descended from Mercian), spoken between the Thames and the Humber and usually divided into East and West Midland; Southern, or South Western (descended from West Saxon), spoken south of the Thames except in Kent; and Kentish, or South Eastern (descended from Kentish), spoken in Kent and its environs.

London was in the East Midland area, and its variety of East Midland as spoken by the court, governmental officials, and university men (both Oxford and Cambridge are in the East Midland area) became the basis for standard English. By the end of the Middle Ages it was victorious and was gradually depressing the other dialects, except for Scottish, which has continued a lively existence as a literary and standard language down to today, though not uninfluenced by the London dialect.

It should be noted that the proper Old English ancestor of standard English is not the Wessex dialect, in which practically all our Old English documents are written, but the Mercian (for London was in Mercia), in which little is preserved. However, in spite of this break, we can still trace our English vocabulary back to Old English with confidence.

The position of the London dialect was further strengthened, though not determined, because it was the language in which Chaucer, Gower, and Lydgate, the major writers of England in the later Middle Ages, wrote. After a lapse of some 350 years, England again had a standard language; but the battle of the vernacular was not yet won.

Middle English in its later forms is recognizably English, and a modern speaker could certainly understand a fair amount of it, although there are traps to be avoided. Some words still used today no longer have the same meaning—for example, *hope*, meant "expect," and *edify* meant "build"—and some words have disappeared. Yet the vocabulary is basically familiar. The following passage from Chaucer's Prologue to *The Canterbury Tales*, written about 1387, is not unrepresentative and is clearly English:

> Ther was also a Nonne, a Prioresse,
> That of hir smylyng was ful symple and coy;
> Hir gretteste ooth was but by Seinte Loy;
> And she was cleped [called] madame Eglentyne.
> Ful weel she soong the service dyvyne.

The spelling of Middle English is much more phonetic than that of Modern English, so that the strange orthography often indicates differences in pronunciation from the way we speak today. A final *e*, when not before a vowel, was sounded as a separate syllable, the phonetic value being that of the *a* in Modern English *sofa*. All the consonants were pronounced; for example, the *k* and *gh* in *knight*, and the *l* in *walked*. Yet almost any passage from Chaucer is felt as English, as Old English is not.

A series of major vowel changes from about 1350 to 1550 marks the shift from Middle English to Modern English, and is usually termed the Great Vowel Shift. It is the demarcation between the older stages of the language, strange to modern ears, and the later, which are recognizable as essentially what we speak today. Readers of Shakespeare are aware that his English is not the same as ours, but feel that it is close to our kind of English. The Great Vowel Shift in effect moved the long stressed vowels forward in the mouth and diphthongized long *i* and long *u* to (aī) and (au) respectively, so that Middle English *I*, pronounced (ē), became the Modern English pronunciation of the first person singular pronoun, and Middle English *hous*, pronounced (hōōs), became Modern English *house*. Printing, introduced into England by William Caxton in the midst of this shift, tended to preserve the old Middle English spelling and thus helped to put our orthography into the rather disorganized state from which it has suffered down to our day.

As English was called upon to perform a wider and wider variety of functions, and above all to increase its vocabulary to cope with tasks formerly left to Latin, it modified itself to fit the new needs. The Renaissance period is noted for its great influx of vocabulary, especially from the classical languages, and from French and Italian. Englishmen adopted words right and left; and although some words did not survive, enough did to make the vocabulary of English perhaps the largest of any language. This has created certain difficulties. For example, adjectives and nouns referring to the same thing may be unrelated in root to each other (*oral/mouth; ocular/eye*). But the wide borrowing has produced a rich store of synonyms from different linguistic sources (for example, *royal, kingly,* and *regal*).

A good example of this lexical movement may be seen in Andrew Borde's prologue to his *Breviary of Healthe*, written in 1552: "Egregious doctours and maysters of the Eximiouse and Archane Science of physicke, of your Urbanitie Exasperate not your selfe agaynste me for makyinge of this lytle volume of Phisycke." These "inkhorn" terms, as they were called, provoked some indignation, yet the demands made upon English led to the adoption of many of these words. *Eximiouse* (which meant "excellent") has disappeared, but *exasperate* is a word heard every day, and *egregious* is not rare, although its meaning has shifted from "distinguished" to "flagrant." We now have thousands of long and short, hard and easy, Germanic and Romance (that is, derived from Latin) words in our language, each with its particular powers. Shakespeare can be as moving when he writes "the multitudinous seas incarnadine" as when he writes "to be or not to be." English has extensive resources, both concrete and abstract, everyday and elegant or academic, to satisfy various kinds of users and various goals.

American English is descended from that variety of English brought over to the colonies in the 17th century. It developed on its own to some extent—obviously in the matter of names for new objects, peoples, and flora and fauna—without ever losing contact with its base in England. The American and British varieties of the language have persisted, and seem in this era of mass communications and easy travel to be getting closer to each other. The fate of a language is closely bound up with the political fate of its speakers, and the world role of the United States in the past 30 years has strengthened the position of American English.

The regional dialects of English in America have traditionally been called New England, General American, and Southern; and although there has been some questioning of this categorization in recent years, it still seems more useful than the Northern, Midland, and Southern division some favor. In any event, the mobility of modern life and communication devices such as radio and television are profoundly affecting regional dialects, and they seem on the way to merging with each other. Social dialects, on the other hand, are extremely persistent, especially in England and to some extent in America. We are very much aware of the problem of ghetto and urban dialects today, and consequently of the value of bidialectism as well as of bilingualism. It is sufficient merely to mention the other major dialects of English: Canadian English, Irish English, Australian English, Scottish, Indian English—each, it must be emphasized, with its own subdialects.

In spite of some differences, there has been a basic stability in the rules or inner regulations of English over the centuries. As Professor Ian Gordon has written in *The Movement of English Prose:* "The segmented English sentence, stressed in word-groups, each word-group separated from its neighbour by a boundary-marker, the major stress of each group falling on the semantically important word in the group, the groups occurring in a relatively fixed order, the words in each group generally falling in a precisely fixed order—all this, plus the continuity of the original vocabulary and the preservation of the original structural words, has ensured an underlying stability in English speech, and in the prose which is based upon it."

With the establishment of a standard dialect in the late 14th century and the acquisition of an adequate vocabulary in the 16th and 17th centuries, it was left to the 18th and 19th centuries to create adequate grammars and dictionaries, so that by about 1800 English was fully ready to assume the international responsibility that the cultural, scientific, and political importance of England and America was to thrust upon it. English in 1750 was a language of more or less minor importance in the world; by 1850 it was a world language. Since then it has spread all over the globe and is the international language par excellence. If there are more speakers of some varieties of Chinese than English, a fact not completely established, Chinese does not have the world authority, the geographic spread, the important literature and scientific writings, or the commercial significance of English. English opens gates to great literature and philosophy and makes possible the universality of science. Although this high eminence is not fundamentally because of its innate superiority, it is certainly well fitted for its eminence and for the task of bringing various peoples together and establishing ties rather than severing them.

We have seen, then, how Modern English has developed a vocabulary of great extent and richness, drawn from many languages of the world. Its inflections are few, but its syntactic rules are probably as intricate as those of any language. Its verbal system presents great complexities, making for subtle distinctions. It is both a very concrete and an abstract language. It favors sibilants over other sounds, and yet possesses a wide phoneme repertory. Its spelling is fairly irregular, although not without some patterns and rules. Above all it is a supple and variegated language, which its native speakers should cherish and which provides them with their hold on the past, their contact with the present, and their claim on the future. Finally, it makes possible their view of the world and of themselves.

Robert Benchley

A Good Old-Fashioned Christmas

Sooner or later at every Christmas party, just as things are beginning to get good, someone shuts his eyes, puts his head back and moans softly: "Ah, well, this isn't like the old days. We don't seem to have any good old-fashioned Christmases any more." To which the answer from my corner of the room is: "All right! That suits me!"

Just what they have in mind when they say "old-fashioned Christmas" you never can pin them down to telling. "Lots of snow," they mutter, "and lots of food." Yet, if you work it right, you can still get plenty of snow and food today. Snow, at any rate.

Then there seems to be some idea of the old-fashioned Christmas being, of necessity, in the country. It doesn't make any difference whether you were raised on a farm or whether your ideas of a rural Christmas were gleaned from pictures in old copies of "Harper's Young People," you must give folks to understand that such were the surroundings in which you spent your childhood holidays. And that, ah, me, those days will never come again!

Well, supposing you get your wish some time. Supposing, let us say, your wife's folks who live up in East Russet, Vermont, write and ask you to come up and bring the children for a good old-fashioned Christmas, "while we are all still together," they add cheerily with their flair for putting everybody in good humor.

Hurray, hurray! Off to the country for Christmas! Pack up all the warm clothes in the house, for you will need them up there where the air is clean and cold. Snow-shoes? Yes, put them in, or better yet, Daddy will carry them. What fun! Take along some sleigh-bells to jangle in case there aren't enough on the pung. There must be jangling sleigh-bells. And whisky for frost-bite. Or is it snake-bite that whisky is for? Anyway, put it in! We're off! Good-by, all! Good-by! JANGLE-JANGLE-JANGLE-Jangle-Jangle-Jangle-jangle-jangle-jangle-jangle-jangle-jangle!

In order to get to East Russet you take the Vermont Central as far as Twitchell's Falls and change there for Torpid River Junction, where a spur line takes you right into Gormley. At Gormley you are met by a buckboard which takes you back to Torpid River Junction again. By this time a train or something has come in which will wait for the local from Besus. While waiting for this you will have time to send your little boy to school, so that he can finish the third grade.

At East Russet Grandpa meets you with the sleigh. The bags are piled in and Mother sits in front with Lester in her lap while Daddy takes Junior and Ga-Ga in back with him and the luggage. Giddap, Esther Girl!

Esther Girl giddaps, and two suitcases fall out. Heigh-ho! Out we get and pick them up, brushing the snow off and filling our cuffs with it as we do so. After all, there is nothing like snow for getting up one's cuffs. Good clean snow never hurt anyone. Which is lucky, because after you have gone a mile or so, you discover that Ga-Ga is missing. Never mind, she is a self-reliant little girl and will doubtless find her way to the farm by herself. Probably she will be there waiting for you when you arrive.

The farm is situated on a hill about eleven hundred miles from the center of town, just before you get into Canada. If there is a breeze in winter, they get it. But what do they care for breezes, so long as they have the Little Colonel oil-heater in the front room, to make everything cozy and warm within a radius of four inches! And the big open fireplace with the draught coming down it! Fun for everybody!

You are just driving up to the farmhouse in the sleigh, with the entire right leg frozen where the lap robe has slipped out. Grandma is waiting for you at the door and you bustle in, all glowing with good cheer. "Merry Christmas, Grandma!" Lester is cross and Junior is asleep and has to be dragged by the hand upstairs, bumping against each step all the way. It is so late that you decide that you all might as well go to bed, especially as you learn that breakfast is at four-thirty. It usually is at four, but Christmas being a holiday everyone sleeps late.

As you reach the top of the stairs you get into a current of cold air which has something of the quality of the temperature in a nice well-regulated crypt. This is the Bed Room Zone, and in it the thermometer never tops the zero mark from October fifteenth until the middle of May. Those rooms in which no one sleeps are used to store perishable vegetables in, and someone has to keep thumbing the tomatoes and pears every so often to prevent their getting so hard that they crack.

The way to get undressed for bed in one of Grandpa's bedrooms is as follows: Starting from the foot of the stairs where it is warm, run up two at a time to keep the circulation going as long as possible. Opening the bedroom door with one hand, tear down the curtains from the windows with the other, pick up the rugs from the floor and snatch the spread from the top of the bureau. Pile all these on the bed, cover with the closet door which you have wrenched from its hinges, and leap quickly underneath. It sometimes helps to put on a pair of rubbers over your shoes.

And even when you are in bed, you have no guarantee of going to sleep. Grandpa's mattresses seem to contain the overflow from the silo, corn-husks, baked-potato skins and long, stringy affairs which feel like pipe cleaners. On a cold night, snuggling down into these is about like snuggling down into a bed of damp pine cones out in the forest.

Then there are Things abroad in the house. Shortly after you get into bed, the stairs start snapping. Next something runs along the roof over your head. You say to yourself: "Don't be silly. It's only Santa Claus." Then it runs along the wall behind the head of the bed. Santa Claus wouldn't do that. Down the long hall which leads into the ell of the house you can hear the wind sighing softly, with an occasional reassuring bang of a door.

The unmistakable sound of someone dying in great pain rises from just below the window-sill. It is a sort of low moan, with just a touch of strangulation in it. Perhaps Santa has fallen off the roof. Perhaps that story you once heard about Grandpa's house having been a hang-out for Revolutionary smugglers is true, and one of the smugglers has come back for his umbrella. The only place at a time like this is down under the bedclothes. But the children become frightened and demand to be taken home, and Grandpa has to be called to explain that it is only Blue Bell out in the barn. Blue Bell has asthma, and on a cold night they have to be very patient with her.

Christmas morning dawns cloudy and cold, with the threat of plenty more snow, and, after all, what would Christmas be without snow? You lie in bed for one hour and a quarter trying to figure out how you can get up without losing the covers from around you. A glance at the water pitcher shows that it is time for them to put the red ball up for skating. You think of the nice warm bathroom at home, and decide that you can wait until you get back there before shaving.

This breaking the ice in the pitcher seems to be a feature of the early lives of all great men which they look back on with tremendous satisfaction. "When I was a boy, I used to have to break the ice in the pitcher every morning before I could wash," is said with as much pride as one might say, "When I was a boy I stood at the head of my class." Just what virtue there is in having to break ice in a pitcher is not evident, unless it lies in their taking the bother to break the ice and wash at all. Anytime that I have to break ice in a pitcher as a preliminary to washing, I go unwashed, that's all. And Benjamin Franklin and U.S. Grant and Rutherford B. Hayes can laugh as much as they like. I'm nobody's fool about a thing like that.

Getting the children dressed is a lot of fun when you have to keep pumping their limbs up and down to keep them from freezing out stiff. The children love it and are just as bright and merry as little pixies when it is time to go downstairs and say "Good morning" to Grandpa and Grandma. The entire family enters the dining-room purple and chattering and exceedingly cross.

After breakfast everyone begins getting dinner. The kitchen being the only warm place in the house may have something to do with it. But before long there are so many potato peelings and turkey feathers and squash seeds and floating bits of pie crust in the kitchen that the women-folk send you and the children off into the front part of the house to amuse yourselves and get out of the way.

Then what a jolly time you and the kiddies and Grandpa have together! You can either slide on the horse-hair sofa, or play "The Wayside Chapel" on the piano (the piano has scroll-work on either side of the music rack with yellow silk showing through), or look out the window and see ten miles of dark gray snow. Perhaps you may even go out to the barn and look at the horses and cows, but really, as you walk down between the stalls, when you have seen one horse or one cow you have seen them all. And besides, the cold in the barn has an added flavor of damp harness leather and musty carriage upholstery which eats into your very marrow.

Of course, there are the presents to be distributed, but that takes on much the same aspect as the same ceremony in the new-fashioned Christmas, except that in the really old-fashioned Christmas the presents weren't so tricky. Children got mostly mittens and shoes, with a sled thrown in sometimes for dissipation. Where a boy today is bored by three o'clock in the afternoon with his electric grain-elevator and miniature pond with real perch in it, the old-fashioned boy was lucky if he got a copy of "Naval Battles of the War of 1812" and an orange. Now this feature is often brought up in praise of the old way of doing things. "I tell you," says Uncle Gyp, "the children in my time never got such presents as you get today." And he seems proud of the fact, as if there were some virtue accruing to him for it. If the children of today can get electric grain-elevators and tin automobiles for Christmas, why aren't they that much better off than their grandfathers who got only wristlets? Learning the value of money, which seems to be the only argument of the stand-patters, doesn't hold very much water as a Christmas slogan. The value of money can be learned in just about five minutes when the time comes, but Christmas is not the season.

But to return to the farm, where you and the kiddies and Gramp' are killing time. You can either bring in wood from the woodshed, or thaw out the pump, or read the books in the bookcase over the writing-desk. Of the three, bringing in the wood will probably be the most fun, as you are likely to burn yourself thawing out the pump, and the list of reading matter on hand includes "The Life and Deeds of General Grant," "Our First Century," "Andy's Trip to Portland," bound volumes of the Jersey Cattle Breeders' Gazette and "Diseases of the Horse." Then there are some old copies of "Round the Lamp" for the years 1850–54 and some colored plates showing plans for the approaching World's Fair at Chicago.

Thus the time passes, in one round of gayety after another, until you are summoned to dinner. Here all caviling must cease. The dinner lives up to the advertising. If an old-fashioned Christmas could consist entirely of dinner without the old-fashioned bedrooms, the old-fashioned pitcher, and the old-fashioned entertainments, we professional pessimists wouldn't have a turkey-leg left to stand on. But, as has been pointed out, it is possible to get a good dinner without going up to East Russet, Vt., or, if it isn't, then our civilization has been a failure.

And the dinner only makes the aftermath seem worse. According to an old custom of the human race, everyone overeats. Deliberately and with considerable gusto you sit at the table and say pleasantly: "My, but I won't be able to walk after this. Just a little more of the dark meat, please, Grandpa, and just a dab of stuffing. Oh, dear, that's too much!" You haven't the excuse of the drunkard, who becomes oblivious to his excesses after several drinks. You know what you are doing, and yet you make light of it and even laugh about it as long as you *can* laugh without splitting a seam.

And then you sit and moan. If you were having a good new-fashioned Christmas you could go out to the movies or take a walk, or a ride, but to be really old-fashioned you must stick close to the house, for in the old days there were no movies and no automobiles and if you wanted to take a walk you had to have the hired man go ahead of you with a snow-shovel and make a tunnel. There are probably plenty of things to do in the country today, and just as many automobiles and electric lights as there are in the city, but you can't call Christmas with all these improvements "an old-fashioned Christmas." That's cheating.

If you are going through with the thing right, you have got to retire to the sitting-room after dinner and *sit*. Of course, you can go out and play in the snow if you want to, but you know as well as I do that this playing in the snow is all right when you are small but a bit trying on anyone over thirty. And anyway, it always began to snow along about three in the afternoon an old-fashioned Christmas day, with a cheery old leaden sky overhead and a jolly old gale sweeping around the corners of the house.

No, you simply must sit indoors, in front of a fire if you insist, but nevertheless with nothing much to do. The children are sleepy and snarling. Grandpa is just sleepy. Someone tries to start the conversation, but everyone else is too gorged with food to be able to move the lower jaw sufficiently to articulate. It develops that the family is in possession of the loudest-ticking clock in the world and along about four o'clock it begins to break its own record. A stenographic report of the proceedings would read as follows:

"Ho-hum! I'm sleepy! I shouldn't have eaten so much."
"Tick-tock-tick-tock-tick-tock-tick-tock—"
"It seems just like Sunday, doesn't it?"
"Look at Grandpa! He's asleep."
"Here, Junior! Don't plague Grandpa. Let him sleep."
"Tick-tock-tick-tock-tick-tock—"
"Junior! Let Grandpa alone! Do you want Mamma to take you up-stairs?"
"Ho-hum!"
"Tick-tock-tick-tock-tick-tock—"

Louder and louder the clock ticks, until something snaps in your brain and you give a sudden leap into the air with a scream, finally descending to strangle each of the family in turn, and Grandpa as he sleeps. Then, as you feel your end is near, all the warm things you have ever known come back to you, in a flash. You remember the hot Sunday subway to Coney, your trip to Mexico, the bull-fighters of Spain.

You dash out into the snowdrifts and plunge along until you sink exhausted. Only the fact that this article ends here keeps you from freezing to death, with an obituary the next day reading:

"DIED suddenly, at East Russet, Vt., of an old-fashioned Christmas."

Berton Roueché

A Pig from Jersey

Among those who passed through the general clinic of Lenox Hill Hospital, at Seventy-sixth Street and Park Avenue, on Monday morning, April 6, 1942, was a forty-year-old Yorkville dishwasher whom I will call Herman Sauer. His complaint, like his occupation, was an undistinguished one. He had a stomach ache. The pain had seized him early Sunday evening, he told the examining physician, and although it was not unendurably severe, its persistence worried him. He added that he was diarrheic and somewhat nauseated. Also, his head hurt. The doctor took his temperature and the usual soundings. Neither disclosed any cause for alarm. Then he turned his attention to the manifest symptoms. The course of treatment he chose for their alleviation was unexceptionable. It consisted of a dose of bismuth subcarbonate, a word of dietetic advice, and an invitation to come back the next day if the trouble continued. Sauer went home under the comforting impression that he was suffering from nothing more serious than a touch of dyspepsia.

Sauer was worse in the morning. The pain had spread to his chest, and when he stood up, he felt dazed and dizzy. He did not, however, return to Lenox Hill. Instead, with the inconsistency of the ailing, he made his way to Metropolitan Hospital, on Welfare Island. He arrived there, shortly before noon, in such a state of confusion and collapse that a nurse had to assist him into the examining room. Half an hour later, having submitted to another potion of bismuth and what turned out to be an uninstructive blood count, he was admitted to a general ward for observation. During the afternoon, his temperature, which earlier had been, equivocally, normal, began to rise. When the resident physician reached him on his evening round, it was a trifle over a hundred and three. As is customary in all but the most crystalline cases, the doctor avoided a flat-footed diagnosis.

A PIG FROM JERSEY From *Eleven Blue Men* by Berton Roueché, by permission of Little, Brown and Co. Copyright 1950 by Berton Roueché; originally appeared in *The New Yorker*.

In his record of the case, he suggested three compatible possibilities. One was aortitis, a heart condition caused by an inflammation of the great trunk artery. The others, both of which were inspired by an admission of intemperance that had been wrung from Sauer in the examining room, were cirrhosis of the liver and gastritis due to alcoholism. At the moment, the doctor indicated, the last appeared to be the most likely.

Gastritis, aortitis, and cirrhosis of the liver, like innumerable other ailments, can seldom be repulsed by specific medication, but time is frequently effective. Sauer responded to neither. His fever held and his symptoms multiplied. He itched all over, an edema sealed his eyes, his voice faded and failed, and the seething pains in his chest and abdomen advanced to his arms and legs. Toward the end of the week, he sank into a stony, comalike apathy. Confronted by this disturbing decline, the house physician reopened his mind and reconsidered the evidence. His adaptability was soon rewarded. He concluded that he was up against an acute and, to judge from his patient's progressive dilapidation, a peculiarly rapacious infection. It was an insinuating notion, but it had one awkward flaw. The white-blood-cell count is a reliable barometer of infection, and Sauer's count had been entirely normal. On Wednesday, April 15th, the doctor requested that another count be made. He did not question the accuracy of the original test, but the thought had occurred to him that it might have been made prematurely. The report from the laboratory was on his desk when he reached the hospital the following day. It more than confirmed his hunch. It also relieved him simultaneously of both uncertainty and hope. Sauer's white count was morbidly elevated by a preponderance of eosinophiles, a variety of cell that is produced by several potentially epidemic diseases but just one as formidably dishevelling as the case in question. The doctor put down the report and called the hospital superintendent's office. He asked the clerk who answered the phone to inform the Department of Health, to which the appearance of any disease of an epidemiological nature must be promptly communicated, that he had just uncovered a case of trichinosis.

The cause of trichinosis is a voracious endoparasitic worm, *Trichinella spiralis*, commonly called trichina, that lodges in the muscle fibres of an animal host. It enters the host by way of the alimentary canal, and in the intestine produces larvae that penetrate the intestinal walls to enter the blood stream. The worm is staggeringly prolific, and it has been known to remain alive, though quiescent, in the body of a surviving victim for thirty-one years. In general, the number of trichinae that succeed in reaching the muscle determines the severity of an attack. As such parasitic organisms go, adult trichinae are relatively large, the males averaging one-twentieth of an inch in length and the females about twice that. The larvae are less statuesque. Pathologists have found as many as twelve hundred of them encysted in a single gram of tissue. Numerous animals, ranging in size from the mole to the hippopotamus, are hospitable to the trichina, but it has a strong predilection for swine and man. Man's only important source of infection is pork. The disease is perpetuated in swine by the practice common among hog raisers of using garbage, some of which inevitably contains trichinous meat, for feed. Swine have a high degree of tolerance for the trichina, but man's resistive powers are feeble. In 1931, in Detroit, a man suffered a violent seizure of trichinosis as a result of merely eating a piece of bread buttered with a knife that had been used to slice an infected sausage. The hog from which the sausage was made had appeared to be in excellent health. Few acute afflictions are more painful than trichinosis, or more prolonged and debilitating. Its victims are occasionally prostrated for many months, and relapses after apparent recoveries are not uncommon. Its mortality rate is disconcertingly variable. It is usually around six per cent, but in some outbreaks nearly a third of those stricken have died, and the recovery of a patient from a full-scale attack is almost unheard of. Nobody is, or can be rendered, immune to trichinosis. Also, there is no specific cure. In the opinion of most investigators, it is far from likely that one will ever be found. They are persuaded that any therapeutic agent potent enough to kill a multitude of embedded trichinae would probably kill the patient, too.

Although medical science is unable to terminate, or even lessen the severity of, an assault of trichinosis, no disease is easier to dodge. There are several dependable means of evasion. Abstention from pork is, of course, one. It is also the most venerable, having been known, vigorously recommended, and widely practiced for at least three thousand years. Some authorities, in fact, regard the Mosaic proscription of pork as the pioneering step in the development of preventive medicine. However, since the middle of the nineteenth century, when the cause and nature of trichinosis were illuminated by Sir James Paget, Rudolf Virchow, Friedrich Albert von Zenker, and others, less ascetic safeguards have become available. The trichinae are rugged but not indestructible. It has been amply demonstrated that thorough cooking (until the meat is bone-white) will make even the wormiest pork harmless. So will refrigeration at a maximum temperature of five degrees for a minimum of twenty days. So, just as effectively, will certain scrupulous methods of salting, smoking, and pickling.

Despite this abundance of easily applied defensive techniques, the incidence of trichinosis has not greatly diminished over the globe in the past fifty or sixty years. In some countries, it has even increased. The United States is one of them. Many epidemiologists are convinced that this country now leads the world in trichinosis. It is, at any rate, a major health problem here. According to a compendium of recent autopsy studies, approximately one American in five has at some time or another had trichinosis, and it is probable that well over a million are afflicted with it every year. As a considerable source of misery, it ranks with tuberculosis, syphilis, and undulant fever. It will probably continue to be one for some time to come. Its spread is almost unimpeded. A few states, New York among them, have statutes prohibiting the feeding of uncooked garbage to swine, but nowhere is a very determined effort made at enforcement, and the Bureau of Animal Industry of the United States Department of Agriculture, although it assumes all pork to be trichinous until proved otherwise, requires packing houses to administer a prophylactic freeze to only those varieties of the meat—frankfurters, salami, prosciutto, and the like—that are often eaten raw. Moreover, not all processed pork comes under the jurisdiction of the Department. At least a third of it is processed under local ordinances in small, neighborhood abattoirs beyond the reach of the Bureau, or on farms. Nearly two per cent of the hogs slaughtered in the United States are trichinous.

Except for a brief period around the beginning of this century, when several European countries refused, because of its dubious nature, to import American pork, the adoption of a less porous system of control has never been seriously contemplated here. One reason is that it would run into money. Another is that, except by a few informed authorities, it has always been considered unnecessary. Trichinosis is generally believed to be a rarity. This view, though hallucinated, is not altogether without explanation. Outbreaks of trichinosis are seldom widely publicized. They are seldom even recognized. Trichinosis is the chameleon of diseases. Nearly all diseases are anonymous at onset, and many tend to resist identification until their grip is well established, but most can eventually be identified by patient scrutiny. Trichinosis is occasionally impervious to bedside detection at any stage. Even blood counts sometimes inexplicably fail to reveal its presence at any stage in its development. As a diagnostic deadfall, it is practically unique. The number and variety of ailments with which it is more or less commonly confused approach the encyclopedic. They include arthritis, acute alcoholism, conjunctivitis, food poisoning, lead poisoning, heart disease, laryngitis, mumps, asthma, rheumatism, rheumatic fever, rheumatic myocarditis, gout, tuberculosis, angioneurotic edema, dermatomyositis, frontal sinusitis, influenza, nephritis, peptic ulcer, appendicitis, cholecystitis, malaria, scarlet fever, typhoid fever, paratyphoid fever, undulant fever, encephalitis, gastroenteritis, intercostal neuritis, tetanus, pleurisy, colitis, meningitis, syphilis, typhus, and cholera. It has even been mistaken for beriberi. With all the rich inducements to error, a sound diagnosis of trichinosis is rarely made, and the diagnostician cannot always take much credit for it. Often, as at Metropolitan Hospital that April day in 1942, it is forced upon him.

The report of the arresting discovery at Metropolitan reached the Health Department on the morning of Friday, April 17th. Its form was conventional—a postcard bearing a scribbled name, address, and diagnosis —and it was handled with conventional dispatch. Within an hour, Dr. Morris Greenberg, who was then chief epidemiologist of the Bureau of Preventable Diseases and is now its director, had put one of his fleetest agents on the case, a field epidemiologist named Lawrence Levy. Ten minutes after receiving the assignment, Dr. Levy was on his way to the hospital, intent on tracking down the source of the infection, with the idea of alerting the physicians of other persons who might have contracted the disease along with Sauer. At eleven o'clock, Dr. Levy walked into the office of the medical superintendent at Metropolitan. His immediate objective was to satisfy himself that Sauer was indeed suffering from trichinosis. He was quickly convinced. The evidence of the eosinophile count was now supported in the record by more graphic proof. Sauer, the night before, had undergone a biopsy. A sliver of muscle had been taken from one of his legs and examined under a microscope. It teemed with *Trichinella spiralis*. On the basis of the sample, the record noted, the pathologist who made the test estimated the total infestation of trichinae at upward of twelve million. A count of over five million is almost invariably lethal. Dr. Levy returned the dossier to the file. Then, moving on to his more general objective, he had a word with the patient. He found him bemused but conscious. Sauer appeared at times to distantly comprehend what was said to him, but his replies were faint and rambling and mostly incoherent. At the end of five minutes, Dr. Levy gave up. He hadn't learned much, but he had learned something, and he didn't have the heart to go on with his questioning. It was just possible, he let himself hope, that he had the lead he needed. Sauer had mentioned the New York Labor Temple, a German-American meeting-and-banquet hall on East Eighty-fourth Street, and he had twice uttered the word "*Schlachtfest.*" A *Schlachtfest*, in Yorkville, the Doctor knew, is a pork feast.

Before leaving the hospital, Dr. Levy telephoned Dr. Greenberg and dutifully related what he had found out. It didn't take him long. Then he had a sandwich and a cup of coffee and headed for the Labor Temple, getting there at a little past one. It was, and is, a shabby yellow-brick building of six stories, a few doors west of Second Avenue, with a high, ornately balustrated stoop and a double basement. Engraved on the façade, just above the entrance, is a maxim: "Knowledge Is Power." In 1942, the Temple was owned and operated, on a non-profit basis, by the Workmen's

Educational Association; it has since been acquired by private interests and is now given over to business and light manufacturing. A porter directed Dr. Levy to the manager's office, a cubicle at the end of a dim corridor flanked by meeting rooms. The manager was in, and, after a spasm of bewilderment, keenly cooperative. He brought out his records and gave Dr. Levy all the information he had. Sauer was known at the Temple. He had been employed there off and on for a year or more as a dishwasher and general kitchen helper, the manager related. He was one of a large group of lightly skilled wanderers from which the cook was accustomed to recruit a staff whenever the need arose. Sauer had last worked at the Temple on the nights of March 27th and 28th. On the latter, as it happened, the occasion was a *Schlachtfest*.

Dr. Levy, aware that the incubation period of trichinosis is usually from seven to fourteen days and that Sauer had presented himself at Lenox Hill on April 6th, motioned to the manager to continue. The *Schlachtfest* had been given by the Hindenberg Pleasure Society, an informal organization whose members and their wives gathered periodically at the Temple for an evening of singing and dancing and overeating. The arrangements for the party had been made by the secretary of the society—Felix Lindenhauser, a name which, like those of Sauer and the others I shall mention in connection with the *Schlachtfest*, is a fictitious one. Lindenhauser lived in St. George, on Staten Island. The manager's records did not indicate where the pork had been obtained. Probably, he said, it had been supplied by the society. That was frequently the case. The cook would know, but it was not yet time for him to come on duty. The implication of this statement was not lost on Dr. Levy. Then the cook, he asked, was well? The manager said that he appeared to be. Having absorbed this awkward piece of information, Dr. Levy inquired about the health of the others who had been employed in the kitchen on the night of March 28th. The manager didn't know. His records showed, however, that, like Sauer, none of them had worked at the Temple since that night. He pointed out that it was quite possible, of course, that they hadn't been asked to. Dr. Levy noted down their names—Rudolf Nath, Henry Kuhn, Frederick Kreisler, and William Ritter—and their addresses. Nath lived in Queens, Kreisler in Brooklyn, and Kuhn and Ritter in the Bronx. Then Dr. Levy settled back to await the arrival of the cook. The cook turned up at three, and he, too, was very cooperative. He was feeling fine, he said. He remembered the *Schlachtfest*. The pig, he recalled, had been provided by the society. Some of it had been ground up into sausage and baked. The rest had been roasted. All of it had been thoroughly cooked. He was certain of that. The sausage, for example, had been boiled for two hours before it was baked. He had eaten his share of both. He supposed that the rest of the help had, too, but there was no knowing. He had neither seen nor talked to any of them since the night of the feast. There had been no occasion to, he said.

Dr. Levy returned to his office, and sat there for a while in meditation. Presently, he put in a call to Felix Lindenhauser, the secretary of the society, at his home on Staten Island. Lindenhauser answered the telephone. Dr. Levy introduced himself and stated his problem. Lindenhauser was plainly flabbergasted. He said he was in excellent health, and had been for months. His wife, who had accompanied him to the *Schlachtfest*, was also in good health. He had heard of no illness in the society. He couldn't believe that there had been anything wrong with that pork. It had been delicious. The pig had been obtained by two members of the society, George Muller and Hans Breit, both of whom lived in the Bronx. They had bought it from a farmer of their acquaintance in New Jersey. Lindenhauser went on to say that there had been twenty-seven people at the feast, including himself and his wife. The names and addresses of the company were in his minute book. He fetched it to the phone and patiently read them off as Dr. Levy wrote them down. If he could be of any further help, he added as he prepared to hang up, just let him know, but he was convinced that Dr. Levy was wasting his time. At the moment, Dr. Levy was almost inclined to agree with him.

Dr. Levy spent an increasingly uneasy weekend. He was of two antagonistic minds. He refused to believe that Sauer's illness was not in some way related to the *Schlachtfest* of the Hindenberg Pleasure Society. On the other hand, it didn't seem possible that it was. Late Saturday afternoon, at his home, he received a call that increased his discouragement, if not his perplexity. It was from his office. Metropolitan Hospital had called to report that Herman Sauer was dead. Dr. Levy put down the receiver with the leaden realization that, good or bad, the *Schlachtfest* was now the only lead he would ever have.

On Monday, Dr. Levy buckled down to the essential but unexhilarating task of determining the health of the twenty-seven men and women who had attended the *Schlachtfest*. Although his attitude was half-hearted, his procedure was methodical, unhurried, and objective. He called on and closely examined each of the guests, including the Lindenhausers, and from each procured a sample of blood for analysis in the Health Department laboratories. The job, necessarily involving a good deal of leg work and many evening visits, took him the better part of two weeks. He ended up, on April 30th, about equally reassured and stumped. His findings were provocative but contradictory. Of the twenty-seven who had feasted together on the night of March 28th, twenty-five were in what undeniably was their normal state of health. Two, just as surely, were not. The exceptions were George Muller and Hans Breit, the men who had provided the pig. Muller was at home and in bed, suffering sorely from what his family physician had uncertainly diagnosed as some sort of intestinal upheaval. Breit was in as bad a way or worse, in Fordham Hospital. He had been admitted there for observation on April 10th. Several diagnoses had been suggested, including rheumatic myocarditis, pleurisy, and grippe, but none had been formerly retained. The nature of the two men's troubles was no mystery to Dr. Levy. Both, as he was subsequently able to demonstrate, had trichinosis.

On Friday morning, May 1st, Dr. Levy returned to the Bronx for a more searching word with Muller. Owing to Muller's debilitated condition on the occasion of Dr. Levy's first visit, their talk had been brief and clinical in character. Muller, who was now up and shakily about, received him warmly. Since their meeting several days before, he said, he had been enlivening the tedious hours of illness with reflection. A question had occurred to him. Would it be possible, he inquired, to contract trichinosis from just a few nibbles of raw pork? It would, Dr. Levy told him. He also urged him to be more explicit. Thus encouraged, Muller displayed an unexpected gift for what appeared to be total recall. He leisurely recounted to Dr. Levy that he and Breit had bought the pig from a farmer who owned a place near Midvale, New Jersey. The farmer had killed and dressed the animal, and they had delivered the carcass to the Labor Temple kitchen on the evening of March 27th. That, however, had been only part of their job. Not wishing to trouble the cook and his helpers, who were otherwise occupied, Muller and Breit had then set about preparing the sausage for the feast. They were both experienced amateur sausage makers, he said, and explained the process—grinding, macerating, and seasoning—in laborious detail. Dr. Levy began to fidget. Naturally, Muller presently went on, they had been obliged to sample their work. There was no other way to make sure that the meat was properly seasoned. He had taken perhaps two or three little nibbles. Breit, who had a heartier taste for raw pork, had probably eaten a trifle more. It was hard to believe, Muller said, that so little—just a pinch or two—could cause such misery. He had thought his head would split, and the pain in his legs had been almost beyond endurance. Dr. Levy returned him sympathetically to the night of March 27th. They had finished with the sausage around midnight, Muller remembered. The cook had departed by then, but his helpers were still at work. There had been five of them. He didn't know their names, but he had seen all or most of them again the next night, during the feast. Neither he nor Breit had given them any of the sausage before they left. But it was possible, of course, since the refrigerator in which he and Breit had stored the meat was not, like some, equipped with a lock. . . . Dr. Levy thanked him, and moved rapidly to the door.

Dr. Levy spent the rest of the morning in the Bronx. After lunch, he hopped over to Queens. From there, he made his way to Brooklyn. It was past four by the time he got back to his office. He was hot and gritty from a dozen subway journeys, and his legs ached from pounding pavements and stairs and hospital corridors, but he had tracked down and had a revealing chat with each of Sauer's kitchen colleagues, and his heart was light. Three of them—William Ritter, Rudolf Nath, and Frederick Kreisler —were in hospitals. Ritter was at Fordham, Nath at Queens General, and Kreisler at the Coney Island Hospital, not far from his home in Brooklyn. The fourth member of the group, Henry Kuhn, was sick in bed at home. All were veterans of numerous reasonable but incorrect diagnoses, all were in more discomfort than danger, and all, it was obvious to Dr. Levy's un-clouded eye, were suffering from trichinosis. Its source was equally obvious. They had prowled the icebox after the departure of Muller and Breit, come upon the sausage meat, and cheerfully helped themselves. They thought it was hamburger.

Before settling down at his desk to compose the final installment of his report, Dr. Levy looked in on Dr. Greenberg. He wanted, among other things, to relieve him of the agony of suspense. Dr. Greenberg gave him a chair, a cigarette, and an attentive ear. At the end of the travelogue, he groaned. "Didn't they even bother to cook it?" he asked.

"Yes, most of them did," Dr. Levy said. "They made it up into patties and fried them. Kuhn cooked his fairly well. A few minutes, at least. The others liked theirs rare. All except Sauer. He ate his raw."

"Oh," Dr. Greenberg said.

"Also," Dr. Levy added, "he ate two."

William Faulkner

Dry September

I

Through the bloody September twilight, aftermath of sixty-two rainless days, it had gone like a fire in dry grass—the rumor, the story, whatever it was. Something about Miss Minnie Cooper and a Negro. Attacked, insulted, frightened: none of them, gathered in the barber shop on that Saturday evening where the ceiling fan stirred, without freshening it, the vitiated air, sending back upon them, in recurrent surges of stale pomade and lotion, their own stale breath and odors, knew exactly what had happened.

"Except it wasn't Will Mayes," a barber said. He was a man of middle age; a thin, sand-colored man with a mild face, who was shaving a client. "I know Will Mayes. He's a good nigger. And I know Miss Minnie Cooper, too."

"What do you know about her?" a second barber said.

"Who is she?" the client said. "A young girl?"

"No," the barber said. "She's about forty, I reckon. She ain't married. That's why I don't believe—"

"Believe, hell!" a hulking youth in a sweat-stained silk shirt said. "Won't you take a white woman's word before a nigger's?"

"I dont believe Will Mayes did it," the barber said. "I know Will Mayes."

"Maybe you know who did it, then. Maybe you already got him out of town, you damn niggerlover."

"I dont believe anybody did anything. I dont believe anything happened. I leave it to you fellows if them ladies that get old without getting married dont have notions that a man cant—"

"Then you are a hell of a white man," the client said. He moved under the cloth. The youth had sprung to his feet.

"You dont?" he said. "Do you accuse a white woman of lying?"

The barber held the razor poised above the half-risen client. He did not look around.

"It's this durn weather," another said. "It's enough to make a man do anything. Even to her."

Nobody laughed. The barber said in his mild, stubborn tone: "I aint accusing nobody of nothing. I just know and you fellows know how a woman that never—"

"You damn niggerlover!" the youth said.

"Shut up, Butch," another said. "We'll get the facts in plenty of time to act."

"Who is? Who's getting them?" the youth said. "Facts, hell! I—"

"You're a fine white man," the client said. "Aint you?" In his frothy beard he looked like a desert rat in the moving pictures. "You tell them, Jack," he said to the youth. "If there aint any white men in this town, you can count on me, even if I aint only a drummer and a stranger."

"That's right, boys," the barber said. "Find out the truth first. I know Will Mayes."

"Well, by God!" the youth shouted. "To think that a white man in this town—"

"Shut up, Butch," the second speaker said. "We got plenty of time."

The client sat up. He looked at the speaker. "Do you claim that anything excuses a nigger attacking a white woman? Do you mean to tell me you are a white man and you'll stand for it? You better go back North where you came from. The South dont want your kind here."

"North what?" the second said. "I was born and raised in this town."

"Well, by God!" the youth said. He looked around with a strained, baffled gaze, as if he was trying to remember what it was he wanted to say or to do. He drew his sleeve across his sweating face. "Damn if I'm going to let a white woman—"

"You tell them, Jack," the drummer said. "By God, if they—"

The screen door crashed open. A man stood in the floor, his feet apart and his heavy-set body poised easily. His white shirt was open at the throat; he wore a felt hat. His hot, bold glance swept the group. His name was McLendon. He had commanded troops at the front in France and had been decorated for valor.

"Well," he said, "are you going to sit there and let a black son rape a white woman on the streets of Jefferson?"

Butch sprang up again. The silk of his shirt clung flat to his heavy shoulders. At each armpit was a dark halfmoon. "That's what I been telling them! That's what I—"

"Did it really happen?" a third said. "This aint the first man scare she ever had, like Hawkshaw says. Wasn't there something about a man on the kitchen roof, watching her undress, about a year ago?"

"What?" the client said. "What's that?" The barber had been slowly forcing him back into the chair; he arrested himself reclining, his head lifted, the barber still pressing him down.

McLendon whirled on the third speaker. "Happen? What the hell difference does it make? Are you going to let the black sons get away with it until one really does it?"

"That's what I'm telling them!" Butch shouted. He cursed, long and steady, pointless.

"Here, here," a fourth said. "Not so loud. Dont talk so loud."

"Sure," McLendon said; "no talking necessary at all. I've done my talking. Who's with me?" He poised on the balls of his feet, roving his gaze.

The barber held the drummer's face down, the razor poised. "Find out the facts first, boys. I know Willy Mayes. It wasn't him. Let's get the sheriff and do this thing right."

McLendon whirled upon him his furious, rigid face. The barber did not look away. They looked like men of different races. The other barbers had ceased also above their prone clients. "You mean to tell me," McLendon said, "that you'd take a nigger's word before a white woman's? Why, you damn niggerloving—"

The third speaker rose and grasped McLendon's arm; he too had been a soldier. "Now, now. Let's figure this thing out. Who knows anything about what really happened?"

"Figure out hell!" McLendon jerked his arm free. "All that're with me get up from there. The ones that aint—" He roved his gaze, dragging his sleeve across his face.

Three men rose. The drummer in the chair sat up. "Here," he said, jerking at the cloth about his neck; "get this rag off me. I'm with him. I dont live here, but by God, if our mothers and wives and sisters—" He smeared the cloth over his face and flung it to the floor. McLendon stood in the floor and cursed the others. Another rose and moved toward him. The remainder sat uncomfortable, not looking at one another, then one by one they rose and joined him.

The barber picked the cloth from the floor. He began to fold it neatly. "Boys, dont do that. Will Mayes never done it. I know."

"Come on," McLendon said. He whirled. From his hip pocket protruded the butt of a heavy automatic pistol. They went out. The screen door crashed behind them reverberant in the dead air.

The barber wiped the razor carefully and swiftly, and put it away, and ran to the rear, and took his hat from the wall. "I'll be back as soon as I can," he said to the other barbers. "I cant let—" He went out, running. The two other barbers followed him to the door and caught it on the rebound, leaning out and looking up the street after him. The air was flat and dead. It had a metallic taste at the base of the tongue.

"What can he do?" the first said. The second one was saying "Jees Christ, Jees Christ" under his breath. "I'd just as lief be Will Mayes as Hawk, if he gets McLendon riled."

"Jees Christ, Jees Christ," the second whispered.

"You reckoned he really done it to her?" the first said.

II

She was thirty-eight or thirty-nine. She lived in a small frame house with her invalid mother and a thin, sallow, unflagging aunt, where each morning between ten and eleven she would appear on the porch in a lace-trimmed boudoir cap, to sit swinging in the porch swing until noon. After dinner she lay down for a while, until the afternoon began to cool. Then, in one of the three or four new voile dresses which she had each summer, she would go downtown to spend the afternoon in the stores with the other ladies, where they would handle the goods and haggle over the prices in cold, immediate voices, without any intention of buying.

She was of comfortable people—not the best in Jefferson, but good people enough—and she was still on the slender side of ordinary looking, with a bright, faintly haggard manner and dress. When she was young she had had a slender, nervous body and a sort of hard vivacity which had enabled her for a time to ride upon the crest of the town's social life as exemplified by the high school party and church social period of her contemporaries while still children enough to be unclassconscious.

She was the last to realize that she was losing ground; that those among whom she had been a little brighter and louder flame than any other were beginning to learn the pleasure of snobbery—male—and retaliation—female. That was when her face began to wear that bright, haggard look. She still carried it to parties on shadowy porticoes and summer lawns, like a mask or a flag, with that bafflement of furious repudiation of truth in her eyes. One evening at a party she heard a boy and two girls, all schoolmates, talking. She never accepted another invitation.

She watched the girls with whom she had grown up as they married and got homes and children, but no man ever called on her steadily until the children of the other girls had been calling her "aunty" for several years, the while their mothers told them in bright voices about how popular Aunt Minnie had been as a girl. Then the town began to see her driving on Sunday afternoons with the cashier in the bank. He was a widower of about forty—a high-colored man, smelling always faintly of the barber shop or of whisky. He owned the first automobile in town, a red runabout; Minnie had the first motoring bonnet and veil the town ever saw. Then the town began to say: "Poor Minnie." "But she is old enough to take care of herself," others said. That was when she began to ask her old schoolmates that their children call her "cousin" instead of "aunty."

It was twelve years now since she had been relegated into adultery by public opinion, and eight years since the cashier had gone to a Memphis bank, returning for one day each Christmas, which he spent at an annual bachelors' party at a hunting club on the river. From behind their curtains the neighbors would see the party pass, and during the over-the-way Christmas day visiting they would tell her about him, about how well he looked, and how they heard that he was prospering in the city, watching with bright, secret eyes her haggard, bright face. Usually by that hour there would be the scent of whisky on her breath. It was supplied her by a youth, a clerk at the soda fountain: "Sure; I buy it for the old gal. I reckon she's entitled to a little fun."

Her mother kept to her room altogether now; the gaunt aunt ran the house. Against that background Minnie's bright dresses, her idle and empty days, had a quality of furious unreality. She went out in the evening only with women now, neighbors, to the moving pictures. Each afternoon she dressed in one of the new dresses and went downtown alone, where her young "cousins" were already strolling in the late afternoons with their delicate, silken heads and thin, awkward arms and conscious hips, clinging to one another or shrieking and giggling with paired boys in the soda fountain when she passed and went on along the serried store fronts, in the doors of which the sitting and lounging men did not even follow her with their eyes any more.

III

The barber went swiftly up the street where the sparse lights, insect-swirled, glared in rigid and violent suspension in the lifeless air. The day had died in a pall of dust; above the darkened square, shrouded by the spent dust, the sky was as clear as the inside of a brass bell. Below the east was a rumor of the twice-waxed moon.

When he overtook them McLendon and three others were getting into a car parked in an alley. McLendon stooped his thick head, peering out beneath the top. "Changed your mind, did you?" he said. "Damn good thing; by God, tomorrow when this town hears about how you talked tonight—"

"Now, now," the other ex-soldier said. "Hawkshaw's all right. Come on, Hawk; jump in."

"Will Mayes never done it, boys," the barber said. "If anybody done it. Why, you all know well as I do there aint any town where they got better niggers than us. And you know how a lady will kind of think things about men when there aint any reason to, and Miss Minnie anyway—"

"Sure, sure," the soldier said. "We're just going to talk to him a little; that's all."

"Talk hell!" Butch said. "When we're through with the—"

"Shut up, for God's sake!" the soldier said. "Do you want everybody in town—"

"Tell them, by God!" McLendon said. "Tell every one of the sons that'll let a white woman—"

"Let's go; let's go: here's the other car." The second car slid squealing out of a cloud of dust at the alley mouth. McLendon started his car and took the lead. Dust lay like fog in the street. The street lights hung nimbused as in water. They drove on out of town.

A rutted lane turned at right angles. Dust hung above it too, and above all the land. The dark bulk of the ice plant, where the Negro Mayes was night watchman, rose against the sky. "Better stop here, hadn't we?" the soldier said. McLendon did not reply. He hurled the car up and slammed to a stop, the headlights glaring on the blank wall.

"Listen here, boys," the barber said; "if he's here, dont that prove he never done it? Dont it? If it was him, he would run. Dont you see he would?" The second car came up and stopped. McLendon got down; Butch sprang down beside him. "Listen, boys," the barber said.

"Cut the lights off!" McLendon said. The breathless dark rushed down. There was no sound in it save their lungs as they sought air in the parched dust in which for two months they had lived; then the diminishing crunch of McLendon's and Butch's feet, and a moment later McLendon's voice:

"Will . . . Will!"

Below the east the wan hemorrhage of the moon increased. It heaved above the ridge, silvering the air, the dust, so that they seemed to breathe, live, in a bowl of molten lead. There was no sound of nightbird nor insect, no sound save their breathing and a faint ticking of contracting metal about the cars. Where their bodies touched one another they seemed to sweat dryly, for no more moisture came. "Christ!" a voice said; "let's get out of here."

But they didn't move until vague noises began to grow out of the darkness ahead; then they got out and waited tensely in the breathless dark. There was another sound: a blow, a hissing expulsion of breath and McLendon cursing in undertone. They stood a moment longer, then they ran forward. They ran in a stumbling clump, as though they were fleeing something. "Kill him, kill the son," a voice whispered. McLendon flung them back.

"Not here," he said. "Get him into the car." "Kill him, kill the black son!" the voice murmured. They dragged the Negro to the car. The barber had waited beside the car. He could feel himself sweating and he knew he was going to be sick at the stomach.

"What is it, captains?" the Negro said, "I aint done nothing. 'Fore God, Mr John." Someone produced handcuffs. They worked busily about the Negro as though he were a post, quiet, intent, getting in one another's way. He submitted to the handcuffs, looking swiftly and constantly from dim face to dim face. "Who's here, captains?" he said, leaning to peer into the faces until they could feel his breath and smell his sweaty reek. He spoke a name or two. "What you all say I done, Mr John?"

McLendon jerked the car door open. "Get in!" he said.

The Negro did not move. "What you all going to do with me, Mr John? I aint done nothing. White folks, captains, I aint done nothing: I swear 'fore God." He called another name.

"Get in!" McLendon said. He struck the Negro. The others expelled their breath in a dry hissing and struck him with random blows and he whirled and cursed them, and swept his manacled hands across their faces and slashed the barber upon the mouth, and the barber struck him also. "Get him in there," McLendon said. They pushed at him. He ceased struggling and got in and sat quietly as the others took their places. He sat between the barber and the soldier, drawing his limbs in so as not to touch them, his eyes going swiftly and constantly from face to face. Butch clung to the running board. The car moved on. The barber nursed his mouth with his handkerchief.

"What's the matter, Hawk?" the soldier said.

"Nothing," the barber said. They regained the highroad and turned away from town. The second car dropped back out of the dust. They went on, gaining speed; the final fringe of houses dropped behind.

"Goddamn, he stinks!" the soldier said.

"We'll fix that," the drummer in front beside McLendon said. On the running board Butch cursed into the hot rush of air. The barber leaned suddenly forward and touched McLendon's arm.

"Let me out, John," he said.

"Jump out, niggerlover," McLendon said without turning his head. He drove swiftly. Behind them the sourceless lights of the second car glared in the dust. Presently McLendon turned into a narrow road. It was rutted with disuse. It led back to an abandoned brick kiln—a series of reddish mounds and weed- and vine-choked vats without bottom. It had been used for pasture once, until one day the owner missed one of his mules. Although he prodded carefully in the vats with a long pole, he could not even find the bottom of them.

"John," the barber said.

"Jump out, then," McLendon said, hurling the car along the ruts. Beside the barber the Negro spoke:

"Mr Henry."

The barber sat forward. The narrow tunnel of the road rushed up and past. Their motion was like an extinct furnace blast: cooler, but utterly dead. The car bounded from rut to rut.

"Mr Henry," the Negro said.

The barber began to tug furiously at the door. "Look out, there!" the soldier said, but the barber had already kicked the door open and swung onto the running board. The soldier leaned across the Negro and grasped at him, but he had already jumped. The car went on without checking speed.

The impetus hurled him crashing through dust-sheathed weeds, into the ditch. Dust puffed about him, and in a thin, vicious crackling of sapless stems he lay choking and retching until the second car passed and died away. Then he rose and limped on until he reached the highroad and turned toward town, brushing at his clothes with his hands. The moon was higher, riding high and clear of the dust at last, and after a while the town began to glare beneath the dust. He went on, limping. Presently he heard cars and the glow of them grew in the dust behind him and he left the road and crouched again in the weeds until they passed. McLendon's car came last now. There were four people in it and Butch was not on the running board.

They went on; the dust swallowed them; the glare and the sound died away. The dust of them hung for a while, but soon the eternal dust absorbed it again. The barber climbed back onto the road and limped on toward town.

IV

As she dressed for supper on that Saturday evening, her own flesh felt like fever. Her hands trembled among the hooks and eyes, and her eyes had a feverish look, and her hair swirled crisp and crackling under the comb. While she was still dressing the friends called for her and sat while she donned her sheerest underthings and stockings and a new voile dress. "Do you feel strong enough to go out?" they said, their eyes bright too, with a dark glitter. "When you have had time to get over the shock, you must tell us what happened. What he said and did; everything."

In the leafed darkness, as they walked toward the square, she began to breathe deeply, something like a swimmer preparing to dive, until she ceased trembling, the four of them walking slowly because of the terrible heat and out of solicitude for her. But as they neared the square she began to tremble again, walking with her head up, her hands clenched at her sides, their voices about her murmurous, also with that feverish, glittering quality of their eyes.

They entered the square, she in the center of the group, fragile in her fresh dress. She was trembling worse. She walked slower and slower, as children eat ice cream, her head up and her eyes bright in the haggard banner of her face, passing the hotel and the coatless drummers in chairs along the curb looking around at her: "That's the one: see? The one in pink in the middle." "Is that her? What did they do with the nigger? Did they—?" "Sure. He's all right." "All right, is he?" "Sure. He went on a little trip." Then the drug store, where even the young men lounging in the doorway tipped their hats and followed with their eyes the motion of her hips and legs when she passed.

They went on, passing the lifted hats of the gentlemen, the suddenly ceased voices, deferent, protective. "Do you see?" the friends said. Their voices sounded like long, hovering sighs of hissing exultation. "There's not a Negro on the square. Not one."

They reached the picture show. It was like a miniature fairyland with its lighted lobby and colored lithographs of life caught in its terrible and beautiful mutations. Her lips began to tingle. In the dark, when the picture began, it would be all right; she could hold back the laughing so it would not waste away so fast and so soon. So she hurried on before the turning faces, the undertones of low astonishment, and they took their accustomed places where she could see the aisle against the silver glare and the young men and girls coming in two and two against it.

The lights flicked away; the screen glowed silver, and soon life began to unfold, beautiful and passionate and sad, while still the young men and girls entered, scented and sibilant in the half dark, their paired backs in silhouette delicate and sleek, their slim, quick bodies awkward, divinely young, while beyond them the silver dream accumulated, inevitably on and on. She began to laugh. In trying to suppress it, it made more noise than ever; heads began to turn. Still laughing, her friends raised her and led her out, and she stood at the curb, laughing on a high, sustained note, until the taxi came up and they helped her in.

They removed the pink voile and the sheer underthings and the stockings, and put her to bed, and cracked ice for her temples, and sent for the doctor. He was hard to locate, so they ministered to her with hushed ejaculations, renewing the ice and fanning her. While the ice was fresh and cold she stopped laughing and lay still for a time, moaning only a little. But soon the laughing welled again and her voice rose screaming.

"Shhhhhhhhhhh! Shhhhhhhhhhhhhhh!" they said, freshening the ice-pack, smoothing her hair, examining it for gray; "poor girl!" Then to one another: "Do you suppose anything really happened?" their eyes darkly aglitter, secret and passionate. "Shhhhhhhhhh! Poor girl! Poor Minnie!"

V

It was midnight when McLendon drove up to his neat new house. It was trim and fresh as a birdcage and almost as small, with its clean, green-and-white paint. He locked the car and mounted the porch and entered. His wife rose from a chair beside the reading lamp. McLendon stopped in the floor and stared at her until she looked down.

"Look at that clock," he said, lifting his arm, pointing. She stood before him, her face lowered, a magazine in her hands. Her face was pale, strained, and weary-looking. "Haven't I told you about sitting up like this, waiting to see when I come in?"

"John," she said. She laid the magazine down. Poised on the balls of his feet, he glared at her with his hot eyes, his sweating face.

"Didn't I tell you?" He went toward her. She looked up then. He caught her shoulder. She stood passive, looking at him.

"Don't, John. I couldn't sleep . . . The heat; something. Please, John. You're hurting me."

"Didn't I tell you?" He released her and half struck, half flung her across the chair, and she lay there and watched him quietly as he left the room.

He went on through the house, ripping off his shirt, and on the dark, screened porch at the rear he stood and mopped his head and shoulders with the shirt and flung it away. He took the pistol from his hip and laid it on the table beside the bed, and sat on the bed and removed his shoes, and rose and slipped his trousers off. He was sweating again already, and he stooped and hunted furiously for the shirt. At last he found it and wiped his body again, and, with his body pressed against the dusty screen, he stood panting. There was no movement, no sound, not even an insect. The dark world seemed to lie stricken beneath the cold moon and the lidless stars.

Questions

Diction and Structure

1. Morton Bloomfield's brief history of the English language is divided into five parts. What special function is served by the first part? By the last? How are the central three sections related to each other? To the opening and closing parts?

2. Is the Bloomfield essay a simple chronological progression from prehistory to the present? Does the author follow any fixed principle for combining narrative and expository materials?

3. Are the changes in language outlined by Bloomfield concerned more with spoken or written English? What connections does Bloomfield suppose to exist between the two?

4. Bloomfield uses the term *Frenchified* and he defines *edify*. Look up the meanings of the suffixes *-fied* and *-ized* in the dictionary. What determines how they are used? Are such American neologisms as *finalize, compartmentalize, diversify,* and *hospitalize* acceptable by established principles of usage?

5. Is Benchley's "A Good Old-Fashioned Christmas" a simple chronological account of events (imaginary, to be sure) or does it use some other ordering structural principle: fact vs. fiction, past vs. present, narrative plus flashback, etc.?

6. How does the tone of Benchley's essay depend for its humorous effect on the words he chooses? Is the humor purely verbal or something more? If so, what?

7. Notice Benchley's use of dialogue. In how many different ways does he utilize dialogue? For what effects?

8. "A Pig from Jersey" was first published in a widely read, popular magazine. Many of the terms used by Roueché are highly technical: *eosinophiles, endoparasitic, angioneurotic edemas*. Are these terms necessary? Why does he use them? Look up their root meanings and compare their technical significations with the terms from which they derive.

9. Apart from technical terminology, what levels of diction does Roueché use? Point out examples.

10. Roueché's essay begins *in medias res*. Why? Could it have been more clearly or effectively organized?

11. Faulkner's fictional narrative is divided into sections and numbered; can you suggest what purpose is served? How are the sections related in time? What is the nature of section II?

12. Examine the opening sentence of "Dry September" closely. Which words imply the events that follow? What key metaphors in the first sentence reappear later on?

13. For what specific reasons does Faulkner use dialect in his story? In what different ways does it aid characterization? What is the effect of the combination of clichés in the dialogue and a highly connotative, descriptively poetic style in the narrative itself?

Style and Rhetoric

1. How much time is covered in Bloomfield's essay? How does the author use historical events to assist his account of the development of English?

2. Point out places where Bloomfield uses each of these rhetorical techniques: definition, classification, comparison and contrast, cause and effect, illustration.

3. What principles of inference does Bloomfield establish in his opening section to guide his theories about how language develops? Does he consistently follow these principles? Are they valid principles, by R. G. Davis's criteria?

4. Benchley's Christmas is imaginary in many respects. What specific details give it *verisimilitude* (the appearance of reality)?

5. How does Benchley keep his imaginary events within a logical time framework? What is the function of Christmas itself? The references to the Revolution? The clock?

6. Notice how Benchley manages to account for the passage of time. How much time does he cover? Which periods of time— long or brief—are covered in greater detail? Give instances.

7. "A Pig from Jersey" begins as an obvious narrative of events; then a long expository account of trichinosis is given. Can you suggest why? If the exposition had been eliminated what later passages would have lost their point or humor or even have become unintelligible?

8. Notice Roueché's preoccupation with timing every movement of Dr. Levy beginning on Friday, April 17th. Is such a scrupulous attention to time essential to the narrative? How is chronology intrinsically related to the central idea and message of the essay?

9. Why does Roueché end his narrative with the dialogue between the two medical examiners?

10. How much time elapses between the opening event and the

closing one in Faulkner's story "Dry September"? How much time is covered by the expository passages? How do the successive descriptions of the moon work in furthering the narrative? In creating tone and mood?

11. From what point of view is "Dry September" told? Is the narrator a participant in the events that take place? Is this fact important? If so, explain why.

12. There are several main characters in Faulkner's story: the barber, McLendon, Butch, Miss Minnie, Will Mayes the Negro, plus a few minor ones. What different devices of characterization does the author use to develop each?

13. "Dry September" ostensibly treats extremely violent and cruel events, but the most violent actions, such as the actual lynching, are not described and are deemphasized by Faulkner's style. Why does Faulkner maintain such a low-key style? Is he essentially more interested in actions or emotions, events or psychological causes? Is "Dry September" as a whole a specimen of characterization? What might Faulkner be characterizing?

Theme and Viewpoint

1. How does Morton Bloomfield's concern with the English language differ from that of Leo Rosten? Which of them deals more with the speculative aspects of language history? Are their methods substantially alike or unalike?

2. Does Bloomfield's essay on the development of language lend strength to Herbert Muller's assertion that all definition is assumptive and arbitrary, if not accidental?

3. Does Bloomfield give any evidence of agreeing with Eric Fromm about the symbolic qualities of language? Is Bloomfield interested in the psychology of language? Explain. In this essay does he consider language as anything more than an instrument of communication?

4. Do the entries for "prose" from the Oxford English Dictionary bear out Bloomfield's contentions about the way the English language changed from Chaucer's time to the nineteenth and twentieth centuries?

5. Robert Benchley humorously describes a family reunion in his essay on an old-fashioned Christmas; Margaret Mead describes New Year's as a birthday for the human family as they reunite. Is Benchley implicitly making fun of Mead's assumptions about human fellowship with his bickering family and the strangulation of Grandpa? Does Benchley agree with Mead's idea

of the mythic symbolism of holidays like Christmas and New Year's or not?

6. Compare Benchley's descriptive use of the cold with Faulkner's use of heat in "Dry September" to create an emotional mood for his narrative. Both Benchley and Faulkner narrate events leading to a murder. Why is one funny and the other tragic or horrifying?

7. Compare Benchley's point of view toward families with those of the authors in the section on Characterizing. Is Benchley's family more like the Trumans or the Ginsbergs? How so?

8. As Berton Roueché recounts it, is the method of tracking down the source of a trichinosis epidemic "scientific" in the way John Steele outlines the "scientific method"? Which of the logical processes outlined by Robert Gorham Davis does Dr. Levy use in his investigation?

9. In "A Pig from Jersey," Roueché deals with one type of biological relationship between animals and human beings; how do his interests and emphases compare with those of Julian Huxley? Of Alan Devoe? Of Thoreau?

10. Is William Faulkner's portrayal of racial hatred in "Dry September" illustrative of the psychological premises contained in James Baldwin's essay or not? Do Faulkner's characters display the characteristics of prejudice as Ian Stevenson describes them?

11. Faulkner's story has violence as its central theme. Does he share Arthur Miller's definition of violence? Does he agree with Miller's theories of what causes violence? Are McLendon and Butch (and the other members of the lynch mob) "bored and violent"?

12. Is the character of Miss Minnie in "Dry September" an exemplification in any way of Theodor Reik's theories about love and lust?

13. Compare and contrast Faulkner's portrayal of Southerners with those of James Agee and Katherine Anne Porter. How do the three writers differ in their presentations of Southerners as shown here? (All were themselves from the South.) Are they interested in different aspects of Southerners as a group or do they fundamentally differ in their assumptions about Southerners?

14. Compare and contrast the portrayal of relations between white and black Southerners by Faulkner and Porter. Are they in basic disagreement or not? Is one or the other of them more in accord with James Baldwin's views?

Explanation:
showing relationships

Explanation, in its most basic sense, means to spread out or make smooth: that is, to unfold something in order to make it intelligible. The prose writer who explains is concerned with showing relationships: how and why a phenomenon is composed in a certain way and works as it does. Relationships are often very intricate and subtle, as anyone knows who finds that his maternal grandmother is the sister-in-law of his great-aunt on his father's side. Family trees, drawn on paper with connecting lines to show kinship, are a graphic form of explanation. So are road maps, business and organizational tables, the chemist's periodic charts, and the astronomer's maps. Spread out, these illustrated patterns provide the means of demonstrating relationships. Prose explanation unfolds relationships in words.

As a scientific method (and a logical approach), explanation takes some fairly specified forms, notably those dealing with causation and deductive thinking. Showing causality and deducing must follow certain logical rules (including those discussed by Robert Gorham Davis above); and the kinds of explanation involving them must be logically accurate. Less rigorous types of explanation are still subject to the tests of reason. Classifying, analyzing, exemplifying and illustrating—all ways of thinking and writing—may be an aid to the explanatory essayist; and they all should observe the regulations with which you have already become acquainted. The explanation that omits essential data, misinterprets connections, or misconstrues causes will "explain" very little. Definition is also necessary. The speaker who opens a talk by saying he or she will explain some movement of the stars as gravitational clusters had better be sure the audience knows what gravity is. Likewise, a teacher who discusses Donne's lyric poems as combinations of scholastic deduction will get nowhere without defining the scholastic method.

As a discursive mode, explanation may well adopt some of the features of exposition and narration; and it will certainly incorporate in some combination or other every one of the rhetorical methods outlined in Part One. The methods used must depend on whether the topic is material or abstract, an object or a process, simple or compound in kind. Also, certain logical procedures—inductive, deductive, and analogous—will be employed by the writer to help the reader to understand.

Explanatory prose may treat its subject in analytical terms, taking a process such as teaching literature and breaking it down into its component parts, intellectual and verbal, defining and illustrating the parts through successive examples, qualifying them at last into some resolving statement of how the basic process is limited by its elements. Thus Northrop Frye discusses the methods of approaching literature, identifying two levels of understanding, outlining the premises upon which the categories rest, then explicating in detail the nature of understanding, literature, language, and the teacher's utilization of these. His explanation depends upon his categories of comprehension and how criticism of literature must be related to them.

Or the essayist may identify a principle that is basic to a way of doing something, discuss its variations, show why some depart too far from the original principle, and assign reasons why the principle is still valid whereas some of the procedures are not. Walter Lippmann explains the principle of political and intellectual dissent in this manner, showing why mere "toleration" is not enough for "opposition" to perform its inherent moral, emotional, and political purpose.

By collecting several data within a particular field of experience, then hypothesizing about their common elements, the writer may present an explanation inductively established, then go on to qualify it with other, apparently irrelevant data, and thus explicate a complex psychological relationship, between groups and within one's self. Norman Podhoretz looks at some episodes in his childhood that account for his prejudices against Negroes; hypothesizes about their relevance; turns them around to apply to Negroes; and so explains how very illogical and confused prejudice is.

Or through many illustrations, comparisons, and contrasts, the writer may combine causality and description in a more or less continuous narrative to explain how the mind operates. Jacquetta Hawkes uses evolution, stars, lobsters, Marcel Proust, cellular structure, music, and magic to explain the infinite range and variety of human consciousness.

To limit explanatory prose to a few specific types or approaches is impossible, for it is almost unlimited in its variability. About all that may be said by way of definition is that the explanatory mode of writing unfolds relationships so that they become comprehensible. Beyond that, attempts to define tend to overlook the more sophisticated ways of explaining.

Northrop Frye

Criticism, Visible and Invisible

There is a distinction, certainly as old as Plato and possibly as old as the human mind, between two levels of understanding. I say levels, because one is nearly always regarded as superior to the other, whether in kind or in degree. Plato calls them, in his discussion of the divided line in the *Republic*, the level of *nous* and the level of *dianoia*, knowledge of things and knowledge about things. Knowledge about things preserves the split between subject and object which is the first fact in ordinary consciousness. "I" learn "that": what I learn is an objective body of facts set over against

CRITICISM, VISIBLE AND INVISIBLE By Northrop Frye. From *College English*, Vol. 26, No. 1 (October 1964). Reprinted with the permission of the National Council of Teachers of English and Northrop Frye.

me and essentially unrelated to me. Knowledge of things, on the other hand, implies some kind of identification or essential unity of subject and object. What is learned and the mind of the learner become interdependent, indivisible parts of one thing.

Three principles are involved in this conception. First, learning about things is the necessary and indispensable prelude to the knowledge of things: confrontation is the only possible beginning of identity. Second, knowledge about things is the limit of teaching. Knowledge of things cannot be taught: for one thing, the possibility that there is some principle of identity that can link the knower and the known in some essential relation is indemonstrable. It can only be accepted, whether unconsciously as an axiom or deliberately as an act of faith. He who knows on the upper level knows that he knows, as a fact of his experience, but he cannot impart this knowledge directly. Third, *nous* is (or is usually considered to be) the same knowledge as *dianoia*: it is the relation between knower and known that is different. The difference is that something conceptual has become existential: this is the basis of the traditional contrast between knowledge and wisdom.

This distinction is of great importance in religion: Maritain's *Degrees of Knowledge* is one of many attempts to distinguish a lower comprehension from a higher apprehension in religious experience. When St. Thomas Aquinas remarked on his deathbed that all his work seemed to him so much straw, he did not mean that his books were worthless, but that he himself was passing from the *dianoia* to the *nous* of what he had been writing about. I mention the religious parallel only to emphasize a principle which runs through all education: that what Plato calls *nous* is attainable only through something analogous to faith, which implies habit or consistent will, the necessary persistence in pursuing the goals of the faith.

I am dealing here, however, only with the application of the principle of two levels of knowledge to the ordinary learning process. Here the clearest illustration is that of a manual skill. In beginning to learn a skill like driving a car, a conscious mind comes in contact with an alien and emotionally disturbing object. When the skill is learned, the object ceases to be objective and becomes an extension of the personality, and the learning process has moved from the conscious mind to something that we call unconscious, subconscious, instinctive, or whatever best expresses to us the idea of unmediated unity. We think of this subconscious, usually, as more withdrawn, less turned outward to the world, than the consciousness: yet it is far less solipsistic. It is the nervous novice who is the solipsist: it is the trained driver, with a hidden skill that he cannot directly impart to others, who is in the community of the turnpike highway, such as it is.

Literature presents the same distinction. There is the *dianoia* of literature, or criticism, which constitutes the whole of what can be directly taught and learned about literature. I have explained elsewhere that it is impossible to teach or learn literature: what one teaches and learns is criticism. We do not regard this area of direct teaching and learning as an end but as a means to another end. A person who is absorbed wholly by knowledge about something is what we ordinarily mean by a pedant. Beyond this is the experience of literature itself, and the goal of this is something that we call vaguely the cultivated man, the person for whom literature is a possession, a possession that cannot be directly transmitted, and yet not private, for it belongs in a community. Nothing that we can teach a student is an acceptable substitute for the faith that a higher kind of contact with literature is possible, much less for the persistence in that faith which we call the love of reading. Even here there is the possibility of pedantry: literature is an essential part of the cultivated life, but not the whole of it, nor is the form of the cultivated life itself a literary form.

The great strength of humanism, as a conception of teaching literature, was that it accepted certain classics or models in literature, but directed its attention beyond the study of them to the possession of them, and insisted on their relevance to civilized or cultivated life. We spoke of pedantry, and there was undoubtedly much pedantry in humanism, especially at the level of elementary teaching, but not enough to destroy its effectiveness. Browning's grammarian was not a pedant, because he settled *hoti's* business and based *oun* in the light of a blindingly clear vision of a community of knowledge. The act of faith in literary experience which humanism defended was closely associated with a more specific faith in the greatness of certain Greek and Latin classics. The classics were great, certainly, and produced an astonishingly fertile progeny in the vernaculars. But the conception of literature involved tended to be an aristocratic one, and had the limitations of aristocracy built in to it. It saw literature as a hierarchy of comparative greatness, the summit of which provided the standards for the critics.

In the philologists of the nineteenth century, dealing with the vernaculars themselves, one sometimes detects a late humanistic pedantry which takes the form of critical arrogance. All too often the philologists, one feels, form an initiated clique, with literary standards and models derived (at several removes) from the "great" poets, which are then applied to the "lesser" ones. Old-fashioned books on English literature which touch on "lesser" poets, such as Skelton and Wyatt in the early sixteenth century, maintain an attitude toward them of slightly injured condescension. Criticism of this sort had to be superseded by a democratizing of literary experience, not merely to do justice to underrated poets, but to revise the whole attitude to literature in which a poet could be judged by standards derived from another poet, however much "greater." Every writer must be examined on his own terms, to see what kind of literary experience he can supply that no one else can supply in quite the same way. The objection "But Skelton isn't as great a poet as Milton" may not be without truth, but it is without critical point. Literary experience is far more flexible and varied than it was a century ago, but hierarchical standards still linger, and the *subjection* of the critic to the uniqueness of the work being criticized is still not a wholly accepted axiom. Also, the relevance to criticism of what used to be regarded as sub-literary material, primitive myths and the like, is still resisted in many quarters.

All teaching of literature, which is literary *dianoia* or criticism, must point beyond itself, and cannot get to where it is pointing. The revolution in the teaching of English associated with the phrase "new criticism" began by challenging the tendency (less a tendency of teachers, perhaps, than of examination-haunted students) to accept knowledge about literature as a substitute for literary experience. The new critics set the object of literary experience directly in front of the student and insisted that he grapple with it and not try to find its meaning or his understanding of it in the introduction and footnotes. So far, so good. No serious teaching of literature can ever put the object of literary experience in any other position. But new criticism was criticism too: it developed its own techniques of talking about the work, and providing another critical counterpart of the work to read instead. No method of criticism, as such, can avoid doing this. What criticism can do, to point beyond itself, is to try to undermine the student's sense of the ultimate objectivity of the literary work. That, I fear, is not a very intelligible sentence, but the idea it expresses is unfamiliar. The student is confronted by an alien structure of imagination, set over against him, strange in its conventions and often in its values, a mysterious and stylized "verbal icon." It is not to remain so: it must become possessed by and identified with the student. Criticism cannot make this act of possession for the student; what it can do is to weaken those tendencies within criticism that keep the literary work objective and separated. Criticism, in order to point beyond itself, must be more than merely aware of its limitations: it needs to be actively iconoclastic about itself.

The metaphor of "taste" expresses a real truth in criticism, but no metaphor is without pitfalls. The sense of taste is a contact sense: the major arts are based on the senses of distance, and it is easy to think of critical taste as a sublimation, the critic being an astral gourmet and literature itself being, as Plato said of rhetoric, a kind of disembodied cookery. This gastronomic metaphor is frequently employed by writers, for instance at the opening of *Tom Jones*, though when recognized as a metaphor it is usually only a joke. It suggests that the literary work is presented for enjoyment and evaluation, like a wine. The conception of taste is a popular one because it confers great social prestige on the critic. The man of taste is by definition a gentleman, and a critic who has a particular hankering to be a gentleman is bound to attach a good deal of importance to his taste. A generation ago the early essays of Eliot owed much of their influence and popularity to their cavalierism, their suggestion that the social affinities of good poetry were closer to the landed gentry than to the Hebrew prophets. Taste leads to a specific judgment: the metaphor of the critic as "judge" is parallel to the metaphor of taste, and the assumption underlying such criticism is usually that the test of one's critical ability is a value-judgment on the literary work.

If this is true, the critic's contribution to literature, however gentlemanly, seems a curiously futile one, the futility being most obvious with negative judgments. Ezra Pound, T. S. Eliot, Middleton Murry, F. R. Leavis, are only a few of the eminent critics who have abused Milton. Milton's greatness as a poet is unaffected by this: as far as the central fact of his importance in literature is concerned, these eminent critics might as well have said nothing at all. A journal interested in satire recently quoted a critic as saying that satire must have a moral norm, and that Fielding's *Jonathan Wild* was a failure because no character in it represented a moral norm. The question was referred to me, and I said, somewhat irritably, that of course a moral norm was essential to satire, but that it was the reader and not the satirist who was responsible for supplying it. My real objection however was to the critical procedure involved in the "X is a failure because" formula. No critical principle can possibly follow the "because" which is of any importance at all compared to the fact of *Jonathan Wild's* position in the history of satire and in eighteenth-century English culture. The fact is a fact about literature, and, as I have tried to show elsewhere, nothing can follow "because" except some kind of pseudo-critical moral anxiety. Thus: "*King Lear* is a failure because it is indecorous to represent a king on the stage as insane." We recognize this statement to be nonsense, because we are no longer burdened with the particular social anxiety it refers to, but all such anxieties are equally without content. Matthew Arnold decided that "Empedocles on Etna" was a failure because its situation was one "in which the suffering finds no vent in action; in which a continuous state of mental distress is prolonged, unrelieved by incident, hope, or resistance; in which there is everything to be endured, nothing to be done." These phrases would exactly describe, for instance, Eliot's "Prufrock," one of the most penetrating poems of our time, or a good deal of Arnold's contemporary, Baudelaire. We cannot question Arnold's sincerity in excluding his poem from his 1853 volume, but all he demonstrated by excluding it was his own anxious fear of irony.

The attitude that we may call critical dandyism, where the operative conceptions are vogue words of approval or the reverse, like "interesting" or "dreary," is an extreme but logical form of evaluating criticism, where the critic's real subject is his own social position. Such criticism belongs to the wrong side of Kierkegaard's "either-or" dialectic: it is an attitude for which the work of art remains permanently a detached object of contemplation, to be admired because the critic enjoys it or blamed because he does not. Kierkegaard himself was so impressed by the prevalence of this attitude in the arts that he called it the aesthetic attitude, and tended to identify the arts with it. We do not escape from the limitations of the attitude by transposing its judgments from an aesthetic into a moral key. F. R. Leavis has always commanded a good deal of often reluctant respect because of the moral intensity he brings to his criticism, and because of his refusal to make unreal separations between moral and aesthetic values. Reading through the recent reprint of *Scrutiny*, one feels at first that this deep concern for literature, whether the individual judgments are right or wrong, is the real key to literary experience, and the real introduction that criticism can make to it. But as one goes on one has the feeling that this concern, which is there and is a very real virtue, gets deflected at some crucial point, and is prevented from fully emerging out of the shadow-battles of anxieties. Perhaps what the point is is indicated by such comments of Leavis himself as "the poem is a determinate thing: it is *there*," and, "unappreciated, the poem isn't 'there.'" An insistence on the "there-ness" or separation of critic and literary work forces one, for all one's concern, to go on playing the same "aesthetic" game. The paradox is that the "aesthetic" attitude is not a genuinely critical one at all, but social: concern makes the social reference more impersonal, but does not remove it.

Evaluating criticism is mainly effective as criticism only when its valuations are favorable. Thus Ezra Pound, in the middle of his *Guide to Kulchur*, expresses some disinterested admiration for the lyrical elegies of Thomas Hardy, and the effect, in that book, is as though a garrulous drunk had suddenly sobered up, focused his eyes, and began to talk sense. But, of course, if my argument suggests that everything which has acquired some reputation in literature should be placed "beyond criticism," or that histories of literature should be as bland and official as possible, I should merely be intensifying the attitude I am attacking, turning the verbal icon into a verbal idol. My point is a very different one, and it begins with the fact that the work of literature is "beyond criticism" now: criticism can do nothing but lead into it.

There are two contexts in which a work of literature is potential, an internal context and an external one. Internally, the writer has a potential

theme and tries to actualize it in what he writes. Externally, the literary
work, actualized in itself, becomes a potential experience for student,
critic, or reader. A "bad" poem or novel is one in which, so the critic feels,
a potential literary experience has not been actualized. Such a judgment
implies a consensus: the critic speaks for all critics, even if he happens to
be wrong. But an actualized work of literature may still fail to become an
actualized experience for its reader. The judgment here implies withdrawal
from a consensus: however many critics may like this, I don't. The first
type of judgment belongs primarily to the critical reaction to contemporary
literature, reviewing and the like, where a variety of new authors are struggling to establish their authority. The second type belongs primarily to
the tactics of critical pressure groups that attempt to redistribute the traditional valuations of the writers of the past in order to display certain new
writers, usually including themselves, to better advantage. There is no
genuinely critical reason for "revaluation." Both activities correspond in
the sexual life to what Freud calls the "polymorphous perverse," the pre-
liminaries of contact with the object. Judicial criticism, or reviewing, is
necessarily incomplete: it can never free itself from historical variables,
such as the direct appeal of certain in-group conventions to the sophisticated critic. The kind of criticism that is expressed by the term "insight,"
the noticing of things in the literary work of particular relevance to one's
own experience, is perhaps the nearest that criticism can get to demonstrating the value of what it is dealing with. Insight criticism of this kind,
however, is a form of divination, an extension of the principle of *sortes
Virgilianae*: it is essentially random both in invention and in communication.

In short, all methods of criticism and teaching are bad if they encourage the persisting separation of student and literary work: all methods
are good if they try to overcome it. The tendency to persistent separation
is the result of shifting the critical attention from the object of literary experience to something else, usually something in the critic's mind, and this
deprives criticism of content. I know that I have said this before, but
the same issues keep turning up every year. This year the issue was raised
by Professor Rowse's book on Shakespeare. The questions usually asked
about Shakespeare's sonnets, such as who was W. H. and the like, have
nothing to do with Shakespeare's sonnets or with literary criticism, and
have only got attached to criticism because, owing to Shakespeare's por-
tentous reputation, critics have acquired an impertinent itch to know more
about his private life than they need to know. It seemed to Professor
Rowse that such questions were properly the concern of a historian, and
he was quite right. True, he had no new facts about the sonnets and added
nothing to our knowledge of this alleged subject, but his principle was

sound. But Professor Rowse went further. It occurred to him that perhaps literary criticism was not a genuine intellectual discipline at all, and that there could be no issues connected with it that could not be better dealt with by someone who did belong to a genuine discipline, such as history. One of his sentences, for instance, begins: "A real writer understands better than a mere critic." Literary criticism ought to be profoundly grateful to Professor Rowse for writing so bad a book: it practically proves that writing a good book on Shakespeare is a task for a mere critic. Still, the fact that a responsible scholar in a related field could assume, in 1964, that literary criticism was a parasitic pseudo-subject with no facts to build with and no concepts to think with, deserves to be noted.

I do not believe, ultimately, in a plurality of critical methods, though I can see a division of labor in critical operations. I do not believe that there are different "schools" of criticism today, attached to different and irreconcilable metaphysical assumptions: the notion seems to me to reflect nothing but the confusion in critical theory. In particular, the notion that I belong to a school or have invented a school of mythical or archetypal criticism reflects nothing but confusion about me. I make this personal comment with some hesitation, in view of the great generosity with which my books have been received, but everyone who is understood by anybody is misunderstood by somebody. It is true that I call the elements of literary structure myths, because they are myths; it is true that I call the elements of imagery archetypes, because I want a word which suggests something that changes its context but not its essence. James Beattie, in *The Minstrel*, says of the poet's activity:

> From Nature's beauties, variously compared
> And variously combined, he learns to frame
> Those forms of bright perfection

and adds a footnote to the last phrase: "General ideas of excellence, the immediate archetypes of sublime imitation, both in painting and in poetry." It was natural for an eighteenth-century poet to think of poetic images as reflecting "general ideas of excellence"; it is natural for a twentieth-century critic to think of them as reflecting the same images in other poems. But I think of the term as indigenous to criticism, not as transferred from Neoplatonic philosophy or Jungian psychology. However, I would not fight for a word, and I hold to no "method" of criticism beyond assuming that the structure and imagery of literature are central considerations of criticism. Nor, I think, does my practical criticism illustrate the use of a patented critical method of my own, different in kind from the approaches of other critics.

The end of criticism and teaching, in any case, is not an aesthetic but an ethical and participating end: for it, ultimately, works of literature are not things to be contemplated but powers to be absorbed. This completes the paradox of which the first half has already been given. The "aesthetic" attitude, persisted in, loses its connection with literature as an art and becomes socially or morally anxious: to treat literature seriously as a social and moral force is to pass into the genuine experience of it. The advantage of using established classics in teaching, the literary works that have proved their effectiveness, is that one can skip preliminary stages and clear everything out of the way except understanding, which is the only road to possession. At the same time it is easy for understanding to become an end in itself too. The established classics are, for the most part, historically removed from us, and to approach them as new works involves a certain historical astigmatism: but to consider them as historical documents only is again to separate student and literary work. In teaching manual skills, such as car-driving, an examination can test the skill on the higher level; but an examination in English literature cannot pass beyond the level of theoretical knowledge. We may guess the quality of a student's literary experience from the quality of his writing, but there is no assured way of telling from the outside the difference between a student who knows literature and a student who merely knows about it.

Thus the teaching of literature, an activity of criticism which attempts to cast its bread on the waters without knowing when or how or by whom it will be picked up, is involved in paradox and ambiguity. The object of literary experience must be placed directly in front of the student, and he should be urged to respond to it and accept no substitutes as the end of his understanding. Yet it does not matter a tinker's curse what a student thinks and feels about literature until he can think and feel, which is not until he passes the stage of stock response. And although the cruder forms of stock response can be identified and the student released from them, there are subtler forms that are too circular to be easily refuted. There is, for instance, critical narcissism, or assuming that a writer's "real" meaning is the critic's own attitude (or the opposite of it, if the reaction is negative). There is no "real" meaning in literature, nothing to be "got out of it" or abstracted from the total experience; yet all criticism seems to be concerned with approaching such a meaning. There is no way out of these ambiguities: criticism is a phoenix preoccupied with constructing its own funeral pyre, without any guarantee that a bigger and better phoenix will manifest itself as a result.

A large part of criticism is concerned with commentary, and a major work of literature has a vast amount of commentary attached to it. With writers of the size of Shakespeare and Milton, such a body of work is a proper and necessary part of our cultural heritage; and so it may be with, say, Melville or Henry James or Joyce or T. S. Eliot. The existence of a large amount of commentary on a writer is a testimony to the sense of the importance of that writer among critics. As the first critic in *The Pooh Perplex* says, on the opening page of the book: "Our ideal in English studies is to amass as much commentary as possible upon the literary work, so as to let the world know how deeply we respect it." An important critical principle is concealed in this remark. It is an illusion that only great literature can be commented on, and that the existence of such commentary proves or demonstrates its greatness. It is a writer's merits that make the criticism on him rewarding, as a rule, but it is not his merits that make it possible. The techniques of criticism can be turned loose on anything whatever. If this were not so, a clever parody like *The Pooh Perplex* could hardly make its point. Hence a mere display of critical dexterity or ingenuity, even as an act of devotion, is not enough: criticism, to be useful both to literature and to the public, needs to contain some sense of the progressive or the systematic, some feeling that irrevocable forward steps in understanding are being taken. We notice that all the contributors to *The Pooh Perplex* claim to be supplying the one essential thing needed to provide this sense of progress, though of course none of them does. Thus the piling up of commentary around the major writers of literature may in itself simply be another way of barricading those writers from us.

Yeats tells us that what fascinates us is the most difficult among things not impossible. Literary criticism is not in so simple a position. Teaching literature is impossible; that is why it is difficult. Yet it must be tried, tried constantly and indefatigably, and placed at the center of the whole educational process, for at every level the understanding of words is as urgent and crucial a necessity as it is on its lowest level of learning to read and write. Whatever is educational is also therapeutic. The therapeutic power of the arts has been intermittently recognized, especially in music since David played his harp before Saul, but the fact that literature is essential to the mental health of society seldom enters our speculations about it. But if I am to take seriously my own principle that works of literature are not so much things to be studied as powers to be possessed, I need to face the implications of that principle.

I wish all teachers of English, at very level, could feel that they were concerned with the whole of a student's verbal, or in fact imaginative, experience, not merely with the small part of it that is conventionally called literary. The incessant verbal bombardment that students get from conversation, advertising, the mass media, or even such verbal games as Scrabble or cross-word puzzles, is addressed to the same part of the mind that literature addresses, and it does far more to mold their literary imagination than poetry or fiction. It often happens that new developments in literature meet with resistance merely because they bring to life conventions that the critics had decided were sub-literary. Wordsworth's *Lyrical Ballads* met with resistance of this kind, and in our day teachers and critics who think literature should be a matter of direct feeling and are prejudiced against the verbal puzzle find that their students, unlike themselves, are living in the age of *Finnegans Wake*. There is a real truth, for all of what has been said above, in the belief that the critic is deeply concerned with evaluation, and with separating the good from the bad in literature. But I would modify this belief in three ways. First, as just said, the area of literature should not be restricted to the conventionally literary, but expanded to the entire area of verbal experience. Hence the evaluating activity should not be concerned solely with civil wars in the conventionally literary field. Second, the distinction of good and bad is not a simple opposing of the conventionally literary to the conventionally sub-literary, a matter of demonstrating the superiority of Henry James to Mickey Spillane. On the contrary, it seems to me that an important and neglected aspect of literary teaching is to illustrate the affinities in structure and imagery between the "best" and the "worst" of what every young person reads or listens to.

Third, if I am right in saying that literature is a power to be possessed, and not a body of objects to be studied, then the difference between good and bad is not something inherent in literary works themselves, but the difference between two ways of using literary experience. The belief that good and bad can be determined as inherent qualities is the belief that inspires censorship, and the attempt to establish grades and hierarchies in literature itself, to distinguish what is canonical from what is apocryphal, is really an "aesthetic" form of censorship. Milton remarked in *Areopagitica* that a wise man would make a better use of an idle pamphlet than a fool would of Holy Scripture, and this, I take it, is an application of the gospel principle that man is defiled not by what goes into him but by what comes out of him. The question of censorship takes us back to the metaphor of taste by a different road, for censorship is apparently based on an analogy between mental and physical nourishment, what is censorable being inherently poisonous. But there is something all wrong with this analogy: it has often been pointed out that the censor himself never admits to being adversely affected by what he reads. We need to approach the problem that censorship fails to solve in another way.

In primitive societies art is closely bound up with magic: the creative impulse is attached to a less disinterested hope that its products may affect the external world in one's favor. Drawing pictures of animals is part of a design to catch them; songs about bad weather are partly charms to ensure good weather. The magical attachments of primitive art, though they may have stimulated the creative impulse, also come to hamper it, and as society develops they wear off or become isolated in special ritual compartments. Many works of art, including Shakespeare's *Tempest*, remind us that the imaginative powers are released by the renunciation of magic. In the next stage of civilization the magical or natural attachment is replaced by a social one. Literature expresses the preoccupations of the society that produced it, and it is pressed into service to illustrate other social values, religious or political. This means that it has an attachment to other verbal structures in religion or history or morals which is allegorical. Here too is something that both hampers and stimulates the creative impulse. Much of Dante's *Commedia* and Milton's *Paradise Lost* is concerned with political and religious issues that we regard now as merely partisan or superstitious. The poems would never have been written without the desire to raise these issues, and as long as we are studying the poems the issues are relevant to our study. But when we pass from the study to the possession of the poems, a dialectical separation of a permanent imaginative structure from a mass of historical anxieties takes place. This is the critical principle that Shelley was attempting to formulate in his *Defence of Poetry*, and in fact the Romantic movement marks the beginning of a third stage in the attachments of the arts, and one that we are still in.

This third stage (to some extent "decadent," as the first one is primitive, though we should be careful not to get trapped by the word) is both social and magical, and is founded on the desire to make art act kinetically on other people, startling, shocking, or otherwise stimulating them into a response of heightened awareness. It belongs to an age in which kinetic verbal stimulus, in advertising, propaganda, and mass media, plays a large and increasing role in our verbal experience. Sometimes the arts try to make use of similar techniques, as the Italian Futurist movement did, but more frequently the attempt is to create a kind of counter-stimulus. In the various shocking, absurd, angry, and similar conventions in contemporary art one may recognize a strong kinetic motivation. Even in the succession of fashions there is something of this, for the succession of vogues and movements in the arts is part of the economy of waste. Most cultivated people realize that they should overlook or ignore these attachments in responding to the imaginative product itself, and meet all such assaults on their sense of decorum with a tolerant aplomb that sometimes infuriates the artist still more. Here again, the attachment begins as a stimulus and may eventually become a hindrance, unless the artist is astute enough to detach himself at the point where the hindrance begins.

It is the critic's task, in every age, to fight for the autonomy of the arts, and never under any circumstances allow himself to be seduced into judging the arts, positively or negatively, by their attachments. The fact that, for instance, Burroughs' *Naked Lunch* is written in the convention of the psychological shocker does not make it either a good or a bad book, and the fashion for pop-art painting is neither good because painters ought to rediscover content nor bad because they ought not. But an essential part of the critic's strategy, to the extent that the critic is a teacher, is in leading his sudents to realize that in responding to art without attachments they are at the same time building up a resistance to kinetic stimulus themselves. Literary education is not doing the whole of its proper work unless it marshals the verbal imagination against the assaults of advertising and propaganda that try to bludgeon it into passivity. This is a battle that should be fought long before university, because university comes too late in a student's life to alter his mental habits more than superficially. I think of a public school teacher I know who got his grade eight students to analyze the rhetorical devices in a series of magazine advertisements. The effect was so shattering that he thought at first he must be working with too young an age group: children who were contemptuous of Santa Claus and the stork were still not ready to discover that advertising was no more factual than the stories they told their parents. Eventually, however, he realized that he was right, and that he had uncovered a deeper level of literary response than literature as such can ordinarily reach at that age.

The direct response to a verbal kinetic stimulus persists into adult life, and is, of course, what makes the propaganda of totalitarian states effective for their own people. Such response is not an inability to distinguish rhetorical from factual statement, but a will to unite them. Even though a Communist, for example, understands the difference between what is said and the political necessity of saying it, he has been conditioned to associate rhetoric and fact when they are produced in a certain area of authority, not to separate them. In the democracies we are not trained in this way, but we are continually being persuaded to fall into the habit, by pressure groups trying to establish the same kind of authority, and by certain types of entertainment in which the kinetic stimulus is erotic. I recently saw a documentary movie of the rock-and-roll singer Paul Anka. The reporter pried one of the squealing little sexballs out of the audience and asked her what she found so ecstatic about listening to Anka. She said, still in a daze: "He's so *sincere*." The will to unite rhetorical and direct address is very clear here.

The central activity of criticism, which is the understanding of literature, is essentially one of establishing a context for the works of literature being studied. This means relating them to other things: to their context in the writer's life, in the writer's time, in the history of literature, and above all in the total structure of literature itself, or what I call the order of words. Relation to context accounts for nearly the whole of the factual basis of criticism, the aspect of it that can progress through being verified or refuted by later criticism. This central activity itself has a further context, a lower and an upper limit, with which I have been mainly concerned in this paper. On the lower limit is criticism militant, a therapeutic activity of evaluation, or separating the good from the bad, in which good and bad are not two kinds of literature, but, respectively, the active and the passive approaches to verbal experience. This kind of criticism is essentially the defence of those aspects of civilization loosely described as freedom of speech and freedom of thought. On the higher limit is criticism triumphant, the inner possession of literature as an imaginative force to which all study of literature leads, and which is criticism at once glorified and invisible.

We remember the discussion in Joyce's *Portrait* in which the characteristics of beauty are said to be *integritas, consonantia,* and *claritas;* unity, harmony, and radiance. Poet and critic alike struggle to unify and to relate; the critic, in particular, struggles to demonstrate the unity of the work of literature he is studying to relate it to its context in literature. There remains the peculiar *claritas* or intensity, which cannot be demonstrated in either literature or criticism, though all literature and criticism point toward it. No darkness can comprehend any light; no ignorance or indifference can ever see any *claritas* in literature itself or in the criticism that attempts to convey it, just as no saint in ordinary life wears a visible gold plate around his head. All poet or critic can do is to hope that somehow, somewhere, and for someone, the struggle to unify and to relate, because it is an honest struggle and not because of any success in what it does, may be touched with a radiance not its own.

Walter Lippmann

The Indispensable Opposition

1

Were they pressed hard enough, most men would probably confess that political freedom—that is to say, the right to speak freely and to act in opposition—is a noble ideal rather than a practical necessity. As the case for freedom is generally put to-day, the argument lends itself to this feeling. It is made to appear that, whereas each man claims his freedom as a matter of right, the freedom he accords to other men is a matter of toleration. Thus, the defense of freedom of opinion tends to rest not on its substantial, beneficial, and indispensable consequences, but on a somewhat eccentric, a rather vaguely benevolent, attachment to an abstraction.

It is all very well to say with Voltaire, "I wholly disapprove of what you say, will defend to the death your right to say it," but as a matter of fact most men will not defend to the death the rights of other men: if they disapprove sufficiently what other men say, they will somehow suppress those men if they can.

So, if this is the best that can be said for liberty of opinion, that a man must tolerate his opponents because everyone has a "right" to say what he pleases, then we shall find that liberty of opinion is a luxury, safe only in pleasant times when men can be tolerant because they are not deeply and vitally concerned.

Yet actually, as a matter of historic fact, there is a much stronger foundation for the great constitutional right of freedom of speech, and as a matter of practical human experience there is a much more compelling reason for cultivating the habits of free men. We take, it seems to me, a naïvely self-righteous view when we argue as if the right of our opponents to speak were something that we protect because we are magnanimous, noble, and unselfish. The compelling reason why, if liberty of opinion did not exist, we should have to invent it, why it will eventually have to be restored in all civilized countries where it is now suppressed, is that we must protect the right of our opponents to speak because we must hear what they have to say.

We miss the whole point when we imagine that we tolerate the freedom of our political opponents as we tolerate a howling baby next door, as we put up with the blasts from our neighbor's radio because we are too peaceable to heave a brick through the window. If this were all there is to freedom of opinion, that we are too good-natured or too timid to do anything about our opponents and our critics except to let them talk, it would be difficult to say whether we are tolerant because we are magnanimous or because we are lazy, because we have strong principles or because we lack serious convictions, whether we have the hospitality of an inquiring mind or the indifference of an empty mind. And so, if we truly wish to understand why freedom is necessary in a civilized society, we must begin by realizing that, because freedom of discussion improves our own opinions, the liberties of other men are our own vital necessity.

We are much closer to the essence of the matter, not when we quote Voltaire, but when we go to the doctor and pay him to ask us the most embarrassing questions and to prescribe the most disagreeable diet. When we pay the doctor to exercise complete freedom of speech about the cause and cure of our stomachache, we do not look upon ourselves as tolerant and magnanimous, and worthy to be admired by ourselves. We have enough common sense to know that if we threaten to put the doctor in jail because we do not like the diagnosis and the prescription it will be unpleasant for the doctor, to be sure, but equally unpleasant for our own stomachache. That is why even the most ferocious dictator would rather be treated by a doctor who was free to think and speak the truth than by his own Minister of Propaganda. For there is a point, the point at which things really matter, where the freedom of others is no longer a question of their right but of our own need.

The point at which we recognize this need is much higher in some men than in others. The totalitarian rulers think they do not need the freedom of an opposition: they exile, imprison, or shoot their opponents. We have concluded on the basis of practical experience, which goes back to Magna Carta and beyond, that we need the opposition. We pay the opposition salaries out of the public treasury.

In so far as the usual apology for freedom of speech ignores this experience, it becomes abstract and eccentric rather than concrete and human. The emphasis is generally put on the right to speak, as if all that mattered were that the doctor should be free to go out into the park and explain to the vacant air why I have a stomachache. Surely that is a miserable caricature of the great civil right which men have bled and died for. What really matters is that the doctor should tell *me* what ails me, that I should listen to him; that if I do not like what he says I should be free to call in another doctor; and that then the first doctor should have to listen to the second doctor; and that out of all the speaking and listening, the give-and-take of opinions, the truth should be arrived at.

This is the creative principle of freedom of speech, not that it is a system for the tolerating of error, but that it is a system for finding the truth. It may not produce the truth, or the whole truth all the time, or often, or in some cases ever. But if the truth can be found, there is no other system which will normally and habitually find so much truth. Until we have thoroughly understood this principle, we shall not know why we must value our liberty, or how we can protect and develop it.

2

Let us apply this principle to the system of public speech in a totalitarian state. We may, without any serious falsification, picture a condition of affairs in which the mass of the people are being addressed through one broadcasting system by one man and his chosen subordinates. The orators speak. The audience listens but cannot and dare not speak back. It is a system of one-way communication; the opinions of the rulers are broadcast outwardly to the mass of the people. But nothing comes back to the rulers from the people except the cheers; nothing returns in the way of knowledge of forgotten facts, hidden feelings, neglected truths, and practical suggestions.

But even a dictator cannot govern by his own one-way inspiration alone. In practice, therefore, the totalitarian rulers get back the reports of the secret police and of their party henchmen down among the crowd. If these reports are competent, the rulers may manage to remain in touch with public sentiment. Yet that is not enough to know what the audience feels. The rulers have also to make great decisions that have enormous consequences, and here their system provides virtually no help from the give-and-take of opinion in the nation. So they must either rely on their own intuition, which cannot be permanently and continually inspired, or, if they are intelligent despots, encourage their trusted advisers and their technicians to speak and debate freely in their presence.

On the walls of the houses of Italian peasants one may see inscribed in large letters the legend, "Mussolini is always right." But if that legend is taken seriously by Italian ambassadors, by the Italian General Staff, and by the Ministry of Finance, then all one can say is heaven help Mussolini, heaven help Italy, and the new Emperor of Ethiopia.

For at some point, even in a totalitarian state, it is indispensable that there should exist the freedom of opinion which causes opposing opinions to be debated. As time goes on, that is less and less easy under a despotism; critical discussion disappears as the internal opposition is liquidated in favor of men who think and feel alike. That is why the early successes of despots, of Napoleon I and of Napoleon III, have usually been followed by an irreparable mistake. For in listening only to his yes men—the others being in exile or in concentration camps, or terrified—the despot shuts himself off from the truth that no man can dispense with.

We know all this well enough when we contemplate the dictatorships. But when we try to picture our own system, by way of contrast, what picture do we have in our minds? It is, is it not, that anyone may stand up on his own soapbox and say anything he pleases, like the individuals in Kipling's poem who sit each in his separate star and draw the Thing as they see it for the God of Things as they are. Kipling, perhaps, could do this, since he was a poet. But the ordinary mortal isolated on his separate star will have an hallucination, and a citizenry declaiming from separate soapboxes will poison the air with hot and nonsensical confusion.

If the democratic alternative to the totalitarian one-way broadcasts is a row of separate soapboxes, then I submit that the alternative is unworkable, is unreasonable, and is humanly unattractive. It is above all a false alternative. It is not true that liberty has developed among civilized men when anyone is free to set up a soapbox, is free to hire a hall where he may expound his opinions to those who are willing to listen. On the contrary, freedom of speech is established to achieve its essential purpose only when different opinions are expounded in the same hall to the same audience.

For, while the right to talk may be the beginning of freedom, the necessity of listening is what makes the right important. Even in Russia and Germany a man may still stand in an open field and speak his mind. What matters is not the utterance of opinions. What matters is the confrontation of opinions in debate. No man can care profoundly that every fool should say what he likes. Nothing has been accomplished if the wisest man proclaims his wisdom in the middle of the Sahara Desert. This is the shadow. We have the substance of liberty when the fool is compelled to listen to the wise man and learn; when the wise man is compelled to take account of the fool, and to instruct him; when the wise man can increase his wisdom by hearing the judgment of his peers.

That is why civilized men must cherish liberty—as a means of promoting the discovery of truth. So we must not fix our whole attention on the right of anyone to hire his own hall, to rent his own broadcasting station, to distribute his own pamphlets. These rights are incidental; and though they must be preserved, they can be preserved only by regarding them as incidental, as auxiliary to the substance of liberty that must be cherished and cultivated.

Freedom of speech is best conceived, therefore, by having in mind the picture of a place like the American Congress, an assembly where opposing views are represented, where ideas are not merely uttered but debated, or the British Parliament, where men who are free to speak are also compelled to answer. We may picture the true condition of freedom as existing in a place like a court of law, where witnesses testify and are cross-examined, where the lawyer argues against the opposing lawyer before the same judge and in the presence of one jury. We may picture freedom as existing in a forum where the speaker must respond to questions; in a gathering of scientists where the data, the hypothesis, and the conclusion are submitted to men competent to judge them; in a reputable newspaper which not only will publish the opinions of those who disagree but will reëxamine its own opinion in the light of what they say.

Thus the essence of freedom of opinion is not in mere toleration as such, but in the debate which toleration provides: it is not in the venting of opinion, but in the confrontation of opinion. That this is the practical substance can readily be understood when we remember how differently we feel and act about the censorship and regulation of opinion purveyed by different media of communication. We find then that, in so far as the medium makes difficult the confrontation of opinion in debate, we are driven towards censorship and regulation.

There is, for example, the whispering campaign, the circulation of anonymous rumors by men who cannot be compelled to prove what they say. They put the utmost strain on our tolerance, and there are few who do not rejoice when the anonymous slanderer is caught, exposed, and punished. At a higher level there is the moving picture, a most powerful medium for conveying ideas, but a medium which does not permit debate. A moving picture cannot be answered effectively by another moving picture; in all free countries there is some censorship of the movies, and there would be more if the producers did not recognize their limitations by avoiding political controversy. There is then the radio. Here debate is difficult: it is not easy to make sure that the speaker is being answered in the presence of the same audience. Inevitably, there is some regulation of the radio.

When we reach the newspaper press, the opportunity for debate is so considerable that discontent cannot grow to the point where under normal conditions there is any disposition to regulate the press. But when newspapers abuse their power by injuring people who have no means of replying, a disposition to regulate the press appears. When we arrive at Congress we find that, because the membership of the House is so large, full debate is impracticable. So there are restrictive rules. On the other hand, in the Senate, where the conditions of full debate exist, there is almost absolute freedom of speech.

This shows us that the preservation and development of freedom of opinion are not only a matter of adhering to abstract legal rights, but also, and very urgently, a matter of organizing and arranging sufficient debate. Once we have a firm hold on the central principle, there are many practical conclusions to be drawn. We then realize that the defense of freedom of opinion consists primarily in perfecting the opportunity for an adequate give-and-take of opinion; it consists also in regulating the freedom of those revolutionists who cannot or will not permit or maintain debate when it does not suit their purposes.

We must insist that free oratory is only the beginning of free speech; it is not the end, but a means to an end. The end is to find the truth. The practical justification of civil liberty is not that self-expression is one of the rights of man. It is that the examination of opinion is one of the necessities of man. For experience tells us that it is only when freedom of opinion becomes the compulsion to debate that the seed which our fathers planted has produced its fruit. When that is understood, freedom will be cherished not because it is a vent for our opinions but because it is the surest method of correcting them.

The unexamined life, said Socrates, is unfit to be lived by man. This is the virtue of liberty, and the ground on which we may best justify our belief in it, that it tolerates error in order to serve the truth. When men are brought face to face with their opponents, forced to listen and learn and mend their ideas, they cease to be children and savages and begin to live like civilized men. Then only is freedom a reality, when men may voice their opinions because they must examine their opinions.

3

The only reason for dwelling on all this is that if we are to preserve democracy we must understand its principles. And the principle which distinguishes it from all other forms of government is that in a democracy the opposition not only is tolerated as constitutional but must be maintained because it is in fact indispensable.

The democratic system cannot be operated without effective opposition. For, in making the great experiment of governing people by consent rather than by coercion, it is not sufficient that the party in power should have a majority. It is just as necessary that the party in power should never outrage the minority. That means that it must listen to the minority and be moved by the criticisms of the minority. That means that its measures must take account of the minority's objections, and that in administering measures it must remember that the minority may become the majority.

The opposition is indispensable. A good statesman, like any other sensible human being, always learns more from his opponents than from his fervent supporters. For his supporters will push him to disaster unless his opponents show him where the dangers are. So if he is wise he will often pray to be delivered from his friends, because they will ruin him. But, though it hurts, he ought also to pray never to be left without opponents; for they keep him on the path of reason and good sense.

The national unity of a free people depends upon a sufficiently even balance of political power to make it impracticable for the administration to be arbitrary and for the opposition to be revolutionary and irreconcilable. Where that balance no longer exists, democracy perishes. For unless all the citizens of a state are forced by circumstances to compromise, unless they feel that they can affect policy but that no one can wholly dominate it, unless by habit and necessity they have to give and take, freedom cannot be maintained.

Norman Podhoretz

My Negro Problem—and Ours

If we and . . . I mean the relatively conscious whites and the relatively conscious blacks, who must, like lovers, insist on, or create, the consciousness of the others—do not falter in our duty now, we may be able, handful that we are, to end the racial nightmare, and achieve our country, and change the history of the world.

James Baldwin

Two ideas puzzled me deeply as a child growing up in Brooklyn during the 1930's in what today would be called an integrated neighborhood. One of them was that all Jews were rich; the other was that all Negroes were persecuted. These ideas had appeared in print; therefore they must be true. My own experience and the evidence of my senses told they were not true, but that only confirmed what a day-dreaming boy in the provinces—for the lower-class neighborhoods of New York belong as surely to the provinces as any rural town in North Dakota—discovers very early: *his* experience is unreal and the evidence of his senses is not to be trusted. Yet even a boy with a head full of fantasies incongruously synthesized out of Hollywood movies and English novels cannot altogether deny the reality of his own experience—especially when there is so much deprivation in that experience. Nor can he altogether gainsay the evidence of his own senses—especially such evidence of the senses as comes from being repeatedly beaten up, robbed, and in general hated, terrorized, and humiliated.

And so for a long time I was puzzled to think that Jews were supposed to be rich when the only Jews I knew were poor, and that Negroes were supposed to be persecuted when it was the Negroes who were doing the only persecuting I knew about—and doing it, moreover, to *me*. During the early years of the war, when my older sister joined a left-wing youth organization, I remember my astonishment at hearing her passionately denounce my father for thinking that Jews were worse off than Negroes. To me, at the age of twelve, it seemed very clear that Negroes were better off than Jews—indeed, than *all* whites. A city boy's world is contained within three or four square blocks, and in my world it was the whites, the Italians and Jews, who feared the Negroes, not the other way around. The Negroes were tougher than we were, more ruthless, and on the whole they were better athletes. What could it mean, then, to say that they were badly off and that we were more fortunate? Yet my sister's opinions, like print, were sacred, and when she told me about exploitation and economic forces I believed her. I believed her, but I was still afraid of Negroes. And I still hated them with all my heart.

It had not always been so—that much I can recall from early childhood. When did it start, this fear and this hatred? There was a kindergarten in the local public school, and given the character of the neighborhood, at least half of the children in my class must have been Negroes. Yet I have no memory of being aware of color differences at that age, and I know from observing my own children that they attribute no significance to such differences even when they begin noticing them. I think there was a day—first grade? second grade?—when my best friend Carl hit me on the way home from school and announced that he wouldn't play with me any more because I had killed Jesus. When I ran home to my mother crying for an explanation, she told me not to pay any attention to such foolishness, and then in Yiddish she cursed the *goyim* and the *schwartzes*, the *schwartzes* and the *goyim*. Carl, it turned out, was a *schwartze*, and so was added a third to the categories into which people were mysteriously divided.

Sometimes I wonder whether this is a true memory at all. It is blazingly vivid, but perhaps it never happened: can anyone really remember back to the age of six? There is no uncertainty in my mind, however, about the years that followed. Carl and I hardly ever spoke, though we met in school every day up through the eighth or ninth grade. There would be embarrassed moments of catching his eye or of his catching mine—for whatever it was that had attracted us to one another as very small children remained alive in spite of the fantastic barrier of hostility that had grown up between us, suddenly and out of nowhere. Nevertheless, friendship would have been impossible, and even if it had been possible, it would have been unthinkable. About that, there was nothing anyone could do by the time we were eight years old.

Item: The orphanage across the street is torn down, a city housing project begins to rise in its place, and on the marvelous vacant lot next to the old orphanage they are building a playground. Much excitement and anticipation as Opening Day draws near. Mayor LaGuardia himself comes to dedicate this great gesture of public benevolence. He speaks of neighborliness and borrowing cups of sugar, and of the playground he says that children of all races, colors, and creeds will learn to live together in harmony. A week later, some of us are swatting flies on the playground's inadequate little ball field. A gang of Negro kids, pretty much our own age, enter from the other side and order us out of the park. We refuse, proudly and indignantly, with superb masculine fervor. There was a fight, they win, and we retreat, half whimpering, half with bravado. My first nauseating experience of cowardice. And my first appalled realization that there are people in the world who do not seem to be afraid of anything, who act as though they have nothing to lose. Thereafter the playground becomes a battleground, sometimes quiet, sometimes the scene of athletic competition between Them and Us. But rocks are thrown as often as baseballs. Gradually we abandon the place and use the streets instead. The streets are safer, though we do not admit this to ourselves. We are not, after all, sissies—that most dreaded epithet of an American boyhood.

Item: I am standing alone in front of the building in which I live. It is late afternoon and getting dark. That day in school the teacher had asked a surly Negro boy named Quentin a question he was unable to answer. As usual I had waved my arm eagerly ("Be a good boy, get good marks, be smart, go to college, become a doctor") and, the right answer bursting from my lips, I was held up lovingly by the teacher as an example to the class. I had seen Quentin's face—a very dark, very cruel, very Oriental-looking face—harden, and there had been enough threat in his eyes to make me run all the way home for fear that he might catch me outside.

Now, standing idly in front of my own house, I see him approaching from the project accompanied by his little brother who is carrying a baseball bat and wearing a grin of malicious anticipation. As in a nightmare, I am trapped. The surroundings are secure and familiar, but terror is suddenly present and there is no one around to help. I am locked to the spot. I will not cry out or run away like a sissy, and I stand there, my heart wild, my throat clogged. He walks up, hurls the familiar epithet ("Hey, mo'f——r"), and to my surprise only pushes me. It is a violent push, but not a punch. Maybe I can still back out without entirely losing my dignity. Maybe I can still say, "Hey, c'mon Quentin, whaddya wanna do *that* for? I dint do nothin' to *you*," and walk away, not too rapidly. Instead, before

I can stop myself, I push him back—a token gesture—and I say, "Cut that out, I don't wanna fight, I ain't got nothin' to fight about." As I turn to walk back into the building, the corner of my eye catches the motion of the bat his little brother has handed him. I try to duck, but the bat crashes colored lights into my head.

The next thing I know, my mother and sister are standing over me, both of them hysterical. My sister—she who was later to join the "progressive" youth organization—is shouting for the police and screaming imprecations at those dirty little black bastards. They take me upstairs, the doctor comes, the police come. I tell them that the boy who did it was a stranger, that he had been trying to get money from me. They do not believe me, but I am too scared to give them Quentin's name. When I return to school a few days later, Quentin avoids my eyes. He knows that I have not squealed, and he is ashamed. I try to feel proud, but in my heart I know that it was fear of what his friends might do to me that had kept me silent, and not the code of the street.

Item: There is an athletic meet in which the whole of our junior high school is participating. I am in one of the seventh-grade rapid-advance classes, and "segregation" has now set in with a vengeance. In the last three or four years of the elementary school from which we have just graduated, each grade had been divided into three classes, according to "intelligence." (In the earlier grades the divisions had either been arbitrary or else unrecognized by us as having anything to do with brains.) These divisions by IQ, or however it was arranged, had resulted in a preponderance of Jews in the "1" classes and a corresponding preponderance of Negroes in the "3's," with the Italians split unevenly along the spectrum. At least a few Negroes had always made the "1's," just as there had always been a few Jewish kids among the "3's" and more among the "2's" (where Italians dominated). But the junior high's rapid-advance class of which I am now a member is overwhelmingly Jewish and entirely white—except for a shy lonely Negro girl with light skin and reddish hair.

The athletic meet takes place in a city-owned stadium far from the school. It is an important event to which a whole day is given over. The winners are to get those precious little medallions stamped with the New York City emblem that can be screwed into a belt and that prove the wearer to be a distinguished personage. I am a fast runner, and so I am assigned the position of anchor man on my class's team in the relay race. There are three other seventh-grade teams in the race, two of them all Negro, as ours is all white. One of the all-Negro teams is very tall—their anchor man waiting silently next to me on the line looks years older than I am, and I do not recognize him. He is the first to get the baton and crosses the finishing line in a walk. Our team comes in second, but a few minutes later we are declared the winners, for it has been discovered that the anchor man on the first-place team is not a member of the class. We are awarded the medallions, and the following day our home-room teacher makes a speech about how proud she is of us for being superior athletes as well as superior students. We want to believe that we deserve the praise, but we know that we could not have won even if the other class had not cheated.

That afternoon walking home, I am waylaid and surrounded by five Negroes, among whom is the anchor man of the disqualified team. "Gimme my medal, mo'f——r," he grunts. I do not have it with me and I tell him so. "Anyway, it ain't yours," I say foolishly. He calls me a liar on both counts and pushes me up against the wall on which we sometimes play handball. "Gimme my mo'f——n' medal," he says again. I repeat that I have left it home. "Le's search the li'l mo'f——r," one of them suggests, "he prolly got it *hid* in his mo'f——n' *pants*." My panic is now unmanageable. (How many times had I been surrounded like this and asked in soft tones, "Len' me a nickel, boy." How many times had I been called a liar for pleading poverty and pushed around, or searched, or beaten up, unless there happened to be someone in the maurading gang like Carl who liked me across that enormous divide of hatred and who would therefore say, "Aaah, c'mon, le's git someone else, *this* boy ain't got no money on 'im.") I scream at them through tears of rage and self-contempt, "Keep your f——n' filthy lousy black hands offa me! I swear I'll get the cops." This is all they need to hear, and the five of them set upon me. They bang me around, mostly in the stomach and on the arms and shoulders, and when several adults loitering near the candy store down the block notice what is going on and begin to shout, they run off and away.

I do not tell my parents about the incident. My team-mates, who have also been waylaid, each by a gang led by his opposite number from the disqualified team, have had their medallions taken from them, and they never squeal either. For days, I walk home in terror, expecting to be caught again, but nothing happens. The medallion is put away into a drawer, never to be worn by anyone.

Obviously experiences like these have always been a common feature of childhood life in working-class and immigrant neighborhoods, and Negroes do not necessarily figure in them. Wherever, and in whatever combination, they have lived together in the cities, kids of different groups have been at war, beating up and being beaten up: micks against kikes against wops against spics against polacks. And even relatively homogeneous areas have not been spared the warring of the young: one block against another, one gang (called in my day, in a pathetic effort at gentility, an "S.A.C.," or social-athletic club) against another. But the Negro-white conflict had—and no doubt still has—a special intensity and was conducted with a ferocity unmatched by intramural white battling.

In my own neighborhood, a good deal of animosity existed between the Italian kids (most of whose parents were immigrants from Sicily) and the Jewish kids (who came largely from East European immigrant families). Yet everyone had friends, sometimes close friends, in the other "camp," and we often visited one another's strange-smelling houses, if not for meals, then for glasses of milk, and occasionally for some special event like a wedding or a wake. If it happened that we divided into warring factions and did battle, it would invariably be half-hearted and soon patched up. Our parents, to be sure, had nothing to do with one another and were mutually suspicious and hostile. But we, the kids, who all spoke Yiddish or Italian at home, were Americans, or New Yorkers, or Brooklyn boys: we shared a culture, the culture of the street, and at least for a while this culture proved to be more powerful than the opposing cultures of the home.

Why, *why* should it have been so different as between the Negroes and us? How was it borne in upon us so early, white and black alike, that we were enemies beyond any possibility of reconciliation? Why did we hate one another so?

I suppose if I tried, I could answer those questions more or less adequately from the perspective of what I have since learned. I could draw upon James Baldwin—what better witness is there?—to describe the sense of entrapment that poisons the soul of the Negro with hatred for the white man whom he knows to be his jailer. On the other side, if I wanted to understand how the white man comes to hate the Negro, I could call upon the psychologists who have spoken of the guilt that white Americans feel toward Negroes and that turns into hatred for lack of acknowledging itself as guilt. These are plausible answers and certainly there is truth in them. Yet when I think back upon my own experience of the Negro and his of me, I find myself troubled and puzzled, much as I was as a child when I heard that all Jews were rich and all Negroes persecuted. How could the Negroes in my neighborhood have regarded the whites across the street and around the corner as jailers? On the whole, the whites were not so poor as the Negroes, but they were quite poor enough, and the years were years of Depression. As for white hatred of the Negro, how could guilt have had anything to do with it? What share had these Italian and Jewish immigrants in the enslavement of the Negro? What share had they —downtrodden people themselves breaking their own necks to eke out a living—in the exploitation of the Negro?

No, I cannot believe that we hated each other back there in Brooklyn because they thought of us as jailers and we felt guilty toward them. But does it matter, given the fact that we all went through an unrepresentative confrontation? I think it matters profoundly, for if we managed the job of hating each other so well without benefit of the aids to hatred that are supposedly at the root of this madness everywhere else, it must mean that the madness is not yet properly understood. I am far from pretending that I understand it, but I would insist that no view of the problem will begin to approach the truth unless it can account for a case like the one I have been trying to describe. Are the elements of any such view available to us?

At least two, I would say, are. One of them is a point we frequently come upon in the work of James Baldwin, and the other is a related point always stressed by psychologists who have studied the mechanisms of prejudice. Baldwin tells us that one of the reasons Negroes hate the white man is that the white man refuses to *look* at him: the Negro knows that in white eyes all Negroes are alike; they are faceless and therefore not altogether human. The psychologists, in their turn, tell us that the white man hates the Negro because he tends to project those wild impulses that he fears in himself onto an alien group which he then punishes with his contempt. What Baldwin does *not* tell us, however, is that the principle of facelessness is a two-way street and can operate in both directions with no difficulty at all. Thus, in my neighborhood in Brooklyn, *I* was as faceless to the Negroes as they were to me, and if they hated me because I never looked at them, I must also have hated them for never looking at *me*. To the Negroes, my white skin was enough to define me as the enemy, and in a war it is only the uniform that counts and not the person.

So with the mechanism of projection that the psychologists talk about: it too works in both directions at once. There is no question that the psychologists are right about what the Negro represents symbolically to the white man. For me as a child the life lived on the other side of the playground and down the block on Ralph Avenue seemed the very embodiment of the values of the street—free, independent, reckless, brave, masculine, erotic. I put the word "erotic" last, though it is usually stressed above all others, because in fact it came last, in consciousness as in importance. What mainly counted for me about Negro kids of my own age was that they were "bad boys." There were plenty of bad boys among the whites—this was, after all, a neighborhood with a long tradition of crime as a career open to aspiring talents—but the Negroes were *really* bad, bad in a way that beckoned to one, and made one feel inadequate. We all went home every day for a lunch of spinach-and-potatoes; *they* roamed around during lunch hour, munching on candy bars. In winter *we* had to wear itchy woolen hats and mittens and cumbersome galoshes; *they* were bare-headed and loose as they pleased. We rarely played hookey, or got into serious trouble in school, for all our street-corner bravado; *they* were defiant, forever staying out (to do what delicious things?), forever making disturbances in class and in the halls, forever being sent to the principal and returning uncowed. But most important of all, they were *tough*; beautifully, enviably tough, not giving a damn for anyone or anything. To hell with the teacher, the truant officer, the cop; to hell with the whole of the adult world that held *us* in its grip and that we never had the courage to rebel against except sporadically and in petty ways.

This is what I saw and envied and feared in the Negro: this is what finally made him faceless to me, though some of it, of course, was actually there. (The psychologists also tell us that the alien group which becomes the object of a projection will tend to respond by trying to live up to what is expected of them.) But what, on his side, did the Negro see in me that made me faceless to *him*? Did he envy me my lunches of spinach-and-potatoes and my itchy woolen caps and my prudent behavior in the face of authority, as I envied him his noon-time candy bars and his bare head in winter and his magnificent rebelliousness? Did those lunches and caps sell for him the prospect of power and riches in the future? Did they mean that there were possibilities open to me that were denied to him? Very likely they did. But if so, one also supposes that he feared the impulses within himself toward submission to authority no less powerfully than I feared the impulses in myself toward defiance. If I represented the jailer to him, it was not because I was oppressing him or keeping him down: it was because I symbolized for him the dangerous and probably pointless temptation toward greater repression, just as he symbolized for me the equally perilous tug toward greater freedom. I personally was to be rewarded for this repression with a new and better life in the future, but how many of my friends paid an even higher price and were given only gall in return.

We have it on the authority of James Baldwin that all Negroes hate whites. I am trying to suggest that on their side all whites—all American whites, that is—are sick in their feelings about Negroes. There are Negroes, no doubt, who would say that Baldwin is wrong, but I suspect them of being less honest than he is, just as I suspect whites of self-deception who tell me they have no special feeling toward Negroes. Special feelings about color are a contagion to which white Americans seem susceptible even when there is nothing in their background to account for the susceptibility. Thus everywhere we look today in the North we find the curious phenomenon of white middle-class liberals with no previous personal experience of Negroes—people to whom Negroes have always been faceless in virtue rather than faceless in vice—discovering that their abstract commitment to the cause of Negro rights will not stand the test of a direct confrontation. We find such people fleeing in droves to the suburbs as the Negro population in the inner city grows; and when they stay in the city we find them sending their children to private school rather than to the "integrated" public school in the neighborhood. We find them resisting the demand that gerrymandered school districts be re-zoned for the purpose of overcoming de facto segregation; we find them judiciously considering whether the Negroes (for their own good, of course) are not perhaps pushing too hard; we find them clucking their tongues over Negro militancy; we find them speculating on the question of whether there may not, after all, be something in the theory that the races are biologically different; we find them saying that it will take a very long time for Negroes to achieve full equality, no matter what anyone does; we find them deploring the rise of black nationalism and expressing the solemn hope that the leaders of the Negro community will discover ways of containing the impatience and incipient violence within the Negro ghettos.[1]

But that is by no means the whole story; there is also the phenomenon of what Kenneth Rexroth once called "crow-jimism." There are the broken-down white boys like Vivaldo Moore in Baldwin's *Another Country* who go to Harlem in search of sex or simply to brush up against something that looks like primitive vitality, and who are so often punished by the Negroes they meet for crimes that they would have been the last ever to commit and of which they themselves have been as sorry victims as any of the Negroes who take it out on them. There are the writers and intellectuals and artists who romanticize Negroes and pander to them, assuming a guilt that is not properly theirs. And there are all the white liberals who permit Negroes to blackmail them into adopting a double standard of moral judgment, and who lend themselves—again assuming the responsibility for crimes they never committed—to cunning and contemptuous exploitation by Negroes they employ or try to befriend.

And what about me? What kind of feelings do I have about Negroes today? What happened to me, from Brooklyn, who grew up fearing and envying and hating Negroes? Now that Brooklyn is behind me, do I fear them and envy them and hate them still? The answer is yes, but not in the same proportions and certainly not in the same way. I now live on the upper west side of Manhattan, where there are many Negroes and many Puerto Ricans, and there are nights when I experience the old apprehensiveness again, and there are streets that I avoid when I am walking in the

---

[1] For an account of developments like these, see "The White Liberal's Retreat" by Murray Friedman in the January 1963 *Atlantic Monthly.*

dark, as there were streets that I avoided when I was a child. I find that I am not afraid of Puerto Ricans, but I cannot restrain my nervousness whenever I pass a group of Negroes standing in front of a bar or sauntering down the street. I know now, as I did not know when I was a child, that power is on my side, that the police are working for me and not for them. And knowing this I feel ashamed and guilty, like the good liberal I have grown up to be. Yet the twinges of fear and the resentment they bring and the self-contempt they arouse are not to be gainsaid.

But envy? Why envy? And hatred? Why hatred? Here again the intensities have lessened and everything has been complicated and qualified by the guilts and the resulting over-compensations that are the heritage of the enlightened middle-class world of which I am now a member. Yet just as in childhood I envied Negroes for what seemed to me their superior masculinity, so I envy them today for what seems to me their superior physical grace and beauty. I have come to value physical grace very highly, and I am now capable of aching with all my being when I watch a Negro couple on the dance floor, or a Negro playing baseball or basketball. They are on the kind of terms with their own bodies that I should like to be on with mine, and for that precious quality they seem blessed to me.

The hatred I still feel for Negroes is the hardest of all the old feelings to face or admit, and it is the most hidden and the most overlarded by the conscious attitudes into which I have succeeded in willing myself. It no longer has, as for me it once did, any cause or justification (except, perhaps, that I am constantly being denied my right to an honest expression of the things I earned the right as a child to feel). How, then, do I know that this hatred has never entirely disappeared? I know it from the insane rage that can stir in me at the thought of Negro anti-Semitism; I know it from the disgusting prurience that can stir in me at the sight of a mixed couple; and I know it from the violence that can stir in me whenever I encounter that special brand of paranoid touchiness to which many Negroes are prone.

This, then, is where I am; it is not exactly where I think all other white liberals are, but it cannot be so very far away either. And it is because I am convinced that we white Americans are—for whatever reason, it no longer matters—so twisted and sick in our feelings about Negroes that I despair of the present push toward integration. If the pace of progress were not a factor here, there would perhaps be no cause for despair: time and the law and even the international political situation are on the side of the Negroes, and ultimately, therefore, victory—of a sort, anyway— must come. But from everything we have learned from observers who ought to know, pace has become as important to the Negroes as substance. They want equality and they want it *now*, and the white world is yielding to their demand only as much and as fast as it is absolutely being compelled to do. The Negroes know this in the most concrete terms imaginable, and it is thus becoming increasingly difficult to buy them off with rhetoric and promises and pious assurances of support. And so within the Negro community we find more and more people declaring—as Harold R. Isaacs recently put it in an article in *Commentary*—that they want *out*: people who say that integration will never come, or that it will take a hundred or a thousand years to come, or that it will come at too high a price in suffering and struggle for the pallid and sodden life of the American middle class that at the very best it may bring.

The most numerous, influential, and dangerous movement that has grown out of Negro despair with the goal of integration is, of course, the Black Muslims. This movement, whatever else we may say about it, must be credited with one enduring achievement: it inspired James Baldwin to write an essay which deserves to be placed among the classics of our language. Everything Baldwin has ever been trying to tell us is distilled in *The Fire Next Time* into a statement of overwhelming persuasiveness and prophetic magnificence. Baldwin's message is and always has been simple. It is this: "Color is not a human or personal reality; it is a political reality." And Baldwin's demand is correspondingly simple: color must be forgotten, lest we all be smited with a vengeance "that does not really depend on, and cannot really be executed by, any person or organization, and that cannot be prevented by any police force or army: historical vengeance, a cosmic vengeance based on the law that we recognize when we say, 'Whatever goes up must come down.'" The Black Muslims Baldwin portrays as a sign and a warning to the intransigent white world. They come to proclaim how deep is the Negro's disaffection with the white world and all its works, and Baldwin implies that no American Negro can fail to respond somewhere in his being to their message: that the white man is the devil, that Allah has doomed him to destruction, and that the black man is about to inherit the earth. Baldwin of course knows that this nightmare inversion of the racism from which the black man has suffered can neither win nor even point to the neighborhood in which victory might be located. For in his view the neighborhood of victory lies in exactly the opposite direction: the transcendence of color through love.

Yet the tragic fact is that love is not the answer to hate—not in the world of politics, at any rate. Color is indeed a political rather than a human or personal reality and if politics (which is to say power) has made it into a human and personal reality, then only politics (which is to say power) can unmake it once again. But the way of politics is slow and bitter, and as impatience on the one side is matched by a setting of the jaw on the other, we move closer and closer to an explosion and blood may yet run in the streets.

Will this madness in which we are all caught never find a resting-place? Is there never to be an end to it? In thinking about the Jews I have often wondered whether their survival as a distinct group was worth one hair on the head of a single infant. Did the Jews have to survive so that six million innocent people should one day be burned in the ovens of Auschwitz? It is a terrible question and no one, not God himself, could ever answer it to my satisfaction. And when I think about the Negroes in America and about the image of integration as a state in which the Negroes would take their rightful place as another of the protected minorities in a pluralistic society, I wonder whether they really believe in their hearts that such a state can actually be attained, and if so *why* they should wish to survive as a distinct group. I think I know why the Jews once wished to survive (though I am less certain as to why we still do): they not only believed that God had given them no choice, but they were tied to a memory of past glory and a dream of imminent redemption. What does the American Negro have that might correspond to this? His past is a stigma, his color is a stigma, and his vision of the future is the hope of erasing the stigma by making color irrelevant, by making it disappear as a fact of consciousness.

I share this hope, but I cannot see how it will ever be realized unless color does *in fact* disappear: and that means not integration, it means assimilation, it means—let the brutal word come out—miscegenation. The Black Muslims, like their racist counterparts in the white world, accuse the "so-called Negro leaders" of secretly pursuing miscegenation as a goal. The racists are wrong, but I wish they were right, for I believe that the wholesale merger of the two races is the most desirable alternative for everyone concerned. I am not claiming that this alternative can be pursued programmatically or that it is immediately feasible as a solution; obviously there are even greater barriers to its achievement than to the achievement of integration. What I am saying, however, is that in my opinion the Negro problem can be solved in this country in no other way.

I have told the story of my own twisted feelings about Negroes here, and of how they conflict with the moral convictions I have since developed, in order to assert that such feelings must be acknowledged as honestly as possible so that they can be controlled and ultimately disregarded in favor of the convictions. It is *wrong* for a man to suffer because of the color of his skin. Beside that clichéd proposition of liberal thought, what argument can stand and be respected? If the arguments are the arguments of feeling, they must be made to yield; and one's own soul is not the worst place to begin working a huge social transformation. Not so long ago, it used to be asked of white liberals, "Would you like your sister to marry one?" When I was a boy and my sister was still unmarried I would certainly have said no to that question. But now I am a man, my sister is already married, and I have daughters. If I were to be asked today whether I would like a daughter of mine "to marry one," I would have to answer: "No, I wouldn't *like* it at all. I would rail and rave and rant and tear my hair. And then I hope I would have the courage to curse myself for raving and ranting, and to give her my blessing. How dare I withhold it at the behest of the child I once was and against the man I now have a duty to be?"

Jacquetta Hawkes

An Aside on Consciousness

Proust holds himself like a naked nerve at the centre of a trembling web of remembered consciousness. No sound or smell or physical detail of his surroundings escapes him; his awareness of the complexity of emotion, thought and association in himself and in others is almost too sensitive to be endured.

Newton and Einstein drive their minds into regions untouched by experience; Mozart appears as a man born without some obstruction that prevents ordinary people from communicating with a stupendous world of understanding. All of them represent the furthest achievements of an evolutionary process which relates them to the chemical constituents of the planet.

It has been thought that solar radiation acting upon sea water first enabled matter to reproduce itself and life thus to begin. Now it seems that drying mud is a more likely cradle. I had always imagined that the earliest essays in life would be microscopically small, but, on the contrary,

AN ASIDE ON CONSCIOUSNESS   From *A Land* by Jacquetta Hawkes. Reprinted by permission of The Cresset Press, London.

it was probably in quite large masses of matter that reproduction began. Whatever the size of these first pieces of life, whether they preferred sea water or mud, nothing but some fifteen hundred million years separate them from their outcome in Proust. They have grown also into butterflies, into the elaborate lobster and the simple worm. But the dominant, the significant process in those millions of years has been the heightening of consciousness. It remains the only visible opening for significant development in the future. Among the earliest creatures known from the Cambrian rocks are the trilobites, a large family of primitive crustaceans, which for an immense span of time were the aristocrats of life. To-day the lobster is a very fine fellow whether he promenades the sea-floor in flashing blue or lies pink and opulent in an entrée dish; whether he eats men under water or is eaten by them in their world of air. But he has gone too far. Imprisoned in his splendid, his fantastic external skeleton he has no expanding future. If man leaves the feast he will not arise from the dish to make himself master of some new region of life. It is no better with the birds. Though in their isolation the wrens of St. Kilda[1] may have grown longer tails than the wrens of the mainland, they cannot achieve anything much more significant. The birds burnt all their boats when they left the ground; so it has been with all our fellow creatures—they have committed themselves too far. The gazelle is given over to fleetness, the rhinoceros to strength, the giraffe, though he can reach the topmost leaves, already looks impossible.

It seems, although certainly it is only we in our ignorance who say so, that our minds alone are free to go forward to something significantly new. There may be a time when all school teachers can expect to have sitting before them children of the capacities of Newton and Einstein, Mozart and Proust, while the men of genius move in a country far beyond our present guessing. There may be, or it may prove that brain development must be likened to that of the horn of *Synthetoceras*.[2]

It has been a diverse yet constant process, this heightening of consciousness. I shall not attempt to interpret the experiences of the first cells when they suffered fission, but will begin with the trilobites that represented the most complex and shapely form life had achieved by the end of Cambrian times. To secure food was the first duty of consciousness, and the trilobites, some of which had as many as three eyes of a rough and ready sort, were sufficiently aware of matter looming towards them through the water to move in pursuit. For the first time an image, however blurred, was being received by a living organism.

---

1 An island in the Outer Hebrides, west of Scotland.
2 An archaic deer-like mammal, with grotesquely large horns.

This most vital faculty was advanced by the fishes who must have seen a dim, flat world but one that contained distinct shapes, and shapes that were related to one another. When the reptiles left the water life in the air was a tremendous stimulus towards the refinement of the senses. *Diplodocus* was ninety feet long and had a brain the size of a small kitten's; nevertheless the brain was there in the heavy skull and, helped out by a smaller nerve centre above the hips, controlled the vast, straggling nervous system. The toed feet could feel the ground, be aware of the different texture of sand, wet stone or slime as they waded into the water. The lidless eyes as they swung at the end of a neck as long as a crane recorded bright, meaningless pictures of lagoons and fern trees. The nose, too, was sensitive, and made its own arrangement of the smells coming from mud, from crushed vegetation and from animals dead and living.

It was among the early reptiles that consciousness gained a new incentive and a tremendous new agency for its own perfection. For the first time the male had to seek and take the female. Perhaps it is too gross, too crude a piece of sensationalism, to claim for those reptilian couplings, all slime or scale, some part in the creation of Heloise and Abelard, yet it is the truth. There is something more here than sexual selection, immensely powerful as that has been in the evolution of life. The forces of attraction and repulsion, of mutuality, in all their forms, have acted like some universal, instinctive artistic genius, creating all that is most highly formed, most brilliantly coloured in the world: all that is furthest from the drab equality of chaos. Insects have intensified the colours of flowers, fighting has set delicate antlers on the stag, courtship has given birds their brightest plumage. Love refines and sharpens human personality and provokes poetry and music.

Before the great reptiles had disappeared, the mammals were there with their keener senses and their far more complex brains. They experienced fear and anger, and, beyond reptilian sex, they knew family life. Even the nest of a tree shrew can do much to incubate consciousness. Before long the small tarsier appeared with his forward-looking eyes—eyes so disproportionately large that he seems still startled by the stereoscopic vision that made the seen world one and gave it a third dimension. The nut was seen to be plump, the receding glade asked to be explored.

And so to apes and men. A long-drawn effort to correlate hand and eye and brain in non-instinctive movement; a complication of emotion tending towards refinements of love and hate; a widening separation of the self from its surroundings. Then, suddenly, the bison painted on the cave wall. What has happened since then but fifty thousand years of the accumulation of experience and an erratic but pitiless sharpening of thought and feeling?

This gathering up of consciousness during time can be followed also through space. It stretches up through time from the placid mass of cells on the drying mud, through reptiles browsing on the branches of trees and the little mammals peeping on them through the leaves, up to Proust in his exquisite, agonizing web. So, too, at this one moment of time I can feel consciousness stretching from the crystalline virus that blights tomato plants, through fish, reptiles and mammals to the minds of men. Indeed, it is obviously only an expedient convention to stop with the forms of life that are earliest in time, or the simplest in space. Consciousness must surely be traced back to the rocks—the rocks which have been here since life began and so make a meeting place for the roots of life in time and space, the earliest and the simplest. Why, indeed, stop with this planet? Even if nothing like the human psyche and intellect have developed elsewhere, it is necessary in an indivisible universe to believe that the principle of consciousness must extend everywhere. Even now I imagine that I can feel all the particles of the universe nourishing my consciousness just as my consciousness informs all the particles of the universe.

At this my own flesh should be clamouring. Why go so far afield when here in the ball of your thumb, in the muscle of your thigh, is unconscious life. Every cell that makes this "me" has its individual life, and if skilfully transplanted to another medium can grow and multiply—might even be made to outlive "me." Similarly I have rehearsed the story in time. Starting from a single cell, I passed one period of my life with gill slits inherited from my fishy ancestry, then for a few weeks sported a tail and was hard to distinguish from an unborn tree shrew. The protest of the flesh is reasonable. Why think of viruses or pre-Cambrian organisms when inside this delicate membrane of my skin, this outline of an individual, I carry the whole history of life. I am a community of countless units, from cells to complex organs, living unconscious lives, yet supporting as their king the invisible power that is enthroned in the brain.

As in the physical being the foetus recapitulates episodes in the history of life, so each individual consciousness, that most fleeting manifestation, carries beneath it, far out of reach of normal memory, episodes in the history of consciousness back to its remotest origins.

Because mind, like the matter in which it is immanent, seeks to continue itself, it suffers the strange pangs of love, love which can serve its end in two ways. Either it leads mind to strive for union with another and so to continue its existence in a new creature, or excites it to creative activity of all kinds, and above all to project itself through the arts. Whereas the new physical creature represents the prolongation of consciousness in the stream of time, these projections—pictures, poems, symphonies—are the perpetuation of a phase of consciousness motionless within the stream.

Fossils of the psyche. So might a dinosaur either lay its leathery eggs and so secure posterity, or allow its own dying body to roll down to the sea bed to be preserved through all time.

We have become very conscious of the individual being, apparently neatly enclosed by its covering of skin, recognizable as "me," a being to be disliked or desired but certainly a distinct and particular entity. It is the natural tendency of our mode of perception. Even a fire we contrive to see as a separate thing rather than as a chemical process affecting a wide area round the visible flames and smoke. A human being is hardly more cut off from its surroundings than is a naked fire. It is continuously exuding gas and moisture and consuming other gas; a variety of waves can pass through a wall, through air and through a human body almost without interruption. It seems that the mind itself can issue waves, or something akin to them, that can penetrate and be received by other minds. Every being is united both inwardly and outwardly with the beginning of life in time and with the simplest forms of contemporary life. "Me" is a fiction, though a convenient fiction and one of significance to the consciousness of which I am the temporary home.

I think that we are returning to an awareness of our unity with our surroundings, but an awareness of a much more exalted kind than anything that has existed before. The primitive tribesman, to go no further back than the early days of our own species, was still so deeply sunk in nature that he hardly distinguished himself from his environment or from his fellows. This sense of oneness shows itself in totemism and in many forms of magic. In the identification of the name or image with the living person; in summoning rain by spitting water, or in the belief that a man by leaping into the air can make the corn grow tall. In this, just as in the foetal gills, the child repeats the development of the species, he does not distinguish—" 'Tis the eye of childhood that fears a painted devil."

It is in this natural unity that the savage may truly be said to be happy. Certainly civilization must always destroy it. In urban, literate surroundings self-consciousness becomes a sharp knife cutting man away from his matrix. It was early sharpened among the Greeks, but the collapse of the classical world before Christianity and tribal barbarism brought a respite. For another thousand years the mind of an agricultural society was rocked by the comforting seasonal rhythm.

If the East threw the knife away, the West retrieved it. After the Renaissance its possession became the mark of Western civilization—*la volonté de conscience et la volonté de découverte.*[3] It was not hard to bear, indeed it could be exhilarating, for man to feel isolated if he also

[3] "The will toward consciousness and the will toward discovery."

felt important in his isolation. But, needlessly perhaps, man allowed himself to be dwarfed by his own discoveries, by his recollection of evolutionary processes and of the humble place of the earth in the material universe. He was left not merely naked and lonely, but apparently insignificant. Perhaps this condition reached its most terrible pitch of sensitivity in the present century with those who, like Proust, accepted it, and those who, like D. H. Lawrence, tried to retreat. Even for the mass of the people for whom the knife was not so finely sharpened, the god who died and was resurrected in the spring had deserted them.

Yet I believe that those who have had the courage to suffer *la volonté de conscience et la volonté de découverte* are now already half assuaged. Mind, which at first denied men their instinctive sense of wholeness, is at last returning such a sense, but on its own mental level. Consciousness is melting us all down together again—earth, air, fire and water, past and future, lobsters, butterflies, meteors, and men. As for me, what other force has driven me to attempt this book?

Questions

Diction and Structure

1. Many of the terms that Northrop Frye uses to explain the nature of criticism are either taken from the Greek or are Greek words in their original form. Examine Frye's use of the following terms, identify the extent to which he assigns them a stipulative meaning, and state as directly as you can what each means: *nous, dianoia,* axiom, aesthetic, icon, myth, kinetic.

2. Frye occasionally uses phrases or words that might not seem consistent with the overall diction in his essay. What is the function of such terms as: "a particular hankering," "critical dandyism," "a garrulous drunk," "a bigger and better phoenix," "squealing little sexballs"?

3. Outline Frye's essay in its major divisions and subdivisions. What aid does the text itself provide for outlining? Are there any sections that do not logically follow from what came before? If such digressions occur, how can they be explained?

4. Does Walter Lippmann primarily use concrete or abstract terms? How is this usage suited to his topic?

5. Are the divisions of Lippmann's essay indicative of separate aspects of his topic, stages of development, or something else?

6. Norman Podhoretz uses some highly connotative slang terms in his explanation of prejudice: wop, kike, polack, mick, spick, and others. Are these emotionally laden words appropriate in a supposedly objective explanation? Explain.

7. Look up the origins of the slang terms listed above in a *Dictionary of Slang* or a specialized reference work such as Leo Rosten's *The Joys of Yiddish*. How did they originate? Were their meanings always derogatory?

8. Look up the word "item." Does Podhoretz use it properly? What does it contribute, if anything, to the organization of his essay? Compare his use with that of Victor Cline (p. 234).

9. To what extent does Jacquetta Hawkes's essay depend on chronological order for its organization? Why does she open the essay as she does?

10. Look closely at the description of the lobster on page 405. What kinds of diction does it use? What purpose does the passage serve? Is it consistent with the rest of the essay?

11. Like other writers, Hawkes sometimes relies on lists to present many details or examples in a brief space. Cite instances where she does this; suggest the possible benefits and limitations of the method; and suggest how it might be especially suited to particular rhetorical methods of development.

Style and Rhetoric

1. Northrop Frye explains what literature is, the standards by which readers criticize it, the process of understanding literature, the nature of education, and the psychology of understanding. What do you think his chief interest is in "Criticism, Visible and Invisible"?

2. How important to Frye's explanation is exemplification? Illustration? Comparison and contrast? Is any one of these techniques more frequently used than the others?

3. Point out instances in which Frye argues deductively, moving from some major premise to a minor premise and conclusion. How valid are his deductive conclusions? Where does he derive his premises?

4. The relationship treated in Lippmann's "The Indispensable Opposition" is political. It is also emotional, economic, moral, or logical? Explain.

5. How important is definition in Lippmann's essay? Exemplification? Comparison and contrast?

6. Examine closely the logical techniques used by Lippmann. Is he dealing with tangible data or theories? Does he apply the right logical methods to his material?

7. How do Norman Podhoretz's opening paragraphs in "My Negro Problem—and Ours" use logical methods? Does Podhoretz suggest any limitations in logical thinking? How would logical fallacies be relevant to Podhoretz's overall theme?

8. Podhoretz's uses both narrative and expository methods to assist in explaining. Point out instances in which explanation combines with these methods to suggest causality.

9. Is Podhoretz interested only in showing racial relationships? What sorts of relationship are explicated by him?

10. Is the chief logical method in "My Negro Problem" one of induction, deduction, analogy, or none of these? Does Podhoretz fall into any logical errors that you can see?

11. Jacquetta Hawkes's "An Aside on Consciousness" traces the biological evolution of life in its examination of how consciousness developed and took its various forms. Is her essay a narrative? Is it concerned with causality?

12. To what extent is description used as an aid to explanation in Hawkes's essay? What use does the author make of analytical methods?

Theme and Viewpoint

1. Both Northrop Frye and Victor Cline are concerned with the extension of individual awareness (or consciousness) and the impact of mass media on young people. Compare their views on one of the above subjects. Do they agree with each other? Which writer rests his premises on the more convincing evidence?

2. In the final paragraph of "Criticism, Visible and Invisible," Frye refers to the three qualities in literature of *integritas, consonantia,* and *claritas.* Compare Frye's critical terms with those of Graham Hough. Does Frye apply to prose as well as poetry, criteria that Hough reserves for poetry? Explain.

3. Frye criticizes the standard of "taste" in judging literature. Examine his reasons for doing so, then reread F. L. Lucas's comments on style. Are Lucas's criteria based on the kind of "gentlemanly taste" that Frye deplores? Justify your answer.

4. Walter Lippmann discusses the function of movies in a

democracy such as America. Does he hold the same ideas about motion pictures and their effects that Cline and other writers do about T.V.? If you think they disagree, can they both be right?

5. Lippmann's discussion of ideological and political opposition uses the term "eccentric" several times. Is the member of the minority an "eccentric" in Louis Kronenberger's terms? Are the minority member's views those of the crank, the eccentric, or the individualist, as Lippmann explains them?

6. Does Norman Podhoretz accept the theories of Ian Stevenson as to why people are prejudiced and how prejudices are formed, or does he reject them? Is there anything in Podhoretz's account of his prejudice that lends support to Stevenson's views?

7. Like William Faulkner, Norman Podhoretz seeks to explain certain features of violence and its relationship to love. Do the two writers see violence as the same thing? Do they view love as the solution to violence?

8. Podhoretz explains his adult bias as an inability to overcome childish fears. Does his experience confirm the views of Smith and Todes or Jane Jacobs or Victor Cline?

9. Jacquetta Hawkes's discussion of consciousness follows repeated references to consciousness by Northrop Frye, Walter Lippmann, and Norman Podhoretz. Examine the earlier essays and decide whether Hawkes's description of consciousness pertains to the earlier uses.

10. Like Stephen Spender and other writers in this collection, Hawkes uses Newton and Mozart as illustrations in her view of consciousness. Compare the uses of these men as examples.

11. Hawkes defines two sorts of love in her essay, one that may be called "inspiration" or "genius" and the other, "desire" or "sexual attraction." Compare and contrast her theories with those of Spender on the former and Theodor Reik on the latter.

12. In explaining the sense of isolation and separation in human beings Hawkes touches on a topic that is highly important to Arthur Miller. Is his "alienation" the same as her "isolation"? Do they agree as to its causes?

13. Both Northrop Frye and Jacquetta Hawkes discuss the relationship of "magic" to consciousness. Do they define "magic" in the same way? Do they disagree in any important ways about the role of magic in human understanding?

14. Norman Podhoretz is the kind of "liberal" that Claire Boothe Luce criticizes as a faulty thinker. He mentions the diet of the Negroes in his school and he is much concerned with their violence. Does he posit diet as the cause of black violence? What causes does he assign?

15. Compare and contrast their Jewish backgrounds as influential in shaping Ann Landers and Norman Podhoretz. Is there any evidence that Landers shares some of the biases of Podhoretz? Does this confirm or refute Ian Stevenson's hypothesis?

16. Notice the examples of Yiddish and its variants in the Podhoretz essay. Does this and the essays of Kramer and Wax support the contentions of Leo Rosten about the effects of Yiddish on English?

Argumentation
and persuasion:
proving opinion

"I don't know what you mean by 'glory,' " Alice said. Humpty Dumpty smiled contemptuously. "Of course you don't—till I tell you. I meant 'there's a nice knock-down argument for you!' "

Unfortunately, many people act as though they agree with Humpty Dumpty that a knock-down argument—what Dryden called "a word and a blow"—is more glorious than calm, rational, and informed exchanges of opinion. Like Thoreau's ants, eager disputants hurl themselves into battle, attacking their opponent's character, taste, education, and hometown—everything but the strength or weakness of the argument. When differences in opinion occur, fists may not always substitute for words; but *ad hominem, ad populum,* or *ignoratio elenchi* verbiage too often replaces rational and ordered definition of the issues under discussion and a careful weighing of evidence, *pro* and *con.*

It is inevitable that disagreements should arise in written as well as spoken discourse. Despite all of the methods we have developed for collecting, arranging, and evaluating data, much of what passes for factual knowledge is really theory that has not been disproved by any contradictory, known evidence. When we define an intangible (*love,* perhaps, or *stress*), we are naming an elusive and variable quality. Classifying species of animals may work well until some presumably extinct creature like the coelocanth appears or the duck-billed platypus confuses mammalian and nonmammalian characteristics. The inherent weaknesses in causation and illustration have already been mentioned. Even description and characterization produce contradictions. No two eyewitnesses to a train wreck will describe it in the same way, viewing it from different vantage points as they must. And characterizing an individual can produce two portraits so unlike that we wonder whether they are of the same person. One biographer shows Lawrence of Arabia as a heroic, altruistic, pure spirited champion of the Arabs; another pictures him as a sexually neurotic, cowardly egomaniac who plotted secretly against his Arab allies.

To err is human; if we are to recognize our errors and correct them, partially if not completely, we must be willing to display our opinions and reassess them periodically by placing them alongside new, relevant evidence or contrasting points of view. Repeating a falsehood again and again will not make it true; nor will outshouting another opinion demonstrate the validity of one's own. There is a famous schoolmaster in Goldsmith's *The Deserted Village* who, "e'en though vanquished, he could argue still . . ." Even if he could prolong the argument after he had been proved wrong, the loquacious schoolmaster probably never *persuaded* anybody but himself that his arguments were valid or his conclusions true. A good argument will be so convincing in its data, in its ways of interpreting and appraising them, and in presenting them logically that it persuades the hearer (reader) to consider it seriously if not accept it entirely.

"An honest man appeals to the understanding, or modestly confides in the internal evidence of his conscience": so wrote Junius, the famous eighteenth-century essayist. His statement is still a serviceable guide to effective argumentation. Matters of conscience—that is, faith, or belief in matters that cannot be conclusively proved true or false—must usually be left unargued. Everything else is susceptible to public and honest reappraisals.

When an argument is presented orally in the form of a debate, it usually observes certain long-established conventions. A long line of "rhetoricians"—from Democritus and Cicero to William Jennings Bryan—followed certain prescribed and sequential stages in arguing a case, whether pro or con. Such Latin nomenclature as *peroratio, confirmatio, confutatio, exordium,* and *postoratio* would presumably demonstrate the tight reasoning of the argument, if rigidly followed by the speaker. Unfortunately, however, logical formulas do not guarantee logical or valid argumentation; and during the past century, perfervid declamations masquerading as reason while covertly appealing to emotion have come under just suspicion. The public orator is now almost a figure of fun—"I stand for Motherhood, America, and a hot lunch for orphans!"—but argumentation goes on, both in public and private places, and it needs to regard a few ground rules if it is to do anything more than release pent-up anger and destroy friendships.

Proper argumentation necessarily includes stating the problem or question under discussion, defining any doubtful terms, marshalling all the evidence that supports some consistent point of view and all the evidence that refutes or contradicts it, and at last coming to an assessment of the comparative merits of all relevant data. If an opinion then needs to be modified or even discarded, this can be done with the fullest possible understanding. An opinion that has been substantially strengthened by the argument will be more useful than before. If, when all evidence has been taken into account, no real, unequivocal decision seems possible, the matter must remain in a state of doubt or be settled temporarily with an acknowledgedly tentative evaluation.

As in other modes of discourse, the argument on an emotionally charged issue—"sexual revolution," "mercy killings," "press freedom," "education for all"—is most likely to shift from the basis of reason to illogical or irrational rhetorical techniques. Successful arguments, however, must resist tendencies to grow emotional, oversimplify, and strengthen a case by ignoring contradictory evidence. Whether the writer assumes that the contradictory viewpoint is commonly known, perhaps widely accepted, or the writer states both sides of an issue, defending one against the other, he or she must be sure that the aim is not to justify personal pride and beliefs but to discover and persuade the reader of the truth.

The following essays, written for a variety of audiences and purposes, illustrate some fundamental kinds of argumentative discourse. Rollo May begins his essay on the New Puritanism with a series of cause and effect relationships and comparisons and contrasts, establishes a dilemma, then through analysis suggests what ought to be the elements in human sexual relationships. Dr. Joseph Fletcher begins his discussion of euthanasia with a paradoxical statement: it is a "success problem." He views death through a series of opposites; sets up two classifications of euthanasia and describes the "passive"; generalizes about attitudes toward ethical values; analyzes three opposing sets of ethical beliefs; gives some exposition about modern dying; and finally tries to define death by defining "human." Others then question his medical and

legal assumptions. John Gardner states two presumably opposing views, redefines to show they are not opposite and irreconcilable, and argues for the necessity of arriving at a working
synthesis of the views. Mark Harris starts his case against
reading newspapers by attacking a generalization ("You ought
to read the news") and giving examples of people's reactions.
He cites an authority (Thoreau); praises *inductive* thinking;
gives a series of analogies; analyzes the modern inability to
think inductively or analytically; criticizes comparison and contrast as a method of thought; gives the causes for poor reporting and declares the news has no "effects"; uses Watergate as
an illustration; and concludes with a series of assertions.

All of the arguments in these selections are cast clearly in
the format of argumentative discourse. Other essays may well
be argumentation masquerading as explanation, narration, or
exposition. Sometimes a writer may deliberately try to deceive
the reader into accepting opinions for fact. Usually, however,
the apparently expositional or explanational essay that is basically an argument is the result of an author's eagerness to
state views in the most persuasive manner possible. It is the
readers' duty—to themselves, primarily, but also to the writer—
always to read so carefully and perceptively that they will not
adopt ideas because of the rhetorical method used but because
these ideas are valid. By now, you have assumed this duty (it
is to be hoped); and in the future it should be your care to
apply the same critical and reasonable standards to your own
writing.

Rollo May

Antidotes for the New Puritanism

There are several strange and interesting dilemmas in which we find our-selves with respect to sex and love in our culture. When psychoanalysis was born in Victorian times half a century ago, repression of sexual im-pulses, feelings, and drives was the accepted mode. It was not nice to feel sexual, one would not talk about sex in polite company, and an aura of sanctifying repulsiveness surrounded the whole topic. Freud was right in pointing out the varied neurotic symptoms to which this repression of sex gave birth.

Then, in the 1920s, a radical change occurred almost overnight. The belief became a militant conviction in liberal circles that the opposite of repression—sex education, freedom of talking, feeling, and expression— would have healthy effects, and was obviously the only stand for the en-lightened person. According to Max Lerner, our society shifted from acting as though sex did not exist to placing the most emphasis on sex of any so-ciety since the Roman.

Partly as a result of this radical change, we therapists rarely get nowa-days in our offices patients who exhibit repression of sex in the pre-World War I Freudian sense. In fact we find just the opposite in the people who come for help: a great deal of talk about sex, a great deal of sexual activ-ity, practically no one complaining of any cultural prohibitions over his going to bed as often or with as many partners as he wishes.

But what our patients *do* complain of is lack of feeling and passion —so much sex and so little meaning or even fun in it! Whereas the Vic-torian person didn't want anyone to know that he or she had sexual feel-ings, now we are ashamed if we do not. Before 1910 if you called a lady "sexy," you insulted her; nowadays the lady accepts the adjective as a

ANTIDOTES FOR THE NEW PURITANISM   Reprinted from *Saturday Review*, based on *Love and Will* by Rollo May. By permission of W. W. Norton & Company, Inc. Copyright © 1969 by W. W. Norton & Company, Inc.

prized compliment. Our patients often have problems of impotence or frigidity, but they struggle desperately not to let anyone know they *don't* feel sexually. The Victorian nice man or woman was guilty if he or she did perform sexually; now we are guilty if we *don't*.

One dilemma, therefore, is that enlightenment has not at all solved the sexual problems in our culture. To be sure, there are important positive results of the new enlightenment, chiefly in increased freedom for the individual. And some external problems are eased—sexual knowledge can be bought in any bookstore, contraception is available almost everywhere outside Boston, and external societal anxiety has lessened. *But internalized anxiety and guilt have increased.* And in some ways, these are more morbid, harder to handle, and impose a heavier burden upon the individual man and woman than external anxiety and guilt.

A second dilemma is that the new emphasis on technique in sex and love-making backfires. It often seems to me that there is an inverse relationship between the number of how-to-do-it books perused by a person, or rolling off the presses in a society, and the amount of sexual passion or even pleasure experienced by the persons involved. Nothing is wrong with technique as such, in playing golf or acting or making love. But the emphasis beyond a certain point on technique in sex makes for a mechanistic attitude toward love-making, and goes along with alienation, feelings of loneliness, and depersonalization.

The third dilemma I propose is that our highly vaunted sexual freedom has turned out to be a new form of puritanism. I define puritanism as a state of alienation from the body, separation of emotion from reason, and use of the body as a machine. These were the elements of moralistic puritanism in Victorian times; industrialism expressed these same characteristics of puritanism in economic guise. Our modern sexual attitudes have a new content, namely, full sexual expression, but in the same old puritan form—alienation from the body and feeling, and exploitation of the body as though it were a machine.

In our new puritanism bad health is equated with sin. Sin used to be "to give in to one's sexual desires"; now it is "not to have full sexual expression." A woman used to be guilty if she went to bed with a man; now she feels vaguely guilty if after a certain number of dates she still refrains. And her partner, who is always completely enlightened—or at least pretends to be—refuses to allay her guilt and does not get overtly angry at her sin of "morbid repression," her refusal to "give." This, of course, makes her "no" all the more guilt-producing for her.

All this means, of course, that people have to learn to perform sexually but at the same time not to let themselves go in passion or unseemly commitment—which latter may be interpreted as exerting an unhealthy demand on the partner. *The Victorian person sought to have love without falling into sex; the modern person seeks to have sex without falling into love.*

Recently I amused myself by drawing an impressionistic picture of the attitude of the contemporary enlightened person toward sex and love. I call it the portrait of the new sophisticate:

> The new sophisticate is not castrated by society but, like Origen, is self-castrated. Sex and the body are for him not something to be and live out, but tools to be cultivated like a TV announcer's voice. And like all genuine Puritans (very passionate men underneath) the new sophisticate does it by devoting himself passionately to the moral principle of dispersing all passion, loving everybody until love has no power left to scare anyone. He is deathly afraid of his passions unless they are kept under leash, and the theory of total expression is precisely his leash. His dogma of liberty is his repression; and his principle of full libidinal health, full sexual satisfaction, are his puritanism and amount to the same thing as his New England forefathers' denial of sex. The first Puritans repressed sex and were passionate; our new man represses passion and is sexual. Both have the purpose of holding back the body, both are ways of trying to make nature a slave. The modern man's rigid principle of full freedom is not freedom at all but a new straitjacket, in some ways as compulsive as the old. He does all this because he is afraid of his body and his compassionate roots in nature, afraid of the soil and his procreative power. He is our latter-day Baconian devoted to gaining power *over* nature, gaining knowledge in order to get more power. And you gain power over sexuality (like working the slave until all zest for revolt is squeezed out of him) precisely by the role of full expression. Sex becomes our tool like the caveman's wheel, crowbar, or adz. Sex, the new machine, the *Machina Ultima*.

It is not surprising that, confronted by these dilemmas, people become more and more concerned about the technical, mechanical aspects of the sexual act. The questions typically asked about the act of love-making are not whether there was passion or meaning or even pleasure, but how well did one perform? Even the sexologists, whose attitude is generally the more the merrier, are raising their eyebrows these days about the anxious overemphasis on achieving the orgasm and the great importance attached to "satisfying" the partner. The man makes a point of asking the woman if she "made it," or is she "all right," or uses some other such euphemism for an experience for which obviously no euphemism is possible. We men are reminded by Simone de Beauvoir and other women who try to interpret the love act to us, that this is the last thing in the world a woman wants to be asked at that moment.

I often get the impression, amid the male flexing of sexual biceps, that men are in training to become sexual athletes. But what is the great prize of the game? Now it is well known in psychotherapeutic circles that the overconcern with potency is generally a compensation for feelings of impotence. Men and women both are struggling to prove their sexual power. Another motive of the game is to overcome their own solitariness. A third motive is often the desperate endeavor to escape feelings of emptiness and the threat of apathy: they pant and quiver to find an answering quiver in someone else's body to prove their own is not dead. Out of an ancient conceit we call this love.

The struggle to find an identity is also a central motive in acting out these sexual roles—a goal present in women as well as men, as Betty Friedan in *The Feminine Mystique* made clear. The point I wish to emphasize here is the connection between this dilemma about potency and the tendency in our society for us to become machines or ledger books even in bed. A psychiatrist colleague of mine tells me that one of his patients brought in the following dream. "I was in bed with my wife. Between us was my accountant. He was going to make love to my wife. Somehow it seemed all right."

Along with the overemphasis upon mechanism there goes, understandably enough, a lessening of passion and of feeling itself, which seems to take the form of a kind of anaesthesia in people who otherwise can perform the mechanical aspects of the sexual act very capably. This is one reason we therapists get a good number of patients these days with problems of impotence, frigidity, and simple lack of feeling in the sexual act. We psychiatrists often hear the disappointed refrain, "We made love, but it wasn't much good."

Sex is the "last frontier," David Riesman meaningfully wrote fifteen years ago in *The Lonely Crowd*. Gerald Sykes in the same vein spoke of sex as the "last green thing." It is surely true that the zest, adventure, the discovering of vast new areas of feeling and passion in one's self, the trying out of one's power to arouse feelings in others—these are indeed "frontier experiences." They are normally present as part of the psycho-sexual development of every individual, and the young person rightly gets a validation of himself from such experiences. Sex in our society did in fact have this power in the several recent decades since the 1920s, when almost every other activity was becoming "other-directed," jaded, emptied of zest and adventure.

But for various reasons—one of them being that sex had to carry by itself the weight for the validation of the personality on practically all other levels as well—the frontier freshness and newness and challenge of sex were more and more lost. We are now living in the post-Riesman age, and are experiencing the difficult implications of the "other-directed," radar behavior. The "last frontier" has become a teeming Las Vegas and no frontier at all.

Young people can no longer get a bootlegged feeling of personal identity out of the sexual revolt, since there is nothing left to revolt against. A study of drug addiction among young people, published recently in the *New York Times*, reports the young people are saying that the revolt against parents and society, the "kick" of feeling their own "oats" which they used to get from sex, they now have to get from drugs. It is not surprising that for many youngsters what used to be called love-making is now so often experienced as a futile "panting palm to palm," in Aldous Huxley's predictive phrase, and that they tell us that it is hard for them to understand what the poets were talking about.

Nothing to revolt against, did I say? Well, there is obviously one thing left to revolt against, and that is sex itself. The frontier, the establishing of identity, can be, and not infrequently is for the young people, a revolt against sexuality entirely. A modern Lysistrata in robot's dress is rumbling at the gates of our cities, or if not rumbling, at least hovering. As sex becomes more machine-like, with passion irrelevant and then even pleasure diminishing, the problem comes full circle, and we find, *mirabile dictu*, a progression from an *anaesthetic* attitude to an *antiseptic* one. Sexual contact itself then tends to be avoided. The sexual revolution comes finally back on itself not with a bang but a whimper.

This is another and surely least constructive aspect of the new puritanism: it returns, finally, to an ascetic attitude. This is said graphically in a charming limerick that seems to have sprung up on some sophisticated campus:

> The word has come down from the Dean,
> That with the aid of the teaching machine,
>   King Oedipus Rex
>   Could have learned about sex
> Without ever touching the Queen.

What are the sources of these dilemmas? Perhaps if we can get some idea of what went wrong, we shall rediscover values in sex and love that will have genuine relevance for our age.

The essential element, I propose, in the dilemmas we have been discussing is the *banalization of sex and love*. Does not the tendency to make sex and love banal and vapid run through our whole culture? The plethora of books on the subject have one thing in common—they oversimplify sex and love, treating the topic like a combination of learning to play tennis and buying life insurance.

I have said above, describing the modern sophisticated man's dilemmas about sex, that he castrates himself "because he is afraid of his body, afraid of his compassionate roots in nature, afraid of the soil and his procreative powers." That is to say, something much more potent is going on in sexuality than one would gather from the oversimplified books on sex and love—something that still has the power to scare people. I believe banalization serves as a defense against this anxiety.

The widespread tendency among young people to "go steady"—premature monogamy, as it has been called—is an egregious illustration of our point. In my frequent visits to different college campuses for lectures, I have discussed this phenomenon with students, and something like the following seems to be going on. In our insecure age when all values are in flux, at least "the steady" is steady. Always having a date with the same fellow or girl on Saturday night, dancing with this same person through the entire party at college dances, always knowing this one is available, allays the anxiety of aloneness. But it also gets boring. This leads naturally enough to early sexuality: sex at least is something we can do when we run out of conversation—which happens often when the partners have not developed enough in their own right to be interesting very long to each other as persons. It is a strange fact in our society that what goes into building a relationship—the sharing of tastes, fantasies, dreams, hopes for the future and fears from the past—seems to make people more shy and vulnerable than going to bed with each other. They are more wary of the tenderness that goes with psychological and spiritual nakedness than they are of the physical nakedness in sexual intimacy.

Now substituting premature sexuality for meaningful intimate relationship relieves the young person's anxiety, but at the price of by-passing opportunity for further development. It seems that going steady, paradoxically, is related to promiscuity. I define "promiscuity" with Webster as the indiscriminate practice of sexuality whether with one person or a number: sex is indiscriminate when used in the service of security, or to fill up an emotional vacuum. But promiscuity is a lonely and alienating business. This loneliness becomes one of the pushes toward early marriage. Grasping each other in marriage gives a kind of security—a legal and social

security at least—which temporarily allays loneliness, but at the price of
the haunting dread of a boring marital future. *Each step in this pattern
has within it the banalization of sex and love.*

Now the question rarely asked is, are not these young people—possibly wiser in their innocence than their culture in its sophistication—fleeing
from some anxiety that is only too real? I propose that what scares them,
like what scares our "new sophisticate," is an element in sex and love
which is almost universally repressed in our culture, namely the *tragic,
daimonic element.*

By "daimonic"—which I hasten to say does not refer to little "de-
mons"—I mean the natural element within an individual, such as the
erotic drive, which has the power to take over the whole person. The
erotic urge pushes toward a general physiological aim, namely sexual release. But it can push the individual into all kinds of relationships without relation to the totality of his self.

But the potentially destructive effects of the daimonic are only the
reverse side of the person's constructive vitality, his passion and other
potentially creative activities. The Greeks used the term "daimon" to
describe the inspired urges of the poet. Socrates, indeed, speaks of his
"daimon" as his conscience. When this power goes awry—when one element takes over the total personality and drives the person into disinte-
grative behavior—it becomes "demon possession," the historical term for
psychosis. The daimonic can be either creative or destructive, but either
way it certainly is the opposite to banalization. The repression of the daimonic, tragic aspects of sex and love is directly related to their banalization in our culture.

The daimonic is present in all nature as blind, ambiguous power. But
only in man does it become allied with the tragic. For tragedy is the self-
conscious personal realization of being in the power of one element; thus
the Greeks defined tragedy as "inordinate desire," "pride," "reaching beyond just boundaries." We have only to call to mind Romeo and Juliet,
Abelard and Héloise, Tristan and Isolde, Helen of Troy, to see the power
of sexual love to seize a man and woman, lift them up into a whirlwind
that defies rational control and may destroy not only themselves but others at the same time. These stories are told over and over again in Western classic literature, and passed down from generation to generation, for
they come from a depth of human experience in sexual love that is profoundly significant. It is a level largely unmentioned in our day, much to
the impoverishment of our talk and writing about sex and love.

If we are to overcome banalization, we must take sex and love on
several different dimensions at once. Consider, as an analogy, Mozart's

music. In some portions of his music Mozart is engaged in elegant play. In other portions his music comes to us as pure sensuous pleasure, giving us a sheer delight. But in other portions, like the death music at the end of *Don Giovanni*, Mozart is profoundly shaking: we are gripped by fate and the daimonic as the inescapable tragedy rises before us. If Mozart had only the first element, play, he would sooner or later be banal and boring. If he presented only pure sensuality, he would become cloying; or if only the fire and death music, his creations would be too heavy. He is great because he writes on all three dimensions; and he must be listened to on all these levels at once.

Sexuality and love similarly have these three dimensions. Sex not only can be play, but probably an element of sheer play should be fairly regularly present. By this token, casual relationships in sex may have their gratification or meaning in the sharing of pleasure, tenderness, and so on. But if one's whole pattern and attitude toward sex is only casual, then sooner or later the playing itself becomes boring. The same is true about sensuality, obviously an element in any gratifying sex: if it has to carry the whole weight of the relationship, it becomes cloying. If sex is only sensuality, you sooner or later turn against sex itself. The third element, the daimonic and tragic, we emphasized here because that is the one almost wholly repressed in our culture, a fact that has much to do with the banalization of sex and love in our day. In a book like Erich Fromm's *Art of Loving*, for example, the daimonic, tragic element is completely missing.

An appreciation of the tragic and daimonic side of sex and love can help us not only to avoid oversimplification but to love better. Let me illustrate the constructive use of the daimonic. Every person, as a separate individual, experiences aloneness and strives to overcome his loneliness, this striving usually being some kind of love. Sexuality and love require self-assertion: if the person is not to some extent an individual in his own right, he will not only have nothing to give, nothing to relate with, but will be unable to assert himself and therefore unable to be genuinely part of the relationship. Both the man and woman need self-assertion in order to breach the separateness and make some kind of union with each other. Thus there is truth in the vernacular expressions about needing to "let oneself go" and "give oneself over" to the sexual act—or to any creative experience for that matter.

The psychotherapist Dr. Otto Rank once remarked in his latter years of practice that practically all the women who came to him had problems because their husbands were not assertive enough. Despite the oversimplified sound of this sentence, it contains a telling point: our effete cultivation of sex can make us so intellectual and detached about it that the simple power of the act evaporates, and we lose—and this loss is especially serious for women—the important elemental pleasure of "being taken," being "carried away." But the self-assertive power must be integrated with the other aspects of one's own personality, and with the total person of the mate; otherwise it becomes daimonic in the destructive sense.

Let us now summarize some values, potential and actual, in sexual love. There is, first, the overall value of enrichment and fulfilment of personality. This comes from expansion of one's awareness of one's self, one's feelings, one's experience of his capacity to give sexual pleasure and other feelings to the other person, and achieve thereby an expansion of meaning in interpersonal relationship. This fulfilment carries us beyond what we are at any given moment; I become in a literal sense more than I was. The most powerful symbol imaginable for this fulfilment is procreation—the possibility that a new being may be conceived and born. The "birth," however, can and does refer at the same time to the birth of new aspects of one's self.

Tenderness is a second value, a tenderness that is much more than indicated in that most unpoetic of all words, "togetherness." The experience of tenderness comes out of the fact that the two persons, longing as all individuals do to overcome the separateness and isolation to which we are all heir because we are individuals, can participate in a relationship that for the moment is not two isolated selves but a union. In this kind of sexual intercourse, the lover often does not know whether a particular sensation of delight is felt by him or by his loved one—and it doesn't make any difference anyway. A sharing takes place which is a new gestalt, a new being, a new field of magnetic force. A gratifying sexual relationship thus has the gestalt of a painting—the various parts, the colors, feelings, forms, unite to become a new whole.

There is the third value which occurs ideally at the moment of climax in sexual intercourse. This is the point when the lovers are carried not only beyond their personal isolation, but when a shift in consciousness seems to occur that unites them also with nature. In Hemingway's novel, *For Whom the Bell Tolls*, the older woman, Pilar, waits for the hero, Robert Jordan, and the girl he loves when they have gone ahead into the mountain to make love; and when they return, she asks, "Did the earth move?" The shaking of the earth seems to be a normal part of the momentary loss of awareness of the self and the surging up of a sudden consciousness that includes the "earth" as well. There is an accelerating experience of touch, contact, union to the point where for a moment the awareness of separateness is lost, blotted out in a cosmic feeling of oneness with nature. I do not wish this to sound too "ideal," for I think it is a quality, however subtle, in all love-making except the most depersonalized sort. And I also do not wish it to sound simply "mystic," for despite limitations in our awareness, I think it is an inseparable part of actual experience in the love act.

This leads us immediately to the fourth value, sex and love as the affirmation of the self. Despite the fact that many people in our culture use sex to get a short-circuited, ersatz sense of identity, sexual love can and ought to provide a sound and meaningful way to the sense of personal identity. We emerge from love-making normally with renewed vitality, a vitality which comes not from triumph or proof of one's strength but from the expansion of awareness. Probably in love-making there is always some element of sadness—as, to use our previous analogy, there is in practically all music no matter how joyful—in the reminder that we have not succeeded absolutely in losing our separateness, nor is the infantile hope that we could recover the womb made into reality, and even our increased self-awareness can also be a poignant reminder that none of us ever overcomes his loneliness completely. But by one's replenished sense of one's own significance in the love act he can accept these unavoidable human limitations.

A final value inheres in the curious phenomenon in love-making: that to be able to give to the other person is essential to one's own full pleasure in the act. This sounds like a banal moralism in our age of mechanization of sex and "release of tension" in sexual objects. But it is not sentimentality but a point which anyone can confirm in his own experience in the love act, that to give is essential to one's own pleasure. Many patients in psychotherapy find themselves discovering, generally with some surprise, that something is missing if they cannot "do something for," give something to the partner—the normal expression of which is the giving in the act of intercourse itself. Just as giving is essential to one's own full pleasure, the ability to receive is necessary in the love interrelationship also. If you cannot receive, your giving will be a domination of the partner. Conversely, if you cannot give, your receiving will leave you empty. The paradox is demonstrably true that the person who can only receive becomes empty, for he is unable actively to appropriate and make his own what he receives. I speak, thus, not of receiving as a passive phenomenon, but of *active receiving*: one knows he is receiving, feels it, absorbs it into his own experience whether he verbally acknowledges it or not, and is grateful for it.

Dr. Joseph Fletcher and others

Euthanasia—Medicine's Success Problem

The issues posed by euthanasia as a policy proposal in modern dying are like nearly all of the really vital and exciting issues which arise in connection with modern medicine: a consequence of medicine's advances and successes and not of its failures.

The question of a responsible control over dying as well as over living takes its shape as a success problem. Perhaps the most searching of the right–wrong, good–evil, desirable–undesirable questions with which we often preoccupy ourselves are problems posed by increasing knowledge and the control which competent knowledge provides over the whole human cycle of conception and health and dying.

There are two kinds of euthanasia. Sometimes exponents of the one refuse to defend the other. I mean, of course, passive or negative or indirect euthanasia; letting the patient go; ceasing and desisting from resuscitative and maintenance procedures, knowing that the consequence of doing so will be that death follows.

This indirect or negative or passive form of euthanasia is almost daily routine now in the hospitals of this land and most modern countries. The question whether or not to let the patient go is a constant practical problem in medical management, and not without its potential traps for the practitioners since, at least conceivably, suits for malpractice, for example, might be brought successfully against physicians who in one form or another might have recorded their decisions to cease and desist. Although on the non-legal side, as we all know, I hope, there is almost a straight across-the-board agreement among theologically oriented moralists—I mean Catholic and Protestant and Jewish and Humanist, in favor of the view that there is no basic ethical objection to this negative or passive euthanasia,

EUTHANASIA—MEDICINE'S SUCCESS PROBLEM Reprinted from the Proceedings of the Third Euthanasia Conference, December 5, 1970, with the permission of the Euthanasia Educational Council, 250 W. 57th Street, New York, N.Y. 10019.

and that we may quite justifiably decide to refrain from the employment of what Pope Pius called "extraordinary" means, given certain situational circumstances.

It is the very warp and woof of our social habits in the Anglo-Saxon culture and perhaps more broadly to think uncritically about value problems and moral questions with an assumption that some acts are intrinsically evil and universally wrong and absolutely unjustifiable. Yet pragmatically, all of us who have had anything like a mature experience of life and its infinite variety and its great endless combination of happiness and of pain, know perfectly well that there are many situations which in terms of a constructive and loving concern for human life, call for actions not logically consistent with the absolute norms by which we imagine we live.

I want to suggest then that there are at bottom three decisive ethical issues: right–wrong, good–evil, desirable–undesirable issues at stake underneath the discourse that a Society like this carries on.

The first of them is the quality of life. How are we to think—for ourselves and in our relations with others; how are we to think about claims of quality as distinguished from the claims of quantity; is quality of life equally important with its quantity, or less so or more so? What say you and why?

This is an issue posed almost as a presupposition. It is characteristic, at least, of a lot of the people we encounter to suppose that if quality of life and quantity—its fullness as over against its duration—should appear to come in conflict, quality is to be subordinated to quantity. But is that so? I would want to argue that it is the reverse proposition which is logically presupposed in all serious defenses of euthanasia as a policy.

The second of these rather bedrock questions is our thinking and in our doing can be put this way: Is death ever a friend? Is death always the enemy: If it is or could be a friend, when?

The third of these three basic and searching problems is whether we human beings are to make decisions about right–wrong, good–evil, and in particular whether to reserve or release a life, situationally, that is to say in terms of the precise and particular case, or abstractly in terms of synthetic generalizations which tend to falsify reality by refusing to recognize its variety.

Death has changed its shape—an observation also worth pulling into the picture of a cultural and anthropological sort. We do not have deathbed scenes anymore much, where the dying gather their family and friends about them and make their last testament of wisdom and advice. People are dying in hospitals now, and in homes, and increasingly of chronic rather than acute illnesses. They die comatose and betubed and sedated and aerated and glucosed and *non compos mentis*. It has come to be a pretty ugly business.

Maybe this is the price we pay for our increased medical control over the conditions of our dying. But even so, the value questions at stake persist and only take a somewhat more complex shape. They are not eliminated.

As a result of this new shape of dying, as we know, the white coat is beginning to lose something of its shine. In the psychology of medicine it is a matter of considerable concern now that people not only approach medicine with higher expectations of successful care and competent care, but also with far more conflicted feelings about what will happen to them in its course than they ever had before.

What does it mean to be human? This is the last question. I have not got nice, neat packaged answers. I do not think any of us do. This is in part what is troubling and also in part what is exciting about our enterprise. What are we to mean by humanness: What is it to be human—a human being? Or, if you like, what does it mean to be alive? Just redefining death in terms of encephalogram readings and deoxygenation of the brain or losses of spontaneous organic function elsewhere in the system and so on—this is not enough.

Is the question of when we have lost the human being—not the biological system, but the human being something that has to be answered in terms of such criteria or components as cerebration, memory, a sense of futurity, some evident clinical capacity for interpersonal relationship, will or purpose; lovingness—is this in the catalogue; a minimum IQ; utilitarian questions about social productivity and its potential?

We all talk rather slickly, especially in the theological and philosophical tradition about the *humanum*, but when you try to get people down to brass tacks to say, to specify, to itemize the component elements of the *humanum*, they fade away. We, in our Society, owe it to our physicians to help them elaborate some kind of rational and operable understanding of this question. At the terminal end of the human cycle is there a human being present or recoverable, and not just life in the biological sense?

I welcome the fact that last April at the American Assembly at Arden House, Dr. Russell Nelson of the American Association of Medical Colleges, and Judge Russell Marvin Frankel of the New York Federal District Court, and such like persons, adopted among other things this statement for public use: "We should make a study of whether suicide and other laws can be modified to enable victims of terminal illnesses to avoid the unwelcomed prolongation of life with assistance and without penalty."

Ours is obviously not by any means either a lost or even neglected cause. We are getting more support all the time.

DISCUSSION AND COMMENT FROM THE FLOOR

CHAIRMAN: Will you please give your name as you ask a question or make a comment.

MR. TROWBRIDGE: I'd like to ask Dr. Fletcher this question. What is the moral and ethical difference between active and passive euthanasia?

DR. FLETCHER: It is often argued, sometimes very skillfully, that our judgment must be influenced by means as well as by the ends we seek, and that a worthy end such as the abatement of useless suffering, good as it is, cannot of itself justify the use of evil means. That is to say—murder. We must decide whether in our ethical thinking we're going to determine the rightness or wrongness of any act, including one of euthanasia. We must also decide whether we are to think in terms of the notion that some acts are intrinsically right or wrong; or in more consequentialist terms and decide the rightness or the wrongness of an act in terms of our estimate of its foreseeable consequences.

My own personal answer to your question would be to override this distinction and to assert over against it that in the last analysis the only way to justify any means is precisely in terms of the end they seek. Since the end sought in both forms of euthanasia is the same, namely release from a life no longer desirable, either of these forms, depending upon the situation could be the right one to adopt.

DR. LEBENSOHN: I would like to ask the medical men on the panel how they could reconcile the two images of the physician; one, the healer and the giver of hope and the preserver of life, with the person who is also the instrument for the termination of life?

It seems to me that this is a very difficult matter to reconcile. Hope— this is one of the physician's greatest tools, one of his greatest instruments. His mere presence in a room is a symbol of hope, whether he has anything to give or not. If he is associated in the mind of the patient or of the public with being also the terminator of life or the instrument for its termination, I think there is going to be a great conflict, fear and distrust, similar to that which occurred in the time of Rome, where the poisoners were very prevalent.

I would like to ask how you can be both the healer and the giver of hope and the terminator of life. How can you reconcile these two?

DR. SAFFRON: I am not sure I can answer this to your satisfaction. I can only speak from my personal experience as a physician. Naturally with my patients, I hope to inspire them with hope and a desire to live. That is the function, the primary obligation of the physician. However, all physicians are eventually confronted with terminal situations such as have been described here. I believe that this is a very personal problem that the physician must wrestle with and come to a decision of his own. Dr. Fletcher gave the impression that there should be a more active method of euthanasia. I am not convinced of this yet. I feel that the passive approach solves many problems. If you stop all active measures, keep the patient comfortable and let him gradually find his release. I think that is what most physicians do anyhow.

Actually, physicians throughout the centuries have been practicing passive euthanasia. Hippocrates himself said that when you realize that you can do no more, you must relax your active therapy. This is not a new concept at all. I believe that's the way we should approach it.

DR. PERCY KLINGENSTEIN: I think that the question that has been raised depends a good deal, too, upon the physician's subconscious reaction to life and death. So many physicians would say, "I will never tell a patient that he has cancer." I think the reason is that he himself is afraid of the possibility that he may be some day faced with it and cannot measure up to it. I think a physician's knowledge and a physician's emotional reactions are in part related to how he will manage the situation. I feel that he would manage it pretty much as Dr. Saffron has said he would—in a more passive than active phase.

I remember many years ago in a hospital for chronically and terminally ill patients, it was only natural that the resident and house staff should in some instances take the law into their own hands and very humanely put an end to the patient's suffering. This got around to the Administration and there was an investigation. These physicians were called upon the carpet and very seriously censured. Nevertheless I am sure that a great deal of this goes on today in hospitals that take care of terminally ill patients. However, it is not done, let me say, in the open.

ABIGAIL VAN BUREN: With regard to suicide, is there a legal voice present who could tell me if there has ever been a precedent of having punished anyone for suicide. If so, what would that legal punishment be?

COMMENT FROM THE FLOOR: I'm not a lawyer, but I can say this. As we all know, when anyone attempts suicide, we rush him to an insane asylum darn quick.

CYRIL MEANS, Professor of Law: In reply to the question whether or not suicide has ever been punished by the law, the answer is yes. In common law it was punished by the forfeiture of the suicide's goods and chattels. This, of course, was posthumous, but it was nevertheless the punishment which the law did impose. This was abolished rather early in the history of this State. Actually, since 1881 suicide itself has not been an offense in New York law; and since 1910, if I remember correctly, attempted suicide by the person himself has not been an offense. However, aiding another person to commit suicide has always been an offense and still is. Although since 1965, there have been two degrees of it; one, which makes it equivalent to murder when your motives are improper; and the other which makes it a very low misdemeanor if the motives are thought to be worthy, which would probably be the case in most instances of aiding a person to commit euthanasia.

John W. Gardner

College and the Alternatives

Who Should Go to College

All of the conflicting and confusing notions which Americans have concerning equality, excellence and the encouragement of talent may be observed with crystal clarity in the current discussions of "who should go to college." In the years ahead these discussions will become more heated. Pressure of enrollments will make it far harder to get into the better colleges, and there will be lively debate over who has a "right" to a college education.

A good deal of this debate will center around issues of quality versus quantity in education. Douglas Bush eloquently enunciated one extreme position in the phrase, "Education for all is education for none."

Arguments about quality in higher education tend to be heated and rather pointless. There are many reasons why such conversations become muddled, the foremost being that they so often degenerate into arguments over "elite" versus "mass" education. People who engage in these arguments are like the two washerwomen Sydney Smith observed leaning out of their back windows and quarreling with each other across the alley: "They could never agree," Smith said, "because they were arguing from different premises." In the case of arguments over "elite" versus "mass" education, I am convinced that both premises should be vacated, because behind the arguments is the assumption that a society must decide whether it wishes to educate a few people exceedingly well *or* to educate a great number of people rather badly.

This is an imaginary dilemma. It is possible to have excellence in education and at the same time to seek to educate everyone to the limit of his ability. A society such as ours has no choice but to seek the development of human potentialities at all levels. It takes more than an educated elite to run a complex, technological society. Every modern, industrialized society is learning that hard lesson.

The notion that so-called quality education and so-called mass education are mutually exclusive is woefully out of date. It would not have survived at all were there not a few remarkably archaic characters in our midst. We all know that some of the people calling most noisily for quality in education are those who were *never* reconciled to the widespread extension of educational opportunity. To such individuals there is something inherently vulgar about large numbers of people. At the other extreme are the fanatics who believe that the chief goal for higher education should be to get as many youngsters as possible—regardless of ability— into college classrooms. Such individuals regard quality as a concept smacking faintly of Louis XIV.

But neither extreme speaks for the American people, and neither expresses the true issues that pose themselves today. It would be fatal to allow ourselves to be tempted into an anachronistic debate. *We must seek excellence in a context of concern for all.* A democracy, no less than any other form of society, must foster excellence if it is to survive; and it should not allow the emotional scars of old battles to confuse it on this point.

Educating everyone up to the limit of his ability does not mean sending everyone to college. Part of any final answer to the college problem must be some revision of an altogether false emphasis which the American people are coming to place on college education. This false emphasis is the source of great difficulties for us. In Virginia they tell the story of the kindly Episcopal minister who was asked whether the Episcopal Church was the only path to salvation. The minister shook his head—a bit sadly, perhaps. "No, there are other paths," he said, and then added, "but no gentleman would choose them." Some of our attitudes toward college education verge dangerously on the same position.

There are some people who seem to favor almost limitless expansion of college attendance. One hears the phrase "everyone has a right to go to college." It is easy to dispose of this position in its extreme form. There are some youngsters whose mental deficiency is so severe that they cannot enter the first grade. There are a number of youngsters out of every hundred whose mental limitations make it impossible for them to get as far as junior high school. There are many more who can progress through high school only if they are placed in special programs which take into account their academic limitations. These "slow learners" could not complete high school if they were required to enroll in a college-preparatory curriculum.

It is true that some who fall in this group would not be there if it were not for social and economic handicaps. But for most of them, there is no convincing evidence that social handicaps are a major factor in their academic limitations. Children with severe or moderate intellectual limitations appear not infrequently in families which are able to give them every advantage, and in which the possibilities of treatment have been exhaustively explored. Such children can be helped by intelligent attention, but the hope that any major change can be accomplished in their academic limitations is usually doomed to disappointment.

With each higher grade an increasing number of youngsters find it difficult or impossible to keep up with the work. Some drop out. Some transfer to vocational or industrial arts programs. A great many never complete high school.

Presumably, college students should only be drawn from the group which is able to get through high school. So the question becomes: "Should all high school graduates go to college?" The answer most frequently heard is that "all should go to college who are qualified for it"— but what do we mean by *qualified?* Probably less than 1 per cent of the college-age population is qualified to attend the California Institute of Technology. There are other colleges where 10, 20, 40 or 60 per cent of the college-age population is qualified to attend.

It would be possible to create institutions with standards so low that 90 per cent of the college-age population could qualify. In order to do so it would be necessary only to water down the curriculum and provide simpler subjects. Pushed to its extreme, the logic of this position would lead us to the establishment of institutions at about the intellectual level of summer camps. We could then include almost all of the population in these make-believe colleges.

Let us pursue this depressing thought. If it were certain that almost all of the eighteen- to twenty-two-year-old population could benefit greatly by full-time attendance at "colleges" of this sort, no one could reasonably object. But one must look with extreme skepticism upon the notion that all high school graduates can profit by continued formal schooling. There is no question that they can profit by continued *education*. But the character of this education will vary from one youngster to the next. Some will profit by continued book learning; others by some kind of vocational training; still others by learning on the job. Others may require other kinds of growth experiences.

Because college has gained extraordinary prestige, we are tempted to assume that the only useful learning and growth comes from attending such an institution, listening to professors talk from platforms, and reproducing required information on occasions called examinations. This is an extremely constricting notion. Even in the case of intellectually gifted individuals, it is a mistake to assume that the only kind of learning they can accomplish is in school. Many gifted individuals might be better off if they could be exposed to alternative growth experiences.

In the case of the youngster who is not very talented academically, forced continuance of education may simply prolong a situation in which he is doomed to failure. Many a youngster of low ability has been kept on pointlessly in a school which taught him no vocation, exposed him to continuous failure and then sent him out into the world with a record which convinced employers that he must forever afterward be limited to unskilled or semi-skilled work. This is not a sensible way to conserve human resources.

Properly understood, the college or university is the instrument of *one kind of further education of those whose capacities fit them for that kind of education*. It should not be regarded as the sole means of establishing one's human worth. It should not be seen as the unique key to happiness, self-respect and inner confidence.

We have all done our bit to foster these misconceptions. And the root of the difficulty is our bad habit of assuming that the only meaningful life is the "successful" life, defining success in terms of high personal attainment in the world's eyes. Today attendance at college has become virtually a prerequisite of high attainment in the world's eyes, so that it becomes, in the false value framework we have created, the only passport to a meaningful life. No wonder our colleges are crowded.

The crowding in our colleges is less regrettable than the confusion in our values. *Human dignity and worth should be assessed only in terms of those qualities of mind and spirit that are within the reach of every human being.*

This is not to say that we should not value achievement. We should value it exceedingly. It is simply to say that achievement should not be confused with human worth. Our recognition of the dignity and worth of the individual is based upon moral imperatives and should be of universal application. In other words, everyone has a "right" to that recognition. Being a college graduate involves qualities of mind which can never be universally possessed. Everyone does not have a right to be a college graduate, any more than everyone has a right to run a four-minute mile.

What we are really seeking is what James Conant had in mind when he said that the American people are concerned not only for equality of opportunity but for equality of respect. Every human being wishes to be respected regardless of his ability, and in moral terms we are bound to grant him that right. The more we allow the impression to get abroad that only the college man or woman is worthy of respect in our society, the more we contribute to a fatal confusion which works to the injury of all concerned. If we make the confusing assumption that college is the sole cradle of human dignity, need we be surprised that every citizen demands to be rocked in that cradle?

The Need for Institutional Diversity

But a scaling down of our emphasis on college education is only part of the answer. Another important part of the answer must be a greatly increased emphasis upon individual differences, upon many kinds of talent, upon the immensely varied ways in which individual potentialities may be realized.

If we develop such an indomitable concern for individual differences, we will learn to laugh at the assumption that a college education is the only avenue to human dignity and social worth. We would educate some youngsters by sending them on to college. We would educate others in other ways. We would develop an enormous variety of patterns to fit the enormous variety of individuals. And no pattern would be regarded as socially superior or involving greater human dignity than any other pattern.

But the plain fact is that college education is firmly associated in the public mind with personal advancement, upward social mobility, market value and self-esteem. And if enough of the American people believe that one must attend college in order to be accorded respect and confidence, then the very unanimity of opinion makes the generalization true.

It is particularly true, unfortunately, in the crude categories of the employment file. A cynical friend of mine said recently, "Everyone has two personalities these days—the one under his hat and the one in his employment file. The latter is the most important—and it is made up of primitive categories. Have you held too many jobs? (Never mind why.) Did you go to a good college? (Never mind if you were the campus beachcomber.)

Does your job record show a steady rise in responsibilities? (Never mind if you played politics every inch of the way.)"

If we are to do justice to individual differences, if we are to provide suitable education for each of the young men and women who crowd into our colleges and universities, then we must cultivate diversity in our higher educational system to correspond to the diversity of the clientele. There is no other way to handle within one system the enormously disparate human capacities, levels of preparedness and motivations which flow into our colleges and universities.

But we cannot hope to create or to maintain such diversity unless we honor the various aspects of that diversity. Each of the different kinds of institutions has a significant part to play in creating the total pattern, and each should be allowed to play its role with honor and recognition.

We do not want all institutions to be alike. We want institutions to develop their individualities and to keep those individualities. None must be ashamed of its distinctive features so long as it is doing something that contributes importantly to the total pattern, and so long as it is striving for excellence in performance. The highly selective, small liberal arts college should not be afraid to remain small. The large urban institution should not be ashamed that it is large. The technical institute should not be apologetic about being a technical institute. Each institution should pride itself on the role that it has chosen to play and on the special contribution which it brings to the total pattern of American higher education.

Such diversity is the only possible answer to the fact of individual differences in ability and aspirations. And furthermore, it is the only means of achieving *quality* within a framework of quantity. For we must not forget the primacy of our concern for excellence. We must have diversity, but we must also expect that every institution which makes up that diversity will be striving, in its own way, for excellence. This may require a new way of thinking about excellence in higher education—a conception that would be applicable in terms of the objectives of the institution. As things now stand, the word *excellence* is all too often reserved for the dozen or two dozen institutions which stand at the very zenith of our higher education in terms of faculty distinction, selectivity of students and difficulty of curriculum. In these terms it is simply impossible to speak of a junior college, for example, as excellent. Yet sensible men can easily conceive of excellence in a junior college.

The traditionalist might say, "Of course! Let Princeton create a junior college and one would have an institution of unquestionable excellence!" That may be correct, but it may also lead us down precisely the wrong path. If Princeton Junior College were excellent, it might not be excellent in the most important way that a community college can be excellent.

It might simply be a truncated version of Princeton. A comparably mean-ingless result would be achieved if General Motors tried to add to its line of low-priced cars by marketing the front half of a Cadillac.

We shall have to be more flexible than that in our conception of excellence. We must develop a point of view that permits each kind of institution to achieve excellence *in terms of its own objectives.*

In higher education as in everything else there is no excellent per-formance without high morale. No morale, no excellence! And in a great many of our colleges and universities the most stubborn enemy of high morale has been a kind of hopelessness on the part of both administration and faculty—hopelessness about ever achieving distinction as an institution. Not only are such attitudes a corrosive influence on morale, they make it virtually certain that the institution will never achieve even that kind of excellence which is within its reach. For there *is* a kind of excellence within the reach of every institution.

In short, we reject the notion that excellence is something that can only be experienced in the most rarified strata of higher education. It may be experienced at every level and in every serious kind of higher education. And not only may it be experienced everywhere, but we must *demand* it everywhere. We must ask for excellence in every form which higher educa-tion takes. We should not ask it lightly or amiably or good naturedly; we should demand it vigorously and insistently. We should assert that a stub-born striving for excellence is the price of admission to reputable educa-tional circles, and that those institutions not characterized by this striving are the slatterns of higher education.

We must make the same challenging demands of students. We must never make the insolent and degrading assumption that young people unfitted for the most demanding fields of intellectual endeavor are in-capable of rigorous attention to *some sort of standards.* It is an appalling error to assume—as some of our institutions seem to have assumed—that young men and women incapable of the highest standards of intellectual excellence are incapable of any standards whatsoever, and can properly be subjected to shoddy, slovenly and trashy educational fare. College should be a demanding as well as an enriching experience—demanding for the brilliant youngster at a high level of expectation and for the less brilliant at a more modest level.

It is no sin to let average as well as brilliant youngsters into college. It *is* a sin to let any substantial portion of them—average or brilliant—drift through college without effort, without growth and without a goal. That is the real scandal in many of our institutions.

Though we must make enormous concessions to individual differences in aptitude, we may properly expect that every form of education be such as to stretch the individual to the utmost of his potentialities. And we must expect each student to strive for excellence in terms of the kind of excellence that is within his reach. Here again we must recognize that there may be excellence or shoddiness in every line of human endeavor. We must learn to honor excellence (indeed to *demand* it) in every socially accepted human activity, however humble the activity, and to scorn shoddiness, however exalted the activity. As I said in another connection: "An excellent plumber is infinitely more admirable than an incompetent philosopher. The society which scorns excellence in plumbing because plumbing is a humble activity and tolerates shoddiness in philosophy because it is an exalted activity will have neither good plumbing nor good philosophy. Neither its pipes nor its theories will hold water."

Opportunities Other Than College

Not long ago the mother of two teen-age boys came to me for advice. "Roger made a fine record in high school," she explained, "and when he was a senior we had exciting discussions of all the colleges he was interested in. Now Bobby comes along with terrible grades, and when the question of his future arises a silence descends on the dinner table. It breaks my heart!"

I knew something about Bobby's scholastic limitations, which were notable, and I asked warily what I might do to help.

"The high school principal says that with his record no college will take him," she said, "and that if one did take him he wouldn't last. I can't reconcile myself to that!"

"Have you discussed any possibilities other than college?" I asked.

She shook her head. "His father says he can get him a job driving a delivery truck. But I think he just says that to jar Bobby."

It took some time for me to explain all that I thought was deplorable in her attitude and that of her husband. Parents of academically limited children should not act as though any outcome other than college is a fate worse than death. By doing so they rule out of discussion a world of significant possibilities; and the failure to think constructively about those possibilities is a disfavor to the young person.

The great prestige which college education has achieved in our society leads us to assume—quite incorrectly—that it is the only form of continued learning after high school. The assumption is that the young person either goes to college and continues to learn, or goes to work and stops learning. Most parents, deans, counselors—indeed the young people themselves—have given little or no thought to the many ways of learning and growing which do not involve college. The result is that the path to college appears to be the only exciting possibility, the only path to self-development. No wonder many who lack the qualifications for college insist on having a try at it.

The young person who does not go on to college should look forward to just as active a period of growth and learning in the post-high school years as does the college youngster.

The nature of this continued learning will depend on the young person's interests and capacities. The bright youngster who has stayed out of college for financial reasons will require a different kind of program from that of the youngster who stayed out for lack of ability.

The majority of young people—at least, of boys—who terminate their education short of college do so because they lack academic ability. Most have had unrewarding experiences in the classroom and have a negative attitude toward anything labeled "learning" or "education." Even if they are not bitter about their school experiences, they are likely to feel that, having tried that path and failed, their salvation lies elsewhere. *What they must recognize is that there are many kinds of further learning outside formal high school and college programs. The fact that they have not succeeded in high school simply means that they must continue their learning in other kinds of situations.*

The opportunities for further education of boys and girls who leave the formal educational system are numerous and varied.

Training programs within industrial corporations have expanded enormously and constitute a respectable proportion of all education today. Apprenticeship systems are not as universal as they used to be in the skilled crafts or trades, but they are still in operation in every major industry, and offer wide opportunities for the ambitious youngster. (He must be warned, however, that in some of the older crafts and trades entry is jealously guarded; indeed in some it is held within family lines as a hereditary right.)

A few labor unions have impressive educational programs. The International Ladies Garment Workers Union, for example, conducts European tours, sponsors lecture series and offers a wide variety of courses.

Various branches of government offer jobs to high school graduates which involve an opportunity to learn while working. The Armed Services offer training in a great many occupational specialties.

Night classes in the public schools are breaking all attendance records; and more than one quarter of present attendance is in trade courses for semi-skilled or unskilled workers. These courses offer a surprising range of interesting opportunities for the young person who wishes to test his aptitudes and to develop various skills.

There also exist, in the amazingly variegated pattern of American education, many special schools—art schools, music schools, nursing schools and the like—which should be considered by the young person not going on to college. The boy who wishes to become an X-ray technician and the girl who wishes to be a practical nurse, for example, will find a great many schools throughout the country at which they may receive training.

Correspondence study offers the most flexible opportunities for study beyond high school, but the young people who do not go on to college usually have little enthusiasm for paper-and-pencil work, and that is what correspondence study amounts to. For those who can overcome this handicap, there is an open door to almost any conceivable subject. One can study accountancy or blueprint reading, creative writing or diesel mechanics, watch repairing or dressmaking, finger-printing or foreign languages, music or petroleum technology. Almost the only limits are one's own interest and ability.

Educational opportunities on radio and television continue to expand. In certain parts of the country the high school graduate can study a considerable range of subjects through this medium—e.g., salesmanship, typing, composition, reading improvement and foreign languages.

Finally, jobs themselves are a form of education. Today most young people have a wide choice of jobs. They should look at the array of jobs available not simply from the standpoint of money and convenience but from the standpoint of their own further growth. If the young man is willing to think hard about his own abilities and interests, and then to look at available jobs as opportunities for self-development, he can look forward to years of learning and growth at least as rewarding as anything a college student might experience.

The possibilities reviewed here are by no means exhaustive, but they suggest the diverse paths open to the noncollege student. Some youngsters will want to get as far away as possible from "book learning" and some will not. Some will want vocational education and others may wish to continue their general education. Some will shun anything labeled a "school" or "course." But all should somehow continue learning.

In order to help young people in this direction, the following steps are essential:

1. We must make available to young people far more information than they now have on post-high school opportunities other than college.

2. Parents, teachers and high school counselors must recognize that if the youngster who is not going to college is to continue his growth and learning he must receive as much sagacious help and counsel as a college-bound student.

3. We must do what we can to alter the negative attitude toward education held by many youngsters who fail to go on to college. They must understand that they have been exposed to only one kind of learning

experience and that the failures and frustrations encountered in school are not necessarily predictive of failure in every other kind of learning.

4. We must enable the young person to understand that his stature as an individual and his value as a member of society depend upon continued learning—not just for four years or a decade, but throughout life.

Mark Harris

Why Read Newspapers?

I seldom read a newspaper, and you shouldn't read one, either; I seldom watch television; seldom pick up a popular magazine, though I read Time magazine almost every week when I lived in Hiroshima in 1957–'58. I listen to FM radio in the car. Last year, a San Francisco professor said to me: "But how would you know about Watergate?" Come on, Leonard (I replied), a man or a woman of instinct knows about Watergate from history, from literature.

Even so, Leonard couldn't believe me. People addicted to the daily amusement of the media become extremely angry with me for tampering with their addiction. They stare at me. They mistrust their ears. They have believed from childhood that it is a civic duty to read the newspapers, a good man "keeps up with the news," just as a good man bathes regularly and slows his car at school crossings.

Once, when I was reporting for a magazine, I went to see Robert Frost. I asked him how he received the news. "From people I know," he said—his main source, I gathered. (His radio, he said, made "a queer streaky noise.")

It's enough. Surrender your addiction and you'll see that you haven't missed a thing. Try it awhile and you'll see how well you'll get along without the *news*, as it is called. "To a philosopher all *news*, as it is called, is gossip, and they who edit and read it are old women over their tea." So said Henry David Thoreau, and in the same passage: "And I am sure that I never read any memorable news in a newspaper. If we read of one man robbed, or murdered, or killed by accident, or one house burned, or one vessel wrecked, or one steamboat blown up, or one cow run over on the Western Railroad, or one mad dog killed, or one lot of grasshoppers in the winter—we never need read of another. One is enough. If you are acquainted with the principle, what do you care for . . . myriad instances and applications?"

I never knew why Leonard seemed unable to cultivate his intuitions. He was of an age to be ready to cease collecting data and begin forming thoughts of his own. For a while, some years ago, I had thought him ready for something else when I saw him traveling about San Francisco in his black beard and long Hindu robe, until the day I spied him standing at a street corner gaping at the headlines on the rack. Behind the beard and under the robe, it was only Leonard requiring myriad instances.

Somewhere George Bernard Shaw called the newspaper the poor man's university, as it may have been in his time. It may still be. It may also be a fire bell, an alarm system, a bulletin of more or less essential data (the weather, the times of the tides, stock-market numbers, ball scores, movie schedules). Above all, it still may be, used with caution, a kind of gross introduction to life for younger people.

Unfortunately, nowadays the media appear also to be the university man's university, his own having failed to impress upon him the possibilities of his own mind. Middle-aged and older people in general underestimate their own powers of observation. They devour the media when in fact they might preserve both time and energy by listening to the outer world with partial attention only. Those of us who have seen the cycles around so many times need no longer be diverted by repetition—unless, of course, it's repetition we care for, as a kind of simple-minded amusement. We are capable of an economy of observation. We know what we can do without. We know that all games are less than "crucial," and we know the difference between a crisis and a merely recurring event. The older we grow the more shrewdly we draw sound conclusions from minimal clues.

The news that really matters will reach us: If it really matters it forces itself upon us. We will be compensated for the lost data by our experienced perceptions. The mind provides surprises once we free it from the sight and sound of the powerful attractions of *today*, permitting it privacy, silence and self-direction. Often we then think past the raucous diversions to the truer issues.

The media are the opiate of the people. They substitute for our minds, which wither every day for lack of the habit of using them. We have permitted the world of the journalist to become more real to us than the world of our senses, thus restricting our options and suffocating our imagination. Once, in San Francisco, I remarked to a professor (not Leonard but another) that I seldom read The Chronicle. He replied: "Oh, you read The Examiner." He began to compare the two newspapers, point for point. To the brain damaged by media, whenever two objects exist they must be placed in competition—cops and robbers, success and failure, Democrats and Republicans, win and lose, guilty and innocent, happy and sad, yes and no. A conflict must always be established, a race, a contest; and, whenever possible, someone must be drawn into the trap of saying something provocative about someone else. Addicts of the media become confined to limited alternatives. No third, no fourth, no limitless possibilities exist, nor even shades of those we have. There isn't time.

The needs of the newsman become the unacknowledged needs of his reader. The newsman must hurry. Why should the reader also hurry? "The viewer will turn it off," says the newsman, to which the viewer should reply: "I won't turn it off; tell me the whole truth, if you can." The newsman replies: "We can't do it that way. We require a mass audience."

To that I say: "For 'can't' read 'won't.' "

Who is this press, this editor, this columnist, this editorialist who selects and evaluates the *news*, as it is called, day by day for us? To what is this anchorman anchored? You who have achieved age, education and experience sufficient to carry you beyond the need for the daily news—the *hourly* news!—are giving your minds to a group called "journalists," who would have appeared to you suave and breathlessly urbane when you were much younger than you are.

Consider the prose you read or hear. Its style disqualifies it. It talks too simplistically, lacking emotional depth or range. It lacks not only a sense of history but even the memory of yesterday. (The story is told of a critic who called a certain work in June "the best of the decade," but, six months later, failed to place it on his list of "the 10 best of the year.")

Long ago, when I was a young reporter for the old International News Service, I was required to work the word "today" into the first sentence of every article. I believed in my mission. Everything happened "today," though people kept telling me about yesterday and tomorrow. I was a brash fellow, invading other people's emotions, demanding answers to my factual questions in the midst of their most awful crisis; all that stopped me were tears. (To news reporters, tears are the ultimate expression.) I was typical of men and women bringing you your *news*, as it is called. What makes reporters think their findings ought to be *your* quest, and why are you fool enough to agree?

Of course, I never "covered" people who intimidated me. I mainly "covered" loud or self-proclaiming people who had no reticence about their sales message. I "covered" the periphery, never the center.

I cannot see that anything has changed since I walked off my beat. Only hard data are useful to the press. Unable to negotiate meditation, the media turn it off. Reporters cannot believe things they cannot instantly absorb, jot down, add up and phone in. This limitation of the media prevents them from bringing to that public which they claim to serve the good ideas of our more deliberate contemporaries. I hear no news of universities except football and nonsense, no news of art except artists' peculiarities. Nor do I note any balance in music on commercial television.

The media treat with cynicism or derision anything they cannot comprehend. Difficult matters cannot be news; there isn't time. "You know," said the playwright Arthur Miller, who knew Marilyn Monroe, "journalists usually come around with an angle. They *have* to. They simply never get the time or the opportunity to hang around long enough to decide anything. Over the years, the angle becomes the easiest thing to do, and it's gotten, in Marilyn's case, to be very fruitful in terms of copy. And they keep pounding her all the time until that thing becomes reality. By that time, it's impossible to imagine anything else."

I cringe to hear that phrase so common among reporters: "In other words. . . ." Even worse: "What you're really saying is. . . ." Reporters are insensitive to the needs, the realities or the deeper aspirations of people they undertake to record. "My grounds for wanting to let him have both fists in succession in the middle of the face," Frost wrote of a certain newspaperman, "are chiefly that he stated me so much worse than I know how to state myself."

"There are two great mental dangers in journalism," wrote Leonard Woolf, whose analysis of the mind of the journalist strikes me as being an analysis of the mind of America submerged in media—media which have atomized our lives into units called days and deprived us of our necessary memories. "The first is most virulent among editors. It creates a kaleidoscopic, chaotic, perpetual motion rhythm of the mind. As soon as you have produced one number of your paper, you have to begin thinking of and planning the next. Your mind gets into the habit of opening and shutting at regular intervals of 24 hours or seven days like the shells of a mussel or the shutter of a camera, and everything in your life gets to be determined and conditioned by this interval. . . .

"The second occupational disease of journalism is closely connected with the first, but it affects all journalists, not merely editors. What you write for a paper you write for a moment of time, the moment being a morning or evening, a day, a week or three months. Whatever the length of the moment, what you produce is written under the shadow of ephe-merality; you write it not in the mould of eternity, but for consumption with the kipper or eggs and bacon at the breakfast table or to distract someone from falling asleep in a railway carriage."

When I was a young reporter for I.N.S. (working the word "today" into every first sentence), I was both the dupe and the beneficiary of that left wing which told us, whatever else it told us, that the newspapers and the radio were wicked organs of the capitalist class. Anything said by the media was therefore a lie.

Poor old innocent left wing—its mistake lay in imagining that the media cared much for principles at all. The first principle of the media is to serve themselves by serving their customer, a nice reconciliation which the customer himself assists. As I developed a tolerance for paradox, I saw that the left wing was always quoting, as needed, the very wicked capitalist press it deplored. People of the left wing, along with people of almost every other wing, view as triumphs any notice taken of them by these very devils of capitalism—their words reported, their photographs taken, their meetings attended, their petitions announced, their issues pondered, their books reviewed, their poems printed. The hippies of San Francisco in re-volt against bourgeois entrapment dashed for blocks on bare feet to be captured by the capitalist television camera.

The villain of 1940 is the hero of 1974: The persistence of the press delivered Watergate, although Frost and Thoreau could have guessed it, and so could you if you weren't an addict. Sophisticated as you are, don't you see that the newspaper is a *business*? And the *news*, as it is called, is the product the business sells—not principles or truth, or beauty, or liberty, or justice.

Watergate was the ultimate in entertainment. The media are not only business but show business, featuring hard plots, clear conflicts, games, a star system. The principles of news coverage are identical with the prin-ciples of dramatic entertainment: Give the people what they want, follow the trends, keep sacred the customer's expectations. Watergate was perfect. In the main, people prefer second-rate drama, action broad rather than deep, nothing subtle. A great many people who like to think of themselves as disdainful of second-rate drama drink their fill of it when it comes dis-guised as news, presumably pregnant with meaning and import.

Watergate-*cum*-impeachment was only the heroism of good business, though the media claimed that the extensive coverage demonstrated to the American people the process of government. If so, at what cost? During the months of Watergate, thousands of people suffered starvation; the world was progressively endangered by military expansion and ecological neglect. By what corruption of values were the crises of Richard Nixon a million times as newsworthy as the facts of human starvation?

Unfortunately, show business calls not for the summoning of our guilts, but for a single character at the center of the action (king, say, or President), and a standard cast drawn from theater as we have known it: aides and lieutenants, Senators and judges, good guys, bad guys, cops, robbers, spies and jesters—or for the modern touch, an intellectual and his psychiatrist, green cash, electronic surveillance, one clean-cut young man under pain of conscience, one older man bathed by religious conversion.

As happens in poor but popular drama, the Watergate plot was extremely easy to follow, no thought was required, and, in any case, mild intricacies were repeatedly explained by the media serving as Greek chorus. The motives of the actors were obvious and uninteresting: They were stealing money in order to possess it. No human complexity was suggested, and the performance thus was made to order for a relaxed mass audience on one hand, and, on the other, for addicts of the media deceiving themselves that this easy amusement was really rich with redeeming social value.

The end of the long evening would be clear. Nothing would be left vague, nothing indefinite. Since the curtain would close upon the clarity of a vote, the addict and everyone would know absolutely who won, who lost, and sink immediately into a slough of anticlimax, as after the Super Bowl or the seventh game of the World Series. Fresh out of long-running shows, the addict would yearn for another—and, indeed, the media would serve one up very soon.

Meanwhile, the unspeakable problems of society remain, not merely ignored but effectively obscured by thousands of reporters roaming the world with a marvelous opportunity for revealing the urgent news of the world if only they were encouraged to do so. True news comes to us very slowly, if at all, though we boast of our incredible advances toward instantaneous communication. It's not news, those awful things: Starving people are bad box-office. In their self-interest, the media speak often of "the people's right to know," which is to say "the right of the press to go wherever it wants to go." Which is to say, finally, the right of the media to conduct their own business in their own profit-taking manner, according to their own rules.

When I was a boy in grade school in Mount Vernon, N.Y., our teachers were skeptical of the press. As I recall, I was raised to think of newspapers, magazines and radio as doubtful sources, partisan, out there in search of something other than truth. It was thought good to be "up on current events," but for that we subscribed to little magazines specially prepared for school children.

Nowadays, I hear of newspapers and magazines adopted or recommended in schools as fine official sources, and here and there I wince to hear allusions to the child's *duty* to read the newspaper and to watch the news on television. Bulletin boards at public schools are laden with newspaper clippings by the ton. To be mentioned in the newspaper is thought to be a mark of distinction: One achieves reality he doesn't have in mere life.

As time passed, my own name appeared in the newspaper, and sometimes, in a clipping, it hung from the bulletin board in my old school. (Now that I was gone, the teachers loved me.) For years, I pasted up scrapbooks showing my name in print. Some years ago, I stopped. The playwright William Gibson, examining "shoeboxes" of "clippings" about him, preserved by his mother, writes simply: "I read hardly a sentence about me which was not in error—and learned upon what lies the populace based its judgments in matters affecting its life and death."

On balance, being noticed did me good, but I am astounded when people say: "The press has treated you well—why knock it?" But trading favor for favor is no path to clarification. One of the most regrettable aspects of the press is its immunity to criticism. Nobody outside the press has its power of magnification, nor is the press above revenge against people who presume to criticize it. I know of nobody so sensitive to criticism as journalists, whose technique of reply is only further evidence of their poor habits: Writers for the press lie low awhile, and then they throw boomerangs. When their victim is struck in the back of the head, he forgets who was angry at him, and why. "I have seen enough of it to be sure their reasons for likes and dislikes are always other than what they give," Frost wrote of a certain magazine's criticism.

I'd prefer to ignore the various media, but they won't go away, and neither will I. Every day, somebody sends me clippings in the mail about something or other he or she thinks I might be interested in. Oh, my poor friends, addicted to the writings of reporters who don't know half of what you know, who don't see half so well or understand half so much as you who are enslaved. My friends drown in a "glut of occurrences" (a phrase from Bernard Weisberger's "The American Newspaperman").

My friends have sunk into passivity. "Cancel your subscription," I want to cry, "let your tube blow. Hear it from people you know. Ignore the issues. You are old enough to know better. Let the news work its way up to you; don't bend or stoop for the paper at your doorstep. Be a high court—don't review daily trivialities. Save your dimes, save your quarters, save your eyes, save your nerves. Stare if you must, but at more distant horizons. Read wider columns than newsprint. Think!"

You, whoever you are, if you *must* buy a newspaper, don't read it.

Save it. Read it in 10 years. You'll see how much you could have skipped, how many hours of your life you will have preserved and how much clearer your perspective will be upon all subjects. You will have freed yourself of your daily addiction to someone else's idea of where the world is. Once, I read in a newspaper about some men trapped in a cave for several days. One man, upon being rescued, said that he had had time underground to think things over and make an important resolution: He would no longer require his daily newspaper. He'd cancel his subscription. But I don't know if he did.

Questions

Diction and Structure

1. Point out instances in Rollo May's essay where he defines terms. What methods does he use? Is his definition of Puritanism conventional or is it stipulative?

2. What are the various connotations of these terms in May's essay: "sexy," "Victorian," "machine," "alienation"?

3. Outline the organizational structure of May's essay. Is it a debate in the traditional use of the word? What logical or rhetorical principle(s) does it follow?

4. By root definition what does the word euthanasia mean? Is it a synonym for "mercy killing" or not? Explain.

5. Dr. John Fletcher's argument for euthanasia in at least one category is remarkably calm in effect. How does his choice of terminology help to achieve this result? Does he use euphemisms? Technical language? Comment.

6. Why does John Gardner use quotation marks for so many terms in his opening paragraphs? How does he use italicized terms?

7. In what stages does Gardner develop his argument? Are the subsections basic divisions in his thought or not?

8. Is Gardner's listing or itemization on page 441 a summary of his previous line of reasoning? If not, what is it and what relationship has it to previous sections?

9. Mark Harris uses an unusually large number of rhetorical

questions in his essay, "Why Read Newspapers?" Why does he do this? Is his language conversational or formal? How does his diction pertain to his argument about the best way of getting important news?

10. Does the Harris essay lend itself to outlining? Why or why not, in your view? Notice the analysis of the essay in the Introduction to this section; is it accurate and complete?

Style and Rhetoric

1. Rollo May appears to change his narrative point of view in "Antidotes for the New Puritanism": he speaks of "you," "we," "they," and "I" in various places. What basic point of view does he utilize? What is the effect of such expressions as "I often get the impression that" and "It seems to me"?

2. How and why does May use comparison and contrast in his opening pages? How is this use related to cause and effect? Is the last section analysis, hypothesis, or neither?

3. Does May violate any principles of logic in making his case against the New Puritanism? Is he refuting the ideas of Erich Fromm, Freud, David Riesman, and Otto Rank; accepting them; or qualifying them?

4. Examine Dr. Joseph Fletcher's argument for logical errors. Does his classification of the kinds of euthanasia beg the question in any way? Are his definitions clear and accurate? Does he appeal to the emotions?

5. John Gardner begins his essay with a discussion of muddled logic. What points are stressed thereby? What does Gardner mean by "an imaginary dilemma"?

6. Notice Gardner's successive uses of definition. What definitive methods does he use? Are his definitions standard ones?

7. To what extent is the Gardner essay concerned with classification? With comparison? With exemplification?

8. Examine "College and the Alternatives" for logical errors. Are any terms left undefined?

9. Look closely at Mark Harris's illustration of Watergate as an instance of unnecessary newspaper reporting. Is it true that we could "know" about the Watergate corruption by thinking inductively or from our knowledge of history?

10. The press has been given credit for forcing Watergate into the public consciousness. Does Harris ignore the question of whether Watergate might have remained hidden if reporters had not persisted in revealing the facts?

11. In his remarks on trivial, vindictive, and unimaginative reporters he has known, is Harris arguing ad hominem or not? Explain.

12. Is Harris's argument sound or not? Is it valid? Do you agree with him? If not, why not?

Theme and Viewpoint

1. Rollo May makes certain assumptions about the nature of human sexuality or what Theodor Reik calls "love and lust." Does May significantly alter Reik's notion of the nature of sexual impulses and their expression or manifestation?

2. May's comments about sexuality and apathy recall the remarks on these phenomena made by Arthur Miller, Tom Wolfe, and Jeff Greenfield. Do May's theories throw any light on juvenile delinquency, the drug cults of the 1960s, or the Beatles?

3. Examine the use of "love" as a slogan of the New Puritanism and its use by the Beatles. Would May consider the Beatles "New Puritans"? Explain.

4. May makes extended use of the image of sexuality as a mechanical process or the body as a machine. Do you see any relationship between May's sexual theorems and the problems of Joey, the mechanical boy?

5. Would Dr. John Fletcher agree with the assertions of Smith and Todes about the abilities and limitations of medical science in prolonging life? Would they agree with his ideas about euthanasia? In what ways would they agree and in what might they differ?

6. Smith and Todes think of life as a circle; would they find euthanasia a "natural" point of death or not?

7. All of the argumentative essays are concerned with learning or with changing attitudes through some educational process based on innovative principles. Compare and contrast May's views in this regard with those of Fletcher, Gardner, and Harris.

8. Like Truman and Hutchins in the section on Reasoning, John Gardner has spent his adult life on the problems of adult education. Does he think college has the same function that they do? Compare and contrast their attitudes toward higher education. Which is the most insistent on the need for such education for large numbers of people? Which is most insistent that higher education is *not* for everybody but for a relatively limited number of people? Do Gardner, Truman, and Hutchins disagree in basic ways?

9. What is Mark Harris's attitude toward T.V.? Do his arguments about ignoring newspapers apply as well to watching T.V.? Can Truman's insistence on "high literacy" be reconciled with never reading newspapers? Would Harris and Truman agree?

10. Which of the rhetorical techniques studied in Part One of this book are the most common in the Argumentative essays here? Which of the logical fallacies outlined by Robert Gorham Davis seem to be most likely to show up in arguments on inflammatory topics? Discuss.

11. Reread these essays as arguments and analyze them logically: "The Crank, the Eccentric, and the Individualist"; "The Fiction of Science"; "People Aren't Born Prejudiced"; "Why Does the Women's Movement Have No Sense of Humor?"; "Mickey Mouse Slouches Toward Bethlehem"; "The Point of Death"; "The Beatles Changed Rock"; "How TV Violence Damages Our Children"; "Down at the Cross"; "The Indispensable Opposition"; "My Negro Problem—and Ours."

A
B 6
C 7
D 8
E 9
F 0
G 1
H 2
I 3
J 4